CULTURESCOPE

HIGH SCHOOL EDITION

THE PRINCETON REVIEW

*Guide to an
Informed Mind*

Books in The Princeton Review Series

Cracking the ACT
Cracking the ACT with Sample Tests on Computer Disk
Cracking the GED
Cracking the GMAT
Cracking the GMAT with Sample Tests on Computer Disk
Cracking the GRE
Cracking the GRE with Sample Tests on Computer Disk
Cracking the GRE Psychology Subject Test
Cracking the LSAT
Cracking the LSAT with Sample Tests on Computer Disk
Cracking the MCAT
Cracking the MCAT with Sample Tests on Computer Disk
Cracking the SAT and PSAT
Cracking the SAT and PSAT with Sample Tests on Computer Disk
Cracking the SAT II: Biology Subject Test
Cracking the SAT II: Chemistry Subject Test
Cracking the SAT II: English Subject Tests
Cracking the SAT II: French Subject Test
Cracking the SAT II: History Subject Tests
Cracking the SAT II: Math Subject Tests
Cracking the SAT II: Physics Subject Test
Cracking the SAT II: Spanish Subject Test
Cracking the TOEFL with Audiocassette
Culturescope Grade School Edition
Culturescope High School Edition
Culturescope College Edition
SAT Math Workout
SAT Verbal Workout
Don't Be a Chump!
How to Survive Without Your Parents' Money
Trashproof Resumes
Grammar Smart
Math Smart
Reading Smart
Study Smart
Word Smart: Building an Educated Vocabulary
Word Smart II: How to Build a More Educated Vocabulary
Word Smart Executive Edition
Word Smart Genius Edition
Writing Smart
Grammar Smart Junior
Math Smart Junior
Word Smart Junior
Writing Smart Junior
Student Access Guide to America's Top Internships
Student Access Guide to College Admissions
Student Access Guide to the Best Business Schools
Student Access Guide to the Best Law Schools
Student Access Guide to the Best Medical Schools
Student Access Guide to the Best 309 Colleges
Student Access Guide to Paying for College
Student Access Guide to Visiting College Campuses
Student Access Guide: The Big Book of Colleges
Student Access Guide: The Internship Bible

Also available on cassette from Living Language
Grammar Smart
Word Smart
Word Smart II

CULTURESCOPE

HIGH SCHOOL EDITION

THE PRINCETON REVIEW

*Guide to an
Informed Mind*

RANDOM HOUSE, INC., NEW YORK 1995

MICHAEL FREEDMAN

Freedman, Michael
Culturescope: the Princeton review guide to an informed mind/by Michael Freedman.
High school ed./1995 ad., 1st ed.
    p.   cm.
    Includes bibliographical references and index.
    ISBN 0-679-75366-4 $20.00
    1. Handbooks. vade-mecums, etc.   I. Title
    AG105.F87   1994   031.02–dc20   94-34392

Manufactured in the United States of America on paper using partially recycled fibers

9 8 7 6 5 4 3 2

First Edition

DEDICATION

This book is dedicated to the memory of Florence Bernstein Freedman.

ACKNOWLEDGMENTS

The author would like to express his thanks first and foremost to his wife, Grace Roegner Freedman, without whose support and expert editing this book would not have been written. He wants to thank his parents, brothers, and grandfather who had to listen to him go on and on about the book. He would also like to thank all those at The Princeton Review who showed faith in his abilities to write this monster, especially John Katzman, Alicia Ernst, and Lee Elliott.

Almost from the start of this project it became clear that a book that hoped to encompass all of the information included between these covers was much more than a one person job. Thanks are not enough for Lee Elliott, Chris Kensler, Kristin Fayne-Mulroy, and Cynthia Brantley, creative editing team extraordinnaire, for taking the original breadth and focus of this book and creating the vision for the work this has become. Together they oversaw armies of researchers and fact-checkers, they single-handedly requisitioned and selected the hundreds of photos adorning these pages, they pared down what needed focusing and, most importantly, they contributed and added material to this book where it was really needed. In addition, they are responsible for creating and writing the majority of the sidebar information contained herein and also for the entertaining photo captions. Their contributions were instrumental to this book and make the book look great. And speaking of looking great, were it not for Julian Ham and Meher Khambata, these myriad elements would not have come together so harmoniously. Their design makes all of our efforts look even better and kudos must go out to the production team of Adam Hurwitz, John Bergdahl, Heather Kern, Dinica Quesada, Glen Pannell, Chris Thomas, Chris Scott, Joe Cavallaro, Lisa Ruyter, Kim Jack Riley, JiSun Chang, Zachary Knower, Joseph McPartland, Sara Kane, Illeny Maaza, Carol Slominski, Peter Jung, Jessica Brockington, Julian Heath, Russel Murray, Michael Recorvits, Dave Romeo, and Ray Suhler, who worked long hours creating art, trimming photos, and tweaking the design for what must have seemed an eternity. This book is as much theirs as anybody's. These were the star performers, but even they needed help.

The editors would like to thank Maria Russo for her meticulous perfectionism; Bruno Butler, Andy Dunn, and Joe Peletier for their insights and help in gathering the facts that we needed; Kate Lardner for making sure we weren't lying; Judy Lyon Davis for her indexing genius; The Bettmann Archive for their incredible assistance and their treasure of over 16 million photos; Rich Thomas and Domenica Macri for their patience sifting through thousands of photos; The New York Historical Society; The Museum of Natural History; The Museum of Modern Art; The Metropolitan Museum; Art Resource; AP/World Wide Photos; The New York Public Library; The Brooklyn Public Library; and Doogie the spastic monkey for keeping our sense of humor going through times of hardship.

TABLE OF CONTENTS

CULTURESCOPE: THE PRINCETON REVIEW GUIDE TO AN INFORMED MIND

Introduction

The other day, a high school senior was helping his mom take care of his two-year-old sister. The little girl kept reaching up and grabbing her big brother's ear, perhaps attracted by his bright rhinestone earring, glimmering in the sunlight. Every time the little girl tugged the teenager's ear, he would push her hand away ever so gently. After about five minutes, an elderly man who had been sitting nearby came up to the teenager and said, "My, young man, you have the patience of Job."

The teenager looked blankly at the old man. We could see the wheels turning in his head—"Joab, uh Bible guy, yeah, no, what does the old geezer mean?"—as he smiled warmly, shrugged his shoulders, and cleaned his little sister's puke off his new Nikes (probably not realizing that his sneakers are named for a goddess in Greek Mythology (p. 456)).

We had witnessed a cultural breakdown. The old man expected the teenager to understand what he meant when he referred to Job. But the teenager had only a vague idea of what the old man was talking about. (Job (p. 371) was the man tortured by the devil in the Bible, who still maintained his belief in God.) The old man didn't expect the kid to have read the Bible, he just expected him to know the gist of the reference.

SOUND FAMILIAR?

Chances are something similar has happened to you. If you were lucky, it was during a meaningless conversation. If you were less fortunate, it might have happened during a job or college interview. You may not even have noticed it, but the person you were talking to certainly did.

Here's a conversation that was reported to us by a woman in the personnel department of a very large New York City bank:

> Setting: *A job interview at a big bank.*
>
> Interviewer: *Ever since the Iron Curtain lifted, our business over there has boomed. Do you have any ideas we can use to help keep the ball rolling?*
>
> Perplexed Potential Employee: *Well, I'm not really up on steel technology, but I do know some of the basic uses of iron.*

The potential employee did not understand the term "Iron Curtain," while the interviewer had heard the phrase batted around for years (the Iron Curtain refers to the symbolic barrier between Eastern and Western European countries during the Cold War (pp. 104-108)). When she hears it, she pictures the Berlin Wall and the Cuban Missile Crisis, Gorbachev and Reagan, Khrushchev and Kennedy. How could she have explained such a complex situation in a job interview? Because of the misunderstanding, the interviewer left the interview with the idea that the interviewee didn't belong in the company. The cultural slip-up cost the potential employee the job.

BUT DON'T THEY TEACH THIS KIND OF STUFF IN SCHOOL?

Schools do teach some areas of culture, but not everything. Most high schools will teach the basics of history, some science, some literature, and some math, but very few schools teach much outside these fields. You will not learn about the Bible or movies or visual arts. Even in the areas that you do study in school, you may not learn all of the basics that are needed for good cultural communication. Your social studies classes teach you a lot of history, but they don't always teach current trends. And even if they did teach you this stuff in school, you may have forgotten some of it anyway.

Most likely, if you have a good knowledge of culture, you have picked it up from your parents or from your own reading. But you probably missed some things.

THAT'S WHY YOU NEED *CULTURESCOPE*

Culturescope—The Princeton Review Guide to an Informed Mind distills American culture down to its most essential elements. Through exhaustive research, we have culled the ideas and facts that you need to know to have "cultural literacy." *Culturescope* alerts you to the areas in which you need work, and helps add to your knowledge in all subjects. By working diligently with this book, you can fill those nagging gaps in your education and plan further cultural explorations.

PROFESSORS WILL LOVE YOU

As you read *Culturescope* and seek out our recommended books and movies, you will be preparing yourself to deal with life in college and beyond. Professors often assume that students have a certain base level of knowledge in a broad range of subjects. If you come to college with this information, you will be better prepared to handle classwork and assignments.

WHAT MAKES THIS BOOK DIFFERENT?

While doing research for the book, we had a chance to look at a few other books that attempt to do the same thing. Almost all of the books presented the information in alphabetical order. You might run across a page that presented Jackie Robinson, Nelson Rockefeller, and *Roe v. Wade* one after the other. Reading these entries is about as fun as reading a dictionary. Besides having to deal with this boring format, you get no sense of the context in which these cultural facts belong.

IT'S ALL ABOUT ATTITUDE

We also found a bunch of authors who seemed to feel that the younger generation was falling behind, that education was failing, and that we would soon be witnessing the fall of the American Empire. Many education experts seem to think that the American educational system is going down the tubes and that without drastic action, things will only get worse. They point to declining SAT scores and other national testing statistics to prove that kids just aren't what they used to be.

We don't believe these so-called experts. The Princeton Review, the nation's leading test-preparation company, has taught thousands and thousands of high school students to question authority and in the process raise their SAT scores. We have found that most of our students are intelligent and motivated and are learning at least as much in school as their parents did. We looked at the data that these "experts" were using, and we found that there was a good deal of misinterpretation going on.

SAT scores *are* declining, but this is more complicated than it seems. First of all, we don't have much faith in SAT scores; they are a biased way of judging a person's skills. The reason that the scores are declining is that a different population of students is taking the tests. In your parents' days most of the people taking the test were the best students with the best chances of going to college. Today, a more diverse population takes the test. If you look at each socioeconomic and ethnic group separately, SAT scores are actually *rising* in those groups.

Also, most national testing, especially that done by the National Assessment for Educational Progress (NAEP), shows that people are learning as much as they were twenty years ago. The only significant difference in abilities that has been measured is that the reading skills of minority students are improving.

We do agree that a lot of people are not learning the facts that they need to be considered "educated." We just don't feel that this is a new thing, and therefore we are not going to spend a lot of time talking about the inadequacies of our educational system and the potential dangers for America.

HOW DOES *CULTURESCOPE* WORK?

Culturescope is arranged in a question-and-answer format. Take the quiz that starts on page eight to get an idea of your general knowledge of culture. Figure out your CQ (Culture Quotient) and see how your knowledge compares to other high school students. The answer key points you to the page in the book where the answer to each question is explained.

THE BOLD AND THE BLUE

As you read, pay special attention to words that are **bold** or blue. Throughout the book, we give cross references to different sections that we feel are related. (The cross references are like the hyper-text connections that appear in multi-media computer software.) For example, when we talk about Sigmund Freud, the founding father of psychoanalysis, we mention his theory of the Oedipus complex. Since we also talk about the story of Oedipus in Greek Mythology, you will see Oedipus appears in blue, followed by a page number, like this: Oedipus (pp. 388-389). At this point, you have a choice. You can continue on the same page, or you can follow the cross-reference wherever it may lead. The cross-references will help you get a feel for the interrelated nature of our culture.

Words that appear in boldface are words that you will see in newspapers and hear in conversation. If a word is unfamiliar, consider making a flash card to help you remember it. Learning words like these can help you impress your teachers and college professors. It's not enough to have a good vocabulary; you also have to know the cultural references that everyone makes in everyday conversation.

WE BE ZOOMIN'

All of culture is hopelessly interrelated. There are levels upon levels to any discussion of anything. Say you're talking about "humans." One way to take the discussion is to "zoom out" and look at what groups of humans have done to change the world over the years. You can also "zoom in" and see what makes a human tick, examine his organs, cells, genes, etc. We "zoom in" and "zoom out" throughout the book to give you an idea of the complexities of culture.

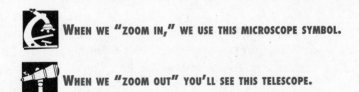

WHEN WE "ZOOM IN," WE USE THIS MICROSCOPE SYMBOL.

WHEN WE "ZOOM OUT" YOU'LL SEE THIS TELESCOPE.

Often, this "zooming around" is what makes learning so damn fun. You'll also notice that these "zooms" appear in blue to offset them from other parts of the text. When a word or phrase appears in black **boldface** in one of these zooms, it indicates a cross-reference just like blue text does in the rest of the book. So if you see something black and bold while you're zooming around, don't be alarmed. It's just another fun and exciting cross-reference!

A MULTI-MEDIA GUIDE

We have loaded *Culturescope* with references to other sources. When we talk about the Roaring Twenties, for example, we recommend that you see *Ragtime*, read *The Great Gatsby*, and listen to a little Cole Porter. These references are illustrated by these icons:

INDICATES GOOD FILMS RELATED TO THE TOPICS AT HAND.

INDICATEZS RECOMMENDED READING FOR FURTHER EXPLORATION OF A TOPIC OR EVENT.

INDICATES MUSIC RELATED TO THE TIME OR EVENTS BEING DISCUSSED.

This way, with a little work on your part, you can bring some of the information in the book to life. Go to the library, the video rental store, or your local music store and check out our recommendations. Rather than listing a large number of sources for each subject, we have been picky and tried to choose the ones that will be appealing to you and instructive at the same time.

DON'T READ IT LIKE A NOVEL

You shouldn't read *Culturescope* straight through. Leave it by your bed and just open it up somewhere and start reading. The answers to the questions that appear in the text appear at the end of each individual section. You *can* read the book from cover to cover, but we think you'll have more fun jumping around (the book, that is). Follow the cross-references wherever they lead. Try out one of the movie recommendations. Read a chapter that particularly interests you. Listen to some of the music. Take your time.

ARE YOU WELL-READ?

In the Humanities sections, we have assembled lists of essential movies, music, and books. We have chosen the works that people refer to a lot and that college professors would expect their incoming students to be familiar with. We have also included reproductions of paintings and sculptures that most educated people will have seen either in person or in books. For example, the painting *American Gothic* (pp. 464-465) is parodied over and over again in art, commercials, and cartoons, so you should know what the original really looks like.

CULTURE IS HIP, COOL, HEP, STUPID, AWESOME, DEF, BAD, ETC.

All this talk about culture obscures one important fact: culture is cool. So, while you work your way through the book, take some time to smell the roses. Read the sidebars, look at the quotes, try out some of the movies and the books. Have a blast.

The *Culturescope* Quiz

Do You Have Cultural Literacy?

The *Culturescope* Quiz is a gauge of your cultural literacy and the launching pad for the rest of the book. The test's questions are arranged in order of difficulty, so the first questions may seem a lot easier than the last. Take the test, mark down your answers on a separate piece of paper, and then compare them with the answers on pages 19-23. As you check your answers, you will notice that we also refer to the page in the book where we talk about the question. If you're curious, go right to the page and read. You will find some interesting stuff.

How's Your CQ?

Instructions for scoring your test are on page 24. You convert the number of questions that you got right into your personal Culture Quotient. If you're curious to see how other high school students from across the country performed on the test, the answer key includes percentages that illustrate how many people got each question right. The results are based on our national survey and you may be surprised by what you and your peers do and don't know. Don't take it too seriously. The quiz is meant to be fun.

1. **Where is the Alamo?**
   (A) Texas
   (B) Louisiana
   (C) Maine
   (D) Alabama

2. **Which of the following people precipitated the Montgomery Bus Boycott?**
   (A) Shirley Chisholm
   (B) Louis Farrakhan
   (C) Rosa Parks
   (D) Booker T. Washington

3. **Which of the following most helps the human body to defend itself against invading organisms?**
   (A) Red blood cells
   (B) White blood cells
   (C) Platelets
   (D) Plasma

4. ***The Empire Strikes Back* is the sequel to which of the following movies?**
   (A) *Star Wars*
   (B) *Enter the Dragon*
   (C) *Empire of the Sun*
   (D) *Millennium*

5. **Who said "float like a butterfly, sting like a bee"?**
   (A) Babe Ruth
   (B) Mohammed Ali
   (C) Tom Clancy
   (D) Robert Frost

6. **Which of the following performers made the song "Respect" famous?**
   (A) Aretha Franklin
   (B) Elvis Presley
   (C) The Rolling Stones
   (D) Billie Holiday

7. **Which of the following events led Europe into World War I?**
   (A) The assassination of Archduke Ferdinand
   (B) The sinking of the Maine
   (C) The sinking of the Lusitania
   (D) The racist policies of Kaiser Wilhelm

8. **What is the primary function of DNA?**
   (A) To protect individuals from disease
   (B) To help in passing different traits from a parent to its offspring
   (C) To mutate the original function of an organism
   (D) To exchange oxygen for energy

9. **In a computer, what is the difference between ROM and RAM?**
   (A) ROM is many times faster than RAM.
   (B) ROM cannot be changed by software, while RAM can.
   (C) ROM and RAM are both the same thing.
   (D) ROM is removable, but RAM is soldered into the motherboard of a computer.

10. What was the Emancipation Proclamation?

    (A) A document created during the Civil War that declared "forever free" the slaves of the rebel states
    (B) A speech given by Martin Luther King Jr. that proclaimed African-Americans as deserving of rights equal to those of whites
    (C) A speech given by Susan B. Anthony asking for universal suffrage
    (D) The words written at the base of the Statue of Liberty

11. What is a mole in chemistry?

    (A) The number of molecules of a gas necessary to take up exactly 22.4 liters of space at standard pressure and temperature
    (B) The number of years it takes for a radioactive particle to decay
    (C) The rate of a chemical reaction
    (D) The gradual warming of the atmosphere as caused by an increase in released carbon dioxide

12. Who killed Julius Caesar in Shakespeare's *Julius Caesar*?

    (A) Othello
    (B) Lear
    (C) Brutus
    (D) Marc Antony

13. Which nation was represented by this flag?

    (A) Israel
    (B) The USSR
    (C) China
    (D) Afghanistan

14. Who painted the painting below?

    (A) Leonardo da Vinci
    (B) Michelangelo
    (C) Rembrandt van Rijn
    (D) Sandro Botticelli

15. Which of the following is the best conductor of electricity?

    (A) Wood
    (B) Aluminum
    (C) Glass
    (D) Plastic

16. What was the name of the actor who said "Frankly my dear, I don't give a damn" in *Gone with the Wind*?

    (A) Frank Sinatra
    (B) Clark Gable
    (C) Jimmy Stewart
    (D) John Wayne

17. What is potential energy?

(A) The energy used to set off a chain reaction in a nuclear power plant

(B) Energy not yet found, such as fossil fuels that are still in the ground

(C) An object's energy of motion

(D) Energy possessed by an object due to its position or condition

18. Icarus is known for

(A) flying too close to the sun

(B) invading Troy during the Trojan war

(C) succeeding Caesar as heir to the throne

(D) joining with Hamlet in attacking his father

19. What longtime leader of the African National Conference won the Nobel Peace Prize?

(A) Nelson Mandela

(B) Idi Amin

(C) Kareem Abdul Jabbar

(D) Poto Doudongo

20. What is a black hole?

(A) A collapsed star with a gravitational field so strong that not even light can escape it

(B) The difference between the money spent by the United States government and the money collected from taxes

(C) The emptiness that exists between different types of matter in space

(D) The shadow cast by one star when its light is blocked by another

	2 He 4.0	Period 1
9 F 19.0	10 Ne 20.0	Period 2
17 Cl 35.5	18 Ar 39.0	Period 3
34 Se 79.0	35 Br 79.9	36 Kr 83.8	Period 4

21. The number 18 above Ar stands for

(A) the number of protons in the nucleus of an atom of Ar

(B) the exact weight of an atom of Ar

(C) the radioactivity of an atom of Ar

(D) the number of electrons in an atom of Ar when it forms a compound with another substance

2 He 4.0	Period 1
10 Ne 20.0	Period 2
18 Ar 39.0	Period 3
36 Kr 83.8	Period 4
54 Xe 131.3	Period 5
86 Rn 222.0	Period 6

22. The substances Ne, Ar, Kr, Xe, and Rn in column 8 of the periodic table share which one of the following properties in common?

(A) They are all radioactive

(B) They are all missing at least one electron

(C) They are all inert gases

(D) They are all easily transformed into superconductors

23. What is the name of the holy book of Islam?
    (A) The Bible
    (B) The Kabbalah
    (C) The Koran
    (D) The Shiite

24. Which of the following rights is NOT guaranteed in the U.S. Constitution?
    (A) The right to bear arms
    (B) The right to free speech
    (C) The right to the pursuit of happiness
    (D) The right to vote

25. What is the approximate temperature of the Earth's core?
    (A) 27° C
    (B) 100° C
    (C) 212° C
    (D) 2450° C

26. Disco music is associated with what decade?
    (A) The fifties
    (B) The sixties
    (C) The seventies
    (D) The eighties

27. What disease caused Franklin Delano Roosevelt to spend his last years in a wheelchair?
    (A) Tuberculosis
    (B) Polio
    (C) Cancer
    (D) Arthritis

28. The Trojan horse
    (A) is a two-time winner of the Kentucky Derby
    (B) is a horse that, although it pulls slowly, gets the job done
    (C) is a wooden horse that concealed Athenian soldiers
    (D) is a horse used to pull chariots in the Roman amphitheaters

29. In what year was the Emancipation Proclamation written?
    (A) 1825
    (B) 1835
    (C) 1863
    (D) 1965

30. If a 2-pound ball and a 20-pound ball of the same size are both dropped from the same height, which will land first? (Assume no air resistance.)
    (A) The 2-pound ball
    (B) The 20-pound ball
    (C) They will both land at the same time.
    (D) It cannot be determined from the information given.

31. At a restaurant, you buy a hamburger and a Coke. The hamburger costs $2.50, and the Coke costs 50 cents. If tax is 6% and you leave a 15% tip, approximately how much money did you part with?
    (A) $3.25
    (B) $3.45
    (C) $3.65
    (D) $3.90

32. Who is the Commander in Chief of the U.S. armed forces?
    (A) The Chairman of the Joint Chiefs of Staff
    (B) The Secretary of State
    (C) The highest ranking general of any of the services
    (D) The President

33. What was the Code of Hammurabi?
    (A) The secret language used by the ancient Mesopotamians
    (B) The ethical structure of Hammurabian civilization
    (C) The legal code of ancient Babylon
    (D) The key to translating hieroglyphics

34. Which of the following substances is used in the H-Bomb?

   (A) Helium
   (B) Gamma rays
   (C) Hydrogen
   (D) Radon

35. The first African-American baseball player in the Major Leagues was

   (A) Babe Ruth
   (B) Hank Aaron
   (C) Jackie Robinson
   (D) Willie Mays

36. Who was the second president of the United States?

   (A) Benjamin Franklin
   (B) John Adams
   (C) Thomas Jefferson
   (D) John Hancock

37. What is Watergate?

   (A) A tourist attraction in the midwest that was damaged in a flood
   (B) A hotel in which illegal actions were undertaken by the Republican party
   (C) A scandal involving the trading of arms for hostages
   (D) The opening mile of the Panama Canal

38. Who painted the Sistine Chapel ceiling?

   (A) Leonardo da Vinci
   (B) Michelangelo
   (C) Raphael
   (D) Lorenzo di Medici

39. In what continent is Cambodia located?

   (A) Africa
   (B) South America
   (C) Asia
   (D) Europe

40. Which of the following people was a former slave who became an abolitionist and an adviser to President Abraham Lincoln?

   (A) Frederick Douglass
   (B) Martin Luther King
   (C) Langston Hughes
   (D) James Weldon Johnson

41. The electricity in your area costs 14¢ per kilowatt-hour. How much does it cost to keep two 100-watt lights on for ten hours?

   (A) 7¢
   (B) 14¢
   (C) 21¢
   (D) 28¢

42. In which centuries did Shakespeare write?

   (A) The fifteenth and sixteenth centuries
   (B) The sixteenth and seventeenth centuries
   (C) The eighteenth and nineteenth centuries
   (D) The nineteenth and twentieth centuries

43. Charlemagne was

   (A) A type of champagne
   (B) An island off the coast of France
   (C) A leader in Europe during the Middle Ages
   (D) A leader of Italy during the Renaissance

44. Which of the following countries shares a border with Tibet?

   (A) Kenya
   (B) Pakistan
   (C) Vietnam
   (D) China

45. What was the policy of the U.S. government in 1939 concerning World War II?

    (A) It was eager to commit American troops to the battle in support of the Allied Powers.
    (B) It was eager to commit American troops to the battle in support of the Axis Powers.
    (C) It was willing to support its allies economically but not militarily.
    (D) American troops were already involved in fighting World War II.

46. The longest river in the United States goes through which of the following states?

    (A) Georgia
    (B) Alabama
    (C) Oklahoma
    (D) Louisiana

47. Which of the following people was NOT at the Yalta conference?

    (A) Joseph Stalin
    (B) Franklin Delano Roosevelt
    (C) Woodrow Wilson
    (D) Winston Churchill

48. What was the "Iron Curtain"?

    (A) Legislation imposed during the 1920s to reduce steel exports
    (B) The symbolic boundary separating Eastern Europe from Western Europe during the Cold War
    (C) The dramatic ending of *Madame Butterfly*
    (D) A shield devised during the 1980s to protect the United States from nuclear missiles

49. What happened to Lot's wife when she turned around to see the destruction at Sodom?

    (A) She burned up instantly
    (B) She was turned into a pillar of salt
    (C) Nothing
    (D) She ran back to save her children

50. Based on Einstein's Special Theory of Relativity it is possible to conclude that

    (A) the maximum velocity attainable is that of light
    (B) some things weigh more than others
    (C) f=ma
    (D) it is impossible to determine the exact location of an electron

51. Which of the following was most responsible for the success of the speakeasies?

    (A) The invention of talkie films
    (B) Prohibition
    (C) The television age
    (D) The "Red Scare"

52. Which of the following people is known for her recording of the song "Crazy"?

    (A) Ella Fitzgerald
    (B) Patsy Cline
    (C) Madonna
    (D) Naomi Judd

53. The book written by Adolf Hitler that described his philosophy was called

    (A) *Mein Kampf*
    (B) *Das Boot*
    (C) *Metamorphosis*
    (D) *Zeitgeist*

54. Which of the following people was a general of the Confederate Army near the end of the Civil War?

    (A) Robert E. Lee
    (B) Ulysses S. Grant
    (C) Stephen Douglas
    (D) John C. Calhoun

55. Windows and MS-DOS for IBM computers and System 7 for Macintosh computers are all
    (A) word processors
    (B) operating systems
    (C) spreadsheets
    (D) hardware

56. "Absolute zero" is
    (A) the number of degrees in a straight line
    (B) the lowest point above sea level
    (C) the temperature at which water freezes
    (D) the temperature at which all molecular motion ceases

57. Which of the following people wrote *The Communist Manifesto*?
    (A) Joseph Stalin and Vladimir Lenin
    (B) Karl Marx and Friedrich Engels
    (C) Leo Tolstoy
    (D) Horace Mann and W. E. B. Du Bois

58. Which of the following people NEVER hung out with Gertrude Stein?
    (A) Pablo Picasso
    (B) Ernest Hemingway
    (C) Harriet Beecher Stowe
    (D) F. Scott Fitzgerald

59. Which of the following political parties was formed as a result of Andrew Jackson's defeat in the election of 1824?
    (A) Democrat
    (B) Republican
    (C) Whig
    (D) Know Nothing

60. Which of the following bands is from the United States?
    (A) The Beatles
    (B) The Rolling Stones
    (C) The Doors
    (D) Led Zeppelin

61. The different temperatures associated with winter and summer are caused by
    (A) the tilt of the earth
    (B) the change in distance between the earth and the sun caused by irregularities in the earth's orbit.
    (C) the jet stream
    (D) evaporation of the ocean

62. Which of the following court cases found the concept of "separate but equal" facilities for whites and blacks unconstitutional?
    (A) Plessy v. Ferguson
    (B) Brown v. Board of Education of Topeka
    (C) Marbury v. Madison
    (D) Roe v. Wade

63. Of the following, who is NOT considered to be a jazz musician?
    (A) Louis Armstrong
    (B) Ella Fitzgerald
    (C) Redd Foxx
    (D) Thelonious Monk

64. What trial focused on whether a teacher could discuss Darwin's theory of evolution in schools?
    (A) Brown v. Board of Education
    (B) The Scopes Trial
    (C) United States v. Butler
    (D) The Spencer Trial

I shall be telling this with a sigh
Somewhere ages and ages hence:
Two roads diverged in a wood, and I—
I took the one less traveled by
And that has made all the difference.

65. Who wrote the poem from which the lines above were taken?

(A) Robert Frost
(B) Emily Dickinson
(C) Walt Whitman
(D) Pat Boone

66. In which of the following ways can a person contract AIDS?

I. Having sex
II. Hugging
III. Giving blood

(A) I only
(B) I and II only
(C) I and III only
(D) I, II, and III

67. Who was an inspiration to the French at the end of the Hundred Years' War?

(A) Joan of Arc
(B) Marie Antoinette
(C) Victor Hugo
(D) Elizabeth II

68. Put in order from smallest to largest:

I. Bit
II. Gigabyte
III. Kilobyte
IV. Megabyte

(A) I, II, III, IV
(B) I, III, II, IV
(C) I, III, IV, II
(D) III, IV, II, I

69. While taking a trip to visit your favorite college, you look at a map in which the scale is 1 inch for every 75 miles. On the map, the distance from where you are to where you have to go is $3\frac{1}{2}$ inches. If you are averaging 50 miles an hour, how long will it take you to get to your destination?

(A) 1 hour and 15 minutes
(B) 3 hours and 15 minutes
(C) 5 hours and 15 minutes
(D) 6 hours

70. Put the following constructions in chronological order according to when they were built:

I. Berlin Wall
II. Chartres Cathedral
III. Great Wall of China
IV. Stonehenge

(A) III, IV, II, I
(B) IV, III, II, I
(C) IV, II, III, I
(D) IV, I, II, III

71. Which branch of government is given the power to declare war?

(A) The executive branch
(B) The legislative branch
(C) The judicial branch
(D) The military branch

72. The Great Salt Lake is in which state?

(A) Utah
(B) New York
(C) Nevada
(D) Michigan

73. MTV first started in which of the following years?

(A) 1972
(B) 1976
(C) 1981
(D) 1986

74. What is the purpose of fiber-optic cable?

(A) To aid in the exchange of digital information
(B) To aid in the transfer of power from electrical lines
(C) To increase the power of intergalactic telescopes
(D) To physically strengthen already existing underwater copper telephone wires

75. Which of the following most accurately describes Reconstruction?

(A) The process of reforming the Union after the Civil War
(B) The rebuilding of Europe after World War II
(C) The buildup of the Union Army near the time of the Civil War
(D) The increase in debt caused by the War of 1812

76. Catherine the Great was a ruler of

(A) France
(B) England
(C) Denmark
(D) Russia

77. The Battle of Bunker Hill occurred in

(A) The American War of Independence
(B) The War of 1812
(C) The Civil War
(D) The Hundred Years' War

78. Put the following in order from most likely to least likely.

I. The likelihood of flipping a coin 10 times and getting heads each time
II. The likelihood of winning a sweepstakes where the odds for winning are 100,000,000 to 1
III. The probability that when two 6-sided dice are rolled, their sum is 7
IV. The probability that when two 6-sided dice are rolled, their sum is 4

(A) I, II, III, IV
(B) IV, III, I, II
(C) III, IV, I, II
(D) III, IV, II, I

79. Who was the first person to fly solo across the Atlantic Ocean?

(A) Charles Lindbergh
(B) Francis Boeing
(C) Amelia Earhart
(D) Orville Wright

80. What was the name of the spacecraft used in the first successful orbit around the earth?

(A) *Enterprise*
(B) *Apollo I*
(C) *Sputnik*
(D) *Perestroika*

81. Who wrote the words "Cogito, ergo sum" (I think, therefore I am)?

(A) Cicero
(B) Plato
(C) René Descartes
(D) Friedrich Nietzsche

82. The artwork pictured above was created during which of the following time periods?

   (A) 1800-1850
   (B) 1850-1900
   (C) 1900-1950
   (D) 1950-present

83. Which of the following is a primary function of mitochondria?

   (A) Asexual reproduction
   (B) Anaerobic respiration
   (C) Energy production
   (D) RNA replication

84. What is "Rosebud" in "Citizen Kane?"

   (A) Kane's girlfriend
   (B) Kane's wife
   (C) Kane's suburban mansion
   (D) Kane's sled

85. Put the following historical figures into chronological order:

   I. Jesus
   II. Abraham
   III. Mohammed
   IV. Buddha

   (A) II, I, IV, III
   (B) II, IV, I, III
   (C) IV, III, I, II
   (D) IV, II, I, III

86. Who was NOT part of the women's suffrage movement?

   (A) Susan B. Anthony
   (B) Elizabeth Cady Stanton
   (C) Carrie Chapman Catt
   (D) Martha Graham

87. What is the name of the theory that lowering taxes on business will increase production and thereby help the economy?

   (A) Supply-side economics
   (B) Supply and demand
   (C) Deficit spending
   (D) Laissez-faire

88. Which of the following presidents was most responsible for implementing supply-side economics?

   (A) Jimmy Carter
   (B) Gerald Ford
   (C) Ronald Reagan
   (D) Bill Clinton

89. What are the values for x, such that $4x^2 + 3x - 7 = 0$

   (A) $(-7/4, 1)$
   (B) $(-4/7, 1)$
   (C) $(-1, 7/4)$
   (D) $(-1, 4/7)$

90. What Nobel Prize-winning author wrote *Song of Solomon*?

   (A) Toni Morrison
   (B) Thomas Pynchon
   (C) Ernest Hemingway
   (D) Charlotte Brontë

91. The movie *Modern Times* was made by

    (A) Charlie Chaplin
    (B) Steven Spielberg
    (C) Howard Hawks
    (D) Orson Welles

92. Put the following people in chronological order:

    I. Ludwig van Beethoven
    II. Johann Sebastian Bach
    III. Wolfgang Amadeus Mozart

    (A) I, II, III
    (B) II, I, III
    (C) III, I, II
    (D) II, III, I

93. Assume that in the year 2000 the annual national deficit has been reduced to one-tenth of what it is now. What would happen to the national debt in the year 2000?

    (A) It would continue to increase.
    (B) It would stay the same.
    (C) It would decrease.
    (D) It cannot be determined from the information given.

Answers to the *Culturescope Quiz*

Question Number	Correct Answer	% of Respondents Answering Correctly	Explanation on Page
1.	A	89	Answer is explained on page 58 (American History)
2.	C	85	Answer is explained on page 111 (American History)
3.	B	87	Answer is explained on page 334 (Science and Technology)
4.	A	91	Answer is explained on page 411 (Humanities)
5.	B	78	Answer is explained on page 469 (Humanities)
6.	A	82	Answer is explained on pages 433-434 (Humanities)
7.	A	75	Answer is explained on page 82 (World History)
8.	B	92	Answer is explained on pages 316-317 (Science and Technology)
9.	B	52	Answer is explained on page 353 (Science and Technology)
10.	A	92	Answer is explained on page 68 (American History)
11.	A	92	Answer is explained on page 296 (Science and Technology)
12.	C	76	Answer is explained on page 396 (Humanities)
13.	B	84	Answer is explained on page 206 (World History)
14.	A	81	Answer is explained on page 453 (Humanities)
15.	B	87	Answer is explained on page 307 (Science and Technology)
16.	B	84	Answer is explained on page 410 (Humanities)
17.	D	76	Answer is explained on page 299 (Science and Technology)
18.	A	66	Answer is explained on page 388 (Humanities)
19.	A	79	Answer is explained on page 212 (World History)
20.	A	77	Answer is explained on pages 303-304 (Science and Technology)
21.	A	84	Answer is explained on page 287 (Science and Technology)

22.	C	79	Answer is explained on page 289 (Science and Technology)
23.	C	79	Answer is explained on pages 378-379 (Humanities)
24.	C	60	Answer is explained on pages 51-52 (American History)
25.	D	63	Answer is explained on page 275 (Science and Technology)
26.	C	80	Answer is explained on page 435 (Humanities)
27.	B	77	Answer is explained on page 94 (American History)
28.	C	82	Answer is explained on page 390 (Humanities)
29.	C	72	Answer is explained on page 68 (American History)
30.	C	70	Answer is explained on page 301 (Science and Technology)
31.	C	75	Answer is explained on pages 357-359 (Science and Technology)
32.	D	71	Answer is explained on pages 50-51 (American History)
33.	C	51	Answer is explained on page 137 (World History)
34.	C	46	Answer is explained on pages 292-293 (Science and Technology)
35.	C	61	Answer is explained on pages 470-471 (Humanities)
36.	B	73	Answer is explained on page 53 (American History)
37.	B	71	Answer is explained on pages 124-125 (American History)
38.	B	70	Answer is explained on page 454 (Humanities)
39.	C	64	Answer is explained on pages 215-216 (World History)
40.	A	74	Answer is explained on page 64 (American History)
41.	D	47	Answer is explained on page 307 (Science and Technology)
42.	B	57	Answer is explained on page 395 (Humanities)
43.	C	75	Answer is explained on pages 152-153 (World History)
44.	D	42	Answer is explained on page 215 (World History)
45.	C	66	Answer is explained on page 95 (American History)
46.	D	65	Answer is explained on page 226 (Geography)

47.	C	56	Answer is explained on pages 99-100 (American History)
48.	B	71	Answer is explained on pages 205-206 (World History)
49.	B	52	Answer is explained on pages 366-367 (Humanities)
50.	A	55	Answer is explained on pages 304-305 (Science and Technology)
51.	B	49	Answer is explained on pages 86-87 (American History)
52.	B	51	Answer is explained on page 433 (Humanities)
53.	A	72	Answer is explained on pages 195-197 (World History)
54.	A	79	Answer is explained on page 67 (American History)
55.	B	58	Answer is explained on page 354 (Science and Technology)
56.	D	65	Answer is explained on page 296 (Science and Technology)
57.	B	53	Answer is explained on page 180 (World History)
58.	C	30	Answer is explained on page 396 (Humanities)
59.	A	27	Answer is explained on pages 57-58 (American History)
60.	C	44	Answer is explained on page 434 (Humanities)
61.	A	52	Answer is explained on page 280 (Science and Technology)
62.	B	42	Answer is explained on pages 109-110 (American History)
63.	C	50	Answer is explained on pages 432-433 (Humanities)
64.	B	41	Answer is explained on pages 88-89 (American History)
65.	A	62	Answer is explained on page 397 (Humanities)
66.	A	39	Answer is explained on page 329 (Science and Technology)
67.	A	59	Answer is explained on pages 156-157 (World History)
68.	C	50	Answer is explained on page 353 (Science and Technology)
69.	C	64	Answer is explained on pages 356-357 (Science and Technology)
70.	B	53	Answer is explained on pages 452-453 (Humanities)
71.	B	39	Answer is explained on page 51 (American History)

72.	A	62	Answer is explained on page 226 (Geography)
73.	C	57	Answer is explained on pages 435-436 (Humanities)
74.	A	47	Answer is explained on page 351 (Science and Technology)
75.	A	30	Answer is explained on page 69 (American History)
76.	D	43	Answer is explained on page 171 (World History)
77.	A	47	Answer is explained on page 44 (American History)
78.	C	53	Answer is explained on pages 359-360 (Science and Technology)
79.	A	53	Answer is explained on page 90 (American History)
80.	C	41	Answer is explained on page 107 (American History)
81.	C	24	Answer is explained on page 169 (World History)
82.	C	25	Answer is explained on page 454 (Humanities)
83.	C	45	Answer is explained on page 321 (Science and Technology)
84.	We're not telling.	33	Answer is explained on page 410 (Humanities)
85.	B	27	Answer is explained on pages 379-380 (Humanities)
86.	D	28	Answer is explained on pages 87-88 (American History)
87.	A	39	Answer is explained on page 128 (American History)
88.	C	34	Answer is explained on page 129 (American History)
89.	A	45	Answer is explained on pages 358-359 (Science and Technology)
90.	A	18	Answer is explained on page 397 (Humanities)
91.	A	32	Answer is explained on pages 409-410 (Humanities)
92.	D	20	Answer is explained on pages 431-432 (Humanities)
93.	A	15	Answer is explained on pages 129-130 (American History)

DETERMINING YOUR SCORE

STEP 1 Using the answers on the next page, determine how many questions you got right.

STEP 2 List the number of correct answers here. This is your raw score.

STEP 3 To determine your real score, take the number from Step 1 above and look it up in the left column of the Score Conversion Table on page 25; the corresponding score on the right is your score on the exam.

THE PRINCETON REVIEW CULTURE QUOTIENT CONVERSION TABLE

Raw Score	Scaled Score	Raw Score	Scaled Score	Raw Score	Scaled Score	Raw Score	Scaled Score
93	800	68	640	43	480	18	320
92	790	67	630	42	470	17	310
91	790	66	630	41	470	16	300
90	780	65	620	40	460	15	290
89	770	64	610	39	460	14	280
88	770	63	610	38	450	13	270
87	760	62	600	37	440	12	260
86	760	61	600	36	440	11	250
85	750	60	590	35	430	10	240
84	740	59	580	34	420	9	230
83	740	58	580	33	420	8	230
82	730	57	570	32	410	7	220
81	720	56	560	31	400	6	220
80	720	55	560	30	400	5	210
79	710	54	550	29	390	4	210
78	700	53	540	28	390	3	200
77	700	52	540	27	380	2	200
76	690	51	530	26	370	1	200
75	690	50	530	25	370	0	200
74	680	49	520	24	360		
73	670	48	510	23	350		
72	670	47	510	22	350		
71	660	46	500	21	340		
70	650	45	490	20	330		
69	650	44	490	19	330		

What Your Score Means

We have given the CQ to high school students throughout the country and scored their tests to give you an SAT-like scale for your cultural literacy. Just like the SAT, your converted score is a number between 200 and 800. The average student gets a 500.

If you score between 710 and 800

You have a profound knowledge of culture. You can carry on a conversation with anyone. Your parents, college professors, and perfect strangers are totally impressed with you. Still, big shot, there are things in this book that you will not know and will find interesting. Pay special attention to the movie and book recommendations and be sure to work on any specific areas that you had trouble with.

If you score between 610 and 700

You have a good understanding of American culture, with a few weak spots. Read the sections where you have the most to learn, make flash cards, and try the movie and book suggestions. You don't have very far to go, so working with *Culturescope* should produce immediate results.

If you score between 510 and 600

There are holes in your cultural education big enough to drive a Mack truck through—but not to worry! We wrote this book with *you* in mind, and boy, are you in for a treat.

Make *Culturescope* your personal Bible. Read it in the car, in the can, on the train, at the basketball game—you get the idea. Don't leave home without it.

IF YOU SCORE BETWEEN 410 AND 500

There are some serious holes in your cultural knowledge, and you will need to spend a good deal of time with this book. But don't worry, you're really going to get your money's worth. Keep the book by your bed, and open it whenever you can. Try some of the recommended movies and books. It won't be long before you, too, are a "cultured" person.

IF YOU SCORE BETWEEN 200 AND 400

Okay, party's over, kid. You've obviously had your fun; now let's get down to business.

The philosopher George Santayana (1863-1952) once said, "Those who cannot remember the past are condemned to repeat it." We agree with George, and add, "Those who cannot remember the past have an incomplete knowledge of current events." Not as catchy as George's *bon mot*, but still true.

American history can be warped to fit almost any argument. For example, some vile rogue may note that women are at an economic disadvantage today because women failed to vote for politicians supportive of their cause in the nineteenth century, and this vile rogue wouldn't really be lying in the strict sense of the word. Women didn't vote for the politicians sympathetic to their plight in the nineteenth century—because they couldn't vote, period. They didn't achieve that right until early this century, after years and years of struggle. Without knowledge of this fact, and facts like this, one can easily be suckered into believing any half-cocked theory.

GIVE US YOUR TIRED, YOUR POOR, YOUR HUDDLED MASSES . . .

America is a country of immigrants. Aside from the Native Americans, everybody here is or has ancestors from a foreign country (including those forced to come here as slaves from Africa). Yet, since people started arriving here from Europe in the seventeenth century, there has been concern about immigration. The first large group to migrate to America were English-speaking Protestants, and they were worried about their capacity to absorb the large group of Germans that began arriving later in the seventeenth century. Then, in the nineteenth century, Irish Catholics came, and everyone was worried that the Anglo-Protestant culture would not be maintainable. Then people from Eastern and Southern Europe came, and guess what? More worries. Laws were passed that restricted immigration, and, by 1924, the number of immigrants allowed in the country was severely restricted. The restrictive laws of the 1920s served to make it difficult for Jews and others to leave Europe in the 1930s when Hitler came to power. Because of these fundamentally racist restrictions, millions of people who could have escaped the Nazis were barred admittance to America and subsequently lost their lives. Today, the same talk continues with many of the people whose ancestors were immigrants--or even whose relatives were kept out by the restrictive laws of the twenties-- advocating for restrictions on the latest wave of immigrants from Asia, Africa, and South America.

With this in mind, our American History section looks at the succession of events on this continent with an eye toward its most influential people, movements, and occurrences. We don't discuss every president (James K. Polk, Franklin Pierce, and Warren G. Harding didn't make the cut), but we do concentrate on people who have become cultural icons, like the industrialist Henry Ford and the teacher John T. Scopes. We don't dwell on the relations between the U.S. and Norway, as interesting as this subject may be, but we give all the "who's," "when's," and "why's" for topics like westward expansion, the civil rights movement, and World Wars I and II.

The American History section starts with the first humans to reach this continent and ends with Bill Clinton. It's full of great stories—some tragic, some inspirational, some hilarious. Hey, it's no fun to go through life being "condemned," so if you believe our old friend George Santayana, you should get reading, and quick.

Pre-Colonial Period

1. **For how long, approximately, have human beings lived on the continent of North America?**

   (A) 500 years
   (B) 1,000 years
   (C) 10,000 years
   (D) More than 15,000 years

2. **The first human beings that came to the Americas got here by**

   (A) crossing over the Bering Strait between present-day Alaska and Russia
   (B) crossing the Pacific Ocean by boat
   (C) crossing the Atlantic Ocean by boat
   (D) traveling north over the frozen Arctic area

 Many people are surprised that the U.S. and Russia are only separated by fifty-five miles. In 1959, during the **Cold War** (pp. 104-108), Alaska became a state after being a territory of the U.S. since 1867. By the time of statehood, more than 200,000 American citizens lived in Alaska.

   Because the first human beings came to America at least 20,000 years ago, it is virtually impossible to determine just how they got here. One

It is usually said that Columbus discovered America, but how *could* he have discovered America? Millions of people were already living here.

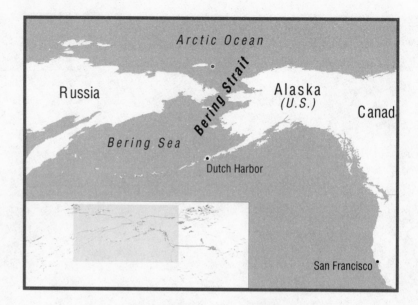

theory is that the first people to come to North America came across the Bering Strait approximately 30,000 years ago. The Bering Strait is fifty-five miles wide and separates Alaska from Russia [see map above]. It is normally frozen from October to June. During the Ice Age, a land bridge is thought to have existed between Asia and North America. Many believe that humans walked over the Bering Strait and then gradually moved south, and that the descendants of these explorers eventually became the people whom **Christopher Columbus** (1451-1506) met when he arrived in the West Indies in 1492.

3. **Prior to the arrival of the Europeans, all of the following cultures existed in what is now the United States EXCEPT**

    (A) the Omaha
    (B) the Iroquois
    (C) the Incas
    (D) the Apaches

Native Community in Montana (undated photo)

All four of these cultures existed in the Americas, but the **Incas** were from Peru in South America. Before the Europeans arrived, many different peoples lived in what is now the U.S. Depending on whom you ask, between one million and sixteen million people lived in America before the arrival of Columbus in 1492.

The arrival of Columbus led to the death of many of these civilizations. Besides being exterminated by the genocide practiced by the Europeans and later by the United States government, many of the original inhabitants of North America died because they did not have resistance to certain diseases (p. 35) (especially smallpox) that the Europeans brought to the **New World.**

Can you name two American Indian Nations in your area?

4. **Who was the first European to "discover" America?**

    (A) Christopher Columbus
    (B) Leif Eriksson
    (C) Bjarni Herjolfsson
    (D) John Cabot

Although we all learned that it was Christopher Columbus who "discovered" America, a few other explorers reached it first. In fact, the Norsemen **Leif Eriksson** (c. AD 1000) and Bjarni Herjolfsson beat Columbus to the New World by some 500 years or so. Herjolfsson reached the New World by accident; he had been blown off course on a trip from Iceland to Greenland. Eriksson tried to establish a colony there and failed.

Columbus's arrival in America is viewed by some as the arrival of an invading force. Peoples adversely affected by Columbus's arrival do not view him as a hero, but as an evildoer.

Yet without Columbus's discovery, most Americans living today would not be here. Columbus's arrival in America led to a grand social experiment, the creation of a nation of immigrants.

NORSE ARE NUMBER ONE

The first child of European parents born in North America was Snorri Karlsfini, the son of members of Norwegian explorer Leif Eriksson's first colony.

Christopher Columbus

WHAT WAS CHRIS REALLY LIKE?

Frankly, Columbus was kind of a jerk. He was a great explorer, but when he reached America he treated the "Indians" poorly. He was amazed at the generosity and naiveté of the Arawak Indians who lived in Haiti, saying that "When you ask for something they have, they never say no. To the contrary, they offer to share with anyone." But soon he required all of them to make regular contributions of gold (of which there was very little in the Caribbean Islands) and those who did not comply had their hands cut off.

When most of us are first taught about the early history of America, we picture the Pilgrims on the Mayflower searching for a better life in a place where they could practice their religion freely. We can sometimes forget that many Europeans saw America solely as a place to make a quick killing. Some came to grab gold and other precious goods while others stayed in Europe and created a system of tariffs and trade that strongly favored the home country. This exploitation was one of the reasons for the Revolutionary War (pp. 42-48).

5. In what half-century were the first successful colonies established by the British in what is now the United States?

(A) 1450-1500
(B) 1500-1550
(C) 1550-1600
(D) 1600-1650

Although Columbus discovered America in 1492 (in 1492, he sailed the ocean blue; you know the rhyme), it wasn't until 1607 that the first successful English colony was established in America. Before that time, other European nations had explored some of what is now the United States, but the English colonies that developed into the United States had not yet been established.

One colony that failed was **Sir Walter Raleigh**'s (c. 1552-1618) on Roanoke Island in 1587. When English ships arrived three years later to bring supplies, the colonists had disappeared. The only trace of the so-called "Lost Colony" was some rusted junk and the word "CROATOAN," carved into a tree. Croatoan was the name of a nearby island, but the colonists were not located there and were never found anywhere.

It's a good idea to get some sense of how long it took to establish the U.S. Columbus landed in Haiti in 1492. Spain and Portugal looted the land from that time on, but it wasn't until 1607 or so that the colonies that would turn into the United States were established. Another 170 years passed before the United States became independent from England.

COLUMBUS— TOO LONG AT SEA?

"I always read that the world, land and water, was spherical.... Now I observed so much divergence, that I began to hold different views about the world and I found it was not round...but pear shaped, round except where it has a nipple, for there it is taller, or as if one had a round ball and, on one side, it should be like a woman's breast, and this nipple part is the highest and closest to Heaven..."

—— Christopher Columbus,
From the log of his third voyage (1498)

6. What was the primary motivation for most European exploration of America during the sixteenth century?

(A) The search for religious freedom
(B) A desire to help the Native Americans
(C) A desire for Native American slaves
(D) The search for gold

Money, money, money. The European adventurers exploring during the sixteenth century were after gold and other valuables. It wasn't until the Puritans arrived in 1620 that Europeans went to

America for other reasons, and even then, the Puritans had reasons for coming to America other than the search for the freedom to practice their religion.

7. **Which of the following European nations first set up colonies in the Americas?**

   (A) Spain
   (B) England
   (C) Germany
   (D) France

Spain was the first country to set up colonies in the Americas. Christopher Columbus had been exploring for the Queen of Spain, and before England had established her first colony, 175,000 Spaniards were living in Central and South America. This is why most of the people currently living in South and Central America speak Spanish.

The colonies that would later become the United States were established by England. All thirteen of the original states were originally English colonies.

8. **What happened to the Native Americans upon the arrival of the Europeans?**

They succumbed to disease and were all but wiped out. Native Americans did not have resistance to many European diseases and were at a serious technological disadvantage—they didn't have guns—and were thus easily conquered. Those that remained were either assimilated into the dominant European societies or gradually pushed off their land as Europeans searched for more space. Many of the Native Americans who are alive today live on reservations where they are relatively autonomous. Many of them still practice elements of their traditional culture, and recently they have been making economic gains.

One of the most frequently asked questions about Native Americans is how many Natives were present before Columbus arrived and how many remain in the United States today. Anthropologist Henry Dobyns released a very thorough study in 1966 in which he estimated that between 9.8 and 12 million Native Americans lived in the area we know now as the United States before the arrival of Columbus (or, one Native American for every three square miles). By 1890 the number had been reduced to 250,000. In the name of freedom, Americans had very nearly wiped out the indigenous people of the United States. Today, according to 1990 census statistics, there are 250,372,000 people living in the United States (or 210 people for every three square miles) and 1,959,235 of those are Native Americans, which represents less than one percent of the population.

ANSWERS

....

1. D   2. A   3. C   4. C   5. D   6. D   7. A

Colonial Times

1. Who were the Puritans?

The **Puritans** were religious separatists who set up a colony in Massachusetts after being persecuted in their native England. The Puritans came over on the *Mayflower* in 1620 and set up their own community in Plymouth. More of their brethren followed and settled in Massachusetts Bay.

The Puritans set up a relatively democratic system of government. Male members of the church were allowed to vote. (Forty percent of the adult male population voted, a higher percentage than in England.) Yet, even though the Puritan community was established in order to avoid religious persecution in England, the Puritans did not establish freedom of religion in their new land. People who held unorthodox beliefs were severely punished. In order to get an idea of what life was like in the time of the Puritans, read *The Scarlet Letter*, by Nathaniel Hawthorne (1804-1864) (pp. 400-401). Although the novel is not entirely historically accurate, it does give a good sense of some of the attitudes of the time, and it explains what is meant by the idea of Puritanism.

The term "puritanical" comes from the Puritans. If someone is puritanical he is rigorous in his observance of religion or some other moral code.

2. **In which of the following cities were nineteen alleged witches put to death?**

   (A) Wichita
   (B) Salem
   (C) Boston
   (D) Atlanta

The Crucible, by Arthur Miller. A good drama depicting the paranoia that fueled the Salem Witch Trials.

One of the most diabolical results of the Puritan theocracy (a theocracy is a church-run government) was the **Salem Witch Trials,** held in Salem, Massachusetts. A group of three girls, aged nine to twelve, who had been acting strangely began to accuse different women of witchcraft. The girls' accusations were taken seriously, and the women were put to trial. In a court that shared much in common with the Spanish Inquisition (p. 155), the accused were asked for their confessions. If they did not confess, they were sentenced to death. Even after the young girls said that they had made up the whole affair for "sport," nineteen women were hanged, and one man, the husband of one of the victims, was stoned to death for refusing to plead.

She's a witch!

PURITAN LOVE

Considering that the image we have of the Puritans is of a rather prudish people, it is interesting to note that in many ways their attitude towards sex was not as puritanical as we might think. The Puritans believed that sex within marriage was a good thing. For example, when James Mattock avoided sleeping with his wife for two years he was expelled from the colony.

They did believe that adulterers should be punished, and certain sexual crimes were punished with death, but the Puritans were much more open about sex than we might have thought.

3. **Which of the following colleges was NOT among the first three established in the United States?**

   (A) Harvard
   (B) Stanford
   (C) William and Mary
   (D) Yale

Harvard (1636), William and Mary (1693), and Yale (1701) were the first three colleges chartered in the United States. (Stanford, located in California, was not chartered until 1885.) A list of the first established colleges looks suspiciously like the current **Ivy League**: Harvard, Yale, Princeton, Brown, Dartmouth, University of Pennsylvania, and Columbia University were all among the first colleges in the United States.

The establishment of these colleges helped create an American identity, which eventually led to the desire for self-rule. Most of these schools started out as seminaries that gave religious education. Only slowly did they become secular universities.

4. **Who were the primary adversaries in the French and Indian War?**

   (A) The French and the Indians
   (B) The French and the English
   (C) The French and the American colonists
   (D) The British and the American colonists

Even though **The French and Indian War** sounds as if it were a war between France and the Indians, it was actually a part of the **Seven Years' War** (1756-1763) in Europe between England and France. The French and Indian War was a conflict over the land west of the Appalachians [see map on following page] to which both England and France felt they had claim. The war was bloody and involved Indians who fought on both sides. The **Iroquois League** was particularly influential, occupying the area between French-ruled Quebec and British-ruled Albany. (People still speak French in Quebec today.)

Even though the French had much success early in the war, the considerable numerical advantage possessed by the British helped them to prevail. There were 1.6 million British colonists compared to 60,000 people living in New France.

The French and Indian War ended with British victory. The ensuing agreement, the Peace of Paris (1763), changed the manner in which

Europeans held control over their different colonies. Before the French and Indian War, France held colonies in India and much of what is now America. The Peace of Paris agreement gave to England all of North America east of the Mississippi River. Since Canada was no longer controlled by the French, the colonies no longer needed to rely heavily on Great Britain for military support. The war also helped the colonists understand the importance of intercolonial cooperation.

The Seven Years' War put England in debt up to its ears. The government of England, believing that the colonies had not contributed enough to the war effort, changed its policies and began to tax the colonies more. This change in policy led to the Revolutionary War (pp. 42-48) and ultimately to the *Declaration of Independence*, which established the United States of America.

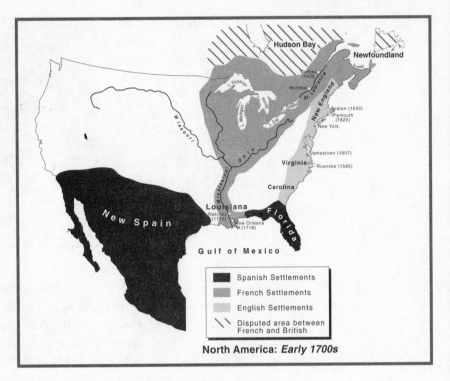

North America: *Early 1700s*

Legend:
- Spanish Settlements
- French Settlements
- English Settlements
- Disputed area between French and British

5. **Which of the following most closely describes imperialism?**

   (A) The belief that an Emperor is given divine power to rule
   (B) The policy of extending power over other countries or areas
   (C) A form of government in which all outlying provinces derive power from the interior
   (D) A form of government in which the government controls the means of production

Imperialism is a type of government in which one country holds control over a bunch of other countries. The word "imperial" comes from the word "empire," which implies that one country rules other countries for its own gain.

Imperialism has been around for a long time (see Roman Empire p. 145). During the sixteenth, seventeenth, and eighteenth centuries, the colonization of America and other lands was an attempt by European countries to establish empires. This is why we refer to the lands held by the British as the British Empire.

Depiction of the French and Indian War

In recent times, the term "imperialism" has taken on a new meaning. It is used to describe the process of **economic imperialism,** in which a country tries to control the policies of a poorer country through economic means. The term "economic imperialism" is used in a negative sense to attack the economic policies of richer nations that result in the strengthening of their powers at the expense of poorer nations.

6. **The idea that a country should regulate its trade to acquire as much precious metal as possible is called**

    (A) Mercantilism
    (B) Laissez-faire
    (C) Free trade
    (D) Industrial policy

The theory of **mercantilism** maintains that a country should set up its economy so there is a balance of trade that brings as much gold and silver into the country's treasury as possible. A country that practices this policy might set up colonies that export raw materials to the mother country while importing the mother country's manufactured goods. The aim of this practice of mercantilism would be to benefit the colonizer at the expense of the colonies.

Mercantilism was the economic policy that the British favored during the colonial period. The British imposed a series of Navigation Acts that basically forbade the colonies from trading with any other European country. These acts incensed the colonies and helped lead to the American Revolution.

7. Which of the following laws did NOT raise taxes on the American Colonists?

(A) The Sugar Act
(B) The Stamp Act
(C) The Northwest Ordinance
(D) The Tea Act

The **Sugar Act,** the **Stamp Act,** and the **Tea Act** were all taxes levied on the colonists by the British before the American Revolution. (The Northwest Ordinance was enacted by America and concerned slavery.)

These acts taxed the colonists in order to raise money for England. The colonists were furious that such taxes were enacted without their consent, and protests were organized. One of these protests resulted in the **Boston Massacre**, in which British troops fired upon demonstrating civilians. Although the word massacre implies a killing of many people, only a few Americans died. The British troops did not fire with the consent of their leader, and the Americans did do some things that provoked the shooting. (For instance, one protester clubbed a British soldier.) Nevertheless, certain rabble-rousing colonists used the massacre as a vehicle to help unify the colonists resisting British policies.

The Boston Tea Party

The Tea Act required colonists to buy tea from only one company. Even though the prices for tea fell as a result, the colonists protested against the Tea Act by refusing to let ships with the tea dock and by staging the **Boston Tea Party** in 1773, in which 150 men dressed as Indians dumped the imported tea into Boston harbor.

All these protests led to considerable unrest within the colonies. Soon the colonies would fight the American War of Independence to sever their relationship with England.

ANSWERS

....

2. B   3. B   4. B   5. B   6. A   7. C

The Revolutionary War
1773–1785

1. In what year was the First Continental Congress formed?

   (A) 1765
   (B) 1774
   (C) 1781
   (D) 1812

No Canada

At the Second Continental Congress, Canada was invited to join as a fourteenth member of the new confederation. Canada declined and remained British.

The First Continental Congress was formed in 1774 to protest certain actions taken by the British government, which the colonists called the Intolerable Acts. It urged the colonies to arm themselves to protect their rights from the encroachment of the British.

The Second Continental Congress was formed in 1775 after the battle of **Lexington and Concord**, and the American War of Independence had begun. The Second Continental Congress produced the **Declaration of Independence** and the **Articles of Confederation**.

Although the Second Continental Congress was able to lead the new nation during the American War of Independence, it was not able to govern effectively when the war ended. Its powers were limited by the Articles of Confederation, which did not provide the national government with much power.

2. **What is the significance of the battle of Lexington and Concord?**
   (A) It was the first battle in the American War of Independence.
   (B) It was the turning point in the American War of Independence.
   (C) It was the first battle in the War of 1812.
   (D) It was the battle at which Benedict Arnold was killed.

IF THEY ONLY HAD A PHONE

Five days after the battles at Lexington and Concord, a number of proposals put forth by England arrived in the colonies. The proposals addressed many of the colonists' complaints, and may have reduced the tensions between the U.S. and England had there been a better way to communicate back then.

The battle of Lexington and Concord was the first battle in the American War of Independence. The British attempted to seize military supplies stored in Concord, but were only partially successful. They succeeded in breaking through the colonists' defenses, but because of **Paul Revere's** (1735-1818) warning, most of the munitions had been secreted away. While attacking Concord, some British **Redcoats** fired at the local **Minutemen**, killing several. As the British soldiers returned to Boston, the Minutemen followed, killing hundreds.

George Washington

The battle of Lexington and Concord served to mobilize the colonists in the preparation for war. The colonists put together a unified army and petitioned the French for help. The battle forced the colonies to work together, and in so doing they realized that a national government might be possible and desirable.

IMAGINE IF THEY HAD SUCCEEDED

A plan was devised to kidnap George Washington during the War of Independence. The governor of New York, along with the mayor of New York City, plotted to kidnap the general to help England win the war. One of Washington's bodyguards who was involved in the plot was court-martialed and hanged on June 28, 1776.

Thomas Paine

The first shot fired in the battle of Lexington is sometimes referred to as **"the shot heard 'round the world."**

3. The Battle of Bunker Hill occurred in

    (A)   The American War of Independence
    (B)   The War of 1812
    (C)   The Civil War
    (D)   The Hundred Years' War

Surprisingly, the **Battle of Bunker Hill** did not take place on Bunker Hill, but instead took place on Breed's Hill during the American War of Independence. A general of the American army was attempting to protect the heights around Boston and sent his men to fortify Bunker Hill, but a mistake was made and they fortified Breed's Hill. The British managed to take Breed's Hill, but only after suffering heavy casualties—228 dead and 826 wounded—in what would be the bloodiest battle of the entire revolution.

After this battle, **George Washington** (1732-1799) was put in charge of the colonists' army.

4. Who wrote *Common Sense*?

    (A)   Thomas Paine
    (B)   George Washington
    (C)   Thomas Jefferson
    (D)   Ethan Allen

Common Sense, a pamphlet written by British-born **Thomas Paine** (1737-1809), gave an eloquent and convincing argument for U.S. secession from England. In *Common Sense*, Paine argues that "until an independence is declared, the continent will feel itself like a man who continues putting off some unpleasant business from day to day, yet knows it must be done, hates to set about it, wishes it over, and is continually haunted with the thoughts of its necessity."

The pamphlet was printed and reprinted and eventually sold half a million copies. Written persuasively, it convinced many people living in the colonies that America must be its own nation.

COMMON SENSE:
ADDRESSED TO THE
INHABITANTS
OF
AMERICA.
On the following interesting
SUBJECTS.

I. Of the Origin and Design of Government in general, with concise Remarks on the English Constitution.
II. Of Monarchy and Hereditary Succession.
III. Thoughts on the present State of American Affairs.
IV. Of the present Ability of America, with some miscellaneous Reflections.

Written by an ENGLISHMAN.
By Thomas Paine

Man knows no Master save creating HEAVEN,
Or those whom choice and common good ordain.
THOMSON.

PHILADELPHIA, Printed
And Sold by R. BELL, in Third-Street, 1776.

TITLE PAGE OF "COMMON SENSE."

5. **Write as much as you can of the first sentence of the Declaration of Independence:**

When in the Course of human Events, it becomes necessary for one People to dissolve the Political Bands, which have connected them with another, and to assume among the Powers of the Earth, the separate and equal Station to which the Laws of Nature and of Nature's God entitle them, a decent Respect to the Opinions of Mankind requires that they should declare the causes which impel them to the Separation.

We hold these Truths to be self-evident, that all Men are created equal, that they are endowed by their Creator with certain unalienable Rights, that among these are Life, Liberty, and the Pursuit of Happiness. . . .

The first few words of the **Declaration of Independence** state eloquently the reasons for the creation of America. The Declaration of Independence set lofty goals for the United States. This was to be a country where people are assumed equal (a rather new concept in the time of European monarchies (pp. 167-170)) and where people had rights including "**Life, Liberty, and the Pursuit of Happiness**."

When **Thomas Jefferson** (1743-1826) wrote these words, he was describing a new purpose for government, a purpose originally described in the philosophy of John Locke (1632-1704) (p. 172). This new form of government was supposed to represent all men, not just the nobility or the church. (Of course, when Jefferson wrote "men," he meant only white men, not women, blacks, or Native Americans, but it was revolutionary nonetheless.)

The Declaration of Independence was signed on **July 4, 1776,** now celebrated as Independence Day. On the same day in England, King George III (1738-1820) wrote in his diary that "nothing of importance happened today."

Founding Father Thomas Jefferson

If you have read anything about the **Vietnam War** (pp. 117-118), all of this will seem somewhat familiar. One of the reasons America had such a hard time fighting in Vietnam was that the enemy was intimately familiar with the lay of the land and thus had a distinct advantage over American troops.

6. How could a ragtag collection of soldiers defeat the well-organized and wealthier British Army?

The British Army was powerful, but it was fighting a war many miles from home. British soldiers had been trained in traditional European warfare, in which large groups of soldiers fought planned battles. So, while the British were good at marching in formation, they were unable to adapt to the guerrilla tactics used by the Americans. The British would win a battle, then be badly shot up in a series of ambushes on their way back to a major city. Remember, the Americans were fighting on their own turf. A Minuteman could shoot a few British soldiers, hide somewhere, and be back home in time for dinner.

The British also had to deal with the size of the American continent. For an occupying force to defeat an army in a territory as massive as the original thirteen colonies, an immense military buildup would be

BENJAMIN FRANKLIN

Benjamin Franklin was a true Renaissance man whose accomplishments could fill several books this size. He was a printer, a writer, a scientist, an inventor, a diplomat, and a philosopher. His accomplishments include negotiating aid from France for the American War of Independence and coining the phrase "Early to bed and early to rise, makes a man healthy, wealthy, and wise." He invented the lightning rod and the rocking chair.

Franklin published Poor Richard's Almanac, *an annual journal, for twenty-five years. In this widely popular magazine of wit and wisdom, he coined many phrases that are still heard today. Among them are:*

> *Necessity never made a good bargain.*
> *Three may keep a secret, if two of them are dead.*
> *God helps them that help themselves.*
> *Experience keeps a dear school, but fools will learn in no other.*

Here are some more Franklin witticisms from other texts:

> *Remember that time is money.*
> *Here Skugg lies snug / As a bug in a rug.*

Franklin is also known for wanting the national bird to be the turkey instead of the bald eagle. He considered the bald eagle "a bird of bad moral character," and the turkey "a much more respectable bird, and withal a true original native of America." If Franklin had lived to see the way in which farming has helped breed the wild turkey into a rather stupid animal, he may have been happy that his advice wasn't heeded.

required—an impossible undertaking considering the distance between England and the American colonies.

These problems were compounded by another British miscalculation: they didn't believe that the colonies were committed to the revolutionary effort. The British assumed there was a large loyalist population and that the revolution was only a revolt sponsored by a few rebels. By the time they realized the extent of support for the colonists' cause, it was too late.

7. **Which of the following countries did NOT provide support for the colonists during the American Revolution?**

   (A) France
   (B) Holland
   (C) Spain
   (D) Germany

IT AIN'T OVER YET

After the war ended, the Continental Congress still had to be careful. No longer in danger from British forces, it was still forced to flee Philadelphia to avoid bloodthirsty American soldiers demanding back pay.

While the guerrilla fighting of George Washington's army was the main reason the colonists prevailed, they also had help from several European countries which were either at odds with England or felt a certain kinship with the colonists. The most help came from France, which secretly provided aid to the colonies at the beginning of the war. The American ambassador at the time, Benjamin Franklin (1706-1790), was immensely popular in Paris. There, he was hailed as the embodiment of the ideals of the enlightenment. France was unwilling to show overt support for the colonists until it knew that the colonists were sure to prevail, but France secretly shipped military supplies and other materials to help the war effort. Franklin was even successful in convincing the almost bankrupt French government to give loans to the Americans.

During the American War of Independence, some of the soldiers who fought against the colonists were from Hesse-Kassel, an area in what is now known as Germany (p. 116), though Germany was not a unified state at the time. The British, unable to find enough of their own

Revolutionaries crossing the Concord Bridge to drive away the British in the Battle of Concord

The tide-turning Battle of Saratoga

soldiers to engage in the war, hired **Hessian Mercenaries** to help their cause. This infuriated the Colonists because the Hessians were known for their brutality in warfare. It all turned out for the best, however. Many of the Hessians stayed on and became citizens in the newly formed United States of America.

8. **Which of the following battles was considered the turning point of the American Revolution?**
   - (A) Lexington and Concord
   - (B) Bunker Hill
   - (C) Saratoga
   - (D) The Battle of Long Island

The turning point of the war was at **Saratoga**, New York, where General John Burgoyne (1722-1792) was forced to surrender 5,000 men to General Horatio Gates (c. 1727-1806) of the American forces. Before this point, France had been helping the colonies covertly, but did not want to commit to making a strong diplomatic statement until the colonists were assured of victory. When France heard of this victory, it recognized the independence of the American colonies on February 6, 1778. France then joined with Spain and Holland in declaring war on its archenemy Great Britain.

With France and Spain on their side, the American colonies were assured of victory. On September 3, 1783, a treaty was signed with Great Britain that recognized the independence of the United States.

YOUNG HICKORY

At the age of fourteen, Andrew Jackson (pp. 56-58) was imprisoned by the British during the Revolutionary War. He then refused to polish a British officer's boots and was punished with a sabre blow that left him marked for life and inspired his lifelong dislike of Great Britain.

ANSWERS

1. A   2. A   3. A   4. A   7. D   8. C

Early U.S. History
1785–1820

1. Which of the following parts of our current governmental structure was defined in the Articles of Confederation?

   (A) The legislative branch
   (B) The executive branch
   (C) The judicial branch
   (D) The military branch

   The Articles of Confederation only provided for a weak central government, without an executive branch or a judicial branch. While the states had their own systems of government, the only national power was a single-chambered Congress. With one vote for each state, it decided whether laws should be put into place. Because of the limited power of the federal government, the Articles of Confederation failed. The national government could not raise taxes and it could not regulate commerce. It was a fundamentally weak government that could not deal with any situation requiring strong leadership. Without a change, unified government of the states was impossible.

The Continental Congress did succeed in passing some legislation about the territories west of the thirteen original states, but because this national government could not levy taxes, it was unable to carry out many of its functions.

2. **Write as much as you can of the first sentence of the Constitution.**

We the People of the United States, in order to form a more perfect union, establish justice, insure domestic tranquillity, provide for the common defence, promote the general welfare, and secure the blessings of liberty to ourselves and our posterity, do ordain and establish this Constitution for the United States of America.

These words, the preamble to the **Constitution of the United States,** established the government of the United States. Two hundred years later the Constitution is still the law of the land.

Considering how well the writers of the Constitution did their job, it is interesting to note just how difficult a time they had in passing it. At the time people were afraid of a document that formed a strong national government. They did not want to be ruled by a despot, and the original Constitution did not have any protection for individual rights. People were also unhappy with the way in which the Constitution was drafted. The Constitution was written in secret with no public record kept of the drafting, and the delegates who wrote the Constitution had not been instructed to form an entirely new type of government.

After much politicking, the Constitution was ratified in June, 1788 by the necessary nine states. Other states soon followed. The last, Rhode Island, ratified the Constitution in May, 1790, after George Washington had taken the oath of office as President.

3. **Who is the Commander in Chief of the U.S. armed forces?**

   (A) The Chairman of the Joint Chiefs of Staff
   (B) The Secretary of State
   (C) The highest ranking general of any of the services
   (D) The President

4. Which branch of government is given the power to declare war?

(A) The executive branch
(B) The legislative branch
(C) The judicial branch
(D) The military branch

The Constitution is an excellent example of **federalism,** the sharing of power between the states and the national government. The Constitution set up three branches of government: the executive, the judicial, and the legislative. Each has different powers.

The executive branch belongs to the president and his aides. The president, who is Commander in Chief of the armed forces, can make appointments to his cabinet and to agencies under his jurisdiction, and he has veto power over legislation. In the Constitution, the states hold the power to elect the president.

The legislative branch is **Congress** and consists of the **Senate**, composed of two legislators per state, and the **House of Representatives,** which is elected in proportion to each state's population. Each Representative (commonly known as Congressman or Congresswoman) is elected by approximately the same number of people, so states with more people have more Representatives. The legislative branch has the power to make laws and to declare war. In the early days of the United States, the legislative branch controlled government because of the power of the purse. Over the years, despite the fact that Congress controls the money, the power has shifted to the president and the executive branch.

The judicial branch interprets the laws passed by Congress and judges whether they follow the rules of the Constitution. The final arbiter of constitutionality is the **Supreme Court.**

5. Which of the following rights is NOT guaranteed in the U.S. Constitution?

(A) The right to bear arms
(B) The right to free speech
(C) The right to the pursuit of happiness
(D) The right to vote

First Lady and early advocate of women's rights, Abigail Adams

FROM THE VOICE OF ABIGAIL ADAMS (1744-1818)

In the new Code of Laws which I suppose it will be necessary for you to make I desire you would Remember the Ladies, and be more generous and favourable to them than your ancestors. Do not put such unlimited powers into the hands of the Husbands. Remember all men would be tyrants if they could. If particular care and attention is not paid to the Ladies, we are determined to foment a Rebellion, and will not hold ourselves bound by any laws in which we have no voice, or Representation.

YOU GOTTA FIGHT FOR THE RIGHT

Many of the rights we take for granted were not in the original U.S. Constitution of 1788. You may be surprised when you see how long it took to correct some of these oversights.

It took seventy-seven years for the United States to abolish slavery (the Thirteenth Amendment, 1865).

After eighty years, the Fourteenth Amendment (1868) guaranteed all persons born in the United States the right to due process and citizenship. These rights were not extended to Native Americans, who were not considered among "all persons" at the time. It took another fifty-six years and an act of Congress for Native Americans to gain their citizenship rights.

After eighty-two years, the Fifteenth Amendment (1870) secured the right of all citizens to vote, regardless of race or creed, but not regardless of gender. It took another fifty years for women to be given the constitutional right to vote. The Nineteenth Amendment (1920) was ratified 132 years after the original Constitution was written.

A poll tax had been constitutional for 176 years until the Twenty-fourth Amendment eliminated the tax in 1964, making it possible for the poor and underprivileged to vote.

People eighteen years of age or older were not given the right to vote until 183 years after the Constitution was written when the Twenty-sixth Amendment was ratified in 1971. It's an important right. Use it.

Actually, none of these rights were guaranteed in the *original* U.S. Constitution, but the right to bear arms, the right to free speech, and the right to vote were all included in the **Bill of Rights** in 1792. ("The pursuit of happiness" is mentioned in the Declaration of Independence.) The Bill of Rights is a series of ten amendments to the Constitution that guarantees the rights of the individual in the U.S.

Besides the above-mentioned rights, the Bill of Rights also guarantees that people do not have to house soldiers, will not be subject to unreasonable searches and seizures, will have due process in criminal cases, will have the right to a speedy trial, will have the right to a jury in suits at law, and will not be unfairly punished for crimes committed.

The Bill of Rights also guarantees that anything not specifically assigned to the national government by the Constitution should be taken care of by the states. This provision divides power between federal and state governments and allows the states a good deal of independence, even while they are still part of the federal system.

6. **The three-fifths compromise was concerned with**
   (A) Land
   (B) Taxes
   (C) Slaves
   (D) Shipping

The **three-fifths compromise** was formed to deal with the issue of slaves in the original states. The House of Representatives is set up with proportional representation—the more people a state has, the more Representatives that state can send to the House. The original framers of the Constitution could not figure out what to do with the whole slavery issue. Counting the slaves as "people" would give slave states undue representation. Yet, this did not seem fair, because the slaves didn't vote. A compromise was reached: Each slave was to be counted as three-fifths of a person in deciding the number of Representatives sent to the House.

Remember, this cynical piece of legislation is part of our original Constitution. The original framers of the Constitution, only twelve years after the Declaration of Independence declared that "all men are created equal," had declared some men only three-fifths equal.

Second President of the U.S., John Adams

7. Who was the second president of the United States?

(A) Benjamin Franklin
(B) John Adams
(C) Thomas Jefferson
(D) John Hancock

John Adams (1735-1826) was the second president of the United States. He was a diplomat during the American Revolution and served as the vice president under George Washington. Adams's presidency proved that a peaceful transition of government was possible. Adams took over after Washington willingly stepped down. Then Adams ceded the power of the government to the opposing party led by **Thomas Jefferson,** the third President, after Jefferson won the election. Incidentally, future presidents were to use Washington as an example for how many terms they should serve. Washington stepped down after two terms, and it wasn't until the 1940s that a president served more terms than Washington (FDR pp. 93-94).

The fear that a peaceful transition was not possible was well founded. During Washington's and Adams' presidencies, the French Revolution (pp. 173-175) was happening in Europe. An incredibly bloody and murderous affair, the French Revolution served as a model of all that could go wrong in a transfer of power. Luckily for us, Jefferson's campaign against Adams, though full of mudslinging and rumor-mongering, was essentially peaceful. No bullets were fired, no bombs exploded, and no heads were chopped off.

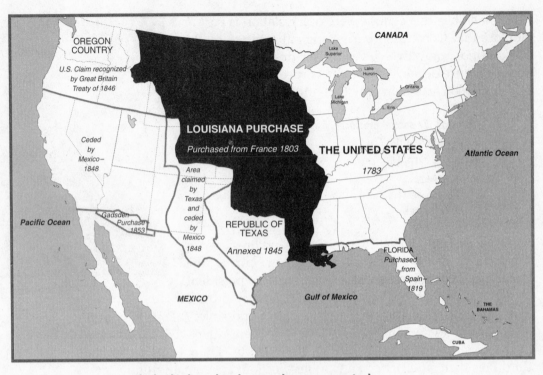

8. **The land indicated in the map above was acquired through**

(A) a purchase
(B) war with a European power
(C) unilateral annexation
(D) war with Native Americans

The area darkened in the map above made up what is called the **Louisiana Purchase.** It was acquired from France in 1803 for approximately fifteen million dollars, a bargain even considering inflation. The Louisiana Purchase consisted of more than 800,000 square miles, which means that it cost $18.75 a square mile or roughly 3¢ an acre.

Thomas Jefferson heard that the French had secretly acquired the Louisiana territory from Spain. He was worried about the possibility that France would not allow free passage on the Mississippi river, so he instructed two emissaries in Paris to negotiate with Napoleon (pp. 176-177) about purchasing the area of Orleans. The emissaries were surprised and delighted when Napoleon offered them the entire Louisiana Territory. Napoleon was having troubles in Haiti and needed money to continue his wars in Europe. Realizing that Haiti was too much trouble to keep, he had no further need for the Louisiana territory.

The Louisiana Purchase practically doubled the size of the United States and allowed for free travel on the Mississippi. It also furthered the idea that the United States might some day extend to the western edge of the continent.

Lewis and Clark

9. What were Lewis and Clark known for?

(A) Crossing the Delaware
(B) Designing a new type of fabric
(C) Exploring Oregon
(D) Leading a series of attacks against the American Indians

Meriwether Lewis (1774-1809) and William Clark (1770-1838) led a year-and-a-half-long exploratory expedition to the Pacific in 1804. The Lewis and Clark expedition strengthened American claims to the Oregon Territory, an area that was also claimed by Great Britain and Spain in the early nineteenth century.

Eventually, the United States acquired a good deal of the Oregon Territory. It was annexed in 1846, with the dividing line between English and American territory set at the latitude of 54° 40′.

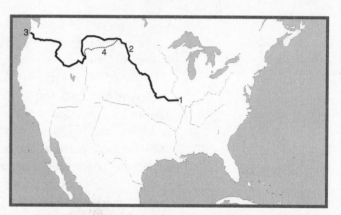

Lewis and Clark's journey: 1. Wintered at St. Louis, 1803-4 2. Wintered at Fort Mandan, 1804-5 3. Wintered at Fort Clatsop, 1805-6 4. Clark returned via the Yellowstone River, 1806

10. What was the War of 1812 about?

The War of 1812 was officially a war with Britain to stop it from seizing American ships and provoking Indian attacks on Western settlers. The war was encouraged by Westerners with expansionist goals who wanted to increase the size of the United States and possibly acquire then-British Canada. The war was opposed by northeastern Federalists who wanted to keep trading with Great Britain.

"54-40 or fight!" was a rallying cry of U.S. soldiers during the War of 1812.

The U.S. was not quite prepared to go to war. The Republican administration had not given much money to the military, and at first things went rather poorly. In a symbolic and devastating early victory, the British succeeding in burning several buildings in Washington, including the Capitol and the president's house. But, in the end, the U.S. did respectably well. One result of the war was an enduring patriotic ditty penned by **Francis Scott Key** (1779-1843). **"The Star-Spangled Banner"** (our national anthem) was written during a battle in which the U.S. prevented the British from entering Baltimore.

11. **Which of the following people was credited by the people of the United States with having won the final battle of the War of 1812?**
   (A) Andrew Jackson
   (B) Thomas Jefferson
   (C) James Madison
   (D) James Monroe

One of the final battles of the War of 1812 provided America's most overwhelming victory. The British, unaware that a peace treaty had been signed, attacked an American position. In what became known as the **Battle of New Orleans**, United States soldiers, under the deft leadership of **Andrew Jackson** (1767-1845), succeeded in inflicting massive losses upon the attacking British soldiers. The Americans only suffered eight deaths compared to over two thousand for the British. Even though the battle took place after the peace treaty with England had been signed—the news had not yet reached Jackson or the British Soldiers—Jackson was proclaimed a hero. The publicity from the event helped catapult him to the presidency a few years later.

The War of 1812, and particularly Jackson's overwhelming victory in the Battle of New Orleans, confirmed in many Americans' minds that the U.S. had a special destiny. If small groups of determined Americans could defeat the world's most powerful army (England had just defeated Napoleon in Europe), God must have special plans for them.

ANSWERS
....
1. A   3. D   4. B   5. C   6. C   7. B   8. A   9. C   11. A

THE MODERN BALAAM AND HIS ASS.

1. **Which of the following political parties was formed as a result of Andrew Jackson's defeat in the election of 1824?**

   (A) Democrat
   (B) Republican
   (C) Whig
   (D) Know Nothing

Andrew Jackson

The **Democratic Party** was formed after Andrew Jackson lost the election in 1824. In the election, Jackson had won a **plurality** of the popular vote and the electoral vote. (A plurality is when someone has the most votes, but not more than fifty percent of those cast.) Because Jackson did not receive a majority, the election was sent to the House of Representatives. There it was decided that the second-place finisher, **John Quincy Adams** (1767-1848), would become president. Henry Clay (1777-1852), the fourth-place finisher, gave his support to Adams. In what

The Democratic Party, begun by supporters of Jackson in 1824, is one of the two dominant parties in American politics today. The style of campaigning started by Jackson's supporters is another of Jackson's lasting legacies: Image, not issues, often wins elections. Jackson is also known for increasing the power of the presidency. He was the first president to use the veto extensively and to cast himself as the representative of the entire population of the United States, embodying the common people as well as the wealthy.

Jackson's supporters considered a dirty political deal, Clay was named secretary of state.

Jackson began his campaign for the 1828 election immediately. He was cast as a tough-minded military man and given the nickname "Old Hickory" (which in those days was a good thing). Rather than concentrating on the issues, Jackson's campaign focused on his personality, much like campaigns do today.

Part of the reason that Jackson's campaign was successful was an increase in the number of people who could vote. Before this time, many states had had property requirements and other barriers to voting. The election of 1828 was one of the first elections in which a high percentage of white men could actually vote.

2. Where is the Alamo?

(A) Texas
(B) Louisiana
(C) Maine
(D) Alabama

The **Alamo** was the scene of a battle between Mexicans and American settlers living in Texas. By the 1830s, Americans outnumbered Mexicans in the state. The Mexican dictator of the time, **Santa Anna,** outlawed slavery and attempted to collect taxes in order to dissuade Americans from living in Texas.

Because of Americans' innate dislike of taxes, and Texans' pro-slavery stance, the settlers rebelled and were soon at war with Santa Anna and his men. At the battle of the Alamo, 182 Americans were vastly outnumbered by over 6,000 Mexican troops. After surviving the Mexican barrage for thirteen days, they were all killed. Even in defeat, however, the soldiers became symbols of the American

Symbol of American bravery, the Alamo

spirit—if you are going to lose a war, you might as well go all out and fight to the last man—and the slogan **"Remember the Alamo!"** became the rallying cry of western expansionists everywhere.

3. **In which year did Mexico become independent from Spain?**
   - (A) 1784
   - (B) 1821
   - (C) 1867
   - (D) 1911

Mexico gained its independence from Spain in 1821, and the newly independent Mexico gradually lost large amounts of territory in skirmishes with the U.S. In 1836, Texas rebelled against Mexico and sought annexation to the U.S., but anti-slavery forces opposed the admission of another slave state. Texas remained an independent republic under its Lone Star flag until its annexation by the U.S. in 1845. (That's what those "Republic of Texas" t-shirts mean.) Mexico refused to recognize Texas as part of the U.S., which led to the Mexican-American War (1846–1848). The U.S. won (again) and claimed land that is now New Mexico and California.

4. **What is "Manifest Destiny"?**
   - (A) The belief that the borders of the United States should extend to the edge of the continent
   - (B) The belief held by communist leaders that they should control the world
   - (C) The American belief that we should continue to dictate policies in Third World nations
   - (D) The belief that French culture should extend to the far reaches of the globe

Manifest Destiny was a belief held by many Americans that the U.S. was destined to extend to the edge of the continent. These Americans believed that areas west of the established states, unsettled except by nomadic tribes, should become part of the nation. This philosophy, although successful, did not take into account Native Americans, who were either forced off their land onto reservations or killed.

Our nation's ethical beliefs were different back then. Indians were savages whose land was free for the taking. Blacks were only good for slavery. We, as a nation, believed in the concept of **pluralism**—the view that decisions are arrived at through the clash of competing interests and ideas—only when it applied to white men of European descent. If one were not a white Christian man with property, one did not have rights in

ANSWERS

....

1. A   2. A   3. B   4. A

Before the Civil War
1840–1860

1. **The Missouri Compromise was a compromise between**

   (A) The U.S. and France
   (B) The U.S. and England
   (C) The northern and southern states
   (D) The northern states and Canada

Gone With the Wind (pp. 414-415) **(1939).** The all-time classic about southern belle Scarlett O'Hara's struggles before and after the Civil War.

The **Missouri Compromise** (1820) was forged between slave states and free states. Before the Civil War, the U.S. was divided almost equally between slave-owning states in the South and states that did not allow slavery in the North. As the U.S. expanded westward and new states joined the union, there was always conflict over whether slavery would be allowed in the new states. The North wanted the new states to make slavery illegal while the South wanted the new states to allow slavery.

The Missouri Compromise was forged when Missouri requested to be admitted into the union. Because Missouri allowed slavery, northern politicians did not want to allow its entrance into the United States.

Different political solutions were attempted, but the problem was solved only when Maine decided to enter simultaneously as a free state. Both states were allowed to join, and the United States remained balanced.

Slavery as an issue divided the United States until (and some might argue well after) the Civil War. The three-fifths clause in the Constitution and the friction caused by the different ways in which black people were treated in the North and the South created a sense that the United States was two different nations. Yet people living in the North were not all fair-minded abolitionists working for an end to slavery. While many northerners felt slavery was immoral, they realized that it was an indispensable part of the southern economy. Until the Civil War, most northerners only wanted to stop the spread of slavery. Many northerners felt that the abolitionists were fanatics who threatened civilized society.

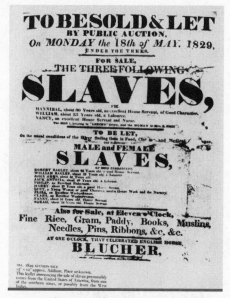

Advertisement for a slave auction complete with descriptions of people, sixteen to forty years old, for sale

2. **Which of the following states borders on the Mason-Dixon line?**

   (A) North Carolina
   (B) Tennessee
   (C) Maryland
   (D) Michigan

Although the Mason-Dixon line is commonly known as the dividing line between northern and southern states, it was originally marked as a dividing line between Pennsylvania and Maryland. In the Missouri Compromise, the line separated the states that allowed slavery and those that did not.

The southern economy was based on a labor-intensive system of agriculture. Cotton and tobacco, both highly profitable cash crops, needed many hands to be cultivated effectively. Slavery provided an inexpensive way in which to grow these crops. However, an increasingly accepted argument holds that slavery actually worked against the South economically by sidetracking the southern states from the economic opportunities afforded the North in manufacturing and trade. In any case, the economic impact of slavery is of secondary importance to the immorality inherent in the subjugation of a race of people because of their skin color, or for any reason. Mistreatment of minority groups is part of our history. Americans must remember this aspect of our past in order to prevent similar tragedies from happening in the future.

Slave laborers on a cotton plantation

THE COTTON GIN

In 1794, the cotton gin was patented by Eli Whitney, a Yale graduate who also maufactured fire arms. The cotton gin revolutionized the cotton industry by automating the process of separating the cotton fibers from the seed bolls, removing the need for hours and hours of slave labor. Although credited with the invention of the cotton gin, it is rumored that Whitney took credit for an idea that was, in fact, the brainchild of a slave.

Numerous movies and television shows have depicted life in the time of slavery. Read the book or watch the television series *Roots*—both are excellent.

3. ***Uncle Tom's Cabin* was written by**

(A) William Lloyd Garrison
(B) Susan B. Anthony
(C) Harriet Beecher Stowe
(D) Herman Melville

Uncle Tom's Cabin, written by **Harriet Beecher Stowe** (1811-1896), was one of the most influential books ever written in America. This fictional account of the lives of slaves gave a human face to the horrors of slavery. Before the novel, many Americans thought of slaves as less than human. The novel's humanistic portrayal of slaves served to galvanize those who did not like slavery and convinced others of slavery's inherent evils. *Uncle Tom's Cabin* was important in convincing northerners who already had some qualms about slavery that it was truly an evil institution. The book also sold well in Europe and became something of an embarrassment to the U.S. Here was the nation of liberty and independence allowing horrible injustice in its midst. When Lincoln met Harriet Beecher Stowe, he is said to have remarked "So you're the little woman who wrote the book that started this great war."

Uncle Tom's author

4. What percentage of southerners owned more than twenty slaves before the Civil War?

(A) 74%
(B) 50%
(C) 25%
(D) 4%

As much as slavery defines the South before the Civil War, not all southerners actually owned slaves. According to census studies of the time, only twenty-five percent owned slaves, while a mere four percent owned more than twenty. Those who did own slaves, mostly wealthy plantation owners, were highly influential in the culture and politics of the South. Besides, it was not necessarily as if the southerners who did not own slaves did not want to own slaves; in many cases they just could not afford them, or did not have enough land to make economical use of them. A strong young black male in the 1850s was valued at $1,800, a considerable sum in those days.

5. **When were the first public efforts made to abolish slavery in America?**

(A) The 1750s
(B) The 1770s
(C) The 1830s
(D) The 1840s

Roots. Alex Haley's engrossing book—later a television series—recounts the history of his ancestors from their lives in Africa to their experiences in America as they were forced into slavery.

Toni Morrison's (p. 397, p. 408) novel *Beloved.*

Although American abolitionist sentiment (among whites) existed in the eighteenth century (individual Quakers were decrying slavery as early as 1726, then as a group during the 1750s), it wasn't until the 1830s that the movement really coalesced. Before that time, some abolitionists advocated a gradual approach that reimbursed owners for the loss of their slaves. In 1831, **William Lloyd Garrison** (1805-1879) began publication of the newspaper *The Liberator*, which advocated a more radical approach. He wanted to end slavery in one grand gesture, freeing all the slaves without compensating the owners.

The strong anti-slavery position in the North given voice by Garrison caused the South to stick to its guns. Before the 1830s, some southern abolitionists argued against slavery. However, in response to radical statements from the North, southerners became more rabidly pro-slavery. Some even argued that slavery was more humane than the treatment given the "wage-slaves" forced to work in factories in the North. Of course these people overlooked the essential difference between a slave and a free worker: A slave who leaves his job is killed; a free worker is still free to try to find another job. This is not to say that "wage-slaves" had easy lives. The early industrial period (pp. 344-345) is not known for its kindness to workers.

IN THE WORDS OF FREDERICK DOUGLASS

What, to the American slave, is your Fourth of July? I answer: A day that reveals to him, more than all other days in the year, the gross injustice and cruelty to which he is the constant victim. To him your celebration is a sham. . . . You profess to believe that "of one blood God made all nations of men to dwell on the face of all the earth"—and hath commanded all men, everywhere, to love one another—yet you notoriously hate (and glory in your hatred!) all men whose skins are not colored like your own!

Frederick Douglass

6. **Which of the following people was a former slave who became an abolitionist and an adviser to President Abraham Lincoln?**

   (A) Frederick Douglass
   (B) Martin Luther King
   (C) Langston Hughes
   (D) James Weldon Johnson

Frederick Douglass (1817-1895), a former slave, went on to become an abolitionist and an adviser to **Abraham Lincoln** (1809–1865). Douglass, an effective orator, was instrumental in convincing people of the evil nature of slavery. He helped convince the union army to allow blacks to fight, and continued to work for reforms for blacks and women until the day he died.

Too often the abolitionist movement is depicted as a struggle between white people who believed in slavery and white people who did not believe in slavery, but in actuality blacks were instrumental in achieving their own freedom. Douglass, **Harriet Tubman** (1821-1913), and even **Nat Turner** (1800-1831), who led a bloody slave revolt that led to the deaths of numerous whites and several slaves killed in retaliation, all furthered the abolitionist cause.

7. **Which of the following most accurately describes the "underground railroad"?**

   (A) The first intercity subway system
   (B) How people paid for slaves without paying taxes
   (C) One way in which slaves escaped to the North
   (D) The first novel by Harriet Beecher Stowe

The underground railroad is a term used to describe the way in which blacks escaped to the North and freedom. The people who helped the blacks, many of whom were Quakers, were referred to as "conductors." They would shelter slaves in their homes, usually putting themselves at great personal risk.

Many times freed slaves would help other slaves to escape. These people would often risk their lives to help others reach freedom. One of the most famous of these conductors was Harriet Tubman, a freed slave, who was responsible for freeing at least 300 others.

8. **With which of the following people did Abraham Lincoln debate in 1858?**

    (A) Stephen Douglas
    (B) John Brown
    (C) James K. Polk
    (D) John Tyler

Stephen Douglas (1813-1861) and Abraham Lincoln engaged in a series of debates during a Senate race in Illinois. Douglas won the race, but Lincoln was catapulted into the national spotlight. The debates were publicized in the newspapers and concerned the question of slavery.

Lincoln's debates with Douglas brought him into the national political arena. Lincoln would eventually go on to win the Presidential election of 1860 and preside over the Civil War. When he became President, his belief that slavery should not be allowed in the new states brought the slavery issue to a head.

Honest Abe

FROM THE VOICE OF ABRAHAM LINCOLN

"A house divided against itself cannot stand. I believe this government cannot endure permanently half slave and half free. I do not expect the Union to be dissolved—I do not expect the house to fall— but I do expect it will cease to be divided. It will become all one thing, or all the other."

ANSWERS

1. C   2. C   3. C   4. D   5. A   6. A   7. C   8. A

The Civil War and Reconstruction
1861–1880

1. Which of the following people was a general of the Confederate Army near the end of the Civil War?

   (A) Robert E. Lee
   (B) Ulysses S. Grant
   (C) Stephen Douglas
   (D) John C. Calhoun

Robert E. Lee (1807-1870) was in charge of all Confederate armies near the end of the Civil War. He was considered the ablest general during the war, and succeeded in taking a southern force that was at a disadvantage and leading it successfully against far superior Union forces.

Confederate General Robert E. Lee

2. **Which of the following people was a general of the Union Army near the end of the Civil War?**

(A) Robert E. Lee
(B) Abraham Lincoln
(C) Thomas J. "Stonewall" Jackson
(D) Ulysses S. Grant

Ulysses S. Grant (1822-1885), and **William Sherman** (1820-1891) were important generals for the Union Army during the Civil War. Sherman is credited with inventing "modern" warfare. He led a vicious "scorch the earth" campaign against the South in which he attacked civilian localities as well as soldiers. Grant later became president.

Union General Ulysses S. Grant

Casualties of the Battle of Gettysburg

During the Civil War, about 560,000 Americans were killed. It changed the American outlook and affected the way black and white Americans in the North and South interacted. The war strengthened the North's industrial economy and crippled the southern economy immeasurably. The campaigns of Sherman and Grant were effective in razing the South, and it took years for the South to regain its strength.

After the North won the war, it imposed a bunch of laws on the South in order to ensure that blacks were treated fairly and to punish the southerners for seceding. This legislation, called Reconstruction (p. 69), ended up causing all kinds of problems.

The 1993 documentary *The Civil War*, directed by Ken Burns, is a thorough and fascinating look at the entire Civil War era. The movie *Glory* (1989) is also entertaining, if not quite as illuminating.

THE GETTYSBURG ADDRESS

"Fourscore and seven years ago our fathers brought forth on this continent a new nation, conceived in Liberty, and dedicated to the proposition that all men are created equal. Now we are engaged in a great civil war, testing whether that nation or any nation so conceived and so dedicated can long endure. We are met on a great battlefield of that war. We have come to dedicate a portion of that field as a final resting-place for those who here gave their lives that that nation might live. It is altogether fitting and proper that we should do this. But in a larger sense, we cannot dedicate, we cannot consecrate, we cannot hallow this ground. The brave men, living and dead, who struggled here have consecrated it far above our poor power to add or detract. The world will little note nor long remember what we say here, but it can never forget what they did here. It is for us the living rather to be dedicated here to the unfinished work which they who fought here have thus far so nobly advanced. It is rather for us to be here dedicated to the great task remaining before us—that from these honored dead we take increased devotion to that cause for which they gave the last full measure of devotion—that we here highly resolve that these dead shall not have died in vain, that this nation under God shall have a new birth of freedom, and that government of the people, by the people, for the people shall not perish from the earth."

3. **Write as much as you can of the first sentence of the Gettysburg Address.**

The **Gettysburg Address** was delivered by Lincoln a few months after the battle of Gettysburg. At the battle of Gettysburg, the northern forces succeeded in turning back and practically destroying Robert E. Lee's army. The speech, one of the best ever given in the English language, honored the soldiers who had died in the battle. (By the way, a score is twenty years.)

4. **In what year was the Emancipation Proclamation written?**
   (A) 1825
   (B) 1835
   (C) 1863
   (D) 1965

5. **What was the Emancipation Proclamation?**
   (A) A document created during the Civil War that declared "forever free" the slaves of the rebel states
   (B) A speech given by Martin Luther King Jr. that proclaimed African Americans as deserving of rights equal to those of whites
   (C) A speech given by Susan B. Anthony asking for universal suffrage
   (D) The words written at the base of the Statue of Liberty

The **Emancipation Proclamation** was written in 1863; it proclaimed that all slaves in rebel states were free. Although the Emancipation Proclamation did not directly free that many slaves—the rebel states had already seceded, and so they did not follow its dictates—it did serve to make slavery an issue in the war.

The Emancipation Proclamation changed the focus of the war. At first, Lincoln's goal during the war was to bring the Union back together. He was not interested in freeing the slaves. But as pressure increased in Congress, the idea of freeing the slaves started to appeal to him. The Emancipation Proclamation helped build momentum for the Thirteenth Amendment, which outlawed slavery.

6. **Which of the following most accurately describes Reconstruction?**

   (A) The process of reforming the Union after the Civil War
   (B) The rebuilding of Europe after World War II
   (C) The buildup of the Union army near the time of the Civil War
   (D) The increase in debt caused by the War of 1812

The Beguiled (1971), starring Clint Eastwood (pp. 423-424) as a wounded Union soldier taken in by the inhabitants of a southern girls' school. Things get strange quickly.

The term "Reconstruction" refers to the period of time immediately after the Civil War when the United States became united again. After the horrors of the war, the victorious North was furious with the South and wanted to impose penalties on them.

Lincoln favored a plan of moderation that did not cause undue pain to the southern states, but Congress, led by radical Republicans, favored a plan that severely punished the South.

One "radical" idea that was passed around Congress was dividing up southern plantations and giving black men land and work animals. The plan fell through and the legislation that would give every black man **40 acres and a mule** failed.

The radical Republicans won out when President Lincoln was assassinated, and they established a plan for Reconstruction that further burdened the already deteriorated southern states.

7. • **Where was Lincoln assassinated?**

   (A) The White House
   (B) Ford's Theatre
   (C) Camp David
   (D) Dallas

Lincoln was attending a play at Ford's Theatre when his bodyguard left him alone for a while. A shot was heard and a man jumped out of Lincoln's box onto the stage, shouting "*Sic semper tyrannis!* (Thus always to tyrants!) The South is avenged!" In jumping, the man broke his shin.

At the same time Lincoln was being assassinated, an attempt was made on the life of **Secretary of State William Seward** (1801-1872). There were also planned attacks on **Vice President Johnson** (1808-1875) and General Grant that were not carried out.

Assassin John Wilkes Booth

Lincoln's killer, **John Wilkes Booth** (1839-1865), was shot or killed himself in a barn twelve days later. Many people entertained conspiracy theories, one of which held that **Jefferson Davis** (1808-1889), the president of the Confederacy, was involved in the shooting.

The last form of "legal" segregation, **apartheid** (apart/same), was abolished in South African (p. 212) elections in 1994.

8. What was the purpose of the Thirteenth Amendment to the Constitution?

(A) To make the purchase of liquor illegal in all states
(B) To increase the power of the President
(C) To give all citizens the right to vote
(D) To make slavery illegal in the United States

The Thirteenth, Fourteenth, and Fifteenth Amendments were passed to give southern blacks more rights. The **Thirteenth Amendment** prohibited slavery. The **Fourteenth Amendment** made all people born in the United States citizens of the United States; in so doing, it contradicted the three-fifths compromise (pp. 52-53). The **Fifteenth Amendment** allowed all male citizens, regardless of race, to vote.

These three amendments helped nullify many biased laws, particularly the three-fifth compromise in the Constitution. They established the basis for legal equality among citizens of the United States, and made meaningless some of the most embarrassing and inequitable provisions of the Constitution. Still, it was a long time before the right to vote was universal in this country. Southerners passed "**Jim Crow**" laws and other legislation to make it hard for black people to vote, and women did not get the right to vote (pp. 87-88) until 1920.

FROM THE VOICE OF JOHN MARSHALL HARLAN (1833-1911) (THE LONE DISSENTING VIEW IN PLESSY V. FERGUSON)

··

"We boast of the freedom enjoyed by our people above all other peoples. But it is difficult to reconcile that boast with a state of the law which, practically, puts the brand of servitude and degradation upon a large class of our fellow citizens, our equals before the law…"

9. What was the result of the Plessy v. Ferguson decision that established the legality of "separate but equal" facilities?

(A) Women and men could both have equal access to certain government institutions.
(B) Blacks could be segregated into inferior schools and hospitals.
(C) The government had to spend the same amount of money on facilities that served blacks as on those that served whites.
(D) The government could deny funding to programs that integrated schools.

Plessy v. Ferguson (1896) basically declared segregation legal. The ruling determined whether a man named Homer Plessy, who was seven-eights Caucasian, could sit in a "whites only" car on a train in Louisiana. The court ruled for Louisiana, saying that there is nothing inherently inequitable about **"separate but equal"** conditions.

This law made legal separate schools, hospitals, and other public institutions, allowing the South to continue to treat blacks as second-class citizens. "Jim Crow" laws were passed to ensure the dominance of white society. Blacks were denied the vote (even though the Fifteenth Amendment of the Constitution gave blacks the vote) through literacy tests, poll taxes, a grandfather clause (saying that only men whose grandfathers had voted could vote), and other means.

FROM THE VOICE OF BOOKER T. WASHINGTON

"You can't hold a man down without staying down with him." Washington believed that an educated black elite should lead blacks to freedom and equality.

10. **How did the views of Booker T. Washington about the goals of blacks after the Civil War differ from those of W. E. B. Du Bois?**

   (A) Washington advocated an immediate exodus to Africa, while Du Bois wanted simple equity.
   (B) Washington advocated economic success first, while Du Bois wanted to agitate immediately for equality.
   (C) Washington concentrated his efforts on education while Du Bois focused on increasing earning power.
   (D) Washington wanted to end white oppression through violent means while Du Bois wanted to use non-violence.

FROM THE VOICE OF W. E. B. DU BOIS (1868-1963)

"The cost of liberty is less than the price of repression."

Du Bois advocated a more forceful approach than Washington and believed that blacks should agitate for complete equality.

Booker T. Washington (1856–1915) was a successful educator who felt that blacks should first achieve economic success before campaigning for political equality. His critics, including **W.E.B. Du Bois** (1868-1963), an early leader of the NAACP and uncompromising advocate of black American rights, complained that Washington was too accommodating concerning current

For more on DuBois, read the Pulitzer Prize-winning biography *W.E.B. Du Bois: Biography of a Race*, by David Levering Lewis.

ANSWERS

1. A 2. D 4. C 5. A 6. A 7. B 8. D 9. B

Western Expansionism
1865-1880

WOUNDED KNEE

*The Native Americans were usually on the losing side of conflicts with U.S. soldiers. One of the most notorious attacks on Native Americans occurred at **Wounded Knee** in South Dakota, where over 150 Sioux were surrounded and killed by soldiers.*

For more on this heinous attack read *Bury My Heart at Wounded Knee*, by Dee Brown.

1. **Who was General Custer fighting when he was killed in 1876?**

   (A) The English
   (B) The Mexicans
   (C) The Sioux and Northern Cheyenne
   (D) The southern states

   General George Custer (1839-1876) led a famous battle against the Sioux and Northern Cheyenne in 1876 **(Custer's Last Stand).** Custer took an army of 250 men against what turned out to be a far superior Native American force. Custer was so sure of his troops' abilities that he did not use reconnaissance to see how many of the enemy he might be facing. When he and his men arrived at the **Little Big Horn** river, they found 3,000 to 4,000 Sioux warriors awaiting his arrival. As you might imagine, the Sioux and Northern Cheyenne, led by **Crazy Horse** (1849-1877) and **Sitting Bull** (c.1834-1893), made short work of Custer's regiment. They

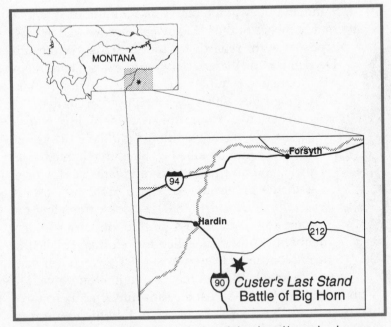

MONTANA

Forsyth

94

Hardin

212

90 *Custer's Last Stand*
Battle of Big Horn

Had Interstate 90 been around in Custer's day, he might have been able to make a hasty retreat.

killed almost all of them in about half an hour. Crazy Horse later said of the battle: "They say we massacred [Custer], but he would have done the same thing to us had we not defended ourselves and fought to the last. Our first impulse was to escape with our squaws and papooses, but we were so hemmed in that we had to fight."

Custer's defeat at the hands of the Sioux and Northern Cheyenne enraged Americans and caused them to redouble their efforts to expand into Native American territory. The U.S. was eventually successful in gaining access to the West and killing off many of the remaining tribes. By holding to the belief that the U.S. had a Manifest Destiny (p. 59) to control the lands to the western edge of the continent, many Americans rationalized their greedy lust for land.

2. Which of the following laws was intended to benefit the American Indians by giving individual Indians land?

(A) The Indian Removal Act (1830)
(B) The Indian Intercourse Act (1834)
(C) The Kansas-Nebraska Act (1854)
(D) The Dawes Severalty Act (1887)

General Custer

SITTING BULL

After Little Big Horn, Sitting Bull retreated to Canada while the U.S. continued to forcibly remove the Sioux and Dakota Indians from land where gold was believed to exist. Sitting Bull returned to the U.S. in 1881 and toured in the Wild West Show of "Buffalo Bill" Cody. The Sioux chief settled on a Dakota reservation, where he was killed in 1893 when soldiers attempted to arrest him on suspicion of subversive acts of Indian agitation. He was shot in the back. In 1980, the Sioux nation was awarded $160 million in compensation for the land that was taken from them more than 100 years earlier.

U.S. Indian policy at the time was a bit muddled. Often, different branches of the U.S. government worked at cross purposes with regard to the Indians. While the Department of War was trying to exterminate them, the Bureau of Indian Affairs was giving Indians hunting rifles which they then used in combat.

The laws from this era involving Native Americans usually outlined different ways the Indians could be killed or forcibly removed from their land and placed on reservations. However, with the publication of Helen Hunt Jackson's *A Century of Dishonor* (1881), a book chronicling the increasing squalidness of life on reservations, many humanitarians called for reforms. This led to the misconceived Dawes Act of 1887, which was supposed to take land from the reservations and give it to individual Indians—and at the same time free up some of that reservation land for the whites. It did little to improve the lot of the Indians.

Most of the violence against settlers was wreaked by the Great Plains Indians, who resisted the settlers' encroachment on their native land. While some tribes, notably the Crow and northern Arapaho, were friendly to whites, the Sioux, Cheyenne, Comanche, Kiowa, Apache, and southern Arapaho did what they could to slow down the spread of "Western Civilization."

One of the most famous Indian warriors was **Geronimo** (1829-1909), an Apache who led many fights against Mexicans and Americans. Geronimo was an excellent fighter, so good that many believed he had supernatural powers and could not be harmed by bullets. (It was this same legendary imperviousness that inspired the U.S. paratroopers of WWII to invoke Geronimo's name as they leapt from their planes into enemy territory.) Eventually, after avoiding capture for years, Geronimo surrendered to U.S. troops and was relocated by the government several times. Sadly, Geronimo's subjugation to the whims of the U.S. government led him, as it did many other Native Americans, to alcoholism. The bitter coda to Geronimo's life saw him fall off his horse and pass out after drinking heavily, the cold night air giving him the pneumonia from which he died.

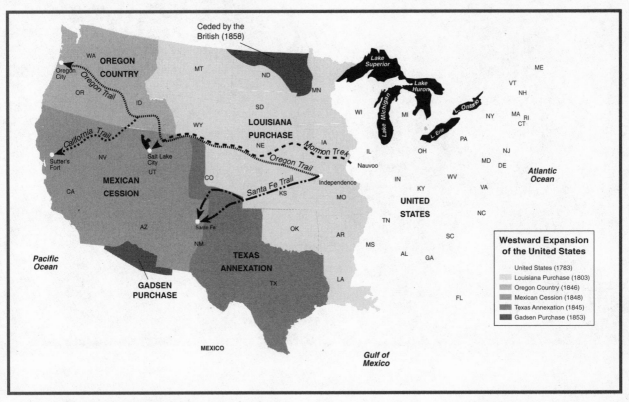

3. **What was the primary drawing point for the U.S. settlers of the West in the 1850s?**

   (A) The availability of cheap land
   (B) The availability of valuable minerals
   (C) The availability of grazing land
   (D) The availability of timber

The Gold Rush (1925) by Charlie Chaplin (pp. 409-410). A comic take on the public's lust for gold, this film is an excellent spoof of the Western Expansionist mentality.

The predominant objective of the first western settlers was finding gold—and lots of it. In 1848, gold was discovered in California, and speculators were soon hightailing it there in search of the valuable mineral.

The **gold rush of 1849** (the football team the San Francisco Forty-Niners are named after all those miners searching for gold) indirectly increased the geographic size of the United States. The miners were the first Americans who went west in search of opportunity. After the miners came the ranchers and then the farmers, and the West was won.

Little Big Man (1970), directed by Arthur Penn, starring Dustin Hoffman. This film recounts the battle of Little Big Horn, and many other historical events, with a comic touch.

ANSWERS

1. B   2. C   3. B

The Rise of Industrialism 1880–1914

 The building of the transcontinental railway system helped increase the efficiency of manufacturing and shipping goods. Companies could make more of a product because it was easier to ship large quantities over long distances. Because they could sell more, companies made their manufacturing systems more efficient, and many companies began to experience enormous growth.

1. **Which of the following methods was the fastest for transporting goods from New York to California from 1880–1930?**

    (A) Trucks
    (B) Railroads
    (C) Ships
    (D) Canals

Railroads were the fastest way to bring goods across America for many years. In 1869, two companies, the Union Pacific and the Central Pacific, were given the job of building the first transcontinental railroad line. The Central Pacific started in California and worked east while the Union Pacific started in Nebraska and worked west. (Railroad lines had already been lain westwardly to Nebraska.) The work started in 1867, and the lines met in Utah two years later, allowing people to ship goods quickly across the country. The railroads were built by a largely immigrant labor force, and many of the laborers stayed and became U.S. citizens.

2. **What is a disadvantage of monopolies?**

(A) They stifle competition.
(B) They are inefficient.
(C) They are usually small companies and are unable to hire enormous numbers of people.
(D) They do not allow for the free practice of government.

A **monopoly** is a company that has exclusive control over the sale or manufacturing of a product. For example, the utility companies that provide your electricity are monopolies. If you don't like the price, you can't get the electricity from somewhere else.

Because a monopoly has no competition, it can set the prices for the services or products that it sells without worrying about whether someone can offer the same good at a lower price. A similar situation occurs when a small group of companies make arrangements to act together to control an industry. This is called an **oligopoly**. When the railroads of the 1880s set up agreements that stifled competition, they could effectively set their own prices. In areas where this sort of agreement reduced competition, the prices were high, but on well-traveled routes where different companies offered the same services and some competition existed, the prices were much lower. The first attempt of government to control this type of activity was in 1887, but that effort was ineffective. The railroads were still able to charge what they wanted.

3. **Which of the following was a goal of the labor unions of the 1880s and 1890s?**

(A) Equal wages for women
(B) The eight-hour work day
(C) Lifting government regulations
(D) The destruction of the capitalist system

Labor unions of the 1880s were concerned with increasing the rights of workers in the newly industrialized economy. The rise in factories brought with it a need for factory workers. But workers in factories did not have the autonomy of skilled craftsmen. Because of this and management's goal of higher profits, workers often were forced to work long hours for low pay. Labor unions were formed to give workers the ability to negotiate with employers over hours, rates of pay, and even insurance.

The labor unions were at a disadvantage. They did not have the influence or the money that industry had, and therefore only had limited

The problem with a monopoly is that prices in capitalist economies are set with the goal of bringing in the most money. If there is a free market, and the prices for a product are too high, another manufacturer will make a similar product and charge less money for it. This way, prices always stay at a fair level. But if one company controls the manufacturing of a particular good, the highest price possible is usually charged. Since nobody is producing a competing good, the price will remain high and consumers will be forced to pay outrageous prices to buy the product. Even today, there is legislation to stop monopolies from forming. In 1982, AT&T was forced to split up in order to allow other companies into the long-distance phone business. Since then, prices for long-distance phone service have dropped significantly.

On the Waterfront (1954), starring Marlon Brando, Karl Malden, and Eva Marie Saint. Winner of eight Oscars, this movie is a harsh account of harbor unions. Brando's famous "I coulda been a contender" line comes from this film.

Although labor unions helped bring about great improvements in working conditions, they are not without scandal. By the 1930s, the major unions like the **Teamsters** (trucking) and the **American Federation of Labor and Congress of Industrial Organizations** (AFL-CIO, a general workers union) had become very powerful, and with power came corruption. One notorious president of the Teamsters was **Jimmy Hoffa** (1913-1975). Convicted on several counts of fraud and jury tampering, Hoffa disappeared in 1975. He is believed dead.

John Steinbeck's (p. 405) *East of Eden* tells a great story set in the era of the railroad. In 1955, it was made into a movie starring James Dean.

methods of achieving their goals. When management cut wages or increased hours, all the labor unions could do was shut down the factory and strike. (A strike is when workers all leave their jobs at the same time in order to prevent the business from operating.) In the 1880s and 90s, there were many strikes (1,500 in 1886 alone), about half of which were won by the unions. Unfortunately for labor, the government usually backed the employers, sometimes sending the military to help keep strikers at work.

Labor unions have been instrumental in creating fair working conditions in factories. In the early part of the Industrial Revolution, workers, including children, worked long hours for little pay in unsafe working conditions. Today such conditions are unacceptable.

Although unions have existed since 1794, it wasn't until the early twentieth century that they gained significant power. Today, the conflict between workers and employers continues. Recently, fewer and fewer workers belong to labor unions, and unions have been forced to make concessions in their demands for benefits since their members are worried about simply keeping their jobs.

ANSWERS

1. B   2. A   3. B

The U.S. as a World Power
1898–1917

1. The Spanish-American War was caused by a disagreement over which of the following territories?

   (A) Puerto Rico
   (B) Cuba
   (C) Venezuela
   (D) Mexico

2. When was the Spanish-American War?

   (A) 1845
   (B) 1864
   (C) 1898
   (D) 1914

Uncle Sam goes off half-cocked.

In 1898, the **Spanish-American War** was fought over Cuba, Spain's chief possession in the late nineteenth century. Unhappy with Spanish rule, the Cuban citizens had rebelled from 1868 to

In this political cartoon (c. 1898), Uncle Sam weighs the pros and cons of war.

1878. Newspapers and pro-war hawks pushed for war with Spain. They argued that Cuba was a western colony fighting for independence, and that it was immoral for the U.S. to sit idly by. Newspapers put forth stories depicting the atrocities of the Spanish, at one point printing a letter written by the Spanish ambassador to the U.S. which depicted then-President **William McKinley** (1843-1901) as feeble minded. Businessmen who wanted a boost for the economy lobbied Congress. Elected officials who wanted to appear strong talked big. Inevitably, after the mysterious sinking of the battleship *Maine*, we were at war with Spain. The U.S. won, "freed" the Cubans, and got possession of the Philippines and Guam in the process.

Yet all this effort aimed at creating an enemy was anything but realistic. Spain was not interested in war with the U.S., and was more than willing to negotiate a settlement. The war cost the lives of more than 5,000 Americans, and the victory was not entirely a good thing. By winning the war, the U.S. acquired all the problems associated with occupying land overseas. **The Philippines** proved to be an especially troubling acquisition. Its people rebelled and eventually killed more Americans than had died in the Spanish-American War. But winning the war and winning some overseas possessions also established the U.S. as a world power. We had taken on a European power and won, and we were starting to flex our expansionist muscle.

FROM THE VOICE OF THEODORE ROOSEVELT

"There is a home-spun adage which runs, 'Speak softly and carry a big stick; you will go far.' If the American nation will speak softly and yet build and keep at a pitch of the highest training a thoroughly efficient navy, the Monroe Doctrine will go far."

3. **Which president won fame for his leadership of the Rough Riders during the Spanish-American War?**

   (A) William McKinley
   (B) Woodrow Wilson
   (C) Andrew Johnson
   (D) Theodore Roosevelt

Theodore Roosevelt (1858-1919) achieved fame for leading the **Rough Riders**, "a cowboy cavalry," in its attack on Spanish Cuba. Roosevelt, then secretary of the Navy, quit his post to lead the troops. Known for his aggressiveness, he led the Rough Riders in several land campaigns, the most famous of which was the battle of San Juan Hill. In this battle, Roosevelt's troops gained control of a strategic spot, and Roosevelt became an instant war hero.

Roosevelt later went on to become president—he was vice-president when McKinley was assassinated. Roosevelt's administration was known for its aggressive foreign policy and progressive ideas. Supporting unions and helping to regulate corporations, the Progressives in Roosevelt's administration believed in changing government so that more people could become involved. One change pushed for by his administration was the direct election of Senators, a policy that went a long way toward giving the electorate the power to affect government.

Under Roosevelt, the U.S. began to throw its weight around, most notably by using American military muscle to acquire the land on which the **Panama Canal** was built. Speaking of throwing weight around, Roosevelt's successor, **William H. Taft** (1857-1930), was the heaviest president so far, weighing in at 354 pounds. (Taft was picked by Roosevelt to be his successor, and his critics said that his name stood for **T**ake **A**dvice **F**rom **T**eddy.)

Teddy and his Rough Riders

4. **How did the Panama Canal get built?**

    (A) The U.S. received the land as a result of the Spanish American War.
    (B) The U.S. threatened Colombia, and then bought the land for a nominal price.
    (C) The U.S. captured the land in an armed attack on communist Panama.
    (D) The U.S. helped Panama revolt from Colombia, and then leased the land.

The Panama Canal cut the travel time between New York and California considerably. Before its construction, ships had to go beyond the tip of South America (see map p. 234). The way in which the U.S. acquired the Panama Canal is typical of U.S. policy in Latin America in the twentieth century. The U.S. wanted to build a canal in Panama, Colombia, but the Colombian government refused U.S. offers in hopes of extracting a higher price for the land. Undaunted, the U.S. sponsored a revolution and helped Panama form its own state. Panama, grateful to the U.S. and having little other choice, gave a ten-mile swath of land to the U.S. for a one-time fee of ten million dollars with a yearly charge of $250,000, and the U.S. then built its canal.

One interesting side-effect of building the Panama Canal was a new understanding of malaria. The canal went through swamps filled with malaria, which killed many workers. Researchers figured that malaria was caused by mosquitoes and learned how to control the dreaded disease.

ANSWERS

1. B   2. C   3. D   4. D

World War I
1917–1919

1. **Which of the following events led Europe into WWI?**

   (A) The assassination of Archduke Ferdinand
   (B) The sinking of the Maine
   (C) The sinking of the Lusitania
   (D) The racist policies of Kaiser Wilhelm

Before **WWI**, countries in Europe were linked in a bunch of **entangling alliances.** If one country was attacked, treaties of protection ensured the others would follow. When **Archduke Ferdinand** (1863-1914) was assassinated in Sarajevo, the Austro-Hungarian Empire declared war on Serbia. Russia backed Serbia and Germany backed Austria-Hungary so Germany attacked France, Russia's ally. Great Britain sided with France and, all of a sudden, there was a world war.

FIRST WORLD WAR (1914–1918)

- The Allies
- The Central Powers
- Neutral Sites
- Areas Occupied by Central Powers
- Areas Occupied by Central Powers (after Brest Litovsk Treaty, 1918)
- Advances of the Allies
- Advances of the Central Powers

President Woodrow Wilson

The world at war

It's important to realize just how long America waited before joining the war. Although business and other interests felt that a war would be good for the economy, most Americans wanted to remain neutral. Also, there were eight million German-Americans living in the U.S. at that time who may not have wanted to see America at war with Germany. The U.S. had pretty much established itself as the chief power in North and South America; it was willing to let events in Europe take care of themselves. But as the war progressed and British propaganda influenced the sentiment of Americans, the U.S. became involved.

2. How eager was the U.S. to enter WWI?

(A) Champing at the bit (very eager)
(B) Ready to rock (somewhat eager)
(C) Straddling the fence (not sure)
(D) Dissing it (totally unwilling)

Initially, the U.S. was not eager to enter the war. **Woodrow Wilson** (1856-1924), the president, made many attempts to achieve a peaceful resolution to the troubles in Europe. His and most Americans' main concern was that the U.S. be allowed to trade with both the Allies and the Central powers. When Great Britain stopped American ships from landing in neutral ports Wilson got upset, but it was German submarine warfare that eventually led to the involvement of the U.S.

Germany's policy was to sink any ships that entered the area around Great Britain and Ireland. In 1915, the **Lusitania,** a British liner, strayed into these waters and was sunk. Twelve-hundred people, including 128 Americans, were killed. The U.S. avoided entering the war immediately through diplomatic negotiations. Wilson's 1916 election campaign stressed the fact that he had kept the U.S. out of war, and he won the campaign on this continued hope.

3. **In what year did the U.S. enter WWI?**
   (A) 1914
   (B) 1915
   (C) 1917
   (D) 1918

The United States did not enter **WWI**, which started in 1914, until 1917. Before that time, it tried to stay neutral and avoid entangling alliances. The U.S. joined the war on the side of the Allied Powers (Great Britain, France, and Russia) because of aggressive acts committed by the Germans and because many Americans felt more closely tied to the French and English than to the Germans.

The trench warfare of WWI resulted in heavy loss of life for minimal gain of enemy territory.

4. What is the name of the treaty signed at the end of WWI?

(A) The Treaty of Versailles
(B) The Peace of Paris
(C) The Bismarck Agreement
(D) The Franco-Russian Agreement

5. Which of the following organizations was formed in the treaty that ended WWI?

(A) The United Nations
(B) The League of Nations
(C) The Iron Curtain
(D) NATO

History proved that Wilson was most likely correct in seeking "peace without victory." The severe punishment inflicted on the Germans and the manner in which their territory had been carved up may have been one factor that led up to WWII. Had Wilson gotten his way, some of the root causes of WWII might have been avoided.

The **Treaty of Versailles,** signed at the end of WWI, contained many punitive measures against the Germans, who lost the war. It required Germany to give up control of its colonies and pay huge sums of **war reparations** to the Allied Powers.

Wilson's plan for a lasting peace consisted of **fourteen points** that straightened out some of the mess in Europe and paved the way for agreements respecting the basic rights of countries and their citizens. It was supposed to ensure **"peace without victory,"** but, unfortunately for Europe, war-bruised France and England wanted peace *with* victory. The Treaty of Versailles did allow for the League of Nations, however, an international group whose purpose was to avoid future world wars.

In a morass of politics, the U.S. Senate did not ratify the treaty and, ironically, and tragically for Wilson, the League of Nations never had the support of the U.S. Because it was not a powerful organization, it could do little to stop the approach of WWII.

There are all kinds of great books and movies about WWI. Ernest Hemingway wrote two of the classics, *In Our Time* and *A Farewell to Arms* (which was made into a movie). Another classic novel, *All Quiet on the Western Front,* written by Erich Maria Remarque, was also made into a great film.

If you want to see a more recent movie about WWI , try *Gallipoli,* starring Mel Gibson.

ANSWERS

1. A   2. D   3. C   4. A   5. B

Between the Wars

1920–1940

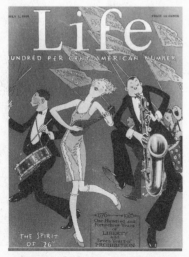

1926 cover of *Life* celebrating "143 years of liberty and seven years of Prohibition"

1. Which of the following was most responsible for the success of the speakeasies?
   (A) The invention of talkie films
   (B) Prohibition
   (C) The television age
   (D) The "Red Scare"

In 1919, the **Eighteenth Amendment** to the Constitution was ratified. The amendment called for a ban on "the manufacture, sale, or transportation of intoxicating liquors" within the United States. Because alcohol was already a part of society, the amendment did not serve to curb drinking, but instead changed the manner in which it was done. By prohibiting something that many Americans did anyway, the law turned law-abiding people into criminals. It created a whole new industry of "**rum runners**" and "**bootleggers**" who sold "**moonshine**" (illegally distilled alcohol), which people drank in "**speakeasies**," private clubs that required pass-words and were often condoned by bribed local policemen. Gangsters like **Al Capone** (1898–1947) made millions of dollars selling and trafficking what used to be a legal substance. The Eighteenth Amendment was repealed in 1933 by the Twenty-first Amendment.

Known as **the Jazz Age**, the twenties were a particularly colorful time in American history. After the horrors of WW I, Americans were ready to return to domestic pursuits, and the life they returned to was a time of prosperity and isolation from world events. Women wore short dresses and bobbed their hair; men wore straw hats and long raccoon coats. People speculated on the stock market and made money easily.

Calvin Coolidge (1872-1933), a conservative who was not a favorite of artists and the media, was president during the first half of the decade. **Dorothy Parker** (1893-1967), a writer from the twenties known for her quips about different subjects, heard about the death of Calvin Coolidge and said, "How can they tell?"

A flapper hams it up

Miller's Crossing (1990), Chicago gangsters during prohibition via the Coen brothers, and *The Untouchables* (1987), starring Robert De Niro as Al Capone, Kevin Costner as Eliot Ness, and Sean Connery. *Public Enemy* (1931) is the story of a prohibition-era gangster as portrayed by James Cagney.

Ragtime by E.L. Doctorow. Another story of gangsters. The movie is also good.

2. **Who was NOT part of the women's suffrage movement?**

   (A)   Susan B. Anthony
   (B)   Elizabeth Cady Stanton
   (C)   Carrie Chapman Catt
   (D)   Martha Graham

The Reconstruction period after the Civil War gave the constitutional right to vote to African-Americans, but women were not granted the right in the Constitution until the **Nineteenth Amendment** of 1919. **Susan B. Anthony** (1820-1906), **Elizabeth Cady Stanton** (1815-1902), and **Carrie Chapman Catt** (1859–1947) were all involved in the women's suffrage movement. (Suffrage means being able to vote.)

The fight for women's suffrage is a good example of the manner in which decisions are made by the U.S. government. The Nineteenth Amendment granting suffrage was passed while Woodrow Wilson was in office. Wilson did not initially support the amendment because a large part of his political support came from the South where support for such a measure was lacking. In the election of 1916, which Wilson won, the women who had won voting rights in many western states voted almost two to one against the Democrat Wilson. By so doing they showed that they could be a viable political force. The Republicans were eager to gain support from women and helped in passing the amendment.

Suffragettes Stanton and Anthony

LEGALIZING BIRTH CONTROL

Women's rights were also helped by the efforts of Margaret Sanger (1883-1966), who coined the phrase "birth control." Appalled by the lot of women who had to choose between either having dangerous back-alley abortions or more children than they could handle, she started a campaign for education on available birth-control methods, especially diaphragms (pp. 327-328) She started a birth control clinic in Brooklyn, New York, and she tried to distribute material on birth control through the mail. Both efforts were considered illegal at the time and the law was always on her trail.

Science and religion have long been at odds. When **Galileo Galilei** (1564-1642) **(p. 269)** came up with his theories of the solar system, he had to fight against the doctrine of the church, which stated that the earth was the center of the universe. The Scopes Trial served to change public opinion about science. Even though Scopes lost, many Americans became convinced that evolution was an important concept.

Women protesting for the right to vote in New York

Considering just how much women's suffrage has become a part of our lives (more women now vote than men), it is rather surprising to find just how long it took to get the Nineteenth Amendment through the governmental process. One of the first recorded attempts at gaining rights for women was from John Adams' wife, Abigail Adams (p. 51). In 1776, she wrote him saying to "remember the Ladies" in his new "code of laws."

The road to the Nineteenth Amendment involved protests and hunger strikes and all kinds of grass-roots politics and infighting. The women took a gradual approach, attempting to get the vote state by state. And in 1916, they succeeded in electing Montana's Jeannette Rankin. As the first woman elected to Congress, she proposed the Nineteenth Amendment.

3. **What trial focused on whether a teacher could teach Darwin's theory of evolution in schools?**

    (A) Brown v. Board of Education
    (B) The Scopes Trial
    (C) United States v. Butler
    (D) The Spencer Trial

Scopes before the judge

John T. Scopes, a high school teacher in Tennessee, taught the theory of evolution in his biology class and was arrested. The ensuing **Scopes Trial** captured the imagination of the nation. Scopes was defended by **Clarence Darrow** (1857-1938), the most famous trial attorney of the time; the prosecution was aided by **William Jennings Bryan** (1860-1925), the Democratic nominee and subsequent loser in three presidential elections. Scopes lost and was fined $100, but the trial served to strengthen the case for teaching science in the schools.

4. **What color was the first mass-produced automobile?**

   (A) Blue
   (B) Brown
   (C) Black
   (D) Green

The 1908 Model T Ford

Although automobiles were invented in the nineteenth century, it wasn't until 1913 that **horseless carriages** could be produced with the efficiency necessary to make them affordable

A Ford factory assembly line circa 1920

to the masses. The first car inexpensive enough to be bought by the average person was the black **Model T** produced by **Henry Ford** (1863-1947), who once said, "They can have whatever color they want, as long as it is black." The son of immigrant farmers, Ford succeeded by taking advantage of engineering breakthroughs and the idea of the **assembly line**. The Model T and subsequent autos made Ford one of the richest men in America. His cars revolutionized the transportation system of the United States and the world.

 The introduction of the automobile made a profound change in many aspects of American life. Besides allowing Americans to travel at will, the automobile was at the center of an enormous new industry. With gas stations, oil exploration, roadside stands, highways, and even traffic cops, the automobile has become one of the driving forces of our economy. And then, of course, there are the social changes that were caused by the automobile. The automobile allowed for the creation of the suburbs, which meant that even the middle class could own land and still work in the city. The auto created pollution and caused urban sprawl.

Lindbergh's Non-Stop Route from New York to Paris

Leaves NY 7:52 AM Friday
New York
Mulgrave 3:05 PM
Meteghan 12:25 PM
Main-A-Dieu 4:00 PM
St. John's 7:15 PM Friday
Atlantic Ocean
Dingle Bay 1:30 PM Saturday
Cherbourg 3:30 PM
★ Paris
Arrives Paris 5:24 NY Time 10:24 Paris Time Saturday

3,600 Miles in 33:32 hours

Ford was not a particularly nice guy, but he is known for doubling the going wage for auto workers. He found that increasing wages was the only way he could keep assembly-line workers from quitting their dreary jobs. He resisted unionization and blamed the Depression on the laziness of workers, saying, "The average worker won't do a day's work unless he is caught and can't get out of it." Ford also published an anti-Semitic newspaper and used "goon squads" to break up worker strikes.

Spirit of St. Louis (1957)
James Stewart recreates Lindbergh's famous flight quite well.

5. Who was the first person to fly solo across the Atlantic Ocean?

(A) Charles Lindbergh
(B) Francis Boeing
(C) Amelia Earhart
(D) Orville Wright

On May 20, 1927, **Charles Lindbergh** (1902-1974) began the first solo flight across the Atlantic ocean in his plane *The Spirit of St. Louis*. He brought a few sandwiches and some water and a few letters of introduction to people in Paris from folks he knew back in the U.S. The flight captured the imagination of the world, and when Lindbergh landed in Paris he received a hero's welcome.

Lindbergh became one of the most famous people in the world—a symbol of American individualism and the "can-do" attitude. Known as "Lucky Lindy," he was a rather shy man who tended to avoid the press when he could. But in 1932 his celebrity led to disaster. His son was kidnapped and held for $50,000. Although the money was paid, the nineteen-month-old child was later found murdered. The event shocked the nation and led to more severe punishments for kidnapping.

6. **Who was the first woman to fly solo across the Atlantic Ocean?**

   (A) Susan B. Anthony
   (B) Amelia Earhart
   (C) Maya Lindbergh
   (D) Maybelle Wright

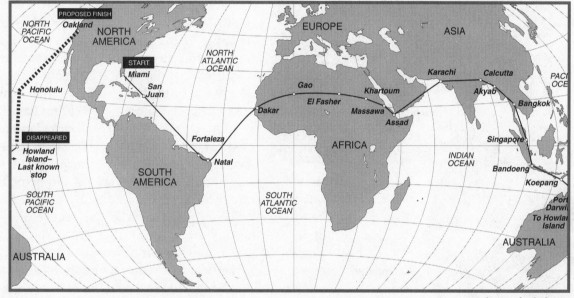

Earhart's unfinished route

The first woman to succeed in a solo flight across the Atlantic Ocean was **Amelia Earhart** (1898-1937) who made the trip in 1932. An adventurer, Earhart planned eventually to make the first flight around the world. Disaster struck during her 1937 attempt to circumnavigate the globe when radio messages from Earhart's plane stopped and she and her navigator disappeared. The plane and her remains have yet to be found, and the cause of the disaster still remains a mystery.

7. **"Black Thursday," the day on which the Stock Market crashed, was**

   (A) March 5, 1896
   (B) June 3, 1903
   (C) October 24, 1929
   (D) November 3, 1945

President Hoover and a "Hooverville," one of the shantytowns that came to bear his name

The stock market collapsed in **1929.** The 1920s had been a period of speculation in stocks and other financial instruments. By buying stocks on **margin** (a small security deposit) rather than at full price, people were able to invest money that they did not really have. A person could borrow 1,000 dollars from the bank and invest it in such a way that it was worth 10,000 dollars on paper. When the market was rising, people had the illusion that they were prosperous. If the stock market came down, there would be major trouble. The people would have to pay that "margin money" back—money they didn't have.

On October 24, 1929, **Black Thursday**, a panic started when people began to sell stocks. Because stockholders were afraid that the market would continue to go down, they sold more shares and helped drive the market down further. By the end of the day many people had lost their entire life savings. The crash itself did not cause the Great Depression, but it was the proverbial straw that broke the economic camel's back. Before the crash, the economy had been having trouble. Farms had become more efficient, thanks in part to the "horseless tractor," and farmers could not sell their crops for enough money. Worldwide production was up and too many goods were being produced. This oversupply of goods led to lower prices and eventually led to the point where manufacturers were saddled with goods they could not sell. This led to layoffs and soon fewer people were working and fewer people had the money to buy any goods. When the stock market crashed, it caused many of these problems to become worse. More people were laid off, investment in new enterprises ceased, and our great nation was suddenly thrown into poverty.

John Steinbeck's *The Grapes of Wrath.* This Pulitzer Prize–winning novel is an American classic and beautifully captures the depression era.

8. Which of the following most accurately describes a "Hooverville"?

    (A) A suburban community linked to the city by highways
    (B) A village of shacks where poor people lived
    (C) The area around the White House where Hoover's advisers were quartered
    (D) A system of mass production often used to produce vacuum cleaners

Hoovervilles were the groups of shacks made out of flattened tin cans, scrap wood, and tar paper that destitute citizens constructed during the **Great Depression. Herbert Hoover** (1874-1964) was president, and the perception that he was doing nothing to help poor people led to his name being attached to these shantytowns.

The Great Depression's effect on America cannot be underestimated. Between twenty-five percent and fifty percent of all people who wanted jobs could not get them. Overfarming in the Midwest had depleted the soil and a drought had caused great clouds of dust to blow across the country, ruining important cash crops and turning the land into a **dustbowl**. People were poor and demoralized, and they believed government was not doing much to help them.

Hoover thought any social program administered by the government was socialist and might lead to communism. He was unwilling to bend his ideology to help the unemployed people throughout the U.S. despite the astronomical unemployment rates. Hoover also seemed out of touch with the suffering of many Americans. He tried to uphold the idea of normality by having gracious parties at the White House. When unemployed people were selling surplus apples given to them by apple growers, he remarked, "Many people have left their jobs for the more profitable one of selling apples." (This sounds a lot like what Marie Antoinette (p. 174) said during the French Revolution (pp. 173-177).)

9. Who said "We have nothing to fear but fear itself?"

    (A) Abraham Lincoln
    (B) Woodrow Wilson
    (C) Herbert Hoover
    (D) Franklin D. Roosevelt

FROM THE VOICE OF FRANKLIN D. ROOSEVELT

"This is pre-eminently the time to speak the truth, the whole truth, frankly and boldly. Nor need we shrink from honestly facing conditions in our country today. This great nation will endure as it has endured, will revive and will prosper. So first of all let me assert my firm belief that the only thing we have to fear is fear itself—nameless, unreasoning, unjustified terror which paralyzes needed efforts to convert retreat into advance."

Franklin Delano Roosevelt (1882-1945) spoke these ringing words in his inaugural address. After four years of Hoover's inability to communicate with the common man, Roosevelt's charisma and warmth stood out. He won the election in a landslide, gaining a mandate to do what was necessary to get the country out of the Depression. Roosevelt called his policies a "new deal" for the "forgotten man." He said, "The country needs and, unless I mistake its temper, the country demands bold, persistent experi-

A lot of different acronyms were used during Roosevelt's administration. There seemed to be one for every social program. There were the CCC (Civilian Conservation Corps), the NIRA (National Industrial Recovery Act), the NRA (National Recovery Administration), the WPA (Works Projects Administration) the PWA (Public Works Administration), the AAA (Agricultural Adjustment Act), and the TVA (Tennessee Valley Authority), to name a few.

mentation. It is common sense to take a method and try it. If it fails, admit it frankly and try another. But above all, try something." And try something he did.

In the first 100 days after his inauguration, Roosevelt sent to Congress a blizzard of proposed legislation, nearly all of which was passed. Roosevelt's **New Deal** for America was based on **Keynesian** economics. **John Maynard Keynes** (1883-1946) believed that the way out of a recession is to spend, spend, spend. The government sponsored many **public works** projects, building dams, roads, bridges, school buildings, and hospitals. The government provided relief for farmers and it helped people who were going to lose their homes.

This approach, the ideal of government helping people and providing for them in hard times, was new to America, so Roosevelt's New Deal drew a great deal of criticism. Many people considered the plan socialist and some of its programs were held as unconstitutional by the Supreme Court. For the most part, though, the New Deal was implemented and it changed the dynamics of American government for good.

10. **What disease caused Franklin Delano Roosevelt to spend his last years in a wheelchair?**

(A) Tuberculosis
(B) Polio
(C) Cancer
(D) Arthritis

Roosevelt contracted **polio** in 1921 when he was thirty-nine. Poliomyelitis is a disease that affects the nervous system, causing paralysis. Roosevelt's bout with the disease put him in a wheelchair, yet he managed to campaign effectively and became one of the nation's greatest presidents. Many people, upon first meeting Roosevelt, were surprised to find out that he was in a wheelchair. Remember, when Roosevelt was president, there was no television. People's only view of Roosevelt was through the newsreels shown in movie theaters, and, if supported by his son or bodyguard, he could stand or walk for short periods using a cane. He also gave explicit orders to the press never to photograph him in his wheelchair.

ANSWERS

1. B   2. D   3. B   4. C   5. A   6. B   7. C   8. B   9. D   10. B

World War II
1941–1945

1. **What was the policy of the U.S. government in 1939 concerning WWII?**
   - (A) It was eager to commit American troops to the battle in support of the Allied Powers.
   - (B) It was eager to commit American troops to the battle in support of the Axis Powers.
   - (C) It was willing to support its allies economically but not militarily.
   - (D) American troops were already involved in fighting World War II.

 Night by Eli Weisel, who was himself a victim of Nazi concentratation camps. A book you"ll not easily forget.

When WWII started, the U.S. government attempted to support Britain and France, the **Allied Powers,** without committing troops. Roosevelt gave the Allies battleships and other weapons of war, but most Americans did not want to fight another war in Europe. The memories of the destruction caused by WWI were still vivid, but as Germany continued to expand, the U.S. government realized that it might have to enter the war and began to prepare.

Was the government in Roosevelt's time anti-Semitic? Maybe, but the U.S. has rarely stood up to governments because of crimes against humanity. Human rights violations have only recently been given as a justification for war. Just as we avoided the Holocaust issue, we now sit idly by as mass killings occur throughout the world. (Cambodia pp. 215-216, El Salvador p. 128, Tibet p. 215)

2. **What was the U.S. government's attitude toward the German government's treatment of Jews and other persecuted groups prior to the entry of the U.S. into the war?**

(A) The U.S. held many of the same policies.
(B) The U.S. threatened Germany with reprisals if it did not change its policies.
(C) The U.S. did not know about the treatment of Jews.
(D) The U.S. expressed some weak condemnation of the German policy.

Concentration camp prisoners at Buchenwald

One horrible feature of Nazi Germany (pp. 195-202) was its treatment of Jews and other groups deemed "enemies of the state," including homosexuals and gypsies. When Adolf Hitler (pp. 195-202) (1889-1945) came to power, he blamed many of Germany's problems on these groups and began to systematically murder them. Hitler's "**final solution**" was to kill Jews, gypsies, homosexuals, and other unwanted minorities as fast as he could. He put these people into concentration camps where, essentially, they were worked to death. When this approach proved too slow, Hitler began to exterminate the groups in death camps, the most infamous of which is Auschwitz (p. 197) This mass murder, now referred to as the Holocaust (p. 197) ranks among the most heinous in history. It stands as a testament to the evil that man is capable of committing.

The American reaction to the Nazi treatment of Jews was not very strong. Roosevelt knew about the Holocaust but did nothing. Even as the U.S. entered the war, the policy did not change.

The devastation at Pearl Harbor

3. **What happened on December 7, 1941?**

   (A) The Japanese bombed Pearl Harbor.
   (B) Hitler invaded Czechoslovakia.
   (C) American and British troops landed in Normandy.
   (D) Roosevelt was reelected for his third term.

FDR addresses the press and the public.

On December 7, 1941, the Japanese bombed **Pearl Harbor** in a surprise attack that killed more than 1,000 American soldiers and wounded 1,178. On the same day, Japan also attacked other U.S. bases in the Philippines. Such an attack would be enough to anger most Americans, but what made it worse was that the Japanese had been making overtures toward peace. The U.S. was outraged, Roosevelt was outraged, Congress was outraged, and all of a sudden we had entered WWII.

4. **When General MacArthur said on March 11, 1942 that "I will return," to where was he planning to return?**

   (A) Japan
   (B) The Philippines
   (C) Paris
   (D) Guadalcanal

FROM THE VOICE OF FRANKLIN DELANO ROOSEVELT

"Yesterday, December 7, 1941—a date which will live in infamy—the United States of America was suddenly and deliberately attacked by naval and air forces of the Empire of Japan."

Historical evidence suggests that some Americans knew when and where the attack on Pearl Harbor was to take place. With this information, the military base of Pearl Harbor could have been more prepared to defend against the attack. But the warnings went unheeded. Several hypotheses have been given for why the military stationed at Pearl Harbor was not prepared for the attack. The most insidious explanation is that Roosevelt needed to marshal support for an all-out war with Germany and Japan in order to stop their expansionist aims. He knew that an attack on Pearl Harbor would piss off most of America and put the country fully behind the war effort. Another, more plausible reason is that the U.S. underestimated the resolve and strength of the Japanese army. People believed Japan would eventually attack the U.S., but they thought that the attack would come in the Philippines. The base at Pearl Harbor was considered too big to be in any danger from Japanese pilots.

5. Did General MacArthur ever return to the place to which he said he would return?

Young General MacArthur (third from the left) with family

General Douglas MacArthur (1880-1964) (pp. 106-107) was leading the defense of the Philippines (an American colony, p. 80) when Roosevelt ordered him to Australia. (The fighting was not going well in the Philippines, and Roosevelt wanted MacArthur to survive so he could continue to lead the troops.) Though the Americans and Filipinos were vastly outnumbered and undersupplied, they managed to hold on for over a year. When they finally surrendered, the survivors were forced to march over one hundred miles in what is now known as the **Bataan Death March.** During this march almost 10,000 prisoners were killed by harsh treatment or starvation. MacArthur did, in fact, return to the Philippines on October 20, 1944, to help engineer a major American victory there.

Go Mom

MacArthur's mom was particularly fond of him, and she let his superiors know it. She would send letters telling them that it was about time for him to become a general.

6. What happens to the pilot after a successful Kamikaze attack?

The **Kamikaze** pilots ("Kamikaze" is Japanese for "divine wind") volunteered for the desperate suicide missions to which the Japanese were driven as the war pressed on. They loaded up their planes with explosives and flew directly into destroyers, battleships, and other American ships. If successful, the pilots died when their planes and the ships exploded.

7. Which of the following actions was NOT taken by the U.S. government to ensure victory in WWII?

(A)   Nationalizing the railroads
(B)   The institution of a draft
(C)   The sale of war bonds
(D)   Internment of Japanese-American citizens

Thirty Seconds Over Tokyo (1944). Oscar-winning special effects are still a stand-out in this exciting WWII film.

The United States pulled out all the stops in preparing for its entry into WWII. Remember, the U.S. had been attempting to stay neutral in the period after WWI. In order to fight WWII, munitions had to be manufactured, planes had to be put together, and boats had to be built quickly. The government imposed rationing, sold war bonds, instituted a draft, and stepped up production in order to meet the challenges of fighting a war overseas. (The country did nationalize the railroads in WWI, but not in

An American tank assembly line

WWII.) The war effort was one of the most effective mobilizations of industrial forces in history. Less than a year after Pearl Harbor, the U.S. had produced more than forty-seven billion dollars worth of war materials: 32,000 tanks, 49,000 airplanes, and eight million tons of ships.

To produce all of this stuff, the U.S. needed labor—and lots of it. Women and African-Americans were given factory jobs because most of the white men (and blacks too) were being shipped off to war. Almost ten million Americans (approximately one out of every seven men) were drafted during WWII. Roosevelt even issued an executive order prohibiting government contractors from practicing racial discrimination.

During the war, 120,000 Japanese-American citizens on the west coast of the U.S. were forced into **internment camps** because the government feared that they would aid the enemy. (We did not put German-American citizens into camps.) These people lost their homes and possessions, yet some of the young men who were relocated went on to serve honorably in the U.S. Army during the war. In fact, one unit of Japanese-Americans, the 442nd Regimental Combat Team, became one of the most highly decorated units of the war.

Hiring women during WWII to do jobs other than typing was a big boost toward the goal of equal opportunity. For the first time, women held jobs requiring physical strength, like driving trucks and riveting. This contradicted the prevailing notion that women were too weak to do physical labor. The gains made in gender equality were short-lived, however. When the veterans returned, women gave up their relatively high-paying jobs to the returning servicemen.

8. **Which of the following people was NOT at the Yalta conference?**

(A) Joseph Stalin
(B) Franklin Delano Roosevelt
(C) Woodrow Wilson
(D) Winston Churchill

The **Yalta** conference, which took place in February 1945, was one of a series of meetings at which Joseph Stalin, leader of the Soviet Union, Winston Churchill, the leader of Great Britain, and Roosevelt discussed future diplomatic relations of the warring countries. In this conference, the leaders agreed on a number of things. They were to divide up the German territory into **American**, **British**, **Soviet**, and **French** sectors after the war and establish the **United Nations.** They also agreed that Poland would have free elections and that all European countries would form democratic governments. (The nations under the USSR's control at the end of the war did not gain their freedom from the USSR, and Europe ended up divided into two hostile camps in what would become known as the Cold War (pp. 104-108).)

The Best Years of Our Lives (1946) One of the truly great American WWII films, this moving story follows the lives of three friends who have returned from battle and how their lives and their country has changed in their absence.

9. **Where was this picture taken?**

    (A) Iwo Jima
    (B) Tokyo
    (C) Berlin
    (D) Hawaii

This picture, an icon of American achievement in WWII, is of six marines raising the American flag on top of Mount Suribachi. The struggle to capture **Iwo Jima** was one of the bloodiest battles of WWII. The marines had 25,000 casualties in the twenty-five days it took them to secure the island. The Japanese fought valiantly and almost to the last man: 21,000 Japanese soldiers were killed, and only 200 surrendered.

10. Which vice president became president after Roosevelt died in 1945?

(A) Dwight D. Eisenhower
(B) Grover Cleveland
(C) John F. Kennedy
(D) Harry S Truman

Roosevelt died in 1945 of a cerebral hemorrhage and was replaced by then-vice president **Harry S Truman** (1884-1972). Roosevelt had been president since 1932, when he led the U.S. out of the Depression. Many Americans could not remember any other president, and his death left America, and the rest of the world, a little disoriented. Roosevelt's fireside chats, and his belief that government could and should provide social programs for the common people, transformed the federal government. His personality and abilities transformed the power of the president.

Truman certainly jumped into a firestorm. Not only did he have to make many fateful decisions on how the U.S. should fight the war, but he also had to deal with the aftermath—a strong Soviet threat that endangered war-torn Europe's future.

The mushroom cloud resulting from the bombing of Nagasaki

11. Hiroshima was significant in WWII because

(A) It provided a stepping stone for the U.S. to attack Japan
(B) It was where the first atomic bomb was dropped
(C) It was the first battleship destroyed by Kamikaze fighters
(D) It was the last battle in which the Japanese army provided significant resistance

Should the United States have unleashed the most destructive weapon ever? Not only did this event usher in a new era of war-making, it established that an atomic bomb could be used in warfare. With one move, a country could effectively be wiped out.

Truman's decision to drop the bomb came after the realization that an invasion of Japan would cost hundreds of thousands of American lives. But did the U.S. have to drop the bomb on an actual city? Why didn't the U.S. just demonstrate the bomb, or at least warn Japan of its awesome new weapon?

There are a number of historical arguments as to why the U.S. did not first demonstrate the power of the bomb to the Japanese. The most logical seems to be that the U.S. did not really grasp the amount of destruction that would be caused by the bomb. Scientists did not understand the dangers of radiation, and they underestimated the destructive capabilities of the new weapon. They also weren't sure that the bomb would work after being dropped from a plane.

Then why did we drop the second bomb? After the first bomb was dropped, Japan did not surrender. So the soldiers dropping the bombs continued their mission and dropped another one on Nagasaki. Because Truman did not say "don't drop the second one," Nagasaki was destroyed.

The crew of the Enola Gay

On August 6, 1945, the *Enola Gay,* a B-29 bomber, dropped the first atomic bomb (p. 292) on **Hiroshima,** Japan. Almost 80,000 people were killed instantly, and ninety-eight percent of the buildings in the city were flattened. Three days later, another bomb, this one made of plutonium instead of uranium, was dropped on **Nagasaki.** The death toll from these two bombs was horrifying. Equally horrifying was the ensuing radiation sickness that also killed many Japanese. Many lucky enough to have survived the initial blast still died slow deaths in which their cells were destroyed from the inside out.

Hiroshima in the aftermath of the bomb

12. **Approximately how many people died as a result of WWII?**

   (A)   500,000
   (B)   Two million
   (C)   Ten million
   (D)   More than thirty-eight million

WWII was the deadliest war ever. More than thirty-eight million people died. To give you an idea of just how many people that is, imagine the city of New York being blown up—*four times*. The destruction wrought by the war was abetted by vast improvements in military technology. From faster ships and better tanks to atomic bombs and land mines, people had learned to kill, and kill well.

A child cries in the rubble of Hiroshima.

 Since World War II, many new weapons have been created. The atomic bomb, which uses **fission (p. 292)**, was replaced by the hydrogen bomb, which uses **fusion (pp. 292-293)**. Today's bombs are up to 100 times more powerful than the bomb used to destroy Hiroshima.

Even worse has been the advancement in land mines. Since World War II, millions of tiny land mines have been spread throughout military zones in Cambodia, Somalia, and Thailand. These mines are virtually impossible to detect, and will be killing and maiming unsuspecting civilians for generations to come.

ANSWERS

1. C   2. D   3. A   4. B   5. Yes   7. A   8. C   9. A   10. D   11. B   12. D

The Cold War Begins
1945–1955

1. Whom did the U.S. battle during "the Cold War"?

(A) Japan
(B) The USSR
(C) South Korea
(D) Panama

 The Cold War describes the relationship between the Soviet Union and the U.S. from 1945 to 1992. The icy relations between the Soviet Union and the U.S. led to troubles of all kinds. Many countries took sides as the USSR and the U.S. tried to block each other's imperialistic (pp. 39-40) tendencies. An understanding of the last forty years of U.S. and world history is impossible without knowledge of the tensions between the USSR and the U.S.

After the Soviet Union and the United States defeated the Nazis (pp. 195-202), it was only one year before a chill in their relationship developed. Winston Churchill (1874-1965)(p. 198), the charismatic prime minister of England who had been instrumental in defeating the Nazis, declared that an "**iron curtain**" had been dropped between Eastern and Western Europe. Any action taken by either side was looked upon by the other with distrust.

The **Cold War** was not a war at all. There was no direct military confrontation between the United States and the Soviet Union. There was, however, a great deal of tension. The communist ideology to which the Soviet Union subscribed held that for communism to be truly effective, it must be universal. That is, for the Soviet Union to develop fully it would have to convert other countries to the cause of communism (p. 180) President Harry S Truman responded to the communist threat with a policy of "**containment**" that became known as the **Truman Doctrine.** This policy pledged U.S. support to non-communist countries so that the "free peoples" of the world could resist communism.

2. **What is a superpower?**

The United States and the Soviet Union were called "**superpowers**" because of their huge influence on world affairs. Both countries had nuclear weapons. At the touch of a button, they could obliterate each other and the rest of the world as well.

3. **What was the Marshall Plan?**

   (A) An economic plan to help European nations devastated during WWII
   (B) A policy of using the military to keep the Soviet Union from expanding its borders
   (C) A plan to make U.S. government more efficient
   (D) A plan to integrate southern colleges

The U.S. decided to help the post-war recovery in the free countries of Europe. This economic help was called the **Marshall Plan,** and its goal was to prevent the "hunger, poverty, desperation, and chaos" that might lead to communist expansion. The Marshall Plan was successful in raising the standard of living in Europe and preventing Soviet expansionism.

4. **What was the name of the Eastern European block of nations that opposed NATO?**

   (A) The Russian Organization
   (B) The Communist Manifesto
   (C) The Warsaw Pact
   (D) The Alliance for Freedom

The countries of Western Europe and the U.S. formed an alliance called **NATO** (North Atlantic Treaty Organization) to protect their interests, while the Eastern European nations allied with the Soviet Union signed a similar treaty at Warsaw, Poland—appropriately named the **Warsaw Pact.** These alliances were at odds with each other during the Cold War.

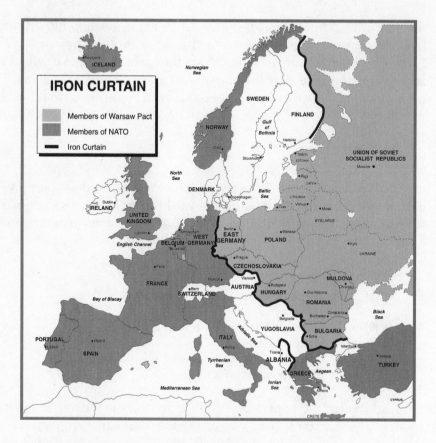

THE KOREAN WAR
1950-1953

United States Supported:

South Korea

Soviet Union Supported:

North Korea

Number Killed:

Over 2,000,000

The Atomic Cafe (1982). Frightening, sometimes hilarious documentary-style film encompassing U.S. propaganda films of the 1950s that sang the praises of the bomb.

5. **Which of the following governments sent troops in support of South Korea during the Korean War?**

   (A) China
   (B) The USSR
   (C) The United States
   (D) Japan

Only a few years after the end of WWII, the **Korean War** started when Soviet-backed North Korean troops invaded South Korea. The United States, committed to its policy of containing communism, convinced the United Nations to set up a force to stop the aggression. The force, which was mainly composed of people from the United States and South Korea, also included soldiers from fifteen other nations. Under the leadership of General Douglas MacArthur (p. 98), the campaign was at first very successful in driving the North Koreans north. But soon, the headstrong MacArthur disobeyed orders and pushed the war even farther north. The newly communist Chinese, worried about U.S. progress up the Korean peninsula, began to amass troops near the northern border of North Korea. When MacArthur got too close, they attacked and succeeded in driving MacArthur's armies almost into the ocean. MacArthur, a staunch anti-communist, called for a nuclear attack on China. But as a result of his refusal to obey orders, he was fired by Truman.

The UN armies regrouped and were successful in recapturing South Korea. The war ended pretty much as it had started, with South Korea occupying land south of the 38th Parallel, and North Korea holding territory to the north. Though it caused the destruction of the Korean economy and resulted in two million casualties, the war did not change the borders of the country. It also established the willingness of the United States to enter a war without actually declaring war: The Korean war was never declared a war. It was fought under the cloak of the United Nations, but this police action (as it is euphemistically called) ended up killing over 100,000 Americans.

Truman later said of canning McArthur, "I fired him because he wouldn't respect the authority of the President. That's the answer to that. I didn't fire him because he was a dumb son of a bitch, although he was, but that's not against the law for generals. If it was, half to three-quarters of them would be in jail."

6. **What was the name of the spacecraft used in the first successful orbit around the earth?**

   (A) *Enterprise*
   (B) *Apollo I*
   (C) *Sputnik*
   (D) *Perestroika*

On October 4, 1957, the Soviet Union succeeded in launching the first successful satellite into space. The *Sputnik* satellite traveled around the earth at a low orbit over populated areas, emitting a constant beeping that could be picked up by radios on earth. This was a public relations coup for the Soviet Union. People throughout the world listened on their ham radios as the beeping became clearer and then faded away. Not only was *Sputnik* important as an engineering breakthrough, it was also a powerful political statement. The Russians had beaten the U.S. in the first heat of the space race. They had launched a satellite, while our Vanguard program was plagued with problems.

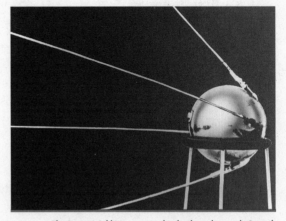
The Soviets' Cold War coup and technological marvel, *Sputnik*

The U.S. response to *Sputnik* was to crank up our own space program. We made the space race a matter of national pride and, in what ranks among the great technological achievements of all time, we were soon successful in putting a man on the moon (p. 122)

TINSELTOWN FIGHTS BACK

Hollywood was a victim of a McCarthy-ite purge launched by the House Un-American Activities Committee in 1947. Several movies ridiculing McCarthy and his ideas were made. Try watching The Manchurian Candidate, *starring Frank Sinatra (1915-), of all people. A McCarthy-sound-alike politician is controlled by a Soviet agent, played by Angela Lansbury (from the television show "Murder, She Wrote").*

 Invasion of the Body Snatchers (1956). Although a sci-fi horror film, Body Snatchers is the definitive Cold War film. It plays on the fears McCarthyism inspired and is a great allegory of the communist threat.

WRESTLEMANIA

At the height of McCarthy's power, all wrestlers in the state of Indiana had to swear they were not communists before being allowed to compete.

McCarthy and Roy Cohn trying to hide their lies in court

7. **The crusade to eliminate Communist influence from the U.S. government in the 1950s was led by**

   (A) Jesse Helms
   (B) Ronald Reagan
   (C) Joseph McCarthy
   (D) Richard Nixon

   In the United States, the Cold War was characterized by an almost irrational fear of the Soviet Union and a sense that communist spies had infiltrated many American institutions. Senator **Joseph R. McCarthy** (1908-1957) led a "crusade" to drive communists out of the government. McCarthy's method, which many have likened to the witch hunts in colonial Salem (p. 37), was to label anyone who disagreed with him a communist sympathizer. These vile tactics soon became known as **McCarthyism.**

ANSWERS

1. B   3. A   4. C   5. C   6. C   7. C

The Civil Rights Movement

1954 to Present

1. **Which of the following court cases found the concept of "separate but equal" facilities for whites and blacks unconstitutional?**

   (A) Plessy v. Ferguson
   (B) Brown v. Board of Education of Topeka
   (C) Marbury v. Madison
   (D) Roe v. Wade

"Strange Fruit," a jazz standard made famous by Billie Holiday (p. 440) concerning a lynching she witnessed as a child.

Invisible Man, by Ralph Ellison (p. 407). A black man struggles for identity. *Autobiography of Malcolm X,* by Alex Haley; *Black Like Me,* by John Howard Griffin.

In 1954, the Supreme Court ruled in the case *Brown v. Board of Education of Topeka* that the principle of "separate but equal" schools for white and black children was unconstitutional. In 1896, the Supreme Court had ruled in the case *Plessy v. Ferguson* (pp. 70-71), that "separate but equal" facilities were constitutional for railroads. Using the 1896 decision as precedent, new laws had been passed to permit the segregation of black people.

Finally, the National Association for the Advancement of Colored People (NAACP) and one of their lawyers, **Thurgood Marshall** (1908-

"Fables of Faubus" from *Mingus Ah Um.* A jazz piece by Charles Mingus (p. 432) about Governor Orville Faubus.

1993) (he later became a Supreme Court Justice) brought several cases against the local and state governments who wanted to keep the schools segregated. The Supreme Court, led by newly appointed Chief Justice **Earl Warren** (1891-1974), arrived at a unanimous decision that "in the field of public education the doctrine of 'separate but equal' has no place. Separate educational facilities are inherently unequal."

On August 28, 1963, over 200,000 people Marched on Washington to show their support for civil rights.

2. To which of the following cities was the federal government forced to send troops to enforce the ruling that allowed for integration of the schools?

    (A) Little Rock, Arkansas
    (B) Atlanta, Georgia
    (C) Jacksonville, Florida
    (D) Kansas City, Missouri

Government troops were sent to **Little Rock, Arkansas** to enforce the Supreme Court ruling *Brown v. Board of Education of Topeka.* The governor of Arkansas, Orville Faubus, had called in National Guard troops to prevent nine black children from entering the Little Rock Central High School. As millions of Americans watched in disgust on TV, an angry mob spit and cursed at the children as they tried to go to school. A federal court ordered Arkansas to let the children into the school, but the state refused. President Eisenhower was forced to place the National Guard under federal control. He sent in additional federal troops to protect the students and, ultimately, allow them to pursue their education.

"Thank You Sister Rosa," by The Neville Brothers. A tribute to Rosa Parks.

3. **Which of the following people precipitated the Montgomery Bus Boycott?**

   (A) Shirley Chisholm
   (B) Louis Farrakhan
   (C) Rosa Parks
   (D) Booker T. Washington

GAY POWER

In 1969, the Gay Rights movement got its start. The police raided the Stonewall Inn, a club in Greenwich Village, New York, known to be frequented by homosexuals. This was not an uncommon occurrence—in fact, it was an all-too-common violation of their rights. On this night the gay patrons of Stonewall stood up to the cops, throwing bottles, hurling invectives, and causing what has come to be known as the Stonewall Riots. Fed up with rampant discrimination, the gay movement "came out of the closet" that night and continues to gain ground in the quest for equal rights.

On her way home from her job as a seamstress at a Montgomery department store, **Rosa Parks** took a seat in the rear section of the bus. In Montgomery, the first ten rows in buses were reserved for whites, the last twenty-six for blacks—but a driver could expand the white section. Parks, seated near the dividing line, refused to give up her seat to a white man when the bus driver instructed her and three other blacks to move back so that he could expand the white section. Parks was arrested. The African-Americans of Montgomery began a boycott of city buses that led to the end of segregation on Montgomery buses in 1956.

The leader of the boycott was a minister named **Martin Luther King, Jr.** (1929-1968). King believed in using non-violent methods to achieve his aims. Having studied the methods of Henry David Thoreau (1817-1862) (pp. 401-402) and Mahatma Gandhi (1869-1948) (pp. 216-217), King was an inspiring and thoughtful orator. His **"I Have a Dream"** speech, delivered in Washington, D.C. in 1963, is regarded as one of the finest ever given.

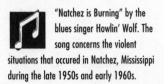

"Natchez is Burning" by the blues singer Howlin' Wolf. The song concerns the violent situations that occured in Natchez, Mississippi during the late 1950s and early 1960s.

4. Why did Malcolm X take "X" as his last name?

(A) His grandfather's last name in Africa was "X."

(B) He did not like his given name, "Little."

(C) He took "X" to convey that through slavery he had lost his true African name.

(D) While in prison, Malcolm took the letter X from his prison identity number, X-137.

Another leader in the Black Civil Rights movement was a fiery reformer named **Malcolm X** (1925-1965), who believed that blacks should take a more forceful role in defending themselves against white violence. After spending six years in prison for burglary, Malcolm X converted to the Muslim religion. He became a leader of the **Black Muslims**—sometimes called the **Nation of Islam** (see Mohammed Ali, p. 469). Born Malcolm Little in Omaha, Nebraska, Malcolm decided to get rid of his "slave name" and took "X" as his last name to represent the idea that he had lost his true African identity. After leading the Nation of Islam for a while, he made a pilgrimage to Mecca (p. 379), after which he became less militant. Before he could spread these more moderate ideas, he was assassinated by members of his own organization.

A National Guardsman keeping the peace during the Watts riots

5. In which of the following cities did the Watts Riot occur?

(A) Newark

(B) Selma

(C) Los Angeles

(D) Miami

The Civil Rights movement, under the leadership of Martin Luther King, Jr., had been relatively peaceful. Using non-violent methods of protest and working through the courts, African-Americans began to make great strides toward gaining equality with whites. But in the sixties, many of the Civil Rights movement's non-violent actions were answered with bullets. Civil Rights activists, both white and black, were killed. Civil Rights activist **Medgar Evers** was shot down in 1963 next to his home in Jackson, Mississippi. (His white assailant was finally convicted in 1994, more than thirty years after the attack.) A Birmingham church was bombed, killing four young black girls. Workers trying to register black voters were killed in Mississippi.

Although the movement was able to achieve many important court victories, many black people lived in ghettos in the inner cities. Even with legal equality, it seemed impossible for blacks to gain economic equality. During the hot summer of 1965, this frustration came to a head when a

 In 1992, after an all-white jury did not convict four white policemen in the beating of Rodney King (King, a parolee, was driving drunk and had led the policemen on a high-speed chase), another riot in Los Angeles materialized. In this case, part of the evidence presented was a videotape showing policemen kicking and hitting the unarmed King with sticks. When the policemen were not convicted of police brutality, the area of South Central Los Angeles erupted in violence.

Aftermath of arson and looting duing the L.A. riots in 1992

black driver was stopped for drunk driving by a white policeman in **Watts,** a section of Los Angeles that was ninety-six percent black. The predominantly white police in Los Angeles were viewed by blacks as an occupying force, and the arrest served to spark a riot. After six days of mayhem, thirty-four people were killed and more than 1,500 injured. Even today, some of the devastation left by the riots is still visible in Los Angeles.

The violence during the Watts riots served to bring the problems of the inner cities to the consciousness of the rest of the United States.

ANSWERS

....

1. B   2. A   3. C   4. C   5. C

The 1960s

John Fitzgerald Kennedy

1. **Whom did John Fitzgerald Kennedy run against in the 1960 presidential election?**

   (A) Richard M. Nixon
   (B) Dwight D. Eisenhower
   (C) Lyndon B. Johnson
   (D) General Douglas MacArthur

John F. Kennedy's (1917-1963) Republican opponent in the 1960 election was **Richard Nixon** (1913-1994), Dwight D. Eisenhower's (1890-1969) vice president. Nixon would later go on to win the 1968 election.

Kennedy's slim victory may have been the first time that television affected the outcome of a presidential race. On September 26, 1959, the two candidates met in the first of a series of face-to-face debates. Kennedy was charismatic, handsome, and the picture of health, while Nixon appeared sinister with his perpetual five o'clock shadow. Nixon just didn't look good on TV. Those polled who had listened to the debate on radio considered it a tie. Those who had televisions overwhelmingly felt that Kennedy had outperformed Nixon.

The televised debate between Nixon and JFK

2. **What was the Bay of Pigs?**

(A) A meat-packing scandal
(B) The location of a failed invasion of Cuba
(C) The location of Kennedy's secret rendezvous with Marilyn Monroe
(D) A Russian military installation

JFK AND MARTIN LUTHER KING, SR.

When Martin Luther King, Jr., was arrested in 1959, Kennedy called King's wife, Coretta, to see if he could help. JFK's brother, Robert Kennedy (1925-1968), helped get King out on bail. King's father decided that he should support Kennedy despite his reservations about voting for a Roman Catholic. When JFK heard of all this he remarked, "Imagine Martin Luther King having a bigot for a father. Well, we all have fathers, don't we?"

The **Bay of Pigs** was the site of a disastrous U.S.-supported invasion of Cuba in April, 1961. Fidel Castro (1927-), the leader of Cuba, had become very troublesome to the U.S. Cuba confiscated American businesses, sent agents to other Latin American countries to start revolts, and aligned itself with the U.S.S.R. and communist China. In early 1960, the Central Intelligence Agency (CIA) began to train and equip a force of anti-Castro Cuban exiles. The plan called for the invasion to serve as a spark for a general uprising. Shortly after Kennedy became president, he reviewed the plan and wanted to call off the whole deal, but his advisors insisted that such a move would anger anti-communist forces in the U.S. Frankly, the CIA did not think that the plan had much of a chance of working, but

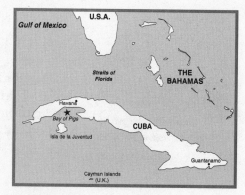

Bay of Pigs Invasion

it was totally doomed when JFK ordered that the planned U.S. Air Force and Navy participation be canceled. When the invasion force landed, it was overwhelmed by superior forces and, without air and naval gun cover, pinned down on the beach. The popular support never appeared since there was no real invading army to join. It all resulted in a great deal of embarrassment for both JFK and the U.S.

3. **Who were the leaders of the U.S. and the USSR during the Cuban Missile Crisis?**
   (A) Eisenhower/Stalin
   (B) Kennedy/Khruschev
   (C) Johnson/Khruschev
   (D) Nixon/Castro

The closest that the U.S. and the USSR ever came to war was during the Cuban Missile Crisis (p. 207) of 1962. Kennedy was president, and the Soviet Union under **Nikita Khruschev (1894-1971)** was secretly building offensive military bases in Cuba. When Kennedy found out that the Soviet missiles were only a few dozen miles away and could be pointing straight at the White House, he enforced a naval quarantine to keep the Soviet Union from bringing more missiles into the Western Hemisphere.

Tensions were high. People knew that a war with the Soviet Union would be devastating. As millions were glued to their television sets, Khruschev relented, and the missiles were dismantled and returned to the Soviet Union.

4. **What symbol of the Cold War was erected in 1961 and destroyed in 1989?**
   (A) The Iron Curtain
   (B) The Berlin Wall
   (C) The Castle of Leningrad
   (D) The Korean War Memorial

The **Berlin Wall** was built in 1961 by the government of East Germany, with support from the Soviet Union, in an effort to keep dissatisfied citizens from fleeing Eastern Europe to the more prosperous West. The Berlin Wall came down in November 1989, and was the symbolic end of the Cold War.

Dr. Strangelove (1964), directed by Stanley Kubrick, starring Peter Sellers and George C. Scott. Black comedy about nuclear war.

Vietnamese children burned by Napalm

THE VIETNAM WAR (1954-1975)

United States Supported:

South Vietnam

Soviet Union Supported:

North Vietnam

Number Killed: **2,000,000-3,000,000**

 Apocalypse Now (1979), Francis Ford Coppola's Vietnam epic based on Joseph Conrad's *Heart of Darkness*. *The Deer Hunter* (1978), a devastating Vietnam film, won five Oscars, including Best Picture, Best Director, and Best Supporting Actor.

5. Did the United States Government consider Vietnam a war?

(A) Yes
(B) No

 "Alice's Restaurant," by Arlo Guthrie, off the album of the same name. "Fixing to die Rag," by Country Joe and the Fish, off the *Woodstock* (p. 446) soundtrack album. "For What It's Worth," by Buffalo Springfield, off the eponymous album *Buffalo Springfield*.

It looked like a war, it smelled like a war, it killed like a war, but it was not technically a war. The Constitution grants only Congress the right to declare war, but the conflict in Vietnam was fought without an official declaration of war from Congress. After a reported incident involving an attack on American ships in the Gulf of Tonkin in 1964, a bill was put through Congress that allowed the president to "take all necessary measures" to defend U.S. forces and to "prevent further aggression." This bill, the **Gulf of Tonkin Resolution**, gave the president far-reaching powers to conduct the "war" in Vietnam without the approval of Congress.

In an attempt to stamp out communism in Southeast Asia, the U.S. first helped the South Vietnamese by sending advisers. Then it began to send troops. Opposed by a committed force that

American soldiers in Vietnam

The Vietnam war has been memorialized in many movies, some of which show U.S. soldiers acting bravely and honorably as they kill off **Viet Cong** (the enemy) in their search for **POWs** (Prisoners of War). Others show U.S. soldiers mercilessly mowing down civilians and participating in other heinous acts. The Vietnam War had its share of both kinds of acts, but one incident should be examined because it demonstrates just how awful modern warfare has become.

In a military action against a village called **My Lai** that took place in 1968, an American unit called Charlie Company was instructed to "clean the village out." But when the company arrived, no enemy military personnel were to be seen, and there was no evidence of any military activity. Charlie Company, nevertheless, killed 560 Vietnamese, most of whom were women and children. The Vietnamese were rounded up into the center of the village and shot with automatic weapons. When word got out about My Lai, the incident came to symbolize that the Vietnam War was an unjust war. We were in Vietnam allegedly to help the Vietnamese free themselves from communist influence, but instead our presence caused as much destruction as an occupying communist one would have.

One of the infamous images of Vietnam, the assassination of a Viet Cong

knew the territory, our army was at a severe disadvantage. Finally, in the seventies, after many protests in the U.S. and many failures on the battlefield, U.S. troops were gradually evacuated from Vietnam. When we left, the North Vietnamese seized power over the rest of the country.

At first, folks at home didn't much understand or care about the conflict in Vietnam, but as President Johnson escalated our military commitments and the draft was reinstated, people took notice. Many college students got involved in protests, and some of the protests led to violence. At **Kent State University** in Ohio in 1970, four student protesters were killed when National Guardsmen opened fire at a demonstration. Even some of the popular music of the time was concerned with the war and its protests. The enormous concert at Woodstock (pp. 446-447) in 1969 contained many references to the war, and if you listen to recordings from it, you will get a good idea of the spirit at the time.

Full Metal Jacket (1987). Stanley Kubrick's sordid and atmospheric Vietnam film presents a different view of the war than most others in the genre. Well worth a look.

"Ohio," by Neil Young from the album *Déja Vu*, by Crosby, Stills, Nash, and Young.

One of the students shot to death by National Guardsmen at Kent State University

Assassination Score Card

Assassin	President	Year	Method	Fatalities	Success	Failure	Motive	Fate
Richard Lawrence	Andrew Jackson	1835	single-shot derringers	0		✔	Insanity	Found criminally insane (prosecuted by F.S. Key
John Wilkes Booth	Abraham Lincoln	1865	handgun	1	✔		Politics	Killed in a barn soon after
Charles J. Guiteau	James A. Garfield	1881	handgun	1	✔		Insanity	Hanged or killed himself
Leon Czolgosz	William McKinley	1901	handgun	1	✔		Politics/personal	Electric chair
Giuseppe Zangara	Franklin Roosevelt	1933	handgun	1		✔	Nihilism Chronic pain	Electric chair
Oscar Collazo & Griselio Torresola	Harry Truman	1950	handguns	4		✔	Politics	GT: killed at scene; OC: death sentence commuted, released '79
Lee Harvey Oswald	John Kennedy	1963	rifle	1	✔		Personal (?)	Killed by Jack Ruby two days later
Samuel Byck	Richard Nixon	1974	airplane, handgun	2		✔	Politics/personal	Suicide at scene
Lynette "Squeaky" Fromme	Gerald Ford	1975	handgun	0		✔	Politics/personal	Life sentence
Sara Jane Moore	Gerald Ford	1975	handgun	0		✔	Politics/personal	Life sentence
John Hinckley, Jr.	Ronald Reagan	1981	handgun	2		✔	Jodie Foster	Committed to mental institution in Washington

Although the assassination of JFK shocked the nation, it was far from unprecedented.

6. **Who killed President John Fitzgerald Kennedy?**

   (A) J. Edgar Hoover
   (B) Lee Harvey Oswald
   (C) Adlai Stevenson
   (D) Fidel Castro

According to the **Warren Commission,** which investigated the shocking assassination of John Fitzgerald Kennedy, **Lee Harvey Oswald** (1939-1963) acted alone in shooting Kennedy. Kennedy was in a Dallas motorcade campaigning for the 1964 election when he was shot. He died and was succeeded by then-vice-president Lyndon B. Johnson. The Warren Commission (a panel chaired by Earl Warren, the Chief Justice of the United States) produced findings that were not universally accepted by the public, and some people still believe that some sort of conspiracy was involved in the planning of the attack.

JFK (1991), starring Kevin Costner, directed by Oliver Stone. Paranoid conspiracy theory at its finest.

Lee Harvey Oswald just seconds before being killed by Jack Ruby

7. Who killed the man who assassinated John Fitzgerald Kennedy?

(A) J. Edgar Hoover
(B) Jack Ruby
(C) Oliver Stone
(D) Barry Goldwater

Jack Ruby (1911-1967) shot Lee Harvey Oswald on national television only two days after he was arrested, making it much more unlikely that the American public would ever be satisfied with any explanation of Oswald's act. What details of JFK's assassination might Oswald have revealed? We will never know.

8. What was the name given to the social programs that President Lyndon B. Johnson put into place in the 1960s?

(A) The Great Society
(B) The New Deal
(C) Freedom For All
(D) A Fair Deal

Lyndon B. Johnson (1908-1973) became president of the United States when Kennedy died. Johnson was re-elected to the presidency a little over a year later in a resounding victory over Republican Barry Goldwater

(1909-). Johnson won with the largest margin ever in a presidential election, receiving 61.2 percent of the popular vote.

This incredible support from the populace gave Johnson tremendous power in getting legislation he wanted passed through Congress. Johnson's idealistic goal was to create a **"Great Society,"** a society that "rests on abundance and liberty for all. It demands an end to poverty and racial injustice, to which we are totally committed in our time." His administration was responsible for Medicare and Medicaid, varied anti-poverty legislation, and several civil rights bills including the Civil Rights Act of 1964, which gave the federal government power to enforce anti-discriminatory laws.

But Johnson also helped bring the U.S. deeper into the unpopular Vietnam War, and within four years, the previously popular Johnson was so discouraged that he decided not to seek re-election.

9. **Which of the following is NOT part of the student movement of the sixties?**

   (A) Anti-war protests
   (B) Increased use of illegal drugs
   (C) More permissive attitudes toward sex
   (D) An increase in membership in churches and
   synagogues

President Lyndon Johnson

Those damn hippies

The sixties are thought of as an idealistic time when students actually cared about stuff, but often showed it by "dropping out." College students, along with many other Americans, marched on Washington for civil rights and an end to the war in Vietnam. Known as **hippies**, these tie-dye-wearing, grass-smoking libertarians burned draft cards, took over campuses in order to gain some control over their education, and practiced pre-marital sex with unprecedented regularity and zeal.

On the Road by Jack Kerouac. Although associated with the 60s, "beat" literature actually began in the 50s. *On the Road* (1957) is considered a classic example of beat literature and of 60s youth culture and attitudes.

Anything by the Grateful Dead. This band, which still tours constantly, is an American institution that began in the 60s.

Easy Rider (1969), starring Jack Nicholson, Peter Fonda, and Dennis Hopper. They all do drugs and ride motorcycles.

10. Who was elected President after Lyndon B. Johnson?

(A) Jimmy Carter
(B) Gerald Ford
(C) Richard Nixon
(D) Ronald Reagan

In the election of 1968, Lyndon B. Johnson chose not to run for a second term, and Republican Richard Nixon eked out a victory over Hubert Humphrey (1911-1978). Nixon, who had served as vice president under Eisenhower and ran unsuccessfully against John F. Kennedy, was a political veteran. Nixon's administration was known for its successes in foreign affairs. He opened up relations with communist China, and a period of détente between the U.S. and USSR began. (Détente is the warming of relations between nations.)

The Right Stuff (1983), starring Dennis Quaid, Ed Harris, and Sam Shepard. A film about how cool and macho the first astronauts were.

11. Who was the first man to set foot on the moon?

(A) John Glenn
(B) Neil Armstrong
(C) Yuri Gagarin
(D) Virgil "Gus" Grissom

Neil Armstrong on the moon, July 20, 1969

The first man to land on the moon was **Neil Armstrong** (1930-) who said upon landing, **"That's one small step for a man, one giant leap for mankind."** *Sputnik* (p. 107) inspired the U.S. to accelerate our space program, and the U.S. and the USSR competed to see who could put the first man into space (the Russian **Yuri Gagarin** (1934-1968) took the honors), and then who could get a man to the moon first. The moon landing was watched by hundreds of millions of people, and it made Americans feel pretty darn good about themselves.

ANSWERS

1. A   2. B   3. B   4. B   5. No   6. B   7. B   8. A   9. D   10. C
11. B

1. **Which of the following Supreme Court decisions led to the legalization of abortion?**

   (A) Munn v. Illinois
   (B) Hammer v. Dagenhart
   (C) Roe v. Wade
   (D) Plessy v. Ferguson

On January 22, 1973, the Supreme Court ruled that a state law prohibiting abortions was unconstitutional. The decision made it legal for a woman to choose abortion in the first trimester (p. 330). The decision was extremely controversial and is still debated vigorously today. People who believe that abortion is murder call themselves "**pro-life**" and argue that life begins at conception. People who believe in the right to abortion call themselves "**pro-choice**." They believe that it is up to the prospective mother to decide whether or not to abort a fetus.

In the late 1980s and 1990s, the abortion issue has gained a lot of press through the extremist acts of different anti-abortion protesters. Their tactics include chaining themselves to the doors of abortion clinics and performing other acts to harass women who have made the choice to get an abortion. Most unfortunately, in 1994, a radical group of pro-lifers were involved in murders. They shot two doctors who performed abortions, making one wonder how they can truly call themselves "pro-life."

Fear and Loathing on the Campaign Trail '72, by Hunter S. Thompson. Thompson, known as a "gonzo" journalist, was (and is) a brilliant satirist and notorious scofflaw. If you like this book, try *Fear and Loathing in Las Vegas.*

2. **What is Watergate?**

   (A) A tourist attraction in the Midwest that was damaged in a flood
   (B) A building in which illegal actions were undertaken by the Republican party
   (C) A scandal involving the trading of arms for hostages
   (D) The opening mile of the Panama Canal

The Nixon administration is most known for the scandal involving the break-in to the **Watergate** Office Building in Washington, D.C., on June 17, 1972. The perpetrators were all employed by Nixon's election campaign. They attempted to tap the phones of Democratic leaders in order to gain knowledge of the Democrats' strategy in the upcoming election. The subsequent cover-up led to the resignation of President Nixon.

Nixon was almost impeached, or officially accused by the House of Representatives of a crime, and would most likely have been con-

Nixon in his victory pose

Watergate fascinated the nation. Much of the investigation by the Senate was televised, and millions of Americans watched in disbelief while one crime after another was exposed. In the course of the investigation, it was revealed that Nixon taped all conversations in the Oval Office, and the investigators subpoenaed the tapes to use in the investigation. Nixon resisted, but finally released the tapes. Some of the tapes had been erased. The investigators cried foul. Soon Nixon was on the verge of impeachment.

Nixon was succeeded by vice president **Gerald Ford** (1913-), who Nixon had appointed when **Spiro Agnew** (1918-) was forced to resign as a result of having taken kickbacks when he was governor of Maryland. Ford pardoned Nixon one month after taking office.

Shaft (1971), starring Richard Roundtree. "Blaxploitation" cop flick indicative of 1970s cinema. The clothes they wear in this movie are fly.

All the President's Men (1976), in which Robert Redford and Dustin Hoffman star as *Washington Post* reporters Woodward and Bernstein, the journalists who exposed Watergate.

3. **Which president was elected in the election held after Nixon resigned?**
   (A) Gerald Ford
   (B) Jimmy Carter
   (C) Ronald Reagan
   (D) Walter Mondale

In the election of 1976, **Jimmy Carter** (1924-) narrowly beat Gerald Ford. The Nixon era was over. Carter's presidency was marked by "stagflation," a condition marked by inflation, high unemployment, and a stagnant economy. He also had the bad luck of presiding over the U.S. during the Iranian hostage crisis.

4. **What happened in Iran when the Shah was overthrown by the Ayatollah Khomeini?**
   (A) A more American-friendly administration came to power in Iran
   (B) Iran became a state with freedom of religion
   (C) The Shah remained in Iran as Ambassador to the United States
   (D) American citizens were taken hostage by militant students

President Carter

On November 4, 1979, approximately 500 militant supporters of the **Ayatollah Khomeini** took over the American embassy in Iran and held most of the employees hostage. The supporters were upset because the former, but despised, leader of Iran, the Shah, was being treated for cancer in the United States. Carter agonized over how to free the hostages, as

WELCOME BACK TO FREEDOM

OPEN

The hostages come home after more than a year.

millions of Americans watched the days tick by on television. Nothing that Carter did seemed to work. There was an aborted rescue attempt. Diplomacy failed. Finally, minutes after Carter left office, the hostages were released. The **Iranian hostage crisis** was one of the reasons that Carter lost in his campaign for reelection.

5. Which commodity was OPEC created to control?

   (A) Wheat
   (B) Oil
   (C) Munitions
   (D) Coal

OPEC (The Organization of Petroleum Exporting Countries) is an organization of states that controls most of the world's oil. The OPEC countries, mostly Arab, first began to flex their muscle during the days of Nixon and Ford. In 1973, they refused to sell oil to the U.S. in reprisal to American support for Israel. The boycott changed a lot of American policies about energy. The U.S. started programs for conservation and alternative fuels. People began to desire fuel-efficient cars. Unfortunately, U.S. automakers in Detroit had not yet come to terms with the idea of a fuel-efficient car, so many Americans started buying smaller foreign cars.

OPEC continued to be a problem throughout Carter's administration as it manipulated the price of oil to maximize profits. But in the early nineties, OPEC's control decreased as instability in the Middle East reduced its power to control prices.

Saturday Night Fever (1977), starring John Travolta. Way seventies disco movie featuring a Bee Gees soundtrack and flared pants.

ANSWERS

1. C   2. B   3. B   4. D   5. B

The 1980s and 1990s

1. Who was elected President in 1980?

   (A) Jimmy Carter
   (B) Gerald Ford
   (C) George Bush
   (D) Ronald Reagan

With America's economy in a recession, high inflation, and all the trouble in the Middle East, it isn't surprising that **Ronald Reagan** (1911-) became president in 1980. He advocated a return to the values that "made America great." While other presidents were often hurt by scandals, the majority of the American public continued to like Reagan—no matter what happened in his administration.

2. **In which of the following countries did the U.S. NOT intervene militarily in the 1980s?**

   (A) Mexico
   (B) El Salvador
   (C) Nicaragua
   (D) Panama

Many of you have probably heard of the Iran-Contra Scandal. It is alleged that certain military personnel and members of the CIA traded arms with Iran and sent the profits to the Contras fighting communist forces in Nicaragua. All transactions were blatantly illegal because they countermanded a congressional order. Presidents Bush and Reagan are both alleged to have been involved.

During the 1980s, the U.S. was embroiled in Central American politics. A lot of people get confused about just who the U.S. was supporting and against whom it was fighting. In general, during the eighties (before the end of the Cold War (pp. 104-108)), the U.S. would support the side in a conflict that proclaimed itself non-communist. Marxist Sandinista guerrillas gained control of the government of Nicaragua in 1979, and the U.S. supplied military aid to the **Contras,** who sought to overthrow the Marxist government.

In El Salvador, the U.S. backed the government and supplied arms and advice to the National army against leftist groups supported by the communists.

And in Panama, in a dispute that did not stem from our government's distaste for communism, but rather from its dislike of anyone who helps sell illegal drugs, the U.S. invaded the country and pushed Manuel Noriega from power.

Valley Girl, starring Nicolas Cage. Totally eighties, like, y'know? I mean "gag me with a spoon"! Very funny stuff. Spiky hair. Awesome sound track.

3. **What is the name of the theory that lowering taxes on business will increase production and thereby help the economy?**

   (A) Supply-side economics
   (B) Supply and demand
   (C) Deficit spending
   (D) Laissez-faire

Supply-side economics (also called "trickle-down economics" or "Voodoo economics" depending on whom you ask) is the theory that if taxes were cut, people would spend more money and thereby create broader prosperity. Because people were making more money, the theory holds that the government would bring in more total taxes.

4. **Which of the following presidents was most responsible for implementing supply-side economics?**

    (A) Jimmy Carter
    (B) Gerald Ford
    (C) Ronald Reagan
    (D) Bill Clinton

Ronald Reagan was a believer in supply-side economics, and he did his best to reduce taxes for the rich. The reduction in taxes served to spur the economy, but it did not increase revenue. In fact, Reagan was responsible for a tremendous increase in the national deficit, the difference between the amount of money coming in and the amount going out. (If you earned $50 and spent $60, your "deficit" would be $10.)

President Bush

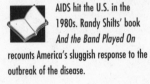

AIDS hit the U.S. in the 1980s. Randy Shilts' book *And the Band Played On* recounts America's sluggish response to the outbreak of the disease.

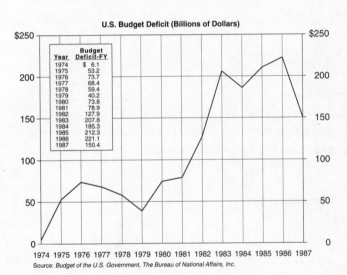

U.S. Budget Deficit (Billions of Dollars)

Year	Budget Deficit-FY
1974	$ 6.1
1975	53.2
1976	73.7
1977	68.4
1978	59.4
1979	40.2
1980	73.8
1981	78.9
1982	127.9
1983	207.8
1984	185.3
1985	212.3
1986	221.1
1987	150.4

Source: *Budget of the U.S. Government, The Bureau of National Affairs, Inc.*

5. **Assume that in the year 2000 the annual national deficit has been reduced to one-tenth of what it is now. What would happen to the national debt in the year 2000?**

    (A) It would continue to increase.
    (B) It would stay the same.
    (C) It would decrease.
    (D) It cannot be determined from the information given.

BLACK MONDAY

*The chart at right shows the events that occurred on October 19, 1987, otherwise known as **Black Monday**, when the stock market crashed. It was the most severe crash since the big one in 1929. However, the U.S. had learned its lesson in 1929; it created the **Securities and Exchange Commission** to regulate trading and insure that events such as those that led up to the crash of 1929 would never happen again.*

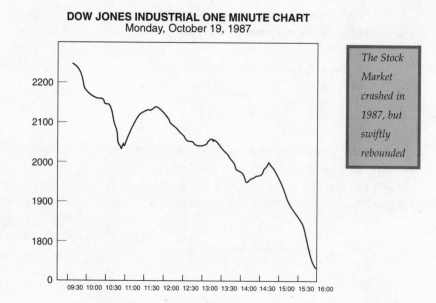

DOW JONES INDUSTRIAL ONE MINUTE CHART
Monday, October 19, 1987

The Stock Market crashed in 1987, but swiftly rebounded

Most people do not have a clear understanding of how the deficit and the debt interact. If a deficit exists, it means that the government is not bringing in enough money to pay its expenses. The debt is the sum total of all the deficits. Eventually, we will have to pay off the debt. So as long as a deficit exists, the debt will continue to grow.

6. **Who was elected President in 1988?**
   (A) Ronald Reagan
   (B) George Bush
   (C) Bill Clinton
   (D) Dan Quayle

The President who succeeded Ronald Reagan was George Bush (1924-), Reagan's vice president for eight years, and before that, director of the CIA from 1976 to 1977.

7. **Whom did we fight during the Persian Gulf War?**
   (A) Saudi Arabia
   (B) Kuwait
   (C) Iraq
   (D) Persia

In a war that did wonders for the stock market and oil prices and did horrors to the Iraqi people and their environment, the U.S. allied itself with Saudi Arabia and Kuwait to drive the Iraqis out of Kuwait. Iraq had basically annexed Kuwait without the Kuwaitis' permission. The U.S. did not like this because Kuwait has a lot of oil, and the U.S. wanted to stop Iraq and its dictator **Saddam Hussein** (1937-) from controlling this oil. The U.S. won the war and Kuwait is again a free country.

Saddam Hussein (above) and tracer fire over Kuwait during the Gulf War

THE MEANINGS OF "CONSERVATIVE" AND "LIBERAL" SHIFT OVER TIME.

Conservative	Liberal
Leans politically "right"	Leans politically "left"
More money for the military	Less money for the military
Pro-life	Pro-choice
Less money for social programs	More money for social programs
Lower taxes	Higher taxes for the rich
Shifting power to the states	More power in the federal government
Everyone should be able to fend for himself	Society should help those who are disadvantaged

Generation X, by Douglas Coupland. A funny book about people born in the sixties.

ANSWERS

1. D   2. A   3. A   4. C   5. A   6. B   7. C

Introduction to European & World History

H.W.10.

plaucicn vo gor

In America, the histories of the world come together. They intermingle, clash, parry, and ultimately co-exist. Aside from the Native Americans, everyone living in this country has come from, or has ancestors from, another country. Therefore, an understanding of world history is integral to a full understanding of the United States. Some snooty foreigners—and snooty Americans—like to say that America has no culture because it has only been around for a couple hundred years. We like to think that America has even more culture than any relatively closed society, no matter how long that closed society has been in existence. There are very few places in the world where people from several divergent cultures live side by side in relative harmony; therefore, there are very few people for whom learning world history is as important as it is for an American, especially a young American like you.

For example, you should know Russian history because many American citizens have Russian and Eastern European ancestors, and Eastern European culture has had a great impact on American culture. You have to know the history of England because America started as an English colony and so much of American culture is an extension of English culture: our national language; our system of government (to an extent); our prevailing Christianity—all of these things came from England and Europe hundreds of years ago.

By learning world history you can also better understand some of the decisions made by the U.S. regarding other nations. Again, if you know the history of Russia, you can better understand why we have been wary of them in this century—and why the future of Russia is anyone's guess. If you know the history of Africa, you will realize why the continent is in such a state of turmoil today, and to what extent that turmoil is the responsibility of our nation and other Western colonizers.

World history has shaped America more than it has any other nation on the planet. America has become the melting pot for the world's cultures, redefining them, altering them, and creating new cultural identities as a result. To be an informed American you must have knowledge of the world history that made our young nation a reality.

In the Beginning

1. Which of the following was NOT an ancient civilization?

   (A) The Sumerians
   (B) The Egyptians
   (C) The Babylonians
   (D) The Elizabethans

A **civilization** is characterized by a complex political system in which there is a high level of cultural and technological achievement. The first civilizations started about 5,000 years ago in the Middle East. Among the first civilizations were the Egyptians, Sumerians, Babylonians, and Phoenicians. The Egyptian civilization developed in the Nile River Valley, just west of an area sometimes known as the Fertile Crescent.

Another area in which early civilizations developed was **Mesopotamia**, an area of land nestled between the Tigris and the Euphrates rivers. In Mesopotamia, the Sumerians wrote laws, studied mathematics, and used a system of writing called **cuneiform**. Mesopotamia traded with other cultures in Egypt and India.

2. **Which of the following civilizations developed pyramids?**

   I. The Aztecs
   II. The Egyptians
   III. The Greeks

(A) I only
(B) II only
(C) I and II only
(D) I, II, and III

Ancient Egyptians are known for the enormous pyramids built by slaves under the direction of the **pharaohs** (or kings) approximately 4,500 years ago. Some people believe that the proportions of the pyramids had some religious significance for the Egyptians. The world's largest pyramid (in ground area), however, was built by the **Aztecs** near what is now Mexico City.

The great Egyptian Pyramids

The Egyptian writing system was called **hieroglyphics**. It used a set of about 700 picture-like symbols that could be used to represent the thing pictured or could be used in combination with other hieroglyphs to represent a series of sounds that made up another word. The system was very different from our phonetic alphabet.

3. **What was the Code of Hammurabi?**

   (A) The secret language used by the ancient Mesopotamians
   (B) The ethical structure of Hammurabian civilization
   (C) The legal code of ancient Babylon
   (D) The key to translating hieroglyphics

The Babylonians followed the Sumerians as the next great civilization in Mesopotamia. **The Code of Hammurabi**, written by Hammurabi, is one of the earliest and most complete recorded systems of laws. These rules of Babylonian society were fairly severe and seem harsh by today's standards: Theft and adultery were both punishable by death. Surprisingly, murder is not mentioned among the crimes discussed by the code. In those days, it was assumed that the victim's family would avenge the murder.

Civilizations seem to have developed independently in other areas of the world. In China, the **Shang** civilization developed around 1600 BC. In India, the **Indus** civilization reached its peak from 2500 to 1700 BC. In the Americas, the **Aztecs**, the **Mayas**, the **Toltecs**, and the **Incas** were all early civilizations.

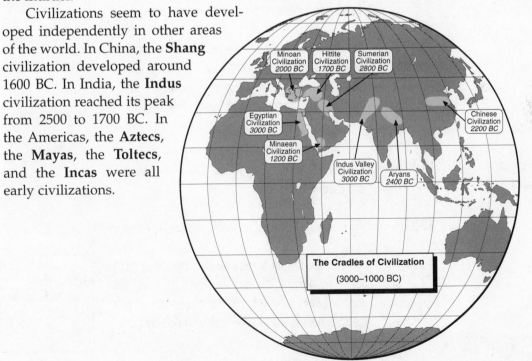

Minoan Civilization 2000 BC

Hittite Civilization 1700 BC

Sumerian Civilization 2800 BC

Egyptian Civilization 3000 BC

Minaean Civilization 1200 BC

Indus Valley Civilization 3000 BC

Aryans 2400 BC

Chinese Civilization 2200 BC

The Cradles of Civilization
(3000–1000 BC)

The following chart shows how weapons technology has developed since the "discovery" of fire. Lands have been conquered, peoples destroyed, and agony inflicted at every turn as new ways of killing people have been invented. Better guns have almost always ensured victory, and from the first civilizations, those who blew up things best were most likely to be on the top of the world political food chain.

WARFARE TECHNOLOGY TIMELINE

(DATES ARE APPROXIMATE)

BC

10000 — Fire developed. Man can guard camps against hostile groups and animals.

2500 — Large-scale stone tool development.

1800 — The chariot, flexible bow, and iron smelting are developed. Military tactics are revolutionized.

600 — The cavalry replaces the chariot. Advances in defensive gear like armor, shields, and helmets will last for the next 2,000 years, along with weaponry such as the mace, ax, dagger, sword, spear, and javelin.

AD

1100 — The Chinese invent gunpowder. Primitive grenades are used in warfare.

1327— The cannon is first used in battle, and proves effective.

1356 — The first metal gun is developed. There is a great outcry from the nobles that the introduction of "the gun" will take all the honor out of combat, as any common person will be able to slay a noble by merely aiming at him.

1400 — Professionalism develops among soldiers. What was once viewed as a short-term dislocation to fight a battle now becomes a full-time profession.

1610 — The development of the telescope allows for long-range reconnaissance.

1792 — The Montgolfier brothers fly their first balloon, leading to improved reconnaissance and the development of aircraft as a military weapon.

1800 — Massive coordination of troops becomes possible with the telegraph, allowing armies of over 100,000 men to keep amazingly precise timetables and execute intricate tactical movements.

1855 — The Gatling gun, forefather of the machine gun, is invented. Thousands are killed in the 1860s in the Civil War, proving its efficacy.

1890 — John Holland develops an underwater craft capable of replenishing its own air supply, adding another element to maritime warfare.

1897 — Massive manufacturing of ammunition becomes possible through other mass-manufacturing technological advances.

1916 –
1918 — World War I tests new inventions of modern weaponry: The flame thrower, the submachine gun, improved accuracy light artillery, and chemical weapons (specifically mustard gas). Following this use, poison gas is discontinued by mutual accord.

1939 — Radar is developed.

1940 — Tanks, in use for over a decade, become deadly when used by the German army. Rommel equips each tank with a two-way radio, allowing for precise information and coordination of attacks. Rommel's Panzer corps becomes the elite crew of the German army.

1943 — Long-range aircraft expand the field of battle to thousands of miles. Warfare becomes accessible from any distance.

1945 — The first atomic bombs are dropped on August 6, 1945 (Hiroshima) and August 8, 1945 (Nagasaki). Many agree that the bombs herald a new age in which a weapon will only be used to prevent war, not for warfare itself. This is the only time that atomic weapons have been used in military conflict.

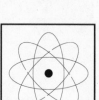

1947 — John von Neumann invents stored programming, paving the way for computers in warfare. For the next 30 years, most major military advances are made based on computer applications—war simulations, orbiting tracking satellites, orbiting weaponry, and automated firing and detection systems.

ANSWERS

1. D   2. C   3. C

Ancient Greece

1. **Which of the following civilizations developed in the same geographical area as the Mycenaean civilization?**

   (A) Egypt
   (B) Greece
   (C) Babylonia
   (D) Inca

Out of the ashes of the Mycenaean civilization (which shared a domain with the Minoan civilization (pp. 387-388)) was born the great civilization of **ancient Greece.** Most of what is European in our heritage can be said to have been developed first by the Greeks (who borrowed a lot from the Egyptians, but the Greeks get most of the credit). You name it, the Greeks helped develop it: science, philosophy, art, literature, and democracy. Most of what we consider our culture has its origins in the ancient Greek cultures of two to three thousand years ago.

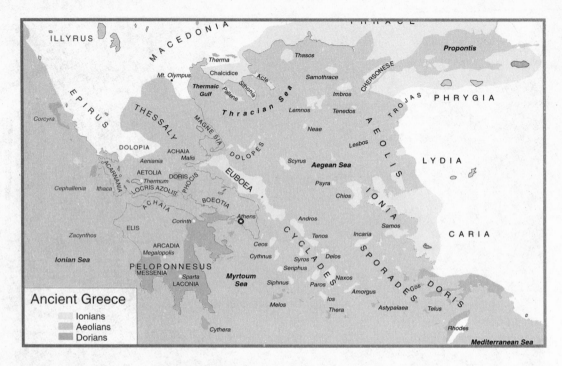

Ancient Greece

Ionians
Aeolians
Dorians

2. Which of the following were rival city-states during most of Greek civilization?

(A)   Athens and Sparta
(B)   Gaul and Florence
(C)   Macedonia and Carthage
(D)   Rome and Acropolis

Socrates gets his thoughts on papyrus.

The two main city centers of ancient Greece were **Athens** and **Sparta**, and each had different philosophies. The people of Athens were concerned with the arts, philosophy, and the natural sciences, while the people of Sparta concerned themselves with the art of war. Think of Athens as the liberal hippie who read philosophy and got beat up after school. Think of Sparta as a rogue gang with rigid war-like ideas. Athens and Sparta fought each other during the Peloponnesian wars. Guess who won.

Most of the Greek artistic tradition (which became our artistic tradition) came out of Athens, where the cultural elite passed the time thinking great thoughts and drinking good wine. **Socrates** (c. 469-399 BC), **Plato** (c. 428-347 BC), and **Aristotle** (384-322 BC) all lived in Athens. In addition, many of the greatest architectural works of the time were built in Athens. The Acropolis, where the Parthenon is located, was the city center.

3. Who wrote the *Republic?*

    (A) Plato
    (B) Socrates
    (C) Machiavelli
    (D) Marx

Perhaps the most important philosopher in the Western tradition is Plato, a student of Socrates. Plato believed every object was only a shadow of its ideal form; this book that you hold in your hand is just a copy of the actual form of "bookness." These and other Platonic theories were expressed beautifully in the form of dialogues between characters. Usually the main character is Socrates, who expresses Plato's beliefs. Reading the dialogues is actually a lot of fun. Some of the dialogues, especially the *Symposium,* deal with everyday life and are quite accessible. The *Symposium* is Plato's take on love and makes fascinating reading.

Plato is also known for his theories on politics, which are best expressed in his **Republic.** In the *Republic,* Plato calls for rule by philosopher-kings, and he denigrates democracy as the lowest form of government.

One of Plato's students, **Aristotle** (384-322 BC), went on to become another of the pillars of Greek thought. Aristotle disagreed with Plato over his "forms,"and his studies in the natural sciences were hugely influential during the Middle Ages and the early Renaissance. Unfortunately, most of Aristotle's writing that was aimed at the general public has disappeared, and our knowledge of him comes from rather difficult texts most likely meant for his colleagues. Aristotle was also Alexander the Great's tutor, and his ideas influenced Christian thought.

Plato makes his point.

4. Alexander the Great was a ruler of which of the following empires?

    (A) The Roman Empire
    (B) The Greek Empire
    (C) The Russian Empire
    (D) The European Empire

The Peloponnesian War, Thucydides. A gripping war story full of blood and guts, written by one of the greatest historians to ever live.

Alexander the Great (356-323 BC) was the son of **Philip of Macedonia** (382-336 BC), who finally succeeded in conquering Greece after centuries in which the Greek civilization was pre-eminent.

Alexander the Great

Alexander the Great succeeded in conquering Persia and ruled the largest empire of the time. When he died, the Grecian empire collapsed and was gradually replaced by the Roman empire.

A WOMAN POET FROM THE PAST

One of the rarest discoveries an archaeologist can make is the finding of ancient Greek texts written by women. One such rare find is the poetry of Sappho, who lived on the island of Lesbos around the year 600 BC. In these short, evocative verses, Sappho boasts, truthfully, about the destiny of her work.

8   *I took my lyre and said:*
     Come now, my heavenly
     tortoise shell: become
     a speaking instrument

9   *Although they are*
     Only breath, words
     which I command
     are immortal

Aristotle, by Raphael Sanzio (1483-1520), an artist from the Renaissance (pp. 159-162)

Zorba the Greek (1964), starring Anthony Quinn and Irene Papas. Oscar-winning movie that takes place in modern Greece.

Medea, a drama by Euripides. The adage that "Hell hath no fury like a woman scorned," from a play by William Congreve (1670-1729), was probably coined with Medea in mind. In *Medea*, written in the fifth century BC, Medea goes on a murderous rampage when her husband decides to leave her for another woman.

TIME	NAME	CONTRIBUTION
Pre-Periclean Age	Homer (Epic Poet)	The Iliad The Odyssey
Periclean Age (5th Century BC)	Hippocrates (c. 460-370 BC)	Medicine
	Socrates (Philosopher)	Rational thought through questioning and answering
Hellenistic Age (4th Century BC)	Plato (Philosopher)	Student of Socrates: "Ideas" can be real.
	Aristotle (Philosopher)	Student of Plato: Only natural world is real.
Also:	Greek Drama Greek Architecture	Comedy and Tragedy The Parthenon

ANSWERS

1. B   2. A   3. A   4. B

The Roman Empire

1. Patricians in ancient Rome are similar to which of the
   following social classes?

   (A) Slaves
   (B) Nobility
   (C) Farmers
   (D) The working class

For much of its 800-year existence, ancient Roman civilization was
split up into three classes of peoples: the **patricians** (nobles); the **plebeians** (free men); and **slaves**. The government was organized as a republic, with two consuls (their leaders chosen annually) who worked in con-
junction with a Senate (made up of patrician families) and an Assembly
(open to all plebeians). Slaves and women had no place in the government.

Rome's early years were characterized by a series of wars with neighboring states. Of these, the most famous are the **Punic Wars** between

I Claudius, by Robert Graves.
A behind-the-scenes look at
the Roman emperors. The
book was made into a riveting PBS
television series, available on videotape.

JULIUS CAESAR

Although Julius Caesar died over twenty centuries ago, his name is still used to denote a powerful ruler. In the twentieth century, both Germany and Austria-Hungary called their leaders "Kaiser," the German spelling of "Caesar." The British ruler of India (until 1947) was called the "Kaiser-i-Hind" and the Russian word "Tsar," or "Czar," comes from Emperor Julius' name. It is not unusual to use the name of an ancient leader to indicate either position or action.

Bust of Julius Caesar

Julius Caesar, by William Shakespeare (p. 396).

Rome and **Carthage.** Rome ended up winning the wars and destroying Carthage.

2. **When Hannibal crossed the Alps, which of the following empires was he trying to conquer?**

    (A) Carthage
    (B) Rome
    (C) Greece
    (D) Egypt

In the second Punic War, **Hannibal** (247-182 BC) crossed the Alps with elephants and surprised the Romans in the northern Po Valley. Hannibal was victorious over the Romans for a time, but the Romans eventually won the war. They built up an enormous empire which stretched over most of Europe and part of Africa and the Middle East.

3. **Which of the following men became the first dictator of Rome in 49 BC?**

    (A) Alexander the Great
    (B) Julius Caesar
    (C) Augustus Caesar
    (D) Constantine

The Roman Republic lasted for hundreds of years, to about 44 BC, when **Julius Caesar** (c. 100-44 BC) declared himself emperor for life. Caesar came to power in a three-part union with Pompey (106-48 BC) and Crassus (108-53 BC), called the **First Triumvirate.** Although Caesar had the support of the lower classes, his disputes with the Senate ultimately shortened his life. He was assassinated by the senators, and his rule was followed by that of the **second triumvirate** of **Augustus** (63 BC-AD 14), **Marc Antony** (83-30 BC), and Lepidus.

4. Which of the following Romans cavorted with Cleopatra VII?

   I. Julius Caesar
   II. Mark Antony
   III. Constantine

   (A) I only
   (B) II only
   (C) I and II only
   (D) I, II, and III

Cleopatra (c. 68-30 BC) is one of the most famous rulers of Egypt. Through the force of her personality and her incredible political skills, she attempted to revive the power of Egypt. She has fascinated writers for centuries: Shakespeare's *Antony and Cleopatra* and George Bernard Shaw's *Caesar and Cleopatra* both tell stories about her life. The thing that draws playwrights to her story was her use of romantic liaisons to attain her goals. Not only did Cleopatra and Caesar have an affair that led to a child, but she also was **Mark Antony**'s mistress. In her attempts to seize politi-

Mark Antony and Cleopatra, Queen of Egypt

Ovid's series of poems on love and courtship, "The Amores," delve into the most minute details of winning and losing love. Even in the time of the Romans, the equivalent of the contemporary captain of the football team was despised by wimpier poets for his success with women.

Does anyone nowadays look up with admiration
  At the liberal arts, or believe
Love-elegies rate a dowry? Time was when poetic talent
  Came dearer than gold, but today
To lack cash is plain vulgar. When my poems please my
     mistress
   They can go in where I can't.
A few pretty compliments, and the front door slams behind
me —
   Me, genius, out in the cold,
Traipsing round like a fool, replaced by some new-rich soldier,
   A bloody oaf who slashed his way to the cash
And a knighthood. Darling, how could you bear to embrace
     him
   With those exquisite arms - much less let him hug you?

cal power, she banded with Antony and attempted to set up a vast kingdom. She hoped the kingdom would be ruled by her children, but the plan failed when her army was defeated by Octavian, later called **Augustus.** Antony committed suicide. He was soon followed by Cleopatra, who, as legend has it, allowed herself to be bitten by an **asp** (a symbol of Egyptian royalty).

5. **The rule of Augustus Caesar in Rome (27 BC–AD 14) was known as**

    (A) Pax Romana
    (B) a particularly violent time
    (C) the fall of the Roman Empire
    (D) Carpe Diem

The Augustine Age of Roman history is known as the Pax Romana *(Roman Peace).* Augustus believed that there could be peace under Roman domination, and he dealt fairly with the conquered territories. He even gave some of the conquered people citizenship rights. His policies were continued even after his death, and under Augustus, the Roman Empire reached its largest geographical proportions. In this period of relative tranquillity, Roman arts and culture flourished.

Spartacus (1960), starring Kirk Douglas and Laurence Olivier. Saga of a Roman slave who leads a revolt against the empire. Fabulous fight scenes. Based on a true story.

6. **The AD that precedes the date stands for**

    (A) Anno Domini
    (B) After Death
    (C) Augustus Dei
    (D) Absolute Date

The AD that precedes any date that is expressed as a positive number means *Anno Domini*—"in the year of our lord." The calendar, devised some 500 years after Jesus was born (c. 4 BC-AD 29 or 30), is supposed to start on the day when he was born. Some historians think that the calendar is a little off, disputing that Jesus was born in AD 1 and suggesting that he was born in about 4 BC (Before Christ).

7. **During the first 200 years after the death of Jesus, Christianity**

   (A) was the dominant religion in Rome
   (B) was outlawed and many of its followers persecuted
   (C) was the first monotheistic religion
   (D) was immediately embraced by Rome's leaders

Although Christianity is practiced by more people today than any other religion, the first few years were not kind to those who practiced it. Since Christians were not willing to accept the Emperor as their supreme leader, they were persecuted and the religion was outlawed. The first Roman leader to legalize Christianity was **Constantine the Great** (c. AD 280-337), who ruled in the fourth century AD. Constantine himself converted during the middle of his reign, which helped the Christian religion to grow. He also helped establish **Constantinople**, an Eastern capital for the Roman Empire.

After Constantine died, the Roman empire split up and was soon destroyed by invading German peoples from the North. The Western half of the empire fell into chaos, and the Middle Ages began. The Eastern Empire became known as the Byzantine Empire, and the Christian church was preserved there. The Roman Empire's former greatness was somewhat restored under the Byzantine emperor **Justinian** (483-565), and the region flourished through trade which, in turn, fostered the arts.

Constantine the Great

FRIENDS, ROMANS, COUNTRYMEN

When we think of ancient Rome, images of feasting, fighting, and feeding people to the lions often come to mind. Nevertheless, many Romans were concerned with ethics, morals, and strict codes of behavior. Marcus Tullius Cicero (106-43 BC), a wealthy politician and brilliant orator, left us a number of ideas on friendship, honor, statesmanship, and the "good" life. Cicero's carefully constructed writing style influences many writers even today.

During the fourth and fifth centuries AD, the Church's power grew because the **Pope**, the leader of the Christian church, did not have to contend with a Roman Empire. Thus the Western church began to take a bigger and bigger role in western affairs, and soon became the predominant power in Europe.

8. **Which of the following religions supplanted Christianity during the Middle Ages in most of the Eastern half of the Roman Empire?**
    (A) Buddhism
    (B) Judaism
    (C) Islam
    (D) Taoism

In the seventh century, the prophet **Mohammed** (c. 570-632) wrote the **Koran** as God's, or **Allah**'s, word; Islam (pp. 378-379), a monotheistic religion, emerged. The religion spread quickly and became the dominant belief system in the Middle East and in Northern Africa. Throughout the Middle Ages, Constantinople was the only area of the former Eastern empire to remain Christian.

ANSWERS

1. B   2. B   3. B   4. C   5. A   6. A   7. B   8. C

The Middle Ages

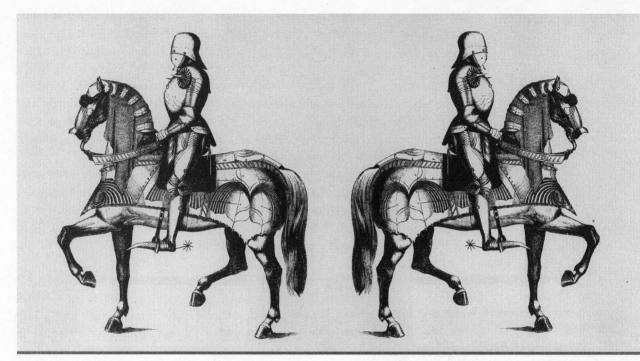

1. In the Middle Ages there was a hierarchical ordering of social classes. Which of the following is a correct order from lowest caste to highest caste?

   (A) Serf, lord, vassal
   (B) Serf, vassal, lord
   (C) Lord, vassal, serf
   (D) Lord, serf, vassal

The **Middle Ages**, sometimes referred to as the "**Dark Ages**," is the period stretching all the way from the fall of the Roman Empire to the fifteenth century. This was the time of knights and lords and kings and chivalry and all that stuff that you see in a Robin Hood movie. The Middle Ages were characterized by a social organization called **feudalism.** Feudalism is a hierarchical organization based on land, wealth, and prestige. The king (pp. 442-443) was at the top of the organization (sort of

The Adventures of Robin Hood (1938), starring Errol Flynn and Olivia de Havilland. This is *the* classic Robin Hood movie. With distressed damsels, oppressed peasants, and brilliant archery, it's hard to beat.

a medieval CEO)—immediately followed by **lords**, **vassals**, and **subvassals**. In the feudal system, the lord granted a **fief**—a plot of land given to a knight in return for military service or given to a vassal in return for money or a percentage of future earnings from the land. The lords called the shots and could decide who the vassal could marry, and all kinds of other stuff. The vassals also had to declare their loyalty to the lords and were obligated to follow a code of honor. To betray your lord or king would be a disloyalty worse than death. (Of course, if a vassal decided to betray his lord, death would surely follow.)

Beneath the vassals were the **peasants** and **serfs**. The peasants were free men who farmed on a fief. They could actually keep some of the harvested food. The serfs were more like slaves. They had no choice but to work for a vassal, and had few rights. As the hardships of the agricultural economy continued, more and more peasants were forced into serfdom.

Even the church got involved. The higher clergy could be feudal lords themselves, often acquiring lands, extracting **tithes** (those payments to the church that Jesus was all up in arms about), and organizing their own vassals and serfs.

2. **Charlemagne was**

    (A) A type of champagne
    (B) An island off the coast of France
    (C) A leader in Europe during the Middle Ages
    (D) A leader of Italy during the Renaissance

After the fall of the Roman Empire, much of Europe was decentralized. Instead of an all-encompassing "government" or "nation," society was organized in small territorial units governed by local kings and lords. There was no single emperor. Each little mini-nation had its own local laws and customs.

In the eighth century, **Charlemagne** (742-814) began to gather together the different fiefdoms under one rule—his. After a series of Bloody (and we mean Bloody with a capital "B") wars, Charlemagne succeeded in conquering many of the surrounding territories. By using a ruthless policy

Emperor Charlemagne

that aimed to subjugate and destroy any opposition, he managed to annex huge amounts of land and to convert many residents of those lands to Christianity. Eventually, he convinced the Pope to declare him **Holy Roman Emperor** in AD 800; with the help of the Church, he managed to rule a huge empire without the benefit of taxes or a large central bureaucracy.

After Charlemagne died, his empire became vulnerable to attack from the **Vikings** of Scandinavia and the **Muslims** of the East and South, and fell apart.

3. **Which of the following events happened in Europe in 1066?**

    (A) The Italian Renaissance started.
    (B) Charlemagne died.
    (C) William the Conqueror invaded England.
    (D) Catherine the Great succeeded in taking over Russia.

In **1066**, **William the Conqueror** (c. 1027-1087) led the Normans (descendants of the Scandinavian Vikings who had attacked Europe in the past) in an invasion of England. Although he introduced feudalism to the region, William was a powerful king—able to avoid the fragmentation that feudalism brought to the rest of the continent. The Normans were highly organized and succeeded in bringing together the different regions of England. Although the English were resentful of the Norman rulers, the stability brought by their reign helped make England into a powerful state.

William the Conqueror

The Lion in Winter (1968), starring Katharine Hepburn, Peter O'Toole, Anthony Hopkins, and Timothy Dalton. Fascinating story of intrigue and double-dealing between Henry II and his wife Eleanor of Aquitaine (Richard the Lionheart's father and mother). Henry keeps Eleanor locked in jail most of the time, but lets her out for Christmas.

4. **The name for the series of wars in which European kings attempted to gain control of the land in which Jesus lived is**

(A) The Jihad
(B) The Crusades
(C) The First World War
(D) The Wars of Holy Recapture

St. Louis and his band of Crusaders

Between the eleventh and fourteenth centuries, the kings in Europe engaged in a series of campaigns to capture the lands where Jesus had lived. These campaigns were called **Crusades,** and those fighting in them had many goals. Aside from the obvious religious reasons, the people fighting these wars were attempting to increase their earning potential. Inheritance was set up so that only the oldest son of a lord would get anything. If the younger sons of a feudal lord wanted to make their way in the world, they could wage war on the infidels. Just like kids today who go to college to make money, the young sons of feudal lords would join a crusade to make their fortunes. It's the same thing! Sort of . . .

The European nations gained a great deal from the Crusades. Not only did they get the goods picked up by the crusaders on their way to Jerusalem, but the nations also benefited from the newly opened trade routes.

Richard the Lionhearted (1157-1199) was King of England during Robin Hood's time. He spent most of his reign crusading.

5. **The enormous stone churches built during the Middle Ages were called**

(A) Pyramids
(B) Cathedrals
(C) Temples
(D) Pantheons

Although the Middle Ages is known for many artistic creations, the most well-known of these are the **cathedrals.** Enormous stone churches that could take centuries to build, these structures were beautiful attempts at bringing a worshipper closer to God. With flying buttresses and pointed arches, these churches were engineering triumphs built without the benefit of bulldozers or trucks. Imagine how hard it would be to lug a huge slab of rock to the top of a 300-foot-high building without the aid of modern machinery.

The cathedrals demonstrate just how much power the church had at the time. These structures required a huge outlay of funds and a great deal of control to be built.

6. **Which of the following most closely describes the Inquisition?**

   (A) The formalized questioning and persecution of heretics
   (B) The process by which a king or queen gives up his or her throne
   (C) The style of philosophy in which truth is achieved through the asking of questions
   (D) The church practice of exchanging money for salvation

The **Inquisition** was a traveling court designed to rid the church—and society in general—of heretics. (A heretic is someone who doesn't follow established church beliefs.) An inquisitor would set up in a town, and anyone who wanted to denounce anyone else could start the ball rolling. Once denounced, a person was considered guilty and was required to confess. If he decided not to, he would be tortured, often on a gruesome device called the rack. If the crime were deemed bad enough and the tormented insisted on his beliefs and did not confess, he would be killed.

The rack

Several famous people were brought before the Inquisition. Joan of Arc and Galileo each had to face it. Galileo (1564-1642) (p. 269) recanted. Joan of Arc (pp. 156-157) was burned at the stake.

7. **What was the importance of the Magna Carta?**

   (A) It increased the power of the monarchy in England.
   (B) It took away power from the monarchy in England.
   (C) It was one of the longest letters ever written.
   (D) It established a long lasting peace between England and France.

From the time of William the Conqueror, England had a tradition of a strong monarchy. Under the rule of King John (1167-1216), the English higher-ups revolted and forced the king to sign the **Magna Carta**, a docu-

STRETCHING THE TRUTH OUT OF YOU

Here is William Lithgow's first-hand description of what it was like to be placed on the rack during the Spanish Inquisition. It is not a pretty sight:

"I was brought to the rack, then mounted on the top of it. My legs were drawn through the two sides of the three-planked rack. A cord was tied about my ankles. As the levers bent forward, the main force of my knees against the two planks burst asunder the sinews of my hams, and the lids of my knees were crushed. My eyes began to startle, my mouth to foam and froth, and my teeth to chatter like the doubling of a drummer's sticks. My lips were shivering, my groans were vehement, and blood sprang from my arms, broken sinews, hands and knees. Being loosed from these pinnacles of pain, I was hand-fast set on the floor, with this incessant imploration: 'Confess! Confess!'"

THE ENGLISH FINGER

The French had an interesting strategy when fighting against the longbow. When they captured a soldier who used this weapon, they cut off the first two fingers of his right hand. To this day, in England, it is considered a strong insult to hold up the first two fingers of your right hand. It is the equivalent of giving "the finger" in the U.S.

ment requiring the king to seek consent from Parliament to raise taxes. The Magna Carta also established that no free man of England could lose his liberty or his property without a trial. Probably the most important legal document since the Code of Hammurabi (p. 137), the Magna Carta established the predominance of law over whim. Some of its strictures (for example, the idea that "due process" was necessary before certain government actions could be taken) eventually led to our Constitution's Bill of Rights (p. 52).

The signing of the Magna Carta

The Magna Carta led to the formation of **Parliament**, a government body similar to our Congress, that helped govern England. Parliament was eventually divided into two branches, the **House of Lords** (nobles and clergy), and the **House of Commons** (knights and wealthy citizens). If you are wondering which house represented the poor, you needn't wonder. The poor didn't have any power.

8. Who was an inspiration to the French at the end of the Hundred Years' War?

   (A) Joan of Arc
   (B) Marie Antoinette
   (C) Victor Hugo
   (D) Elizabeth II

England and France both had strong centralized governments and eventually decided to go to war. The **Hundred Years' War** was fought from 1337 to 1453. At first, because of its financial superiority and the support of the Pope, France was winning. However, with the invention of the **longbow,** the English were able to come back with outstanding victories. The longbow gave the English a huge advantage. They could pick off the French soldiers from far away.

Eventually, however, the French were inspired by **Joan of Arc** (1412-1431), a peasant who had visions that God had chosen her to save France.

Joan of Arc

With her encouragement, the French were able to eke out a victory. Joan wasn't so lucky. She was burned at the stake (p. 155). After her death, Joan was made a saint.

9. Which of the following people led the Mongol army in gaining control of most of Asia and Eastern Europe?

(A) Genghis Khan
(B) Shogun
(C) Emperor Hirohito
(D) Alexander the Great

In the thirteenth century, the **Mongols** under **Genghis Khan** (c. 1167-1227) managed to take over much of Asia and some of Europe to create what was probably the largest empire ever. Through efficiency and organization, the Mongols were able to use their horses to control vast amounts of territory. Imagine, if you can, one nation controlling an area bigger then the U.S., Canada, and Russia combined. The Mongol takeover of Russia helped keep it separated from the rest of Europe.

10. The Black Death was caused by which of the following?

(A) Smallpox
(B) Bubonic plague
(C) Malaria
(D) The measles

Ghengis Khan

The **Black Death**, an epidemic of **bubonic plague** that occurred in Europe in the fourteenth century, killed one-fourth to one-half of the population—about seventy-five million people. Bubonic plague is a horrible disease transmitted from rodents to people by fleas and then from person to person by airborne transmission. The disease was particularly disastrous in the fourteenth century because of the chronic malnutrition of the peasant classes and because of their unsanitary living conditions. Some historians think the capricious nature of the disease, and the inability of humans to protect themselves from it, served to shift civilization's focus away from "otherworldly" matters like the Church and its life-after-death focus toward more human-centered concerns.

The symptoms of bubonic plague are pretty severe. Within a few hours of the first symptoms, a victim becomes gravely sick. He may expe-

The Canterbury Tales, by Geoffrey Chaucer (written in the fourteenth century). Written in what's known as "Middle English," it's even older and harder to understand than Shakespeare, but you can (and should) pick up a copy. The stories are very funny (sometimes bawdy) and you'll have to read it in college anyway.

The Seventh Seal (1957). Directed by the famous Ingmar Bergman. It's black and white and in Swedish (don't worry, there are subtitles), but it's considered a masterpiece. An unhappy knight plays chess with Death.

rience vomiting or delirium. Lymph nodes throughout the body become swollen and filled with pus and the inflammation is extremely painful. If untreated, the vast majority stricken with the disease will die within days. Luckily for us, through improved sanitation and the use of antibiotics, we have kept the plague under control.

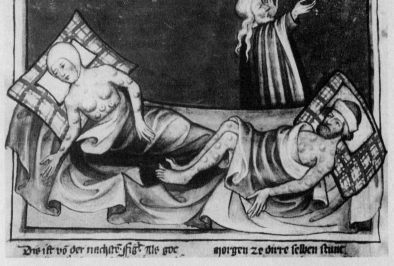

Two unlucky victims of the plague

ANSWERS

1. B   2. C   3. C   4. B   5. B   6 A   7. B   8. A   9. A   10. B

The Renaissance

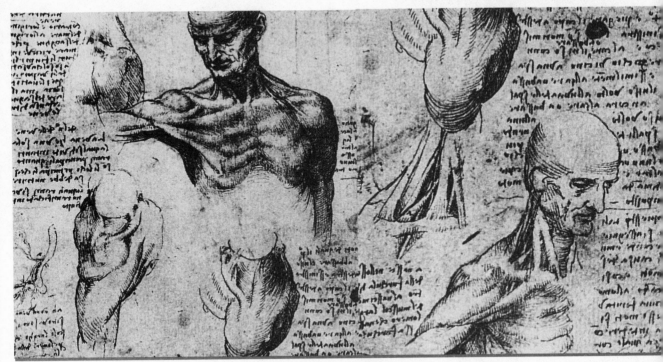

1. **The first printing press with movable type was invented by**

   (A) Antonin Dvorak
   (B) Johannes Gutenberg
   (C) Leonardo da Vinci
   (D) Rene Printemps

The printing press with movable type was one of the most important inventions in the history of humankind. Before the printing press, books were made by the elaborate and time-consuming method of hand-copying. A scribe would slowly copy the words of one book into another, page by page. **Johannes Gutenberg**'s (1400-1468) invention of the printing press allowed for the mass production of books. The first work, of course, was the **Gutenberg Bible** (people were more religious back then). The fact that ideas could be passed among people quickly and relatively cheaply was an important step toward the intellectual achievements of the **Renaissance**.

2. **Which of the following families is known for its support of the Italian Renaissance in the fourteenth and fifteenth centuries?**
   (A) The Russo
   (B) The Castellano
   (C) The Medici
   (D) The Corleone

ANATOMY ON THE SLY

While the study of anatomy is integral to accurate artistic representation, the manner of that study is often debated. Both Leonardo da Vinci and Michelangelo were rumored to have performed dissections on cadavers in order to further their anatomical studies. While these allegations were never proven, Pope Leo heeded them enough to deny da Vinci permission to visit the hospital in Rome in order to study anatomy.

The term Renaissance means "re-birth," and many scholars consider it a rebirth of the artistic and philosophic pursuits of the ancient Romans and Greeks. Considered by some as the high point of artistic achievement, Renaissance art broke new ground in many fields. The artists of the time include Shakespeare (1564-1616) (pp. 395-396), Leonardo da Vinci (1452-1519)(p. 454), Michelangelo (1475-1564) (p. 454), and J. S. Bach (1685-1750)(p. 437). Part of the reason for the success of the Renaissance was the patronage of several rich families, the most famous of which was the Medici family of Florence, who helped support many Italian artists of the time.

3. **Who wrote *The Prince*?**
   (A) Niccolo Machiavelli
   (B) Martin Luther
   (C) Oliver Cromwell
   (D) William Shakespeare

One of the most influential books ever written, **Niccolo Machiavelli**'s (1469-1527) *The Prince* (written 1513, published 1532) extols the benefits of a strong, but sometimes manipulative, leadership. A Machiavellian ruler acts purely out of self-interest, rather than on the basis of vague moral tenets. Machiavelli believed a monarch should be independent of the church and should not have any historical ties. Thus, one of a Machiavellian leader's first steps would be to destroy (i.e., kill) any hereditary princes.

The Prince was the favorite bedtime reading of a number of famous dictators. Among those who cherished the book were Louis XIV, Oliver Cromwell, Napoleon Bonaparte, Otto von Bismarck, Adolf Hitler, and Benito Mussolini. Both Hitler and Louis XIV admitted to keeping the book by their bedside.

4. Which of the following people was among the first Europeans to establish a long-standing relationship with Asia?

   (A) Erasmus
   (B) Marco Polo
   (C) Vasco da Gama
   (D) Cortes

The Renaissance also saw Europe explore distant lands. **Marco Polo** (1254-1324) was one of the first Europeans to travel to Asia and stay for any length of time. His accounts of his adventures, written around 1300, were the only writings on Asia to be written by a European for the next 300 years. He stayed in Mongolia in the court of the emperor **Kublai Khan** (whose grandfather was Genghis Khan (p. 157)) for nearly twenty years. His accounts of life in Asia astonished Europeans and piqued their interest in trade with China and other Eastern countries. The addition of Eastern trading partners also helped provide the money needed to fuel the artistic achievements of the Renaissance.

Niccolo Machiavelli

Gradually, as technologies in shipbuilding, navigation, and **cartography** (map-making) improved, explorers searched for new trade routes and new people to convert to Christianity (p. 372). These explorations, aside from filling the pockets of many adventurous sailors and their champions, also helped shift the power in Europe to the countries with borders on the Atlantic Ocean—England, France, Spain, and Portugal.

FAMOUS RENAISSANCE-ERA EXPLORERS

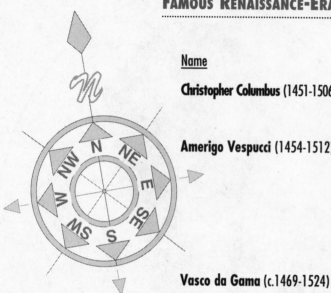

Name	Act of Exploration
Christopher Columbus (1451-1506)	You know, he "discovered" America.
Amerigo Vespucci (1454-1512)	He mapped the Atlantic coast of S. America and convinced many that these lands were not India. Also convinced many that he reached America first. Hence the name.
Vasco da Gama (c.1469-1524)	He sailed to India around the Cape of Good Hope, Africa.
Vasco Balboa (1475-1519)	He was the first European to "sight" the Pacific Ocean.
Ferdinand Magellan (1480-1521)	He was the first to circumnavigate the globe.
Hernán Cortes (1485-1547)	He was a conquistador who conquered the Aztecs.
Francisco Pizarro (c.1475-1541)	He was a conquistador who conquered the Incas of Peru.

ANSWERS

1. B 2. C 3. A 4. B

1. **Which of the following people posted the "Ninety-five Theses," a tract arguing against the practices of the Catholic church?**
   - (A) John the Baptist
   - (B) Martin Luther
   - (C) Pope Innocent III
   - (D) Thomas Hobbes

The sixteenth-century Catholic church was notably corrupt and incredibly rich (it still is among the richest of all institutions). Among its questionable methods of fundraising was the **selling of indulgences.** Indulgences were payments to the church that reduced the punishment due a sinner before he reached heaven, and, as you can imagine, they were a real money-maker. The **Reformation** set out to eradicate all of these unholy practices from the Catholic church.

Martin Luther (1483-1546), a German friar (after whom Martin Luther King, Jr. (pp. 110-112) was named), objected to the sale of indulgences, especially those that allowed a person to wipe out all his sins. So, in the traditional manner of settling theological disputes, Luther posted his **"Ninety-five Theses"** (1517), a statement of his disagreements with the Church and an invitation to debate the points. Fifty years earlier, Luther would have been quickly muzzled by Church authorities, but this was the day of the printing press (p. 159). Copies of the theses, translated into German from Latin, were read all over Germany. Luther soon had significant public support. He even challenged the authority of the Pope, reasoning that no mortal man could have the final say on the interpretation of holy scripture. Luther was **excommunicated** (kicked out of the church), but continued to preach. The "Ninety-five Theses" was highly influential, and eventually led to the creation of the **Protestant church**.

The Protestant church was also influenced by the thinking of **John Calvin** (1509-1564). Calvin believed that God had predetermined the ultimate destiny for all people, and that it was important to live a moral life in order to know that you were marked for salvation. Calvin's ideas, formulated in the 1530s after Luther's, became another cornerstone of the Protestant church.

John Calvin, Protestant reformer.

2. **Which of the following initially led to the forming of the Anglican Church?**

   (A) The Norman invasion of England in 1066
   (B) King Henry VIII's desire for another wife
   (C) English disgust with the sale of indulgences
   (D) A philosophical difference of opinion among English theologians

The Reformation continued in England, but was helped along greatly by **King Henry VIII**'s (1491-1547) desire to have a son. Henry VIII's first

wife, Catherine of Aragon (1485-1536), had not given Henry a son, and he wanted the marriage annulled so he could try with someone else. The Pope refused to give an annulment (which is basically a church-sanctioned divorce), so Henry decided to take matters into his own hands. He declared himself head of the English Church, and the **Anglican Church** was born. Henry married **Anne Boleyn** (1507-1536), with whom he had fallen in love. But she was accused of adultery and incest with her half-brother, and beheaded. His third wife produced a son, but she died shortly after the birth of Edward (1537-1553). Though Henry would never have believed it, his *daughter* by Anne Boleyn, **Elizabeth** (1533-1603), would become one of the most powerful English rulers of all time.

Queen Elizabeth I

3. **Who wrote *Praise of Folly*?**

   (A) Leonardo da Vinci
   (B) Erasmus
   (C) William Shakespeare
   (D) John Calvin

Erasmus (c.1466-1536), one of the most respected scholars of his time, wrote *Praise of Folly* in 1509. This book lampooned many of the institutions of the day with a merciless wit. Erasmus was critical of some of the political moves of the time and was not happy with the way the Catholic church was being run. He was in favor of moving the Church with gentle reason rather than through the more overt revolution favored by Martin Luther and John Calvin.

Erasmus writing *Praise of Folly*

A Man for All Seasons, by Robert Bolt, is a play based on the real-life conflict between Henry VIII and Sir Thomas More. The 1966 film version is also good.

A contemporary and friend of Erasmus, **Sir Thomas More** (1478-1535) of England, wrote a book called *Utopia*. In it he described an ideal society where people would share the wealth and all would have a place to eat and sleep. "Utopia" has come to mean any idealized place or society.

More was an early supporter of Henry VIII, who employed him on foreign embassies, made him a member of the privy council, and finally appointed him Lord Chancellor in 1529. More's meteoric rise was, well, cut short when he refused to recognize Henry VIII as head of the Anglican Church. He was beheaded in 1535.

Sir Thomas More

ANSWERS

1. B   2. B   3. B

Independent Nation States

1. **Which of the following English leaders was a Tudor?**

   (A) Queen Elizabeth I
   (B) Oliver Cromwell
   (C) King Charles I
   (D) Mary, Queen of Scots

Since 1066, six families have occupied the throne of England; the Tudors were the fourth. The Tudor family's reign in England was characterized by peace and prosperity. Henry VIII was a Tudor, as was his daughter **Elizabeth I.** Elizabeth ruled from 1558 to 1603, and she ruled well. The **Elizabethan Age** is known as an especially stable period in which England explored the New World and grew in strength economically. The arts flourished as well. Famous writers William Shakespeare (1564-1616) (pp. 395-396) and **Ben Jonson** (1572-1637) both wrote during this time.

Queen Elizabeth I

BLOODY MARY

Born Mary Tudor, "Bloody Mary" ruled England from 1553-1558. A devout Catholic, she was called "Bloody Mary" because there were 300 Protestants executed during her reign (not because she preferred tomato juice with her vodka).

During Elizabeth's reign, many challenges were made to her control of the throne. One was organized by **Mary, Queen of Scots** (1542-1587), a Catholic (Elizabeth was member of the Church of England) from the **Stuart family** who tried to foster several religious rebellions. Although Elizabeth initially resisted suggestions that she execute Mary, she eventually gave in to ensure stability. A bigger threat to her reign would occur when the Spanish Armada, famed for its superiority on the sea, attacked England. Surprisingly, the Armada was defeated in the English channel, and England remained independent.

Elizabeth, known as the "Virgin Queen," never married, and the Tudor family died out after her death. Although courted at times by many potential suitors, Elizabeth remained single and managed to use this to her political advantage by letting foreign suitors think that they could resolve certain issues through marriage.

After the peace under the Tudor family, the **Stuart family**'s reign was characterized by political and religious conflicts. The most serious of these occurred when **Oliver Cromwell** (1599-1658), a Puritan, led a Parliamentary revolt and succeeded in deposing King Charles I (1600-1649). (This was shocking. A king was supposed to have a **divine right** to rule.) The Puritans (pp. 36-37) were not happy with the Church of England because its doctrines were too close to Catholic doctrines. The Puritans were Protestants who followed Calvinist (p. 164) teachings.

All this instability eventually led to the **Glorious Revolution**, which restored the monarchy of England in such a way that it shared power with Parliament. The king would not have absolute power, but would rule in tandem with Parliament. This political structure, with the king acting as the executive power and the Parliament acting as the legislative power, was highly influential to eighteenth-century political theorists. It is quite similar to the present form of government in the United States (p. 45), which was developed near the end of the eighteenth century.

Oliver Cromwell: Puritan Parliamentarian

2. Who wrote the words "Cogito, ergo sum" ("I think, therefore I am")?

(A) Cicero
(B) Plato
(C) René Descartes
(D) Friedrich Nietzsche

The Three Musketeers, Alexander Dumas père. Swashbuckling at its best. These expert swordsmen are "all for one, one for all" in defense of their king. Many movies have been based on this book. A popular cologne for men is even named after one of the musketeers.

René Descartes (1596-1650) (p. 357) is credited with developing much of modern Western philosophy. If you want to get a sense of how Descartes thought, read his *Meditations*, in which he systematically tears apart the fabric of reality. How can we know what we are seeing is real? How can we know we are not dreaming? Imagine some evil genius is trying to deceive us. Your sense perceptions—what you think you see, hear, and feel—might be false. Descartes successfully showed that even though the nature of our existence is uncertain, we do, in fact, exist because we are thinking about whether or not we exist. If there weren't some "one" to think, thinking couldn't happen. Descartes put it this way: "**I think, therefore I am**" ("**Cogito, ergo sum**" in Latin, if you want to impress someone).

3. The French Huguenots of the sixteenth and seventeenth centuries were

(A) Catholic
(B) Protestant

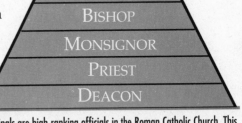

Cardinals are high-ranking officials in the Roman Catholic Church. This pyramid shows the whole ranking system.

Cardinal Richelieu

In France, the **Bourbon dynasty** gave the country a series of able and powerful monarchs. Although the first Bourbon king, Henry IV (1553-1610) was a Huguenot (a French Protestant), he converted to Catholicism upon taking the throne and managed to quell religious tensions. With the help of **Cardinal Richelieu** (1585-1642), a Catholic, he was able to avoid the religious tension that had troubled France in the past and to extend the power of the monarchy. Richelieu was

Louis XIV showing some leg

willing to put the interests of the throne above his religious leanings and even helped the German Protestants in their attack on the Catholic Hapsburgs of Germany. Richelieu helped shore up the French monarchy before the reign of **Louis XIV** (1638-1715), a strong ruler who further weakened any opposition from nobles.

After the destruction wrought by the Thirty Years' War, France became the dominant power on the continent and began to wield that power with a vengeance. Through wars, intrigues, and marriage, Louis XIV managed to extend French rule (p. 174) in Europe and abroad.

4. Where did most of the battles of the Thirty Years' War occur?

(A)   France
(B)   Germany
(C)   Great Britain
(D)   Russia

In Germany, there was a weak centralized government and a group of small, practically independent states that were held loosely together by alliances. The **Hapsburg** family presided over the so-called Holy Roman Empire, but most of the German states were independent, and they all vied for power. When Martin Luther nailed his Ninety-five Theses (p. 164) to a church door in a statement of rebellion against Catholic authority, it gave the German princes who did not like the rule of the Hapsburg family a chance to revolt. They realized the political advantages of becoming Protestant and united to attack the Catholic Hapsburgs.

All of these religious conflicts and power struggles eventually led to the **Thirty Years' War.** Although it started as a war between German Catholics (The Hapsburgs) and German Protestants, the Thirty Years' War eventually came to involve almost all of the countries in Europe. The war was mostly fought in Germany, leaving many parts of the country depopulated and devastated when it ended in 1648.

5. Ivan the Terrible ruled which of the following countries?

(A)   Germany
(B)   Russia
(C)   China
(D)   Spain

In Russia during the sixteenth century, **Ivan the Terrible** (1530-1584, ruled 1547-1584) became the first ruler to use the title "Tsar." The first few years of Ivan's rule were good ones. He extended Russia's borders and began trade with France, England, and the Low Countries (p. 229). But after the death of his wife, Anastasia Romanov, Ivan became a despot. He was convinced that his advisers had been involved in a plot to kill his wife and he threatened to abdicate. The people of Moscow, who had enjoyed his rule for thirteen years, begged him to come back. He said he would if the people consented to a few demands that would strengthen his power. When he returned, he and his henchmen began to kill off the nobility in order to strengthen his control. Estimates vary on the number killed—it's somewhere between 400 and 10,000. But it wasn't just his temper that made Ivan "terrible"—he also managed to leave Russia in a "terrible" state. His clumsy autocratic rule ended with Russia very close to anarchy and economically far behind the other nations of Europe.

6. **Catherine the Great was a ruler of**

   (A) France
   (B) England
   (C) Denmark
   (D) Russia

Ivan the Terrible

Eventually, Russia found good leaders in **Peter the Great** (1672-1725) and **Catherine the Great** (1729-1796), who succeeded in bringing Russia closer to the modern age exemplified in the rest of Europe. By ruling skillfully and borrowing ideas from the West, Peter and Catherine greatly extended the power of the Russian state.

7. **Which of the following theorists believed that man was born with certain inalienable rights?**

   (A) Thomas Malthus
   (B) John Locke
   (C) Louis XIV
   (D) Thomas Hobbes

The period from 1600 to 1770 is usually called the **Enlightenment**, or the **Age of Reason**, because of the work of several French and British philosophers. **John Locke** (1632-1704) was a British theorist who had a great effect on England and France. He believed that mankind was good and that men deserved to have certain inalienable rights. Other theorists

WESTERN PHILOSOPHY IN THE SEVENTEENTH AND EIGHTEENTH CENTURIES

Philospher	Philosophy
Thomas Hobbes (1588-1679)	Best known for **Leviathan**, written in 1651, Thomas Hobbes was the first thinker since Aristotle to attempt a comprehensive theory of nature.
René Descartes (1596-1650)	French philosopher and mathematician René Descartes wrote, "If I am thinking, is it possible for me to doubt that I exist?"
John Locke (1632-1704)	English philosopher John Locke, most noted for **Essay Concerning Human Understanding**, wrote "We can have knowledge no further than we have ideas."
François-Marie Arouet (Voltaire) (1694-1778)	Voltaire believed in deism and devotion to tolerance, justice, and humanity. He wrote **Lettres Philosophiques Sur Les Anglais (Philosophical Letters on the English)** in 1733.
David Hume (1711-1776)	Scottish philosopher David Hume's law reads as follows: "In moral philosophy this law states that it is never possible to deduce evaluative conclusions from factual premises."
Jean-Jacques Rousseau (1712-1778)	French social philosopher Jean-Jacques Rousseau wrote **Du Contrat Social (Social Contract)** in 1762, emphasizing the rights of the people over the rights of the government.
Immanuel Kant (1724-1804)	Immanuel Kant, known for his famous work **Foundations of the Metaphysic of Morals**, wrote, "Act only on the maximum, whereby thou canst at the same time will that it should become a universal law."

included **Voltaire** (1694-1778), who believed in the idea of toleration, **Thomas Hobbes** (1588-1679), who believed that man was selfish (and his life "nasty, brutish, and short") and needed to be controlled by a wise, but absolute monarch, and **Jean-Jacques Rousseau** (1712-1778), who argued that decisions in a society should be made according to "the common will" of the people.

8. **Frederick the Great ruled which of the following countries?**

   (A) Prussia
   (B) Russia
   (C) England
   (D) France

Of the small German states that formed after the end of the Thirty Years' War, Prussia and Austria under the Hapsburgs were among the most powerful. The Prussian state became the strongest through the actions of **Frederick the Great** (1712-1786), known as an **enlightened despot,** who succeeded in ruling his lands with great efficiency and justice. He established religious tolerance and made genuine efforts to improve the lives of the serfs. Prussia eventually succeeded in uniting Germany, and the upper-class Prussians, known as **Junkers**, continued to dominate German politics into the twentieth century.

ANSWERS

1. A 2. C 3. B 4. B 5. B
6. D 7. B 8. A

The French Revolution and Napoleon
1780-1815

1. **Which of the following people would belong to the Third Estate?**

   (A) A priest
   (B) A noble
   (C) A merchant
   (D) A king

In contrast to the straightforward American Revolution (pp. 42-48), where colonists rebelled against foreign control of their country, the **French Revolution** was a complicated affair. It was radical and extremely violent. Many people lost their heads (both literally and figuratively) as different revolutionaries tried different methods to reform the French government. Because of its violence, it changed the entire cultural and political structure of the country.

Before the revolution, the French government was led by a monarch and a governing body that was supposed to represent the people in a manner similar to the English Parliament (p. 156). **The governing body was called the** *Estates-General*, **and was composed of three estates or classes. The First Estate was the clergy, the Second Estate the nobility, and the Third Estate everybody else—the middle-class merchants and the peasants.**

Even though the Third Estate represented about eighty percent of the people, its vote only counted for one-third of the Estates-General. Plus, the First and Second Estates often voted as a block, which further limited the power of the Third Estate. The majority of France, therefore, had little political power. This was not a new thing, of course. Throughout the Middle Ages (pp. 151-158), the peasants had no political power, and only with the rise of the middle class did non-nobility manage to have any money.

Money was among the root causes of the French Revolution. The First and Second Estates were exempt from taxes, so all the money needed by the then-impoverished French government had to be raised by taxing the middle class. Good old Louis XIV (p. 170), who had greatly expanded the French government by waging wars all over the place, had thereby depleted the French treasury. Louis XIV also had a taste for high living. His palace of **Versailles**, which was quite extravagant, is still considered among the greatest architectural achievements in the world.

2. **What was the name of the wife of Louis XVI?**
   (A) Marie Antoinette
   (B) Joan of Arc
   (C) Marie Curie
   (D) Catherine the Great

Louis XIV's great-great-grandson, **Louis XVI** (1754-1793), happened to have bad luck and an unfortunate lack of diplomatic skill at a time when a strong leader was needed to avoid the French Revolution. A man who loved sensual pleasures—especially eating—Louis XVI let the powerful French monarchy fall apart. Louis XVI was married to **Marie Antoinette** (1755-1793). An Austrian who was extravagant, out of touch, and stuck up, Marie was not a favorite among the French people. When informed that the people had not enough bread to eat, Marie is alleged to have responded "**Let them eat cake**." Bad move.

In order to avoid a revolt, Louis XVI allowed the Estates-General to meet and even allowed the voting system to be made more equitable, but somehow the Second Estate still avoided taxation. This infuriated the

Third Estate, which, led by lawyers and powerful businessmen, declared itself the **National Assembly**. At the same time, the peasants revolted and stormed the **Bastille**, a prison which allegedly held political prisoners. Even though only a few political prisoners were released, the storming of the Bastille became a symbol of the French Revolution. Even to this day, **Bastille Day,** July 14, is celebrated in France in much the same way as we celebrate the Fourth of July.

Scaramouche, by Rafael Sabatini. The story of a reluctant French revolutionary.

A Tale of Two Cities, by Charles Dickens. The story of a nobleman's plight in England, and revolutionary France.

3. **Which of the following was a slogan during the French Revolution?**

(A) Live Free or Die
(B) Liberty, Equality, Fraternity
(C) We have nothing to fear but fear itself
(D) Give your hungry cake, your poor bread

Through the storming of the Bastille, the advent of the National Assembly, and the acceptance of the ideas of the Enlightenment (pp. 171-172), a new French government was formed. Using the catchy slogan **"Liberty, Equality, Fraternity,"** it equalized the tax burden and confiscated the land of the Church. But there was dissension within the Third Estate, and there was pressure from foreign governments who were not happy about having a nation with representative government only a short distance away from their autocratic monarchies.

Eventually the revolution got more and more bloody as a few hard-core revolutionaries tried to "save" the revolution from itself by whatever means necessary. The leaders during this time, **Maximilien François Marie Isadore de Robespierre** (1758-1794) and the **Jacobins**, were strict believers in the ideas of equality and in forming a utopia (pp. 195-196). Anyone who didn't believe in these ideals was killed in the **Reign of Terror**, during which both Louis XVI and Marie Antoinette were executed. In fact, anyone with views that differed from those of Robespierre was executed. The blood of numerous revolutionaries, members of the nobility, and royalists was spilled on the ground by the **guillotine**, (a device that is used to cut off heads).

Just call him Robespierre

4. **Which one of the following battlefields was where Napoleon's army was eventually defeated?**

(A) Louisiana
(B) Waterloo
(C) Austerlitz
(D) Wagram

The Scarlet Pimpernel, by the Baroness d'Orczy. A romantic story of a British nobleman who disguises himself as "The Scarlet Pimpernel" and smuggles endangered French nobles out of France.

War and Peace, by Count Lev Nikolayevich Tolstoy. A great book, honest.

After the French Revolution and the Reign of Terror, France was ruled by the **Directory,** a group of five men who attempted to restore a measure of calm to France. The next ruler of France was **Napoleon Bonaparte** (1769-1821), who overthrew the Directory and was reaffirmed by a popular vote. Napoleon at first seemed to be an enlightened ruler, initiating many reforms in agriculture, infrastructure, and education. He even normalized relations with the Church. But Napoleon is best known for his conquests in Europe. He and his troops conquered Austria, Prussia, Spain, and Portugal, and Napoleon crowned himself emperor. (He actually took the crown from the Pope, who traditionally crowned emperors, and put it on himself.)

For a short time, while he was in control of most of Europe, Napoleon *could* think of himself as another Charlemagne (pp. 152-153). But Napoleon lacked the resources necessary to control such a large amount of land. He set up ineffective

Napoleon Bonaparte

leaders (his relatives) in the newly acquired states, and nationalistic uprisings upset his rule. Napoleon then made the stupid decision to invade Russia in winter (as later did Hitler (p. 200)). Napoleon's army did fairly well for a while, but was eventually defeated by the harsh weather and the enormous size of Russia. Only 40,000 of the 450,000 soldiers who invaded Russia made it home. The depleted French armies were soon defeated, and Paris was invaded. Napoleon was forced to abdicate, and was exiled to the island of **Elba**. However, he soon returned and organized an army to attack the English, Dutch, and Prussian forces. He did well for a couple of months, but was resoundingly defeated by the British under the Duke of Wellington at **Waterloo**. Then he was forced to remain in exile in the island of **Saint Helena**. Even today, the name "Waterloo" is sometimes attached to a crushing defeat.

Les Misérables, by Victor Hugo. A man is hunted for twenty years for stealing a loaf of bread. Also a popular Broadway musical.

5. **What was the name of the agreement formed after the defeat of Napoleon I in Europe?**

   (A) The Peace of Paris
   (B) The Congress of Vienna
   (C) The Napoleon Agreement
   (D) The Treaty of Versailles

After defeating Napoleon, the allies all got together at the **Congress of Vienna (1815)** and agreed to establish a Europe in which there was a balance of power. The agreement succeeded in creating a peace that lasted almost forty years—a long time in historically war-torn Europe. France was given the land that it had held before Napoleon took power and was not punished. The Congress of Vienna returned Europe to its state before the French Revolution, restoring the Bourbon dynasty, which was effective in ensuring a lasting peace.

ANSWERS
....

1. C   2. A   3. B   4. B   5. B

The Nineteenth Century

1. Which of the following was responsible for the migration of farm laborers to the cities in nineteenth-century England?

   (A) The end of slavery
   (B) Military unrest in rural areas
   (C) The Industrial Revolution
   (D) The Peace of Paris

The nineteenth century in England brought with it the Industrial Revolution (pp. 344-345). Through better understanding of science and technology, England was able to **mass produce** clothing, pottery, and other staples. In so doing, England increased its wealth and power immensely. The invention of the **steam engine** (p. 344) (actually invented in the eighteenth century but in widespread use by the nineteenth century) increased the ability of people to produce and distribute goods efficiently. Through division of labor, factories could also produce more goods with fewer people.

All this productivity created jobs that drew people from the country into the city. Workers were treated poorly, with eighteen-hour shifts and low wages the norm. But the Industrial Revolution also succeeded in creating the **middle class,** which became important in the struggles of Great Britain. Because of the increased power of the middle class, Great Britain was forced to change the voting laws in 1832, abolish slavery in 1833 (a good deal before the U.S. did), and grant the right to vote to all men in the 1880s.

Oliver Twist by Charles Dickens

The Industrial Revolution also displaced the traditional craftsmen who made their goods by hand from start to finish. These people were not happy with the newfangled factories; one famous group, the **Luddites,** even tried to sabotage the factories. But all this complaining was to no avail. The Industrial Revolution was like a locomotive that would pull Britain and the rest of the world into the technological age.

2. **Which of the following theorists developed the theory of laissez-faire?**

   (A) Karl Marx
   (B) Adam Smith
   (C) Thomas Hobbes
   (D) John Locke

During the nineteenth century, several different "isms" were forwarded by progressive politicians. **Nationalism** was the belief in self-determination for people who shared a similar culture. The kingdoms emerging from the Middle Ages (pp. 151-158) were often made up of several different nationalities, and each of these peoples wanted to have their own distinct country. This desire continues to cause wars in Europe. The states that formed Yugoslavia (pp. 208, 263) split apart a few years ago for religious and ethnic reasons.

The other major beliefs practiced in the nineteenth century are encapsulated under the title of liberalism (p. 181), which was based on the ideas of the Enlightenment. Among the ideas of liberalism was the idea of **capitalism,** which was seen as a noble endeavor. A true believer in capitalism, **Adam Smith** (1723-1790), who wrote *The Wealth of Nations,* argued that government should not interfere with the economy of a nation. He felt that if everyone worked for his own good, a nation's economy would be balanced. This theory, called *laissez-faire,* has become the rallying cry of capitalists everywhere who want to get rid of regulations so that businesses can fend for themselves.

3. Which of the following people wrote *The Communist Manifesto*?

(A) Joseph Stalin and Vladimir Lenin
(B) Karl Marx and Friedrich Engels
(C) Leo Tolstoy
(D) Horace Mann and W. E. B. Du Bois

Adam Smith's *Wealth of Nations* was widely influential, as was *The Communist Manifesto* by **Karl Marx** (1818-1883) and **Friedrich Engels** (1820-1895), which was opposed to unfettered capitalism. Marx believed that history could be looked at as a series of class struggles between the owners of **capital**, called the **bourgeoisie,** and the **working class**, or **proletariat.** He argued that a worker did not receive just compensation for his labor and that workers should revolt. *The Communist Manifesto* is actually reasonably easy to read and has wonderful lines like "Let the governing classes tremble before the communistic revolution. The workers have nothing to lose but their chains. They have the whole world to gain. Workers of the world, unite!"

Marx, by the way, was not Russian. He was German, and he felt that a communist revolution was bound to occur in an industrial state like Germany. (He was wrong; both Russia and China were agricultural states when they turned communist.)

WORKERS OF THE WORLD, UNITE!

A quick look around will show you that the publication of "The Communist Manifesto" was one of the most important moments in the history of politics. Labor unions, minimum wages, worker safety regulations, and eight-hour days are all results of the work of Socialists, Communists, and Progressives over the last century and a half. In the Manifesto, Karl Marx and Friedrich Engels set out the reasoning behind the need for revolution and the steps to be taken in the industrialized nations where revolution (they believed) would occur.

1. *Abolition of property in land and application of all rents of land to public purposes.*
2. *A heavy progressive or graduated income tax.*
3. *Abolition of all right of inheritance.*
4. *Confiscation of the property of all emigrants and rebels.*
5. *Centralization of credit in the hands of the State, by means of a national bank with State capital and an exclusive monopoly.*
6. *Centralization of the means of communication and transport in the hands of the State.*
7. *Extension of factories and instruments of production owned by the State; the bringing into cultivation of waste-lands, and the improvement of the soil generally in accordance with a common plan.*
8. *Equal liability of all to labor. Establishment of industrial armies, especially for agriculture.*
9. *Combination of agriculture with manufacturing industries; gradual abolition of the distinction between town and country, by a more equable distribution of the population over the country.*
10. *Free education for all children in public schools. Abolition of children's factory labor in its present form. Combination of education with industrial production, etc., etc.*

Friedrich Engels and Karl Marx

IMPORTANT 'ISMS

LATE 18TH TO EARLY 19TH CENTURY

	Political Theorist	Theory
Liberalism	Adam Smith	*Laissez-faire*
	Thomas Malthus (1766-1834)	Imminent overpopulation of the world can only be checked by famine and letting the poorer classes starve.
	Herbert Spencer (1820-1903)	Social Darwinism, "the survival of the fittest"
New Liberalism	John Stuart Mill (1806-1873)	Freedom of speech and thought: Clashing opinions yields the best solutions. Wanted to extend the vote to the poor and to women.

MID TO LATE 19TH CENTURY

Socialism	Claude Saint-Simon (1760-1825)	Collective ownership of property, sharing of national wealth and resources. Theory supported by working classes.
Marxism	Karl Marx, Friedrich Engels	Class struggle, the foundation for communism
Anarchism	Pierre-Joseph Proudhon (1809-1865)	The centralized state should be abolished so that all men can be free. These theories led to many assassinations.
Feminism	Elizabeth Cady Stanton (1815-1902) Susan B. Anthony (1820-1906)	Women should be allowed to vote.

 Reds (1981), starring Jack Nicholson, Warren Beatty, and Diane Keaton. The Russians were not the only ones attracted to Communism. Many Western intellectuals and artists (like those portrayed in this movie) were willing to join the Revolution.

Crime and Punishment, by Fyodor Dostoyevsky. The main character in this book decides to see what it feels like to be an Übermensch, and kills someone. The story shows what happens next.

4. **Which philosopher was responsible for the idea of the Übermensch, a superior human being who is not held in check by the boundaries of religion?**

(A) Plato
(B) Friedrich Nietzsche
(C) Thomas Aquinas
(D) Francis Bacon

FREUD AT A GLANCE

Sigmund Freud

Id—Known as the pleasure principle, the id deals with instinctive urges such as eating, drinking, and gaining sexual pleasure.

Superego—Deals with morality as it is learned from one's parents. It represents rules set forth by the parents of an individual and by the society around that individual. At first an act is suppressed through the fear of being caught. Later on in life, an act may be suppressed even when no real punishment exists.

Ego—The ego is called the "reality principle" or the "voice of reason." Balances the superego and the id. The ego distinguishes between desire and reality. It works to satisfy the id, but accomplishes it in a realistic, as opposed to fantastic, way.

Oedipus Complex—(pp. 388-389) A phenomenon, according to Freud, which occurs in young boys, in which they wish to, or believe that they do, partake in sexual acts with their mother. This urge drives the child to reject his father.

Electra Complex—(pp. 390-391) The female version of the Oedipus complex in which a female child has a wish for incest with her father, and therefore rejects her mother out of jealousy.

Dreams—Freud felt that dreams could help a psychoanalyst discover the nature of a patient's subconscious problems, and that they could use the interpretation to deprive the patient of the power to psychosomatically cause his or her own problem.

Friedrich Nietzsche (1844-1900) was a widely influential German philosopher who believed that "God is dead" and that a person should "live dangerously" and become an Übermensch, a person who rises above the masses and uses his passion to become more human. Nietzsche's ideas were distorted by the Nazis (pp. 195-202) as a justification for their acts against humanity.

5. **Which of the following people is primarily associated with the development of psychoanalysis?**

(A) Francis Bacon
(B) Sigmund Freud
(C) Thomas Mann
(D) Voltaire

The most influential person in the development of psychology is **Sigmund Freud (1856-1939)**. Freud determined that many of our actions are due to our unconscious, that psychological problems could be traced to repressed sexual desires from childhood, and that significant improvement in mental health could be made through **psychoanalysis**. Freud based much of his work on studies of people with mental illness and generalized from what he found. He believed that children had strong unconscious sexual desire for their parents, that a boy desires his mother (an Oedipus complex (pp. 388-389)), and that a girl desires her father (an Electra complex (pp. 390-391)). Freud believed that most of a person's later psychological problems could be derived from these early problems. Now increasingly disputed, Freud's beliefs were widely accepted by the psychological community for years, and his ideas have had a huge impact on popular culture. The movie *Psycho* (pp. 420-421), for one, takes as its theme an extreme Oedipus complex.

Rope, directed by Alfred Hitchcock and starring James Stewart. Based on the sensational Leopold & Leob case in which two young men committed murder soley in order to demonstrate superiority to conventional mortality.

6. **Which of the following people was predominantly responsible for the unification of Germany in the 1870s?**
   - (A) Wolfgang Amadeus Mozart
   - (B) Kaiser Wilhelm
   - (C) Otto von Bismarck
   - (D) Friedrich Hegel

The nations that comprised Germany and the Austrian Empire had not been united since Charlemagne in the Middle Ages. In the nineteenth century, a strong nationalistic spirit arose in Germany and throughout Europe. Also, Germans inspired by the French Revolution had attempted similar reforms in Germany, but were stopped by the conservative Hapsburg leader of Austria, **Prince von Metternich (1773-1859)**.

German unification was achieved under **Otto von Bismarck (1815-1898)**, a tough, militaristic Prussian with a strong desire to remove the Hapsburg Austrian influence from German affairs. Through a series of wars, Bismarck—known as the **Iron Chancellor**—succeeded in unifying Germany. Bismarck supported King Wilhelm I of Prussia as the new German Emperor and also saw to it that a governmental body called the **Reichstag** was created. (The Reichstag becomes important in Hitler's (pp. 195-202) reign.)

Prince von Metternich

Germany quickly industrialized after unification, but it did not use the *laissez-faire* approach favored in Great Britain and the United States. Germany's government managed the industrialization of the country and helped create large-scale markets throughout the state.

7. **Who was responsible for the unification of Italy in the nineteenth century?**

   (A) Camillo Cavour
   (B) Leonardo da Vinci
   (C) Pope Innocent III
   (D) Federico Fellini

Italy, like Germany, had been a collection of small states for centuries. During the nineteenth century, Italy had been under the influence of France and Austria. Through the predominantly diplomatic efforts of Count **Camillo Cavour** (1810-1861), Italy finally managed to achieve its Risorgimento—national unity—in the 1870s.

8. **Who lost the Crimean War?**

   (A) Austria
   (B) France
   (C) Russia
   (D) Britain

The Crimean Chronology:
1853—The Balkans are invaded by the Russians. The Turkish Fleet is sunk.
1854—The allied forces invade Crimea declaring war on Russia.
1855—Sardinia declares war on Russia.
1856—Treaty of Paris—War ends.

The **Crimean War** was a result of British and French mistrust of Russia's interest in the Balkans. The war was not particularly well fought even with the development of the telegraph (p. 349) , which allowed people to know almost instantaneously what was going on at the front. The Crimean War also saw the role of women in military activities increase. English nurse **Florence Nightingale** (1820-1910) gained her fame in the Crimean War, reducing the hospital death rate from forty-two percent to two percent. The Russians lost the war. It was considered a symbol of just how far Russia had to go to become as powerful as the other European nations.

9. **Who had the most colonies at the end of the nineteenth century?**
   - (A) England
   - (B) France
   - (C) Germany
   - (D) United States

The end of the nineteenth century saw an increase in imperialism (pp. 39-40). Nearly every European power had expressed some sort of nationalistic spirit, and the act of controlling colonies gave the countries national pride. England held the most colonies (about fifty-five, but an exact number would be hard to pin down), with France a distant second with twenty-nine. Germany, Italy, Russia, and the U.S. got into the game, and together they spread **Western influence** to all parts of the globe. Imperialism bred much resentment against Western nations. Eventually, many of the colonized countries revolted and fought to overcome the Western imperialistic powers.

10. **Who won the Russo-Japanese War?**
   - (A) Russia
   - (B) Japan

The **Russo-Japanese War** (1904-5) was fought over colonization of China. Because of the failure of the Boxer Rebellion (p. 213), China was fair game for colonization, and Russia's attempts to gain influence in China led to war with Japan. The Japanese navy crushed Russia and the defeat fueled social discontent within the beleaguered nation.

ANSWERS

1. C 2. B 3. B 4. B 5. B 6. C 7. A 8. C 9. A 10. B

World War I and Its Aftermath

The Guns of August, by Barbara Tuchman. This Pulitizer Prize-winning novel delves into the root causes of WWI.

YOUR HOLINESS, SIR

Among the more obscure occupations of Popes, Pope John XXIII (of Italy) was an army chaplain in WWI.

1. **Which of the following was NOT a cause of WWI?**
   - (A) The assassination of Archduke Ferdinand
   - (B) Entangling alliances
   - (C) Nationalism
   - (D) The Treaty of Versailles

Due to a system of **entangling alliances** and the buildup of armaments, Europe in the early twentieth century was a powder keg of political tensions ready to explode at any time.

And explode it did. France and Germany had been enemies for a while, mainly because of a dispute over the **Alsace-Lorraine** region that borders the two nations. In 1871, Germany gained control of the region and exacted war reparations from France by winning the **Franco-Prussian War**. Even so, both countries felt that it belonged to them, and in order to bolster their positions, the two countries devised a system of diplomatic alliances with other powerful nations. By the time of WWI, there were two major groups of nations: the **Triple Alliance** of Germany, Austria, and Italy, and the **Triple Entente** of France, England, and Russia. The nations of Europe were also arming themselves at a rapid rate (see the **Warfare Technology Timeline** on pp. 138-40), and all of the larger nations involved had standing armies.

To add to all of this, **Kaiser Wilhelm II,** the ruler of Germany, was doing all kinds of things to antagonize his enemies. He gave speeches expressing strong nationalism and thereby alienated his neighbors. He built up the German navy, thereby threatening British superiority on the seas. Worst of all, he supported Austria's ambitions in the Balkans. So, when **Archduke Ferdinand** (1863-1914) of Austria was assassinated by a Serbian nationalist, a chain of events occurred that led to an enormous European war. Russia, which had pledged to back Serbia in the event of a war with Austria, became involved, and within days the Triple Alliance was at war with the Triple Entente. WWI was incredibly bloody, with new weapons technology and **trench warfare** combining to kill millions of soldiers. Trench warfare was a system of long, dug-out trenches in which soldiers would hide while the fighting raged. Once several lines of trenches were established, the two sides would battle it out attempting to gain control of the land, but usually neither side could move without suffering huge casualties. Because of military innovations like the machine gun and poison gas, it was difficult for an army to break through the trench lines. Millions of men were sent to their deaths in the hope of gaining only a few feet of territory.

Eventually, after much discussion and soul searching, the U.S. entered the war (pp. 83-84) and helped England, France, and Russia achieve victory.

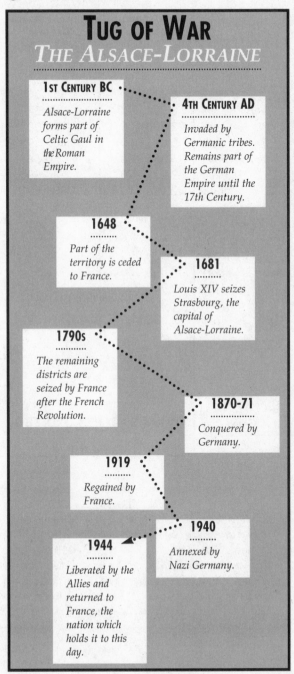

TUG OF WAR
THE ALSACE-LORRAINE

1ST CENTURY BC

Alsace-Lorraine forms part of Celtic Gaul in the Roman Empire.

4TH CENTURY AD

Invaded by Germanic tribes. Remains part of the German Empire until the 17th Century.

1648

Part of the territory is ceded to France.

1681

Louis XIV seizes Strasbourg, the capital of Alsace-Lorraine.

1790s

The remaining districts are seized by France after the French Revolution.

1870-71

Conquered by Germany.

1919

Regained by France.

1940

Annexed by Nazi Germany.

1944

Liberated by the Allies and returned to France, the nation which holds it to this day.

Cost of World War I[1]

	TOTAL FORCE MOBILIZED	MILITARY BATTLE DEATHS[2]	MILITARY WOUNDED	CIVILIAN DEAD[3]	FINANCIAL COST[4]
ALLIES					
France	8,410,000	1,357,800	4,266,000	40,000	49,877
British Empire	8,904,467	908,371	2,090,212[5]	30,633	51,975
Russia	12,000,000	1,700,000[6]	4,950,000	2,000,000	25,600
Italy	5,615,000	462,391	953,886	—[7]	18,143
United States	4,355,000	50,585	205,690	—[7]	32,320
The Rest	2,854,000	500,000	342,000	1,087,000	180,000
Total	42,188,810	4,888,891	12,809,280	3,157,633	193,899
CENTRAL POWERS					
Germany	7,800,000	1,808,546[8]	4,247,143	760,000	58,027
Austria-Hungary	7,800,000	922,500[9]	3,620,000	300,000	23,706
Turkey	2,850,000	325,000[10]	400,000	2,150,000	3,445
Bulgaria	1,200,000[11]	75,844	152,390	275,000	1,015
Total	22,850,000	3,131,889	8,419,533	3,485,000	86,238
NEUTRAL NATIONS					
	—	—	—	—	1,750
Grand Total	**65,038,810**	**8,020,780**	**21,228,813**	**6,642,633**	**281,887**

1. These figures are compiled from various sources and are approximations because official figures are unreliable or absent.

2. Figures represent only those killed in action or from wounds inflicted in battle.

3. Fatalities from epidemics and malnutrition which were not a direct result of the war are included in some of these figures.

4. (S millions) Includes war expenditures, as well as losses in property and commerce.

5. Sixty-five percent of these losses were due to submarine attacks and the remainder to naval and aerial bombardment.

6. 500,000 Polish and Lithuanian citizens are included in these figures.

7. Losses were small and no accurate figures are available.

8. German sources credit the death toll to the Allied blockade of 1919, though a small percent of these deaths were due to Allied aerial bombardment.

9. As much as sixty-five percent of these fatalities were Polish and the rest are attributed to the Allied blockade.

10. Over fifty percent of these deaths were Armenian, with the rest being Syrian and Iraqi.

11. 25,000 or more were non-battle deaths.

SOURCE: R. Ernest Dupuy and Trevor N. Dupuy, The Encyclopedia of Military History, rev. ed. Copyright 1970 by R. Ernest Dupuy and Trevor N. Dupuy. Copyright 1977 by Trevor N. Dupuy. (Reprinted by permission of Harper & Row, Publishers, Inc.)

2. **The Treaty of Versailles, signed at the end of WWI, did all of the following EXCEPT**

   (A)   Make Germany pay war reparations
   (B)   Make Germany give up the Alsace-Lorraine region
   (C)   Establish an international league of nations
   (D)   Allow Germany to keep all of its colonies

As you can tell from the "Cost of World War I" chart, the war was incredibly destructive, with millions dead on both sides. So devastating was the conflict, in fact, that it was referred to as the "**war to end all wars**." Unfortunately, though the war was the fault of all the participants,

The Treaty of Versailles marked the end of WWI

the victors wanted somebody to blame and somebody to pay: Germany. A peace conference was convened in Paris to arrange a settlement. Representatives from the U.S., Italy, France, and England met to decide what the peace treaty would decree. Germany was not invited.

Although President **Woodrow Wilson** (1856-1924) of the U.S. urged moderation in his Fourteen Points plan (p. 85), the representatives of the European nations, and especially **Georges Clemenceau** (1841-1929) of France, wanted to punish Germany severely. The final treaty was neither as harsh as France wanted nor as generous as Wilson wanted, but it still made Germany pick up the tab for the war. Not only did Germany have to pay **war reparations** to the victors, but it had to give up all of its colonies, the disputed Alsace-Lorraine region, all of its armed forces, and a good bit of its pride. The memory of the bitter defeat festered in the collective German consciousness, and later helped Adolf Hitler rise to power.

3. **When did the Union of Soviet Socialist Republics begin its existence?**
   (A) 1890
   (B) 1901
   (C) 1917
   (D) 1945

From the end of the nineteenth century until WWI, Russia experienced growing social problems. Its people wanted a more representative government, but the Russian leaders responded by passing repressive laws and by using military campaigns and imperialism to distract the people from domestic concerns. But when the Russians lost the Russo-Japanese War (p. 185) in 1905, the people lost faith in the government. This discontent led to the **Russian Revolution of 1905,** which began when a peaceful demonstration was ruthlessly suppressed by the Tsar's troops. (This was soon known as **Bloody Sunday**.) The aftermath of Bloody Sunday led to the establishment of a national assembly.

During WWI, Russia faced many problems. Besides the military troubles of dealing with a strong German and Austrian army, the Russians had to deal with problems at home. The Imperial Government was not strong enough to deal with the mounting concerns, and in the **Revolution of 1917,** Tsar Nicholas II (1868-1918) was forced to abdicate. (He was later brutally murdered by the **Bolsheviks**, the socialist party that gained control of the government.) At first, a moderate government was formed.

Vladimir I. Lenin

However, this provisional government was unable to coexist with the more radical **Soviets,** which represented the workers, peasants, and soldiers.

The provisional government wanted to continue to fight with Germany, but the Soviets wanted to get out of the war and set up a communist government. Eventually **Vladimir I. Lenin** (1870-1924), the Marxist leader of the Bolsheviks, mobilized workers and soldiers to overthrow the failing provisional government. Lenin ended the war with Germany and began to nationalize the assets and industries of Russia.

The Russian Revolution of 1905

In the first few years of the new government—called the **Union of Soviet Socialist Republics**—there was a series of civil wars. To overcome the chaos caused by these wars, the Bolsheviks established a strong centralized government. The civil war, combined with the problems that Russia had faced during WWI, encouraged the USSR to set up a strong army. This was done largely through the work of **Leon Trotsky** (1879-1940), a brilliant theorist who influenced people throughout the world.

Leon Trotsky

ANSWERS

1. D   2. D   3. C

The March to World War II

1. **Who became the leader of the Union of Soviet Socialist Republics after the death of V. I. Lenin?**

   (A) Leon Trotsky
   (B) Karl Marx
   (C) Joseph Stalin
   (D) Mikhail Baryshnikov

   After the Russian Revolution of 1917, the USSR became a pariah in Europe. Part of the Marxist philosophy advocated by Lenin stated that for socialism to succeed in Russia, it would have to become the dominant economic policy in the rest of the world. Nothing short of a world-wide revolt of workers would lead to the success of the Soviet system. As you might imagine, this policy alarmed many of the capitalist countries in the rest of the world. The U.S. and other European countries were fearful of communist influences. Over the years, several embarrassing incidents occurred in the Western Nations because of the paranoid persecution of suspected communists (McCarthyism p. 108)

Joseph Stalin

Although Lenin's communism was moderate, allowing for some free enterprise (he allowed farmers to sell some of their grain), his successor, **Joseph Stalin** (1879-1953), was a ruthless leader who assumed total control of the Soviet government. Stalin launched several so-called **Five-Year Plans** that attempted to "collectivize" agriculture and construct large industrial factories. Stalin believed that if he could get the peasants off the farms, he could make them work in the factories. But the peasants resisted, and Stalin ruthlessly forced them to do his bidding. Although his economic plans were relatively successful, he used some unconventional and vicious methods to see them realized. He used terrorist tactics, secret police, and labor camps to punish anyone who might oppose him or his policies. Now known as the **Great Terror,** the period of Stalin's rule is a time in which the USSR killed as many as twenty million of its people in the name of efficient government.

2. **Who was the Italian dictator who led the Fascist state between World War I and World War II?**

    (A) Camillo Cavour
    (B) Benito Mussolini
    (C) Federico Fellini
    (D) Michael Corleone

Corelli's Mandolin by Louis De Bernières. An historical novel recounting the hostile occupation of a Greek island by Italian troops during WWII.

In Italy, after World War I, chaos and poverty prevailed. Unemployed workers, veterans, poor peasants, and a beleaguered middle class all wanted changes. After the elections of 1919 produced an unstable government, a radical socialist named **Benito Mussolini** (1883-1945) invented a new movement called **Fascism.** (The name comes from "the fasces," an ancient Roman symbol of authority.) Mussolini's **Blackshirt** henchmen contributed to the chaos already present in Italy by perpetrating violence. The instability in the country drew Mussolini the support of people who wanted law and order. In 1922, the Fascists marched on Rome, and Mussolini was named prime minister. Four years later, he declared himself the dictator of Italy and outlawed all opposition to him.

Fascism is an ideology that promotes nationalism, glory, and honor under a dictatorship. Surprisingly, in the early years of Mussolini's reign, **"Il Duce"** (his nickname, which means "the leader") was very popular. Mussolini capitalized on the people's desire to bring Italy back to the glory days of Ancient Rome (pp. 145-150). It wasn't until Italy began to fail in its war efforts that people became disgusted with his regime.

3. **The name of the German government supplanted by the Nazi party was**

   (A) The Weimar Republic
   (B) The Heidegger Empire
   (C) Bismarckian Socialism
   (D) Wilhelmian Democracy

Italian dictator, and documented cat hater, Benito Mussolini.

The **Weimar Republic,** the first German experiment with democracy, was not appreciated by the German people. Forced to bow to the conditions of the hated Treaty of Versailles (p. 185), the Weimar government came to be associated with defeat. Also, the economy of Germany was in tatters. With high inflation and the effects of the world-wide depression (pp. 92-93), the Weimar republic couldn't deal with the economic problems of the time. The **Nazi** party, like the Fascists in Italy, inspired thoughts of nationalism. The Nazis also renewed the promise of the long-lost German empire (Europe was united under German control in the days of Charlemagne (pp. 152-153)).

Berlin Stories, by Christopher Isherwood. These stories are about freewheeling Germans and expatriates leading the decadent life in Berlin under the Weimar Republic.

4. **The book written by Adolf Hitler that described his philosophy was called**

   (A) *Mein Kampf*
   (B) *Das Boot*
   (C) *Metamorphosis*
   (D) *Zeitgeist*

The leader of the Nazi party, **Adolf Hitler** (1889-1945)**,** was interested in setting up a vile totalitarian state. Hitler believed that some races were superior to others. He felt that the **Aryan race** (blonde-haired, blue-eyed, fair-skinned, tall people) was better than all other "inferior" races, and he held a special contempt for the Jews, whom he felt were responsible for much of the troubles in Germany. In his utopia (p. 175), all the Jews and other inferior races would be exterminated and a purer German state

Cabaret (1972), starring Liza Minelli, Michael York, and Joel Grey. Based on works by Christopher Isherwood, this Oscar-winning movie shows what life was like when the Nazis were just beginning to exert influence in Germany.

Adolf Hitler

Inside the Third Reich, by Albert Speer. Albert Speer was in Hitler's inner circle and was the chief architect of the Third Reich.

The Producers (1968), starring Gene Wilder and Zero Mostel, directed by Mel Brooks. In this hysterically funny movie, two dishonest Broadway producers try to make money on a play called "Springtime for Hitler."

would result. Most of these beliefs were set forth in the book *Mein Kampf*, which Hitler wrote during a brief stay in prison.

In 1933, Hitler was named Chancellor, just like Bismarck (p. 183), and his Nazi government's main concern was to grab more power. Hitler named his totalitarian government the **Third Reich**, modeling his government on the tradition of Charlemagne (pp. 152-153) and Bismarck. The Nazis killed off any opposition and set up concentration camps where dissidents were incarcerated. Hitler also set up a secret police known as the **Gestapo** that used strong-arm tactics and terrorism to make sure everyone followed the rules.

Hitler was a magnetic speaker, able to whip a crowd into a frenzy. Through the able control of his propaganda minister, Joseph Goebbels (1897-1945), Hitler was able to convince the German people that Nazi Germany was the best place to live in the world.

Under Hitler, the economy was lifted out of its doldrums through the manufacturing of weapons. Jews, Gypsies, homosexuals, and other "outsiders" were plucked out of the German population and put first into ghettos and then into concentration camps, which later became death camps. Before the

A German Jew being arrested by Hitler's Gestapo

Nazi regime toppled at the end of World War II, Hitler had ordered the deaths of more than **six million Jews**.

5. **What was the name of the British Prime Minister who attempted to avoid war with the Nazis by allowing Germany to extend into Czechoslovakia in 1939?**

    (A) Winston Churchill
    (B) Neville Chamberlain
    (C) Sir Thomas More
    (D) Margaret Thatcher

Saying that Germany was overcrowded and that it needed *Lebensraum* (living space), Hitler began to violate the terms of the Treaty of Versailles (p. 185) In 1936, he put German troops in the Rhineland, a territory of Germany that borders France. In 1938, he annexed Austria, and then in 1939, he invaded Czechoslovakia. The other nations of Europe let him get away with this, believing a policy called **appeasement** would help avoid war. The diplomat most associated with this policy is **Prime Minister Neville Chamberlain** (1869-1940) of Great Britain, who helped set up the **Munich Conference** in 1938. In that meeting, Germany was given the right to annex parts of Czechoslovakia. (Hitler claimed that there were a lot of people of German descent in a part of Czechoslovakia called the Sudetenland, and that these people should be allowed to

Germany referred to its plans to exterminate the Jewish population as the **Final Solution** to the Jewish problem. This systematic murder of millions came to be known as the **Holocaust**. The Nazis were ruthlessly efficient killers. You probably haven't spent much time thinking about it, but organizing a mass killing takes a great deal of planning. The Nazis not only had to pick out whom to kill, but they had to do it in such a way that they did not incite a revolt. Through the deception and the complicity of the German population, Hitler was able to kill off the Jews despite several instances of Jewish resistance. The most famous was a revolt in the **Warsaw Ghetto** in Poland, when the Jews managed to hold off better-armed and better-fed Nazi soldiers.

One particularly gruesome tactic used by the Nazis was the **gas chambers** set up in such death camps as **Auschwitz** (other infamous camps include **Dachau** and **Buchenwald**). The Germans would lead the Jews into what looked like showers, but instead of water coming from the plumbing, a poison gas came through. Other inmates were given the job of cleaning up. Inside the chamber, they would find a huge pile of corpses that had died trying to claw their way out the doors.

Grim scene from a Nazi concentration camp

Liberation of concentration camp by U.S. troops

"rejoin" Germany.) Chamberlain declared that the Munich Pact would secure "**peace in our time**," but guess what? He was wrong.

6. **Who is the British Prime minister who led Great Britain through World War II?**

(A) Winston Churchill
(B) Neville Chamberlain
(C) Sir Thomas More
(D) Margaret Thatcher

Prime Minister Neville Chamberlain

Winston Churchill (1874-1965), who would eventually succeed in leading Great Britain to victory in WWII, declared the Munich Pact a "total and unmitigated defeat." And he was right. The British and French appeasement of Hitler served to bolster his leadership and give him reason to believe he could continue to annex the rest of Europe without sanction.

Schindler's List (1993), Steven Spielberg's film adaptation of Thomas Kenealy's novel about the real life German who saved more than 1,000 Jews by letting them work in his factory. Winner of seven Oscars, including Best Picture.

The Diary of Anne Frank, by Anne Frank. Anne Frank was a young Jewish girl hidden from the Nazis. This is her true story, in her own words.
Maus, by Art Spiegelman. A brilliant allegory of Nazism where cats are Nazis and mice are Jews. It sounds strange, but it is a devasting and powerful novel, enhanced by Spielgelman's evocative illustrations.

Prime Minister Winston Churchill

7. **What was the reason behind the Nazi-Soviet Non-Aggression Pact of 1939?**

   (A) To set up an alliance between Germany and the Soviet Union so that they could both attack Great Britain simultaneously
   (B) To allow for Germany and the Soviet Union to invade and split up Poland
   (C) To ensure that anyone attacking Germany would be the enemy of the Soviet Union
   (D) To end the burgeoning Italian threat in Eastern Europe

After taking over Czechoslovakia, Hitler was still looking for elbow room for the German people. So, he signed a secret agreement with Joseph Stalin of the USSR. This **Nazi-Soviet Non-Aggression Pact**, signed in 1939, allowed Germany to invade Poland without fear of Soviet reprisals. It also gave the Soviet Union possession of the Baltic nations. Soon after the agreement, Hitler invaded Poland and quickly conquered a huge area to be added onto Germany. The British and the French had seen enough. They realized that diplomacy was not going to work and declared war on Germany.

8. **What was the name of the Nazi military tactic of using motorized equipment to conquer land very quickly?**

   (A) *Blitzkrieg*
   (B) *Zarathustra*
   (C) *Gestchlozen*
   (D) *Linzertorte*

The German army was extremely successful, conquering large parts of Europe. Using a new form of mechanized warfare in which planes, tanks, and trucks helped move the army quickly through enemy territory, the German army was able quickly to gobble up huge amounts of land. This military tactic, known as *Blitzkrieg,* or "lightning war," would destroy everything in its path with unprecedented speed. Within a year, the **Axis powers**, consisting of Germany and Italy, controlled most of Europe.

At this point, Hitler's only remaining European enemy was Great Britain, so he bombed the hell out of them. But, because of the determined and charismatic leadership of Prime Minister **Winston Churchill,** and the new technology of **radar** that was possessed by the British but not the

EVOLUTION IS WONDERFUL, ISN'T IT?

....

The loss of human life to natural disasters pales beside the loss of human life in war, and the loss of human life in all wars pales beside the loss of human life in World War II. In World War I, the "war to end all wars," nearly ten million people were killed. In World War II, nearly sixty million people died, with nearly twenty million of the dead being Russian. Almost ten percent of the Russian population did not survive WWII. Additionally, between eighteen and twenty-six million prisoners and uninvolved citizens were killed in the Nazi camps. The figures are approximate because in the final days of the war, massive destructions of records took place.

 Countless American movies were made about WWII, both during and after the war. Many of them starred John Wayne ("the Duke"), who was also the star of many westerns. Whether cowboy or soldier, though, Wayne was America's favorite screen hero for decades. Check out *Flying Leathernecks* or *The Sands of Iwo Jima* for some patriotic fervor.

Germans, Great Britain was able to survive the bombings. Radar allowed the British Air Force to know when and where the Germans were attacking and to put up flying resistance. The German pilots couldn't figure out how the Royal Air Force of Great Britain was always lucky enough to be in the right place at the right time.

Then Hitler made a stupid move. He attacked the Soviet Union in the summer in a campaign he thought would be over so quickly he would not need to provide his troops with winter gear. You would think that with a little study of the history and geography of Europe (pp. 227-232) Hitler would have realized that the Soviet Union is a huge country with a devastating winter that can play havoc with attacking troops. By nullifying the Nazi-Soviet Pact, Hitler involved Germany in a **two-front war** (fighting the USSR to the east, and the Allies to the west). Eventually, he was forced to take some of the military pressure off of Great Britain.

9. **Who was Emperor of Japan during World War II?**
    (A) Kurosawa
    (B) Meiji
    (C) Mao Tse-Tung
    (D) Hirohito

Meanwhile, under the leadership of Emperor **Hirohito**, Japan was also feeling like it needed a bit more space. In 1931, Japan invaded Manchuria, now part of China, and struck out against the rest of China in an effort to set up a **"Greater East Asia Co-Prosperity Sphere."** Japan's occupying governments were nasty. Japan is still dealing with Korean claims that Japan set up enormous brothels for the Japanese soldiers, forcing Korean women into prostitution.

Japan became a member of the **Axis** powers and continued its expansions into Asia. Even though the U.S. was not happy with this, it stayed out of the situation because of isolationist policies at home. It wasn't until Japan launched a surprise attack on Pearl Harbor (p. 97) in 1941 that the U.S. got involved in World War II. By forcing the U.S. to enter the war, the Japanese bombing attack ended up ensuring Axis defeat.

10. **When was D-Day?**
    (A) 1939
    (B) 1941
    (C) 1942
    (D) 1944

THE ADVANTAGES OF REMAINING NEUTRAL . . .

During WWII, several countries—Switzerland, Denmark, Norway, Belgium, and the Netherlands—tried to remain neutral, giving no special privileges to Axis or Allied powers. Switzerland managed to remain neutral throughout the war and, for this reason, was a popular place for misguided, damaged or otherwise ill-fated aircraft to land. A total of 250 belligerent airplanes, both American and German, landed or crashed on Swiss soil in the course of the war. The downed airmen, sometimes wounded, were immediately interned by the government and made to live together peacefully, in Switzerland, for the remainder of the war.

After the U.S. entered the war in 1941, the major Allied powers consisted of Great Britain, France, the Soviet Union, and the U.S. The Axis powers included Germany, Italy, and Japan. After the U.S. committed to the war, it took a couple of years to mobilize forces to attack Germany on

D-Day: American soldiers on the fortified beaches of Normandy

the continent of Europe. The Allied forces drove the Axis powers out of North Africa and made ventures into Italy, but the most monumental day in the war was still to come. On June 6, 1944, later termed **D-Day,** the largest and most powerful invasion force in history landed on the shores of **Normandy** and began to re-take Europe. Through deception and an effective counterintelligence organization, the Allied powers were able to convince the Germans that the attack was going to take place somewhere else. The Allies learned that the Germans expected an attack in Calais, so they set up a phantom army that made it appear as if the attack were to take place there.

D-Day was brilliantly conceived. The attack began the night before with paratroopers sent to France to cut off German supply lines. Then the amphibious force set up artificial harbors made out of pontoons and sunken ships to facilitate the landing. Because the Germans expected the attack elsewhere, they were unprepared to deal with such a massive assault. The Allied forces succeeded in landing 150,000 troops in *one day.* The German forces resisted for a month while Allied forces built up to over one million troops within three weeks.

. . . AND MURPHY'S LAW OF REMAINING NEUTRAL

However, remaining neutral during a world war is no guarantee of security. Ironically, in the summer of 1944, a pilotless "Flying Fortress"—the crew having abandoned their crippled aircraft—gradually descended over northern Switzerland. It eventually collided with the tower of a medieval castle, which happened to be the summer residence of professor Max Huber, president of the International Committee of the Red Cross. The plane exploded, spilling flaming gasoline and live ammunition inside the tower, where the professor's library on international peace was located, presumably safe from accidental bombing.

Patton (1970), starring George C. Scott. George Patton was one of the toughest, most controversial generals in U.S. history. The movie focuses on his role in WWII.

IT'S GOOD TO HAVE FRIENDS

Brazil, Australia, Canada, and the governments-in-exile of Poland, Czechoslovakia, and Norway also contributed troops to the Allied effort. In all, there were twenty-six Allied nations.

THE BOMB

A survivor of Hiroshima tells of his experience seeing five teenaged boys running toward him, naked and covered with blood.

"As the boys came near, I saw they were pale, and shaking severely... I have never seen such a horrifying sight as those five shivering boys. Blood was pouring in streams from deep cuts all over their bodies, mingling with their perspiration, and their skin was burned deep red, like the color of cooked lobsters. At first it seemed, strangely, that their burned and lacerated backs and chests were growing green grass! Then I saw that hundreds of blades of sharp grass had been driven deep into their flesh, evidently by the force of the blast."

The invasion of Normandy was the beginning of the end of World War II. The USSR and the Western European forces attacked Germany from two sides, and battled until they reached Berlin. It's thought that when the Allies stormed Berlin, Hitler committed suicide. The European war was over on **V-E Day**, May 8, 1945.

Newly liberated French citizens show their appreciation to a U.S. soldier.

During the last stages of the war, the Allied powers made plans for peace. The most famous of these conferences was the Yalta Conference (p. 100) of 1945, where Franklin Delano Roosevelt (1882-1945), Winston Churchill, and Joseph Stalin discussed plans for future peace. As a result of this conference, the postwar lines of Europe were drawn and the seeds of the Cold War sown.

11. **On which of the following cities was an atomic bomb dropped in World War II?**

    I. Hiroshima
    II. Nagasaki
    III. Tokyo

    (A) I only
    (B) II only
    (C) I and II only
    (D) I, II, and III

Meanwhile, in the Pacific, the U.S. was still engaged in war with Japan. Through a military tactic known as island hopping, the U.S. gradually moved in on the islands of Japan by gaining victories in **Iwo Jima** and **Okinawa**. After seeing the tenacity of the Japanese soldiers, the U.S. realized that a land war victory would claim an enormous number of casualties. Using this rationale, the U.S. decided to use the atomic bomb (p. 292) to force Japan into submission. On August 6, 1945, by order of President Truman, an **atomic bomb** was exploded over **Hiroshima**; a few days later, another bomb was dropped on **Nagasaki**. Japan unconditionally surrendered, and at long last, after forty-five million people had died, World War II was over.

 The Bridge On the River Kwai (1957), starring Alec Guinness, William Holden, and Sessue Hayakawa. In this classic film, British soldiers are held in a Japanese prison camp and forced to build a bridge, which an American spy is sent to destroy. The film won seven Oscars, but ironically, the screenwriters were given no credit because they were blacklisted as Communist sympathizers at the height of the Cold War (pp. 104-108).

A kamikaze attack on a U.S. battleship

12. **What was the name of the war-crimes trials conducted after the end of World War II?**

   (A) The Nazi Trials
   (B) The Nuremberg Trials
   (C) The Normandy Trials
   (D) The Berlin Trials

The Longest Day (1962). This spectacular epic recounts the invasion of Normandy and stars everyone from John Wayne to Sean Connery.

Black Rain (1989). This Japanese film details five years in the life of a family of Hiroshima survivors.

Hiroshima, by John Hersey. Brilliant journalistic account of how survivors coped after the bomb.

After the end of the war, the Allies tried Nazi war criminals in what became known as the **Nuremberg Trials**, held in Nuremberg, Germany. In these trials, twelve Nazis were sentenced to death, including **Hermann Goering** (1893-1946), Hitler's second-in-command. Goering managed to save the executioner the trouble of executing him by committing suicide. One of the defense claims during the trial was that the Nazis were only following Hitler's orders. This claim was not accepted.

In Japan, similar war-crimes trials took place. There, former prime minister **Hideki Tojo,** along with six other military leaders, was sentenced to death.

Nazis stand trial at Nuremberg. Left to right, Front Row: Hermann Goering, Rudolph Hess, Joachim von Ribbentrop, General Wilhelm Keitel. Back Row: Admirals Karl Doenitz and Erich Raeder, Baldur von Schirach, and Fritz Sauckel.

ANSWERS

1. C   2. B   3. A   4. A   5. B   6. A   7. B   8. A   9. D   10. D
11. C   12. B

The Cold War

1. **What was the "Iron Curtain"?**

   (A) Legislation imposed during the 1920s to reduce steel
       exports
   (B) The symbolic boundary separating Eastern Europe from
       Western Europe during the Cold War
   (C) The dramatic ending of *Madame Butterfly*
   (D) A shield devised during the 1980s to protect the United
       States from nuclear missiles

After the war in which the Soviet Union had cooperated with the
Allies and the United States, tensions began to increase between the
Soviet Union and the Western countries. The Soviet Union's brand of
communism (p. 180) required that the entire world must become socialist
for it to succeed. After World War II, both the USSR and the U.S. became
involved in the rebuilding of Europe. Germany was partitioned into
Eastern and Western sectors, and the USSR took neighboring countries

On the Beach (1959),
based on the novel by Nevil
Shute. An all-star cast awaits
the nuclear fallout from an explosion that has
destroyed the rest of the world.

One Day in the Life of Ivan Denisovich (1962), by Alexander Solzhenitsyn (1918-). Semi-autobiographical account of life in a Soviet labor camp. Exiled from the USSR for his anti-Soviet writings, Solzhenitsyn lived in the U.S. for many years.

(Poland, Czechoslovakia, Hungary, Romania, and Bulgaria) into its "sphere of influence." **Winston Churchill**, the former prime minister of England, said in 1946 that "From Stettin in the Baltic to Trieste in the Adriatic an **iron curtain** has descended across the Continent." The expression stuck. The Iron Curtain refers to the political and social barriers the USSR imposed between the nations within its sphere of influence and the rest of the world. People were not allowed to immigrate; eventually, in 1961, this policy reached its symbolic heights with the construction of the Berlin Wall (p. 116), erected to prevent East Germans from seeking asylum in the West.

2. **Which nation was represented by this flag?**

(A) Israel
(B) The USSR
(C) China
(D) Afghanistan

Former Soviet leader, Mikhail Gorbachev

The United States took its own actions to prevent Soviet influence in Western Europe. The **Truman Doctrine,** for instance, set a policy of "**containment,**" with the idea that Soviet influence should remain within the boundaries of the Iron Curtain. The U.S. pledged to "support free peoples who are resisting attempted subjugation by armed minorities or by outside pressures." The U.S. gave economic assistance to the war-torn European nations, a policy known as the **Marshall Plan,** giving Western Europe the economic ability to reestablish free democratic governments. The U.S. also led the military alliance **NATO** (the North Atlantic Treaty Organization). It was directly opposed by its Eastern counterpart, the **Warsaw Pact,** which consisted of eight Eastern European communist countries (see map p. 106).

The Cold War conflict was pretty scary. The stockpiling of nuclear weapons (p. 291-293) on both sides, the Korean War (pp. 106-107), and the Cuban Missile Crisis (p. 116) made people throughout both countries worried that the world would explode in a big mushroom cloud. But tensions eased gradually, and the USSR and the U.S. entered into a period of **détente** during which their relationship was not so sour. Détente lasted for awhile, then the Soviet Union invaded **Afghanistan** in 1979 and the Cold War was back in full swing.

3. **Which of the following leaders of the Soviet Union instituted perestroika?**

(A) Yuri Andropov
(B) Alexander Solzhenitsyn
(C) Mikhail Gorbachev
(D) Nikita Khrushchev

The leader of the Soviet Union who presided over its dissolution was **Mikhail Gorbachev** (1931-), who instituted a policy of *perestroika. Perestroika,* which means "restructuring," was an attempt at economic and political reform. Gorbachev opened up relations with the West and began to open up the political system of the USSR. This eventually led to the break-up of the USSR, the freedom of the satellite countries like Poland, and the end to the Cold War. As of this writing, many of the states that were part of the Soviet Union are independent, including the largest of the states, Russia (geography pp. 262-63). The first leader of the new Russian state was **Boris Yeltsin** (1931-).

4. **Which of the following countries has been independent for more than twenty years?**

(A) Croatia
(B) Kazakhstan
(C) Kyrgyzstan
(D) Hungary

For anyone trying to learn the geography of Europe, the breakup of the Soviet Union poses some interesting problems. In a matter of a few years, the USSR has broken up into several new countries: Russia, Ukraine, Belarus, Kazakhstan, Kyrgyzstan, Tajikistan, Turkmenistan, and

SEE YOU AT THE FUNERAL

Nikita Khruschev (1894-1971) led the Soviet Union through the darkest days of the Cold War, presiding over the Cuban Missile Crisis, the nascent space race, and a host of other altercations involving the two superpowers. No fan of capitalism, Khruschev uttered these now-famous words in 1956:
"About the capitalist states, it doesn't depend on you whether or not we exist. If you don't like us, don't accept our invitations, and don't invite us to come and see you. Whether you like it or not, history is on our side. We will bury you."

The Unbearable Lightness of Being (1984), by Milan Kundera (1929-), later made into a movie starring Daniel Day-Lewis. Like Solzhenitsyn (see previous page), Kundera had to leave his native country, then Communist Czechoslovakia, in order to continue writing.

Uzbekistan; and Armenia, Azerbaijan, Moldova, Georgia, Latvia, Estonia, and Lithuania.

Countries formerly under Soviet influence are also breaking up. As of this writing, Yugoslavia is still in the process of splintering into smaller states through a violent civil war. Now there are five nations vying for the former Yugoslavia's territory: Bosnia and Herzegovina, Croatia, Macedonia, Serbia, and Slovenia. Czechoslovakia split into the Czech Republic and Slovakia. All of this is called "Balkanization." Balkanization is when a nation splits into several different factions, usually along ancient tribal lines.

5. Who is the communist leader of Cuba that came to power after the revolt of 1959?

(A) Fulgencio Batista
(B) Jose Marti
(C) Maximo Gomez
(D) Fidel Castro

Fidel Castro

Many of the Cold War tensions discussed earlier found expression in Latin America. Colonized at almost the same time as the United States, Latin America never reached the prosperity of our country. The U.S. spent a good deal of time and energy making sure Latin America steered clear of communist influence, with limited success.

In the late twentieth century, many regions of Latin America have been relatively unstable, characterized by political revolutions and economic strife. Some countries have adopted communism, most notably **Cuba**. **Fidel Castro** (1926-) ousted dictator Fulgencio Batista in 1959 and installed a communist government. With the dissolution of the Soviet Union, Cuba no longer has the support of an economic superpower, and the nation's people have come under increasingly hard times.

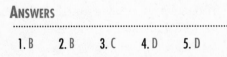

ANSWERS

1. B   2. B   3. C   4. D   5. D

1. In which of the following time periods was much of Africa colonized by European nations?

(A) 1650-1700
(B) 1750-1800
(C) 1820-1850
(D) 1880-1920

Since the Age of Exploration (pp. 161-62), **Africa**'s resources have been exploited and abused by European countries. Its people have been kidnapped and sold into slavery Its natural resources have been taken and used by European countries. Although the slave trade took place from the seventeenth century to the nineteenth century, the African countries were not immediately colonized like the Americas. The geography and the strength of the indigenous African nations made the prospect uneconomical. Although the profits from the slave trade went to the Europeans, the work was mostly controlled by African entrepreneurs who also gained from the sales of African people.

The Gods Must Be Crazy (1981). A very funny movie made in Botswana about a culture clash between people in Southern Africa. It is one of the biggest foreign box-office hits in U.S. history.

Between 1880 and 1914, European nations gained control of Africa and colonized most of the continent. Even though Africa is a mix of different cultures and religions, the colonial powers usually did not respect the divergent cultural roots of the tribes when they established the colonial states. The colonists also tried to convert African "savages" to the ways of Christianity by sending **missionaries.** These people, sometimes lay people and sometimes clerics, would ignore the prevalent culture and try to convince African people to convert to the European way. This kind of colonial dominance is called **cultural imperialism** (imperialism p. 39-40).

2. **Which of the following countries was never a European colony?**

   (A) Zaire
   (B) Ethiopia
   (C) Algeria
   (D) Morocco

Out of Africa (1985), starring Meryl Streep. Based on the life of writer Isak Dinesen, who moved from Denmark to Nairobi.

One of the few African countries to avoid becoming a European colony is **Ethiopia.** It is considered a symbol of African independence, and despite a six-year period during World War II in which it was under the control of fascist Italy (p. 194-95), it has remained an independent nation for centuries. Ethiopia has had a significant Christian population longer than most other countries in the world (its emperor converted in the fourth century).

3. **What is an official language of Kenya?**

   (A) Afrikaans
   (B) Swahili
   (C) Arabic
   (D) Hindi

Juluka, *Scatterlings.* Three Zulu guys make some cool music— both traditional and pop.

Ladysmith Black Mambazo. Anything by this South African group is great. For a good Western-tinged introduction, get Paul Simon's *Graceland.* Ladysmith backs him up.

4. **What is the official language of Nigeria?**

   (A) Swahili
   (B) English
   (C) Nigerian
   (D) Arabic

5. **What is the official language of Egypt?**

    (A) Swahili
    (B) English
    (C) Hebrew
    (D) Arabic

Although many people do not realize it, Africa is an immense and varied continent with many different ethnic groups speaking many different languages. European colonization did not take these ancient tribal divisions into account when drawing the map during colonization, so some countries consist of hundreds of different ethnic groups with hundreds of different languages. Nigeria is an example of one of these countries. Although English is its official language, English is only understood in the largest cities and, at the same time, each ethnic group has its own language.

In Egypt, Arabic is the national language, and in Kenya, both English and Swahili are national languages.

6. **The name of the African country started by freed black slaves is**

    (A) Zaire
    (B) Liberia
    (C) Angola
    (D) South Africa

A Zulu matron in Natal, South Africa

The country of **Liberia** has a fascinating history. In the 1820s, the American Colonization Society was formed to resettle freed blacks in Liberia of South Africa. The Americo-Liberians, despite taking up only a small percentage of the population, ruled the country until 1980 when a **coup d'état** (overthrow of a government) brought about the rule of one of the larger ethnic indigenous groups of Liberia. Since 1980, Liberia has been overrun by civil war and strife.

Former
president of South Africa
F.W. De Klerk . . .

7. Who is the longtime leader of the African National Congress who recently won the Nobel Peace Prize?

(A) Nelson Mandela
(B) Idi Amin
(C) Kareem Abdul Jabbar
(D) Poto Doudongo

South Africa was originally settled by both the British and the Dutch, and the people of the two nations went to war over the gold and diamonds found throughout the country. The Boer War was fought between British and Afrikaner (Dutch) settlers when the Afrikaners tried to wrest control from the British. The British won, but the Afrikaners had a large impact on the political structure of the country. They instituted a policy called apartheid in the 1940s, which stripped blacks of all political powers and even determined where they were allowed to live. Because blacks were the majority in South Africa, white minority rule of the country was not accepted as ethical by much of the rest of the world. Apartheid was condemned by many in the international community, bringing sanctions and other economic penalties to the nation of South Africa in the seventies and eighties.

Arrested as a political prisoner, and kept in jail for 28 years, **Nelson Mandela** (1918-) was one of the original founders of the African National Congress, which became the ruling party in South Africa in 1994. After former President F. W. De Klerk helped get rid of apartheid by establishing universal suffrage, Nelson Mandela became the first official black president of South Africa. Mandela and De Klerk shared the Nobel Peace Prize in 1993 for ending the system of apartheid.

. . . and current president Nelson Mandela

ANSWERS

1. D   2. B   3. B   4. B   5. D   6. B   7. A

1. **What was the cause behind the Opium War between China and Great Britain?**

Until the nineteenth century, China remained fairly isolated from the rest of the world. Despite some exploration in the Middle Ages, China had gradually turned more and more inward through the centuries. In the nineteenth century, China was put under pressure by European nations to trade. The British were dependent on China for tea, but China did not use any British products, so a huge trade imbalance resulted. The British were upset with the negative balance of trade so they "created" a market in China by smuggling opium, made in India, into China. Though the Chinese government was vehemently opposed, the British continued the practice and the conflict led to the **Opium War,** which the British won handily.

In 1900, China again tried to get rid of foreign influence in the **Boxer Rebellion,** which was quashed by a joint effort of British, French, German, Japanese, Russian, and U.S. troops.

Chinese militia chasing Europeans during the Boxer Rebellion.

2. **Who was President of China when the government was overthrown by the communists under Mao Zedong?**

(A) Chiang Kai-shek
(B) Mahatma Gandhi
(C) Zhou En-lai
(D) Marshal Tito

Sun Yat-sen (1866-1925) set up a Nationalist government in 1912. He was succeeded by **Chiang Kai-shek** (1887-1975), who was overthrown in 1949 by **Mao Zedong** (1893-1976). Mao installed a communist government and Chiang Kai-shek fled to Taiwan with two million followers. He set up the non-communist Republic of China, which was recognized by the United States as the official government in China until 1978. President Nixon (pp. 122, 124) began a process of reconciliation with mainland China in 1972, and Communist China was officially recognized in 1978.

Farewell, My Concubine (1993). This absorbing Chinese drama about two male Peking Opera stars spans China's warlord era, the Cultural Revolution, and beyond.

The Last Emperor (1987). Directed by Bernardo Bertolucci, this remarkable film was inspired by the true story of Pu Yi, the last emperor of China.

The leader of Red China, Mao Zedong

3. **Which of the following countries shares a border with Tibet?**

    (A) Kenya
    (B) Pakistan
    (C) Vietnam
    (D) China

4. **The Dalai Lama is the religious and civic leader of which of the following countries?**

    (A) Korea
    (B) Thailand
    (C) Tibet
    (D) Pakistan

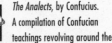

The Analects, by Confucius. A compilation of Confucian teachings revolving around the yin and the yang—the passive and active principles around which Confucianism revolves. These teachings have shaped Chinese society for more than 2000 years.

Most of Tibet, now a province of China, is situated on a plateau 15,000 feet above sea level. Its inaccessibility has allowed Tibet to develop its own distinctive culture and religion. Tibetan Buddhism is a religion that considers the **Dalai Lama** to be its spiritual leader.

In the late 1960s, China began a program to forcibly assimilate the Tibetan people. Monuments and churches were destroyed, books were burned, and Chinese was made the official language of the country. This policy failed, and in the 1980s, the people were once again allowed to practice some aspects of their culture.

5. **In what continent is Cambodia located?**

    (A) Africa
    (B) South America
    (C) Asia
    (D) Europe

The Killing Fields (1984), starring Sam Waterston, Haing S. Ngor, and John Malkovich. A frighteningly realistic movie about war-torn Cambodia, based on a true story.

Cambodia, located in southeast Asia, has been involved in all sorts of wars and revolutions in the last forty years. Most Americans' awareness of our involvement with Cambodia stems from the revelation of secret bombings undertaken during the Vietnam War (pp. 117-118). In 1969, the U.S. bombed Cambodia in an effort to destroy North Vietnamese troops holed up in the country.

In 1975, **Pol Pot** (1925-) and the **Khmer Rouge** took over Cambodia. If there was a hall of evil dictators situated in some dark chamber, Pol Pot would surely rate a bronze bust. With policies as evil as Hitler's, Pol Pot and the Khmer Rouge kicked everybody out of the cities and forced them to work as agricultural workers under the control of Khmer Rouge commanders. More than two million people died from famine, disease, and maltreatment. In 1978, the communist Vietnamese deposed Pol Pot and the Khmer Rouge and set up their own puppet government. When the Vietnamese left, the UN came in and helped diffuse a horrible and dangerous situation. In the largest peace-keeping effort up to the time, the UN succeeded in disarming much of the nation.

But the war and destruction in Cambodia is not over. Besides the millions who have already died, a far more insidious danger rests with the slowly ticking time bomb created by the millions of anti-personnel mines hidden under the soil. Nearly undetectable, these mines are destroying Cambodia's future. Every day, more and more Cambodians (mostly children) are brought to hospitals for care. Designed to maim and not to kill, these bombs are succeeding where Pol Pot left off, creating a nation of amputees, widows, and orphans.

Pol Pot's rule over Cambodia was marked by gross injustice to human rights and mass murder.

6. Who led India to independence in 1947?

(A) Winston Churchill
(B) Mohandas Gandhi
(C) Muhammad Ali Jinnah
(D) Ravi Shankar

Gandhi (1982). Epic film by Sir Richard Attenborough spans the incredible life of Gandhi. It won eight Oscars.

Considered by many to be one of the greatest leaders of the twentieth century, **Mohandas Gandhi** (1869-1948) was successful in liberating India from British rule in 1947. (He is usually referred to as Mahatma Gandhi; Mahatma means "great soul.") India had been conquered by the British in the eighteenth century, but the Indian people were frustrated with British domination. Gandhi championed the concept of **non-violent resistance.** Rather than fighting with weapons, Gandhi and his followers staged peaceful demonstrations and used boycotts and strikes to gain attention.

One example of this tactic was the boycott of machine-made clothing. The British used a mercantile (p. 40) system with India. They imported low-priced natural cotton from India and used it for relatively expensive clothes that were then sold back to the Indian people. Gandhi spun his own yarn and wove his own clothes and encouraged his followers to do the same. This tactic put enormous economic pressure on Britain, because without the demand from India, British factories had a hard time staying in business. It was also nearly impossible to fight. What could the British do—outlaw home-spun clothing? Not really, but they could throw Ghandi in jail, and they did.

When Gandhi was thrown in prison, he refused to eat, garnering sympathy all over the world and embarrassing the British. Gandhi's tactics eventually worked, and India gained independence from Britain in 1947. His one disappointment was that India was split into two countries—**India** and **Pakistan**—because the Muslims and Hindis could not resolve their differences. Gandhi was assassinated in 1948 by a Hindi who thought that his policies favored the Muslims and Pakistan.

Gandhi's methods were incredibly influential. Dr. Martin Luther King, Jr. used many of the same tactics in his campaign for civil rights in the sixties (p. 111)

Mohandas Gandhi advocated passive resistance and employed some of the methods of civil disobedience authored by Henry Thoreau (pp. 401-402)

7. **When was the modern state of Israel first established?**
   (A) 1896
   (B) 1919
   (C) 1948
   (D) 1966

Established after World War II, **Israel** is the world's only Jewish state. The state first declared independence on May 14, 1948, and was attacked one day later by the surrounding **Arab** nations—Egypt, Jordan, Syria, and Lebanon. The tension between Israel and the Arab nations led to a series of wars and general instability in the Middle East. Israeli land gains after some of the wars, especially the Six-Day War in 1966, have resulted in a dispute over the **occupied territories** of the West Bank of the Jordan River and the Gaza Strip—both of which contain mainly Palestinian Arab populations.

Compounding the problems is the strategic importance of the region. Some of the Arab states surrounding Israel have huge reserves of **oil,** and the rest of the world is willing to go to enormous extremes to keep that oil accessible. The oil-producing countries formed a group called **OPEC.** In 1973, OPEC declared a boycott (p. 126) on the U.S., refusing to sell their oil to the U.S. because of our support of Israel. This resulted in the energy crisis (p. 126) of the mid-seventies and was largely responsible for the development of alternative forms of energy.

The Palestinian conflict between the Jewish state of Israel and the Palestinian Arabs has been especially volatile. Defeated and occupied after invading Israel in 1948, the Palestinians recently resisted Israeli domination in an uprising called the *intifada,* which has consisted of stone throwing at Israeli police, boycotts, and terrorism. In 1994, the Palestinians were given control over some of the occupied territories in Israel. It remains to be seen how long this tenuous peace will last.

ANSWERS
....

2. A   3. D   4. C   5. C   6. B   7. C

When older people talk about the failures of the current American educational system, they almost always point to the failure of the younger generation to learn about geography. "When I was young and had to walk three miles to school through the knee-high snow sharing one boot with your great uncle," a grandparent might begin, "we quizzed each other on the capitals of all the states on the way." The old guy will then grill you and discover to his delight that you don't know the capital of North Dakota. Inevitably, he will end the discussion with a sigh and some hackneyed comment like "These kids just ain't what they used to be."

We agree with the old guy that geography is important, but we don't hold that knowing the capital of North Dakota (Fargo) will get you any farther in life (unless, that is, you live in North Dakota). So we have set up this section of *Culturescope* to teach you the important stuff about the lay of the land. Each chapter begins with a blank map and a list of places that we think are important. Give it a try. See how many you can find. The answers are on the page following.

GEOGRAPHY

Each chapter then continues in the same question-and-answer format as the rest of the book. We have discussed aspects of geography that we feel are often referred to and quoted, and we've included brief histories of our planet's most famous topographical treasures.

The United States

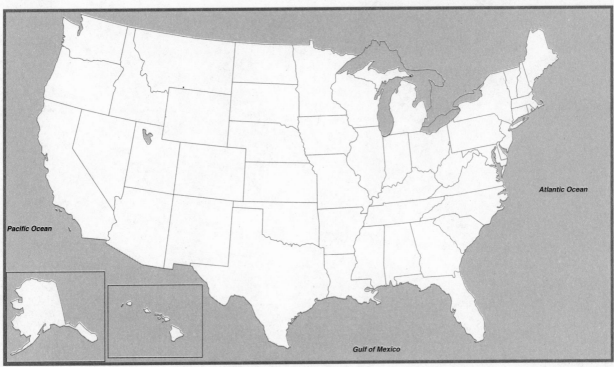

Pacific Ocean

Atlantic Ocean

Gulf of Mexico

Find these states:

New York (NY)
Iowa (IA)
Arizona (AZ)
Nebraska (NE)
Colorado (CO)
Tennessee (TN)
Vermont (VT)
Oklahoma (OK)
Mississippi (MS)
Oregon (OR)
Idaho (ID)
Arkansas (AR)
Indiana (IN)

Find these cities:

Atlanta
Boston
Chicago
Dallas
Detroit
Los Angeles
Miami
New Orleans
New York City
Philadelphia
Phoenix
San Francisco
Washington, D.C.

Find these places:

Plymouth Rock
Salt Lake City
Mt. St. Helens
St. Augustine
The Alamo
The Appalachian Mountains
The Mississippi River
The Grand Canyon
Graceland
Mount Rushmore
Niagara Falls
Disneyworld
Disneyland
Las Vegas
Camp David
The Redwood Forests
The Rocky Mountains
Badlands

GEOGRAPHY

THE UNITED STATES ANSWER MAP

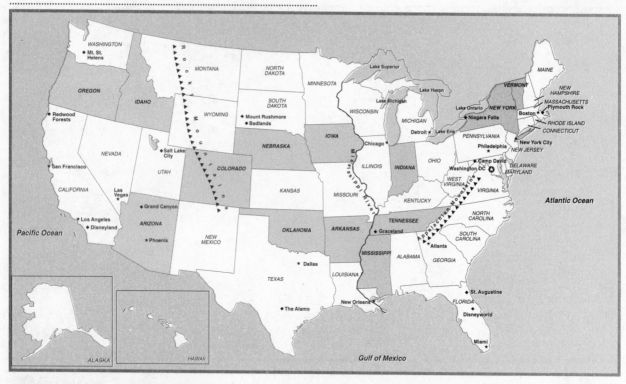

The Empire State Building in midtown Manhattan, c. 1931

1. **Which city's streets served as the model for the game of Monopoly?**

(A) New York City
(B) Atlantic City
(C) Philadelphia
(D) San Francisco

The Parker Brother's Game *Monopoly* takes the names of its streets from those of Atlantic City, New Jersey. Invented in 1933 by Charles Darrow, *Monopoly* is one of the most popular board games ever. Atlantic City has gained in popularity since the introduction of legal gambling in 1978, but the increase in tourism hasn't benefited the city as a whole, as was hoped. Instead, the casino owners have become rich while the rest of the city has slipped ever farther into poverty.

2. **Which of the following places is NOT in New York City?**

   (A) Times Square
   (B) The Bowery
   (C) Broadway
   (D) Independence Hall

Manhattan (1979) starring Woody Allen and Diane Keaton. Beautifully filmed in black and white, this is a sophisticated comedy about New Yorkers.

Taxi Driver (1976) starring Robert De Niro and Jodie Foster. Robert De Niro goes psycho. He's in love with a twelve-year-old.

Probably more than any place on earth, **New York City** is sung about, danced about, talked about, and photographed. It is a city of horrors and romance where over seven million people live. People who don't even live in New York are familiar with many of its landmarks.

Here's a brief rundown:

New York City is made up of five boroughs: Manhattan, Brooklyn, the Bronx, Queens, and Staten Island. When most people think of New York City, they think of **Manhattan**, a narrow island with all the action. Times

Square, an area near the theater district with hundreds of enormous signs advertising this or that, is in Manhattan. Times Square is also known for its New Year's Celebration in which a big apple drops down to mark the beginning of the new year.

Broadway, a street that runs through Times Square, is memorialized in many songs. Often referred to as the "Great White Way" because of its bright marquees, Broadway is where the biggest plays and musicals are performed.

The **Bowery** is an area of New York where those who are down on their luck

Times Square on a rainy night in 1952

"New York, New York,
A hell of a town,
The Bronx is up
And the Battery's down."
– from the song "New York, New York" in
the musical *On the Town*

often end up. Full of missions and soup kitchens, the area has historical-ly been where the down-and-out look for a place to "flop." Recently, the Bowery has been hip-i-fied by young people looking for a cheap place to live in Manhattan. **CBGBs,** a famous joint for hearing punk music, is located in the Bowery.

New York is also the home of the **Statue of Liberty**, **Wall Street**, and **Greenwich Village**.

Chicago's Sears Tower is the world's tallest building at 1,454 feet.

3. **Which of the following cities is known as the "windy city"?**
   (A) Chicago
   (B) Detroit
   (C) Las Vegas
   (D) Dallas

Chicago is known as the "windy city." It is also called **"second city"** because it used to be the second-largest city in the U.S. (Now Los Angeles is the second-largest city; New York is num-ber one.)

4. **In which of the following cities is Hollywood located?**
   (A) Chicago
   (B) New York
   (C) Los Angeles
   (D) Las Vegas

In the early days of film, movies could only be made during the day because they didn't have sufficiently bright artificial light. For this reason, the movie industry developed in **Hollywood,** part of sunny, bright Los Angeles, California. Today, most American movies are still made in Hollywood, and the name of the area has become synonymous with the movie industry.

The Hollywood sign in 1924, before the days of the "talkie" films

5. **Where is the geyser known as "Old Faithful?"**

(A) Yosemite National Park
(B) Grand Teton National Park
(C) Yellowstone National Park
(D) Sequoia National Park

The geyser **"Old Faithful"** is in **Yellowstone National Park**, the country's oldest national park. Established in 1872, Yellowstone has many interesting geological features, including many geysers, underground springs that periodically shoot off a stream of water or steam, and hot springs.

Koyaanisqatsi (1983). A spellbinding non-narrative film that soars across the U.S. in search of beautiful vistas and ecologocal tragedy. Score by Philip Glass. See it in a theater if you can.

GEOGRAPHY

THE EARTH ON ICE

The term "Ice Age" usually refers to the glaciatic activity during the Pleistocene epoch. During this time, Northern Europe was a literal sheet of ice and New York City was covered under two miles of frozen water. There were about twenty "glacial advances," during which glaciers carved out canyons and mountain ranges. The Grand Canyon and Rocky Mountains were formed during the Pleistocene epoch.

6. **The longest river in the United States goes through which of the following states?**

    (A) Georgia
    (B) Alabama
    (C) Oklahoma
    (D) Louisiana

The longest river in the United States, the Mississippi (p. 235), travels through Louisiana on its way to the ocean. Memorialized by the novels of **Mark Twain** (1835-1910), the Mississippi was for many years the lifeblood of the midwestern states. Before the railroad, it was the most efficient way of transporting goods in America.

7. **The Great Salt Lake is in which state?**

    (A) Utah
    (B) New York
    (C) Nevada
    (D) Michigan

The Great Salt Lake is in Utah, and it is so salty that even **Arnold Schwarzenegger** (1947-) could float unaided (muscle weighs more than fat). The lake receives fresh water from a number of sources, and derives its salt content from the minerals in the ground.

ANSWERS

1. B   2. D   3. A   4. C   5. C   6. D   7. A

Europe

North
Atlantic
Ocean

Norwegian
Sea

Gulf
of
Bothnia

North
Sea

Baltic
Sea

English Channel

Bay of Biscay

Tyrrhenian
Sea

Adriatic
Sea

Black
Sea

Aegean
Sea

Mediterranean Sea

Ionian
Sea

Find these countries:

Italy
Spain
France
Ireland
Germany
Finland

Greece
The Balkans
Poland
Switzerland
Belgium

Find these cities:

Madrid
London
Athens
Berlin
Paris
Warsaw

EUROPE ANSWER MAP

1. **Which of the following nations is NOT one of the Low Countries?**

    (A)   The Netherlands
    (B)   Belgium
    (C)   France
    (D)   Luxembourg

The **Low Countries** are the Netherlands, Belgium, and Luxembourg. Called the Low Countries because most of their land is under sea level, these nations have been the battlefield for many major European wars.

The Netherlands, often called Holland, have a rich history as a major trading and shipping center. The Netherlands were one of the first countries to establish colonies in North America; New York City was originally called **New Amsterdam** (Amsterdam is the capital of the Netherlands).

One of the many streets in Holland with a canal cutting through it.

Since most of Holland is under sea level, a series of dikes were constructed to keep the water out. (Remember that story about the little Dutch boy who saves the city by plugging the dike with his thumb?) The bulbs of Holland (bulbs are a method of reproduction used by tulips, irises, and other flowers) are without parallel. Many varieties are available and are exported throughout the world.

2. **Which of the following is the capital of Ireland?**

    (A) Dublin
    (B) Edinburgh
    (C) London
    (D) Guinness

The capital of Ireland is **Dublin**. Known as the cultural and intellectual center of Ireland, Dublin was the home of James Joyce (p. 403), **Jonathan Swift**, and William Butler Yeats.

TALKIN' TURKEY

Istanbul was Constantinople;
Now it's Istanbul, not Constantinople.

*   *   *

Even old New York was once New Amsterdam
Why they changed it I can't say
People just liked it better that way!

*   *   *

Why did Constantinople get the works?
That's nobody's business but the Turks!
—From the song "Istanbul (not Constantinople)"

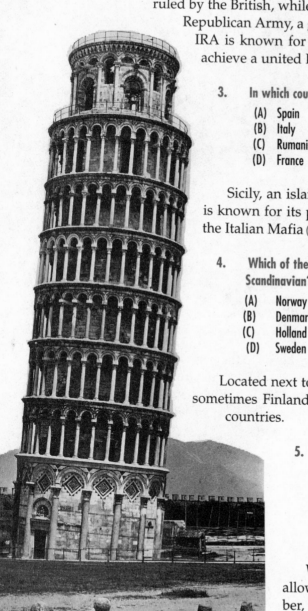

The city of Pisa in Tuscany, Italy is famous for its Leaning Tower, which stands 180 feet tall and leans sixteen-and-a-half feet out of perpendicular.

Ireland, split into Northern Ireland and the Catholic Republic of Ireland in the south, is divided because of religion. Northern Ireland is ruled by the British, while the Republic of Ireland is the home of the Irish Republican Army, a group campaigning for Irish independence. The IRA is known for committing brutal terrorist acts in its effort to achieve a united Ireland.

3. **In which country is Sicily located?**

   (A) Spain
   (B) Italy
   (C) Rumania
   (D) France

Sicily, an island in southern Italy on the Mediterranean Sea, is known for its pizza and its alleged status as the birthplace of the Italian Mafia (*The Godfather*, p. 424).

4. **Which of the following nations is NOT considered Scandinavian?**

   (A) Norway
   (B) Denmark
   (C) Holland
   (D) Sweden

Located next to one another, Norway, Denmark, Sweden, and sometimes Finland and Iceland are all considered **Scandinavian** countries.

5. **Which of the following countries is known for both its chocolate and its banking?**

   (A) France
   (B) Switzerland
   (C) Sweden
   (D) England

With a banking system that ensures privacy by allowing a depositor to be known only by her number, Switzerland has attracted much of the world's capital, especially when the money is meant to stay hidden. Switzerland is also known for its chocolates. Due to its mountainous topography,

Switzerland does not have much military value and was able to stay neutral during both WWI and WWII (pp. 200-201).

6. In which mountain range is the Matterhorn located?
    (A) The Balkans
    (B) The Alps
    (C) The Carpathians
    (D) The Urals

The 14,690 foot peak of the Matterhorn rests on the Swiss-Italian border.

The **Matterhorn,** one of the tallest mountains in Europe, is known for its steep cliffs. Almost 15,000 feet high, the Matterhorn has been the site of more climbers' deaths than any other mountain in the Alps.

7. Which of the following is the smallest country in Europe?

(A) Monaco
(B) Vatican City
(C) Lichtenstein
(D) Luxembourg

The smallest country in the world, the **Vatican** was established as a separate country in a 1920 agreement between the Pope and the Italian government. Located in Rome, the Vatican is home to the Sistine Chapel (p. 454) and Saint Peter's Basilica, two architectural wonders built during the Renaissance (pp. 159-162). It is the center of the Roman Catholic religion and has only 108 acres of land.

ANSWERS

....

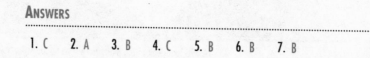

1. C   2. A   3. B   4. C   5. B   6. B   7. B

South America

Find these countries:

Brazil
Peru
Chile
Venezuela
Argentina

Find these places:

Cape Horn
Rio De Janeiro

Geography

SOUTH AMERICA ANSWER MAP

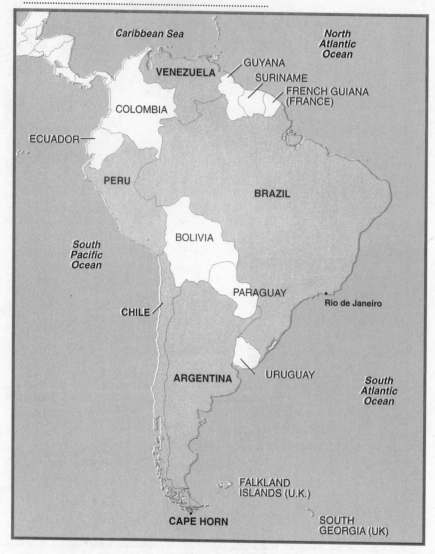

1. Place the following rivers in order from longest to shortest:

   I. Amazon
   II. Rhine
   III. Mississippi

   (A) I, III, II
   (B) II, I, III
   (C) II, III, I
   (D) III, I, II

The two longest rivers in the world are the **Nile** and the **Amazon.** The Amazon (p. 318) is in South America and flows through Brazil; the Nile is in Africa and flows through Egypt. The Amazon has many sources and many mouths, and depending on which way you measure the Amazon, it can either be the longest or the second-longest river. Both rivers are approximately 4,000 miles long, nearly twice the length of the Mississippi and five times the length of the Rhine.

2. **What is the largest city in South America?**

    (A) Brasilia
    (B) Sao Paolo
    (C) Caracas
    (D) Bogota

Fitzcarraldo (German, 1982), Werner Herzog's intense film about a man trying to establish trade routes in the Amazon against amazing odds.

The largest city in South America is **Sao Paolo**, Brazil, with a metropolitan population of almost ten million people. Originated as a Jesuit mission in 1554, Sao Paolo is now South America's leading industrial city, producing electronics, steel, and chemicals.

Sao Paolo is the eighth-largest city in the world with a population (1991) of 9,700,100.

3. **What is the official language of Brazil?**

   (A) Spanish
   (B) Portuguese
   (C) French
   (D) Brazilian

Although you may have thought that the language spoken in all of South America was Spanish, people in Brazil speak Portuguese. Brazil was conquered and first colonized by the Portuguese.

4. **Which city is further east?**

   (A) Atlanta, Georgia
   (B) Bogota, Colombia

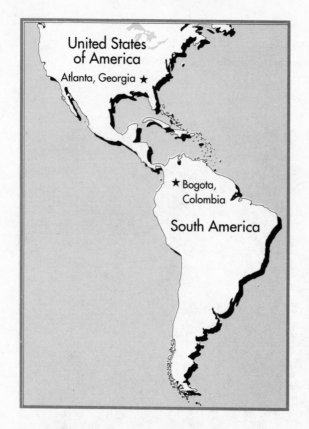

Most people don't realize it, but most of South America is east of the United States. Many picture South America as being directly south of the U.S., but it isn't. Bogota is further east than Atlanta, Georgia.

Central America and the West Indies

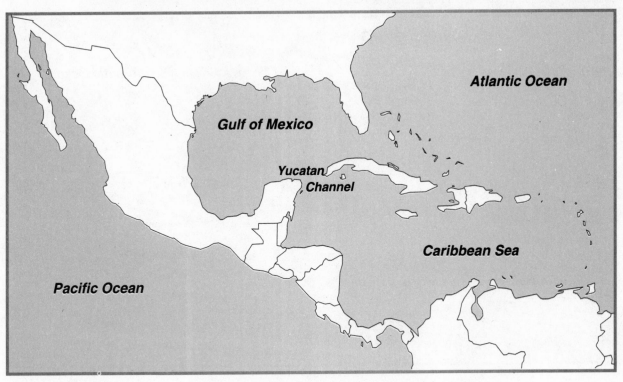

Atlantic Ocean

Gulf of Mexico

Yucatan Channel

Pacific Ocean

Caribbean Sea

Find these countries:
Mexico
Nicaragua
Panama
El Salvador
Cuba
Haiti
Puerto Rico
Jamaica

Find these cities:
Mexico City
Port-Au-Prince

Find these places:
Panama Canal
Cape Horn

GEOGRAPHY

CENTRAL AMERICA AND THE WEST INDIES ANSWER MAP

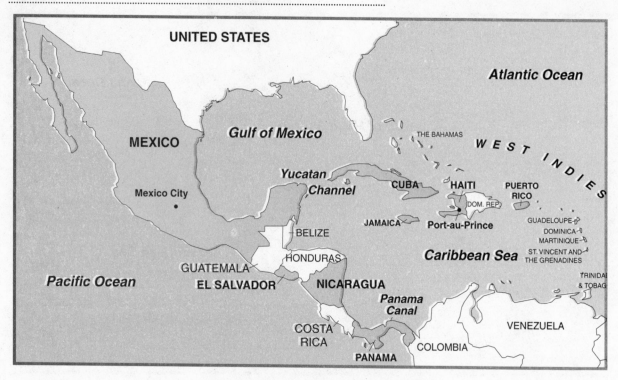

UNITED STATES

Atlantic Ocean

MEXICO

Gulf of Mexico

THE BAHAMAS

WEST INDIES

Mexico City

Yucatan Channel

CUBA

HAITI

PUERTO RICO

DOM. REP.

JAMAICA

Port-au-Prince

GUADELOUPE
DOMINICA
MARTINIQUE
ST. VINCENT AND
THE GRENADINES

BELIZE

HONDURAS

Caribbean Sea

GUATEMALA

Pacific Ocean

EL SALVADOR

NICARAGUA

TRINIDAD
& TOBAGO

Panama
Canal

COSTA
RICA

VENEZUELA

PANAMA

COLOMBIA

1. Which of the following Native American nations was in Mexico before the arrival of Columbus?

(A) The Iroquois
(B) The Seminoles
(C) The Aztecs
(D) The Sioux

Love in the Time of Cholera and *One Hundred Years of Solitude*, two novels in the "magical realism" genre by the Colombian writer Gabriel Garcia Marquez.

Many Native American civilizations flourished in what is now Mexico before the arrival of the Spanish, among them the Maya, the Olmec, the Toltec, and the Aztec. The Mayans are now known for their architecture, including some incredible pyramids that can still be seen in Mexico.

2. The building of the Panama Canal made trips between which of the following two cities quicker?

   (A) New York and London, England
   (B) New York and Caracas, Venezuela
   (C) New York and Los Angeles
   (D) Los Angeles and Tokyo, Japan

Salvador (1986). Based on the true life experiences of journalist Richard Boyle in El Salvador in 1980-81. James Wood stars.

Predator (1987). Arnold battles a crafty, ruthless alien in the jungles of South America. Shot on location, the film shows just how lush this part of the world is.

The Panama Canal (p. 81) runs through Panama in Central America. Undertaken during the presidency of Theodore Roosevelt (pp. 80-81) in 1914, the canal makes it much easier and faster for the U.S. to ship goods from the East Coast to the West Coast. Before its completion, the only way to get from one side of the American Continents to the other was to go through the Strait of Magellan or around Cape Horn, both of which were somewhat treacherous and lengthy routes. (Look at the map to see how the canal shortened travel distances for anyone wishing to ship goods to the two coasts of the U.S.)

Mayan pyramid

Comparative travel distances from Europe to Western North America: Through the Panama Canal vs. around Cape Horn.

3. Which of the following countries is NOT in Central America?

(A) Nicaragua
(B) El Salvador
(C) Guatemala
(D) Chile

Central America is made up of seven small countries—Belize, Guatemala, El Salvador, Honduras, Nicaragua, Costa Rica, and Panama—and Mexico. The narrow isthmus the smaller countries form is strategically located because of its proximity to North and South America. As such it has proved to be a hotbed of political conflicts, almost all of which involved the U.S. trying to ensure stability or stop communism.

ANSWERS

1. C   2. C   3. D

Canada

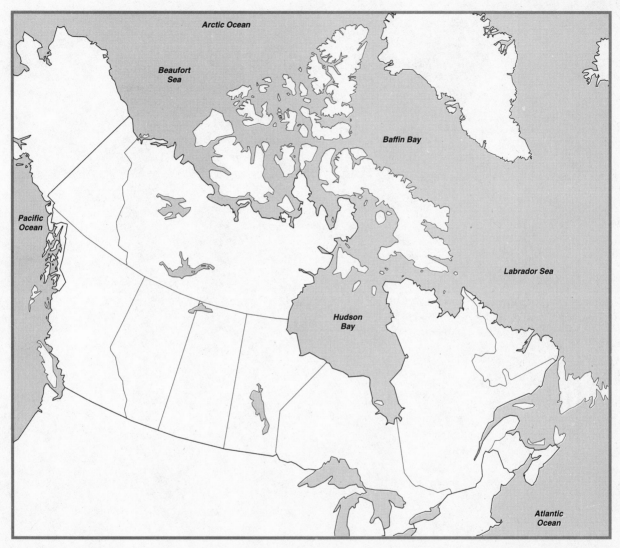

Arctic Ocean

Beaufort
Sea

Baffin Bay

Pacific
Ocean

Labrador Sea

Hudson
Bay

Atlantic
Ocean

Find these provinces:
Ontario
Quebec
British Columbia

Find these cities:
Toronto
Ottawa
Montreal
Vancouver

GEOGRAPHY

CANADA ANSWER MAP

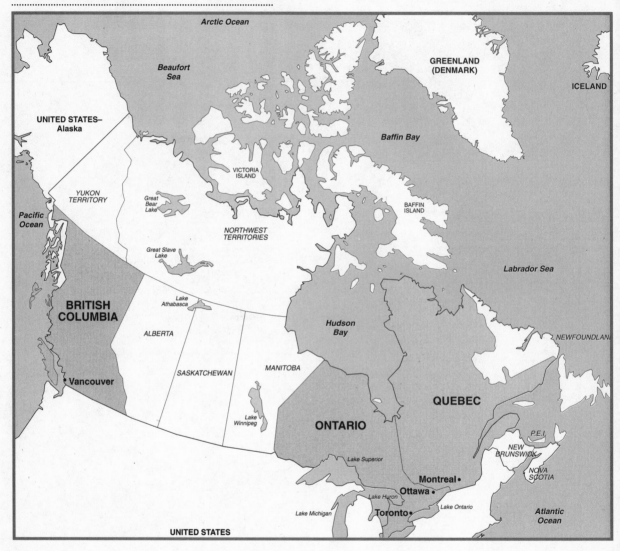

1. **What city is the capital of Canada?**

    (A) Toronto

    (B) Montreal

    (C) Ottawa

    (D) Vancouver

Many Americans know nothing about our largest neighbor. A confederation of different provinces, **Canada** came into being as a unified country in 1867, a little bit after the Civil War. It was not recognized by Britain, its "mother country," until 1931. Canada is the United States's leading trading partner, and the border between the U.S. and Canada is the largest unguarded border in the world. The capital of Canada is **Ottawa**, a city in the province of Ontario. Ottawa became the capital in 1857 despite fierce opposition from other competing cities.

When the moon hits your eye like a big pizza pie, that's Toronto

2. **What is the official language of the Canadian Province of Quebec?**

   (A) English
   (B) Spanish
   (C) French
   (D) Iroquois

The province of Quebec, with its own history and culture, declared French its official language in 1980. Since 1967, there has been a strong movement to create an independent government in Quebec, but the people of Quebec have not yet voted to secede.

3. **Which of the following is NOT a province of Canada?**

   (A) Alberta
   (B) Saskatchewan
   (C) Newfoundland
   (D) Greenland

Just as the United States is a union of fifty states, Canada is the union of ten provinces: Alberta, British Columbia, Manitoba, New Brunswick, Newfoundland, Nova Scotia, Ontario, Prince Edward Island, Quebec, and Saskatchewan. Canada's system of government is modeled after the British triumvirate (pp. 243-244). There is a Senate made up of legislators   . appointed to serve until age seventy-five, a House of Commons

GEOGRAPHY

Canada has produced two of the funniest comedy troupes to hit the small screen in the past twenty years. "SCTV," starring John Candy, Rick Moranis, Martin Short, and a host of other household names in comedy, was popular in the seventies and eighties. If you have cable, you should be able to catch the reruns somewhere. "The Kids in the Hall" is a nineties' phenomenon almost as funny as "SCTV," and well worth a watch.

comprised of legislators elected by popular vote, and a Prime Minister who is the leader of the political party with the most seats in the House of Commons, and therefore the leader of the government itself. Canada's constitution still ties it to England, and the Queen is still nominally the head of state. Canada is a member of the **British Commonwealth of Nations**, a mostly symbolic union of various former British colonies. (The U.S. is not a member.)

Canada has about one-tenth the population of the U.S., with eighty percent of its citizens living within 100 miles of Canada's southern border. Geographically the second largest country in the world after Russia, Canada is largely uninhabited.

4. In which of the following provinces of Canada are Niagara Falls located?

(A) Quebec
(B) Ontario
(C) Alberta
(D) British Columbia

See Niagara Falls! An immense quantity of water crashes down the Horseshoe Falls in Ontario, Canada and the American Falls in New York State. The overwhelming power of nature is made eerily apparent by this breathtaking phenomenon turned tourist trap. Niagara Falls are also known for the crazed antics of fools who think it's fun to fall sixteen stories in a barrel. (Many have tried; some have survived.)

ANSWERS

1. C   2. C   3. D   4. B

Africa

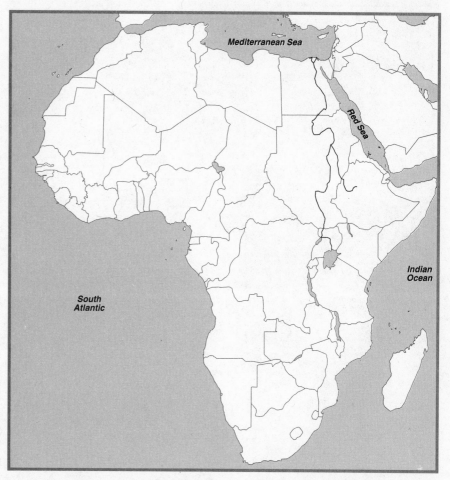

Mediterranean Sea

Red Sea

Indian Ocean

South Atlantic

Find these countries:

Nigeria
Somalia
South Africa
Ethiopia
Egypt
Liberia
Libya
Kenya
Morocco

Find these cities:

Nairobi
Cairo
Johannesburg

Find these places:

The Sahara Desert
The Nile River

GEOGRAPHY

AFRICA ANSWER MAP

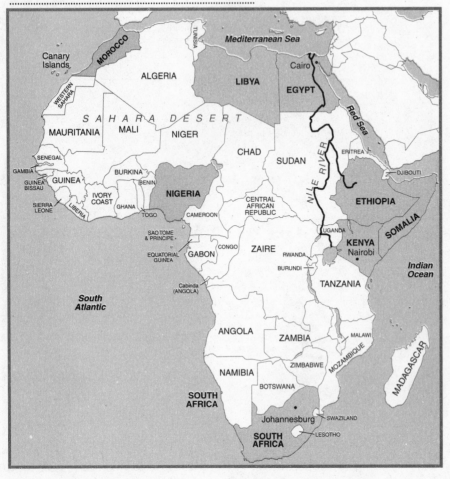

1. **Which direction does the Nile flow?**

    (A) North to South
    (B) East to West
    (C) South to North
    (D) West to East

2. **The Nile river runs through which of the following countries?**

    (A) Sudan
    (B) Somalia
    (C) Angola
    (D) Nigeria

PLATE 1: CAVE PAINTING
ARTIST: UNKNOWN
15,000 – 10,000 BC
REG. No. 261417
COURTESY DEPARTMENT LIBRARY SERVICES,
AMERICAN MUSEUM OF NATURAL HISTORY.

PLATE 2
DISCUS THROWER
ROMAN COPY OF BRONZE
450 BC (ORIGINAL)
SCALA/ART RESOURCE, NY

Plate 3
Nike of Samothrace
Artist: Unknown
200-190 BC
Scala/Art Resource, NY

Plate 4
The Laocoön Group
Artist: Unknown
First century AD after Greek original
Scala/Art Resource, NY

PLATE 8
DAVID
MARBLE, HEIGHT 13'5" (4.08 M)
ARTIST: MICHELANGELO (1475-1564)
1501-4
ART RESOURCE NY, © PHOTO BY ERIC LESSING

PLATE 9
MONA LISA
OIL ON PANEL, 30 ¹/₄" x 21" (77 x 53.5 CM)
ARTIST: LEONARDO DA VINCI
1503-5
SCALA/ART RESOURCE, NY

PLATE 7
THE LAST SUPPER
TEMPERA WALL MURAL, 15'2" x 28'10" (4.6 x 8.8 M)
ARTIST: LEONARDO DA VINCI (1452-1519)
1495-98
SCALA/ART RESOURCE, NY

PLATE 11
SISTINE CHAPEL ALTAR WALL (THE LAST JUDGMENT)
48' x 44' (14.68 x 13.41 M)
ARTIST: MICHELANGELO
1534-1541
SCALA/ART RESOURCE, NY

PLATE 10
SISTINE CHAPEL CEILING (THE CREATION OF ADAM)
9'2" x 18'8" (2.8 x 5.69 M) DETAIL OF ADAM;
ENTIRE CHAPEL CEILING 45' x 128' (13.72 x 39 M)
ARTIST: MICHELANGELO
1508-1512
SCALA/ART RESOURCE, NY

PLATE 12
SELF-PORTRAIT
OIL ON CANVAS, 31 $^5/_8$" x 26 $^1/_2$" (80.3 x 67.3 CM)
ARTIST: REMBRANDT VAN RIJN (1606-1669)
1660
THE METROPOLITAN MUSEUM OF ART, BEQUEST OF BENJAMAN ALTMAN, 1913. (14.40.618)

PLATE 14
DANCERS PRACTICING AT THE BARRE
OIL ON CANVAS, COLORS FREELY MIXED WITH TURPENTINE
29 ³/₄" x 32" (75.6 x 81.3 CM)
ARTIST: EDGAR DEGAS (1834-1917)
1876
THE METROPOLITAN MUSEUM OF ART, BEQUEST OF MRS. H.O. HAVEMEYER, 1929.
THE H.O. HAVEMEYER COLLECTION (29.100.34)

PLATE 15
SUNFLOWERS
OIL ON CANVAS, 17" x 24" (43.2 x 61 CM)
ARTIST: VINCENT VAN GOGH (1853-1890)
1887
SCALA/ART RESOURCE, NY

PLATE 13
WATER LILIES, GIVERNY
OIL ON CANVAS, 6'6 ¹/₂" x 19'7 ¹/₂" (2 x 6 M)
ARTIST: CLAUDE MONET (1840-1926)
1907
MUSEUM OF MODERN ART, NY. MRS. SIMON GUGGENHEIM FUND.
PHOTOGRAPH © 1994 THE MUSEUM OF MODERN ART, NY

PLATE 16
THE SCREAM
TEMPERA AND CASEIN ON CARDBOARD, 36″ x 29″ (91.3 x 73.7 CM)
ARTIST: EDVARD MUNCH (1863-1944)
1893

PLATE 17
ARRANGEMENT IN BLACK AND GRAY: THE ARTIST'S MOTHER
OIL ON CANVAS, 57" x 64 ¹/₂" (144.6 x 163.8 CM)
ARTIST: JAMES MCNEILL WHISTLER (1834-1904)
1871
SCALA/ART RESOURCE, NY

PLATE 18
THE THINKER
BRONZE, HEIGHT 27 ¹/₂" (69.8CM)
ARTIST: AUGUST RODIN (1840-1917)
1879-89
THE METROPOLITAN MUSEUM OF ART.
GIFT OF THOMAS F. RYAN, 1910
(11.173.9)

PLATE 19
LES DEMOISELLES D'AVIGNON
OIL ON CANVAS, 8' x 7'8" (2.43 x 2.33 M)
ARTIST: PABLO PICASSO (1881-1974)
1906-7
MUSEUM OF MODERN ART, NY. ACQUIRED THROUGH THE LILLIE P. BLISS BEQUEST. PHOTOGRAPH © 1994,
THE MUSEUM OF MODERN ART, NY.

PLATE 20
THE DANCE
OIL ON CANVAS, 8'5 ³/₄" x12'9 ¹/₂" (2.59 x 3.9M)
ARTIST: HENRI MATISSE (1869-1954)
1910
MUSEUM OF MODERN ART, NY. GIFT OF NELSON B. ROCKEFELLER IN HONOR OF ALFRED H. BARR, JR. PHOTOGRAPH © 1994, THE MUSEUM OF MODERN ART, NY.

PLATE 22
AMERICAN GOTHIC
OIL ON BEAVERBOARD, 29 $^{7}/_{8}$" x 24 $^{7}/_{8}$" (75.9 x 63.14 CM)
ARTIST: GRANT WOOD (1892-1941)
1930
FRIENDS OF AMERICAN ART COLLECTION, 1930.934

PLATE 21
BLACK IRIS III
OIL ON CANVAS, 36" x 29 $^{7}/_{8}$" (91.4 x 75.9 CM)
ARTIST: GEORGIA O'KEEFFE (1887-1986)
1926
THE METROPLITAN MUSEUM OF ART,
ALFRED STIEGLITZ COLLECTION, 1969. (69.278.1)

PLATE 24
GUERNICA
OIL ON CANVAS, 11'6" x 25'8" (3.5 x 7.8 CM)
ARTIST: PABLO PICASSO (1881-1974)
1937
ART RESOURCE, NY

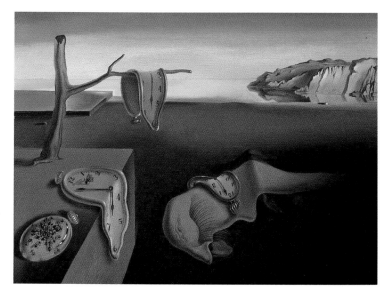

PLATE 23
THE PERSISTENCE OF MEMORY
OIL ON CANVAS, 9 1/2" x 13" (24 x 33 CM)
ARTIST: SALVADOR DALI (1904-1989)
1931
MUSEUM OF MODERN ART, NY. GIVEN ANONYMOUSLY. PHOTOGRAPH © 1994,
THE MUSEUM OF MODERN ART, NY.

PLATE 25
ONE (#31)
OIL AND ENAMEL ON UNPRIMED CANVAS, 8'10" x 17'5 ⅝" (2,69 x 5.32 M)
ARTIST: JACKSON POLLOCK (1912-1956)
1950
MUSEUM OF MODERN ART, NY. SIDNEY AND HARRIET JANNIS COLLECTION. PHOTOGRAPH © 1994,
THE MUSEUM OF MODERN ART, NY.

PLATE 26
CAMPBELL SOUPS
OIL SILK SCREEN ON CANVAS, 36 ⅛" x 24" (91.7
x 60.9 CM)
ARTIST: ANDY WARHOL (1928-1987)
1965
MUSEUM OF MODERN ART, NY. ELIZABETH BLISS PARKINSON FUND.
PHOTOGRAPH © 1994, THE MUSEUM OF MODERN ART, NY.

PLATE 27
THREE FLAGS
ENCAUSTIC ON CANVAS, 30 $^7/_8$" x 45 $^1/_2$" x 5" (78.4 x 115.6 x 12.7 CM)
ARTIST: JASPER JOHNS (1930-)
1958
COLLECTION OF WHITNEY MUSEUM OF AMERICAN ART, NY.
PHOTOGRAPH BY GEOFFREY CLEMENTS, NY.

PLATE 28
LOBSTER TRAP AND FISH TAIL (MOBILE)
PAINTED STEEL WIRE AND SHEET ALUMINUM 8′6″ X 9′6″ (2.6 X 2.9 M)
ARTIST: ALEXANDER CALDER (1989-1976)
1939
MUSEUM OF MODERN ART, NY. COMISSIONED BY THE ADVISORY COMMITTEE FOR THE STAIRWELL OF THE MUSEUM.
PHOTOGRAPH © 1994, THE MUSEUM OF MODERN ART, NY.

The Nile river runs from Burundi and Rwanda through the Sudan and then into Egypt. The river empties into the Mediterranean Ocean, flowing from south to north.

The Nile River Delta is considered one of the most fertile places on earth. It was the foundation of the ancient Egyptian civilization (p. 136) that built the great pyramids and the Sphinx and lasted for thousands of years.

Death on the Nile (1978), starring Peter Ustinov, Bette Davis, and Angela Lansbury. Pretty good mystery about a boatload of potential murderers. Shot on location, so you can see a lot of Egypt.

3. **Which is the largest city in Africa?**

    (A) Cairo
    (B) Lagos
    (C) Johannesburg
    (D) Addis Ababa

The largest city in Africa is **Cairo,** Egypt with a population of over 12 million. The fastest growing city in Africa is **Lagos,** Nigeria.

4. **Which of the following nations does not border on the Mediterranean?**

    (A) Egypt
    (B) Morocco
    (C) Tunisia
    (D) Zaire

Egypt is home to many of the world's endangered species (Referring to the cats, of course, not the "Bug").

Unfortunately for these travelers in the Nairobi desert, camels are not equiped with air conditioning.

Zaire, which is in the center of Africa, does not have access to the Mediterranean. The group of countries in the north of Africa are often considered a different group than those south of the **Sahara Desert.** Countries to the north of the Sahara had contact with Europe throughout their histories and have cultures that are more closely related to the Europeans. Predominantly Muslim, these countries have histories that tie them to Europe. Sub-Saharan Africa, on the other hand, was separated geographically from Europe and the countries to the north by the Sahara Desert. Most of these cultures had only rare interactions with Europe until the nineteenth century. Of course, an exception to this is the slave trade, which generally affected the peoples of Western Africa.

The Sheltering Sky (1949), by Paul Bowles. Set in Morocco, this ethereal novel explores the differences between African and Western cultures.

Carved statue from the Baoulé tribe of Ivory Coast

Asia

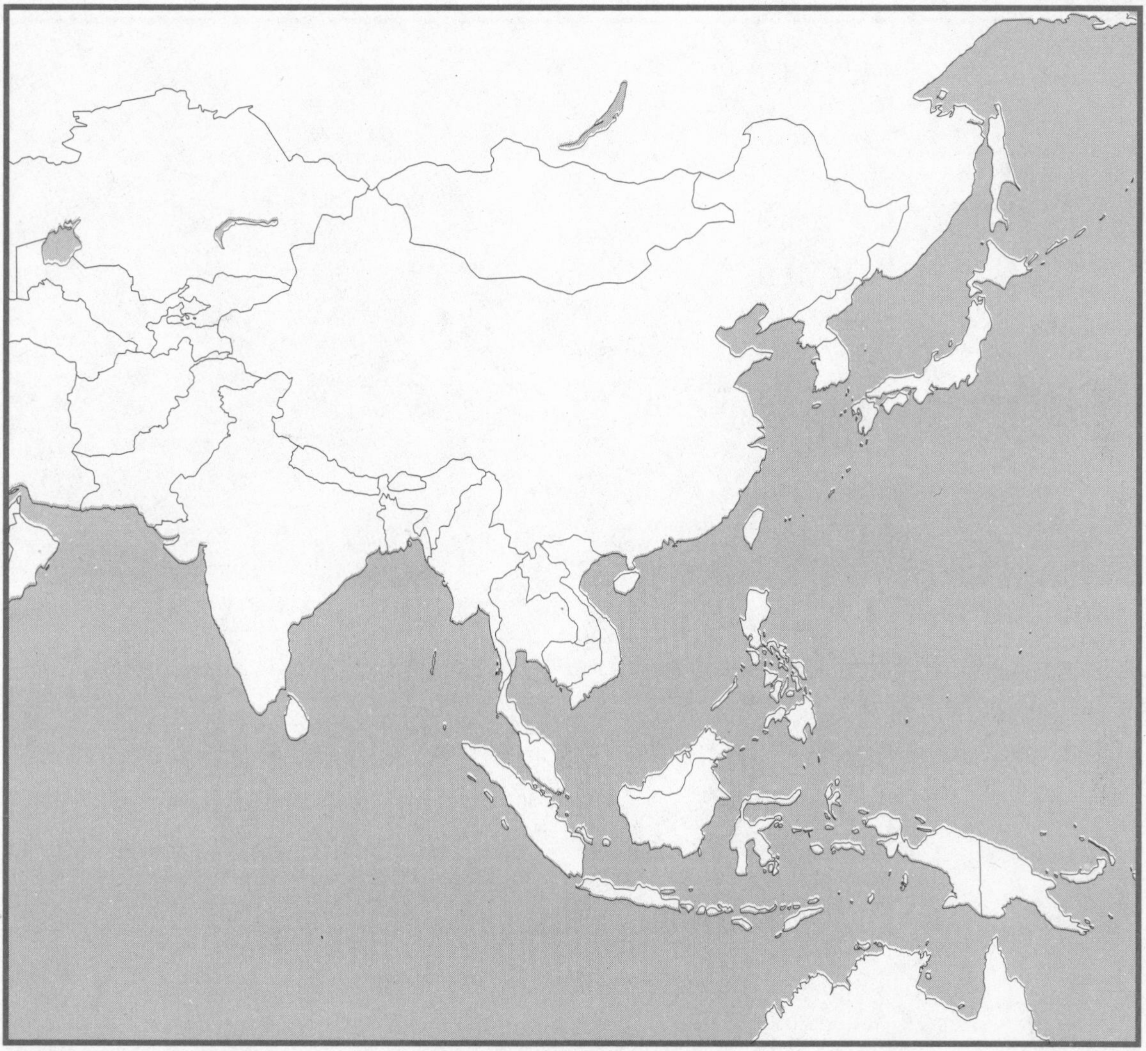

Find these countries:

India	Philippines
Pakistan	Taiwan
Afghanistan	Japan
China	South Korea
Tibet	Vietnam
Thailand	Hong Kong
Vietnam	Bangladesh

Find these cities:

Tokyo
Seoul
Beijing
New Delhi
Hiroshima
Bombay

Find these places:

The Himalayan Mountains

Geography

Asia Answer Map

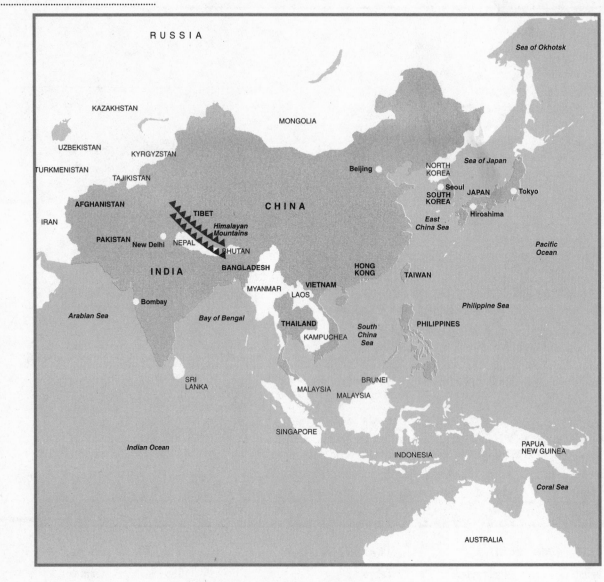

1. Which of the following is the tallest mountain in the world?

   (A) K2
   (B) Mount McKinley
   (C) Mount Everest
   (D) Pikes Peak

Mount Everest, all 29,028 feet of it, is located on the border between Nepal and Tibet in the **Himalayan** mountain range. "Himalaya" is Sanskrit for "snow-home." After Everest was proclaimed the highest mountain in the world in 1856, many attempted to climb it, but the mountain remained unconquered until 1953 when **Edmund Hillary** (1919-) of New Zealand succeeded in reaching the top. Since then, many people have reached the summit of Everest, and most of the world's highest peaks. The highest remaining unconquered mountain is Kankar Punsum on the Bhutan/Tibet border. Standing a mere 24,741 feet tall, it beckons those in search of a most unpleasant vacation.

A busy shopping day on a Tokyo street.

2. **What was the capital of Japan from AD 794-1868?**

    (A) Tokyo
    (B) Hokkaido
    (C) Osaka
    (D) Kyoto

During WWII (p. 202-203), most of the major cities in Japan were destroyed by fire-bombs and nuclear weapons, but the Allies agreed not to bomb the ancient imperial capital of **Kyoto** (capital from 794-1868), where many magnificent monuments—a testament to the creative genius of the feudal Japanese—are concentrated. Today the capital of Japan is **Tokyo**, one of the world's largest cities. With over eleven million people, Tokyo is home to nearly ten percent of Japan's population. Tokyo is so crowded that some commuters travel from suburbs three hours away by train.

3. **What is the official language of China?**

    (A) Cantonese
    (B) Mandarin
    (C) Wu
    (D) Gan

Fireworks in celebration of the Lunar New Year over Hong Kong's Victoria Harbor.

There are many different Chinese **dialects**—a variety of a language separated by grammar and pronunciation from other varieties of the same language—scattered across the country's huge expanse. The most common is **Mandarin**, the official language of China, spoken by almost seventy percent of the population. Another common dialect is **Cantonese**, spoken in **Hong Kong**, a British colony soon to be returned to the control of mainland China. The dialects of China are as different from each other as are the languages of Europe. Just as a person who speaks only French cannot understand Spanish, a person who speaks only Mandarin will not understand Cantonese.

4. **What city used to be called Peking by the West?**

(A) Beijing
(B) Shanghai
(C) Taiwan
(D) Hong Kong

Beijing, the capital of China, was known for years in the West as Peking. The second largest city in China with a population of almost seven million, Beijing has a northeast border that is partly formed by the **Great Wall of China**, the only man-made structure on earth visible from space. Beijing is the site of both the Boxer Rebellion (p. 213) and the 1989 student uprising at **Tiananmen Square,** in which over 1,000 peaceful pro-democracy protesters were massacred by government forces.

The Great Wall, started during the Qin Dynasty in 214 BC, stretches 1,450 miles and is 25 feet tall.

Middle East

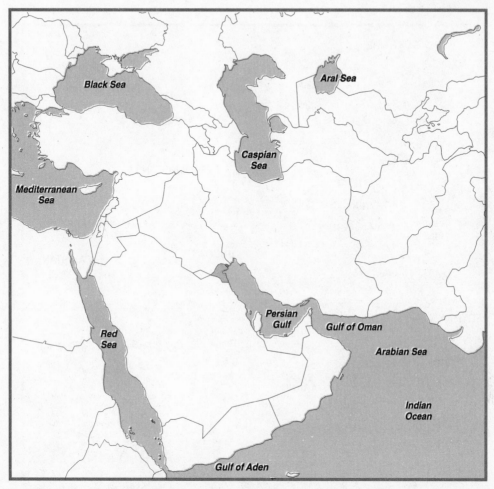

Black Sea

Aral Sea

Caspian Sea

Mediterranean Sea

Persian Gulf

Gulf of Oman

Red Sea

Arabian Sea

Indian Ocean

Gulf of Aden

Find these countries:

Egypt
Iran
Iraq
Israel
Jordan
Kuwait
Saudi Arabia
Syria
Turkey

Find these cities:

Jerusalem
Bethlehem
Baghdad
Beirut
Cairo
Tehran

Find these places:

The Persian Gulf
Mecca

MIDDLE EAST ANSWER MAP

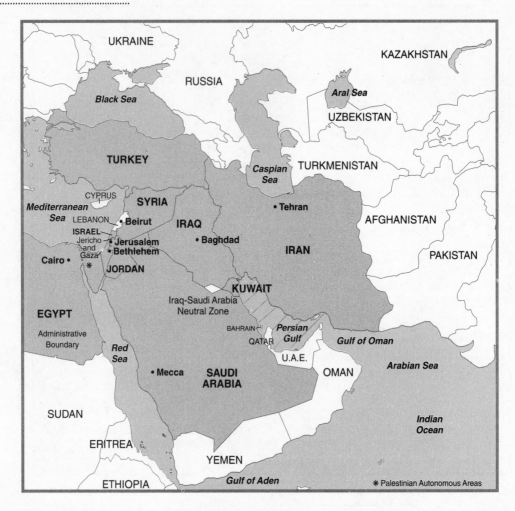

1. **Which of the following nations does NOT have substantial oil reserves?**

    (A) Saudi Arabia
    (B) Jordan
    (C) Kuwait
    (D) Iran

   Many Arab Nations in the Middle East have accumulated vast sums of wealth from their oil reserves. Saudi Arabia, Kuwait, Iran, and Iraq, all original members of OPEC (p. 126), have used the power of petrochemicals (p. 342) for political purposes: these countries once boycotted the sale of oil to the U.S. to protest our support of Israel during the **Yom Kippur War** in 1973. Yet not all Middle Eastern nations have been blessed with oil. Jordan, Israel, and Lebanon must find other ways to generate income.

2. **In which country is Mecca located?**

   (A) Israel
   (B) Iraq
   (C) Saudi Arabia
   (D) India

Mecca (p. 379), the holiest city of the Islamic religion, is located in Saudi Arabia. The heart of the city is the al-Haram, or Great Mosque, which holds the Kaaba, a sacred stone. Because it is holy, the city is open to Muslims only.

3. **What country was formally known as Persia?**

   (A) Iraq
   (B) Iran
   (C) Lebanon
   (D) Saudi Arabia

Iran was renamed "Persia" by the Greeks (pp. 141-144) when it became a province of their empire. In 1935, Iranians changed the name of the country back to its original form. Modern-day Iran has often featured prominently in U.S. politics. From the Iranian hostage crisis (p. 126) to the Iran-Contra scandal (p. 128), the country has been nothing but trouble since the U.S.-backed Shah was deposed and **Ayatollah Khomeini** (1900-1989) took over in 1979.

4. **Where is the Wailing Wall located?**

   (A) Jerusalem
   (B) Alexandria
   (C) Bethlehem
   (D) Tel Aviv

View of Beirut with the Mediterranean in the background.

The Arabian Nights, a group of Arab tales in oral circulation since the tenth century, includes the popular stories of "Ali Baba," "Aladdin," and "Sinbad the Sailor." Legend has it that Scheherazade told her sultan husband a new tale every night, which she only agreed to finish the following night. In this way, she avoided the fate of her predecessors, who were killed the night after their weddings to prevent them from being unfaithful to the sultan.

The city of **Jerusalem** is a spiritual center for three of the world's major religions: Judaism, Islam, and Christianity. For the Jews, it was the home of their ancient temple, and the Wailing Wall is the one remaining remnant of the temple. People still pray at the **Wailing Wall** and place slips of paper with prayers written on them in the cracks of the wall.

For the Christians, Jerusalem was the scene of many of the events in Jesus's (pp. 373-377) life, and for the Muslims, Jerusalem is where Mohammed (p. 150) ascended to heaven. Because of the religious importance of the city, it draws many tourists and pilgrims searching for spirituality.

ANSWERS

1. B   2. C   3. B   4. A

Australia, New Zealand, and Indonesia

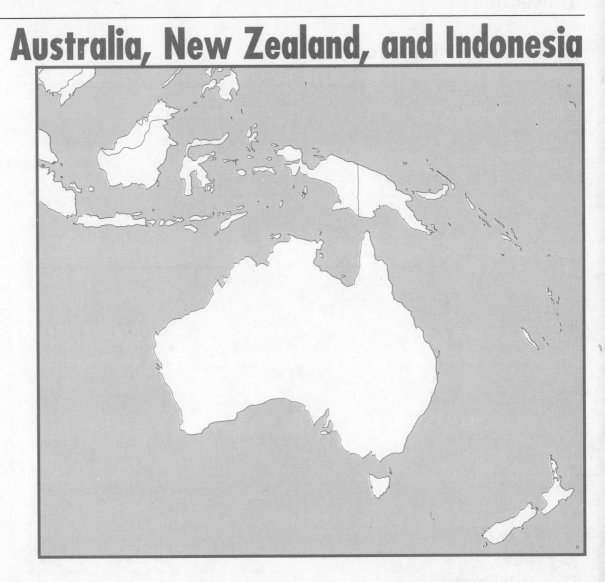

Find these countries:
New Zealand
Australia
Singapore
Malaysia
Indonesia
Philippines
New Guinea

Find these cities:
Sydney
Jakarta
Melbourne
Bali
Auckland

Find these places:
Great Barrier Reef
Tasmania

AUSTRALIA, INDONESIA, AND NEW ZEALAND ANSWER MAP

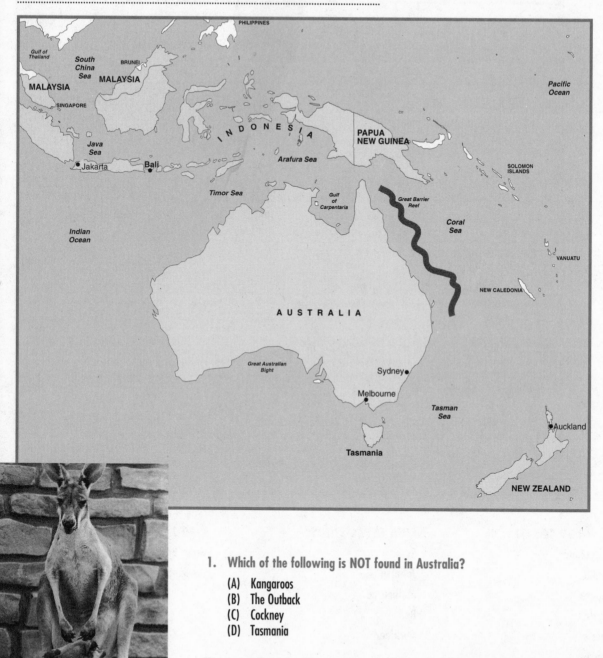

Australia: Kangaroo country

1. **Which of the following is NOT found in Australia?**

   (A) Kangaroos
   (B) The Outback
   (C) Cockney
   (D) Tasmania

First reached by Europeans in 1606, Australia was thought to be several small islands until 1801. Australia was named for the unknown southern continent that had been theorized about for centuries. ("*Terra australis incognita*" is Latin for "unknown southern land.") Vast areas of the interior continent (known as the **outback**) are still unsettled by human beings.

Australia is geographically isolated from the rest of the world. Because of this, all kinds of weird animals and vegetation have developed. Among the most interesting are the marsupials, a special type of mammal that carries its young in a pouch. The most famous marsupial is the kangaroo. Its rear legs have incredible strength: A red kangaroo once jumped forty-two feet in one hop. It's true! Another creature that only exists in Australia is the Tasmanian Devil, named after the island of Tasmania to the southeast of the continent. These creatures are small, with huge, bone-crushing teeth, and have become famous from their appearance in the Bugs Bunny cartoons.

The thriving metropolis of Sydney, Australia

2. **What is the largest structure ever built by living creatures?**
   (A) The Great Wall of China
   (B) The Great Barrier Reef
   (C) The World Trade Center
   (D) The Three Mile Island Nuclear Power Plant

One of the most incredible sites in Australia is the Great Barrier Reef, a 1,260-mile-long structure off the northeast coast of Australia. Covering an area of over 80,000 square miles, the beautiful structure is made up of the bodies, dead and alive, of millions of stony coral.

3. **Rank by population in New Zealand**
   I. Humans
   II. Sheep
   III. Cattle
   (A) I, II, III
   (B) II, I, III
   (C) II, III, I
   (D) III, II, I

WALTZING MATILDA

The national anthem of Australia is an odd choice for an anthem. It doesn't even mention the name of the country or any famous battle, and it's full of strange expressions. Anyway, it's called "Waltzing Matilda," and here it is:

> Once a jolly swagman sat beside a billabong
> Under the shade of a coolibah tree,
> And he sang as he watched and waited till his
>   billy boiled
> "You'll come a-waltzing Matilda with me."
>
> Waltzing Matilda, waltzing Matilda
> You'll come a-waltzing Matilda with me.

A "swagman" is a hobo or tramp, a "billabong" is a waterhole, a "coolibah" tree is a eucalyptus tree, and a "billy" is a tea kettle. To go "waltzing Matilda" doesn't involve a girl or dancing — the term means to carry a backpack (the Matilda) as you wander (waltz) through the countryside.

GEOGRAPHY

 The Year of Living Dangerously (1983), starring Mel Gibson and Sigourney Weaver. A great political drama set in strife-ridden 1960s Indonesia.

New Zealand, located nearly 1,200 miles from Australia, is an industrializing nation that historically has relied on agriculture to make ends meet. The country is the second largest exporter of wool in the world, with nearly twenty times as many sheep as people. There are also more than twice as many cows as people.

4. Approximately how many islands are there in the country of Indonesia?
(A) 10
(B) 300
(C) 800
(D) 3,000

An entrance to an ancient Balinese temple

Indonesia is a nation made up of almost three thousand islands. A Dutch colony for three hundred years until 1945, Indonesia has been ruled by the same leader, General Suharto, since 1967. Modern Indonesia has yet to experience a peaceful transfer of power from one ruler to the next.

ANSWERS
....
1. C   2. B   3. C   4. D

Russia and the Republics

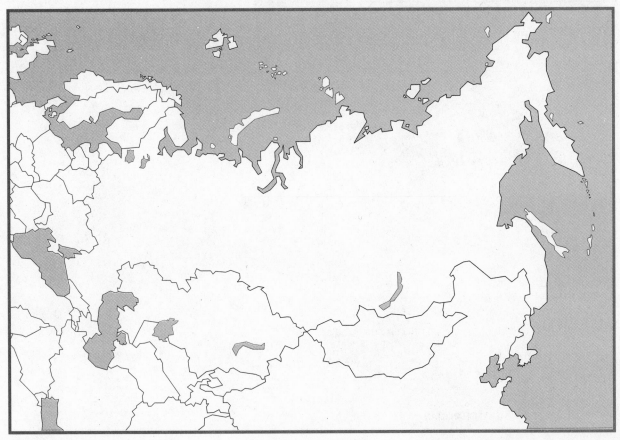

Find these countries:
Estonia
Latvia
Lithuania
Ukraine
Serbia
Kazakhstan
Georgia

Find these cities:
Belarus
Moscow
Chernobyl
Kiev
Odessa
St. Petersburg

Find these places:
Siberia

GEOGRAPHY

RUSSIA AND THE REPUBLICS ANSWER MAP

Key to Numbered Countries

1. ESTONIA   7. AZERBAIJAN
2. LATVIA   8. TURKMENISTAN
3. LITHUANIA   9. UZBEKISTAN
4. BELARUS   10. KYRGYZSTAN
5. GEORGIA   11. TAJIKISTAN
6. ARMENIA

1. **Which of the following was NOT part of the former Soviet Union?**

   (A) The Baltics
   (B) The Balkans
   (C) Georgia
   (D) Kazakhstan

   The breakup of the Soviet Union has thrown the entire map-making world into a tizzy. It used to be so easy! The big monolithic country that ran from Europe into most of Asia was called the USSR (The Union of Soviet Socialist Republics.) When the USSR (p. 207) collapsed in 1991, the so-called union became a commonwealth of independent states, each with its own color on the map. The process of secession is not over yet. The nations continue to split up, forming independent Republics with names that contain far too many consonants.

Some of the first nations to secede from the Soviet Union were the **Baltics**. Located to the northeast of Europe, just next to the Baltic Sea, these nations—Lithuania, Estonia, and Latvia—declared independence soon after the attempted coup on Mikhail Gorbachev (p. 207). Azerbaijan, Belarus, Kyrgyzstan, Moldova, Ukraine, Uzbekistan, Armenia, Kazakhstan, Russia, Tajikstan, and Turkmenistan all broke loose soon afterwards. By the end of 1991, the Soviet Union was dissolved.

Many people confuse the Baltic states with the Balkans. The Balkans are a band of mountains in which the new states of Slovenia, Croatia, Bosnia and Herzegovina, Montenegro, Serbia, Albania, and Macedonia are located.

As the Soviet Union was dissolving in the early 1990s, the country of Yugoslavia was going through its own breakup. Yugoslavia, while not technically a republic of the USSR, was still under its influence. When the USSR was no longer, the republics of Yugoslavia decided to declare their independence—first Croatia, then Slovenia, then Macedonia, and finally Bosnia and Herzegovina (one country with a long name). This left the "new Yugoslavia" of Serbia and Montenegro.

Rocket launchers on parade in Red Square in 1956

The new countries of the former Yugoslavia were not satisfied with their borders and war broke out along ethnic lines. Since the map of this area has been redrawn so many times in the last century, all of the countries have claims to larger "historical" areas. The countries have used these ancient ethnic rivalries as an excuse for the brutal murder and rape that accompanies war. Under the rubric of **"ethnic cleansing,"** unspeakable acts have been committed as the different ethnic groups vie for power.

2. **Which of the following is the former name of St. Petersburg?**

    (A) Moscow
    (B) Marxtown
    (C) Riga
    (D) Leningrad

GEOGRAPHY

Serbian fighters take cover in operations against Bosnian snipers.

After the dissolution of the Soviet Union, the city of St. Petersburg voted to restore its name. From 1924 to 1991, the city had been known as **Leningrad**, to commemorate V. I. Lenin (pp. 191-194), the first leader of the USSR. St. Petersburg is famous for surviving a 900-day siege during WWII.

3. **How far away is Russia from the United States at the closest point?**

   (A) 55 miles
   (B) 155 miles
   (C) 855 miles
   (D) 3,155 miles

An island off the tip of Alaska is only fifty-five miles from Cape Dezhnev in Siberia, just across the Bering Strait (pp. 31-32)

ANSWERS

....

1. B   2. D   3. A

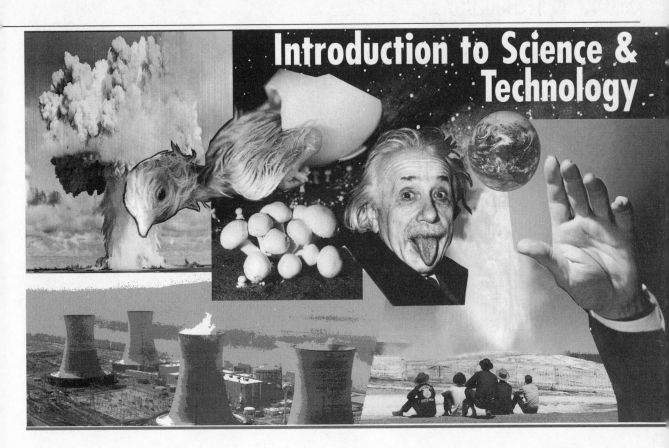

Introduction to Science & Technology

The physical world is breathtakingly complex and interrelated. Consider something as simple as a piece of bread. We eat bread all the time with nary a thought towards its origins. But wheat, which was harvested to form the flour, is a genetic hybrid that would not be able to reproduce without our help. The yeast used to make the bread rise is a unicellular creature that reproduces at a rapid rate and, in the process, produces carbon dioxide. This release of gas in the flour dough creates the little holes that give bread its appealing texture. We eat the bread, and through digestion, it is converted into sugars used by our bodies for energy. Our bodies then get rid of the parts of the bread we can't digest, and in some cases, this waste is turned into fertilizer that is used to grow more wheat.

Not convinced? Consider for a moment the venerable automobile. When you drive down the street, you are using the energy of millions of creatures that died millions of years ago. Your car is converting this energy to kinetic energy through tiny little explosions in the engine. When you brake, the kinetic energy does not "disappear." It is turned into heat energy transferred through the brake pads. If you crush a bug while traveling at high speeds, the bug actually slows down the car a tiny bit.

Science throws light on all of these physical processes. It also enables us to create man-made wonders that rival the natural.

But I Don't Like Science

Even if you are not excited by science, you still need to know some of the basics to get by in this world. For example, if you ever plan to become intimately involved with another person, you had better know how the human sexual and reproductive systems work.

Many of you may feel that science is not an easy thing to learn, that even the simplest concept is complicated enough to send your head spinning. You are partially correct. In the last hundred years or so, there has been a technological and scientific explosion. We know so much about so many things that it is impossible for a single soul to know everything about science and technology, but there are certain basic concepts that are pretty easy to grasp. We hope they provide a foundation for your further exploration of the sciences.

Astronomy

1. **What is the name of the theory that explains how the universe came into being?**

   (A) The Theory of Universal Creation
   (B) The Big Bang Theory
   (C) The Black Theory
   (D) The Andromeda Strain

A Brief History of Time, by Stephen Hawking. Hawking's well-known theory of the origin of the universe.
Genius, by James Gleick. A biography of the offbeat physicist Richard Feynman.
The First Three Minutes, by Steven Weinberg. A hypothetical account of the first three minutes of the universe.

The **Big Bang Theory** of the creation of the universe is the one most accepted by scientists today. The theory states that the universe was created by an event similar to a huge explosion. Evidence showing that the universe is still expanding helps prove this theory.

There's evidence that between ninety and ninety-nine percent of the matter in the universe is not radiating at any wavelength detectable with our present technology. Some scientists suspect the presence of this so-called "dark matter" because of its gravitational effect on matter we can see. Of course, we might have made a colossal error in figuring how gravity (pp. 302-303) operates, but that suggestion isn't popular.

2. Which of the following is the name of our galaxy?

(A) The Milky Way
(B) The Andromeda Galaxy
(C) The Owtadiswald Galaxy
(D) Galaxy Z

When scientists talk about the stars, they inevitably will throw around words like light year and parsecs and such. A light year is the distance that light travels in a year. It may sound a bit weird at first, but a light year is a convenient way of measuring distance. The speed of light is fixed; no matter what happens, light will always move at the same speed (pp. 304-305 relativity). The distance light travels in a year is always about six trillion miles. Because nothing travels faster than light, it is impossible for us to know what is happening now in outer space. Whatever we know about stars is ancient history. The light that reaches us from a star 1,000 light years away is 1,000 years old. Imagine that intelligent life exists in outer space and is attempting to send us a message through the stars. By the time we get the message, it will probably be tens of thousands of years old.

Our galaxy is known as the **Milky Way**. It is one of the larger galaxies thus far observed by man and is about 100,000 light years (p. 271) wide. Our sun is just one of the Milky Way's several billion stars. Another large galaxy observed by humans is the Andromeda Galaxy, which is about 2.2 million light years away.

3. Which of the following scientists published a work in 1543 that indicated that the earth moved around the sun?

(A) Ptolemy
(B) Nicolaus Copernicus
(C) Marie Curie
(D) Isaac Newton

For thousands of years, the accepted scientific thought as developed by **Aristotle** (384-322 BC) and **Ptolemy** (AD 100-170) was that the earth was the center of the solar system and the planets and the sun moved about the earth. In order to describe and predict the motion of the planets, Ptolemy devised elaborate systems in which planets and the sun moved in crazy orbits called epicycles. During the Middle Ages (pp. 151-158), the idea of an earth-centered universe became so pervasive and so much a part of the religious beliefs of the time, that any other theory was considered heresy.

It wasn't as if there were no other theories to describe the motions of the planets. The Pythagoreans and Aristarchus of Samos came up with models that showed the planets going around the sun, but the people of the Middle Ages were so enthralled with Aristotle and Ptolemy's theories that they were unwilling to accept a theory that did not show the earth in the center. Religious leaders believed that the Bible provided support for such a theory. The first Renaissance (p. 159-162) thinker to posit a **helio-centric** (sun-centered) view of the solar system was **Nicolaus Copernicus** (1473-1543). Without making many direct observations himself,

For great science fiction and special effects that are hard to beat, see: *2001: A Space Odyssey* (1968), directed by Stanley Kubrick. Truly a milestone in film making. Also, *Star Wars* (1977), starring Harrison Ford, Mark Hamill, and Carrie Fisher. One of the most popular movies of any sort ever made.

Copernicus was able to take the theories of others and show that a much simpler solution was available. His theory marked the beginning of the scientific revolution that started during the Renaissance.

4. **Which of the following people used observations made through a telescope to prove the theory that the earth revolved around the sun?**
   (A) Nicolaus Copernicus
   (B) Galileo Galilei
   (C) Leonardo da Vinci
   (D) Pope Urban VIII

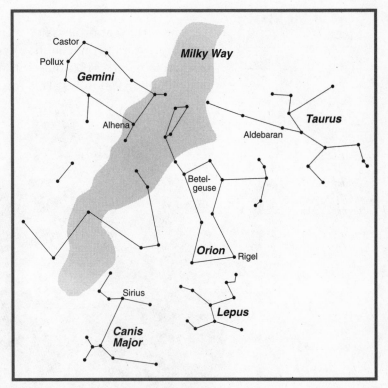

The debate over whether the universe was sun-centered or earth-centered went on for a while, but for the most part, the arguments were based on mathematics. However, when **Galileo Galilei** (1564-1642) invented the telescope, he was able to make observations that proved without a doubt that the earth and other planets revolved around the sun. This theory caused Galileo much trouble, and he was brought in front of the Inquisition (p. 155) where he was made to sign a paper stating he thought no such thing. But Galileo was right, and all the religious arguments in the world could not stand in the way of the truth. The scientific method prevailed, and we now know that the earth and the planets orbit around the sun.

5. **How many miles is it from the sun to the earth?**
   (A) 93,000
   (B) 930,000
   (C) 9,300,000
   (D) 93,000,000

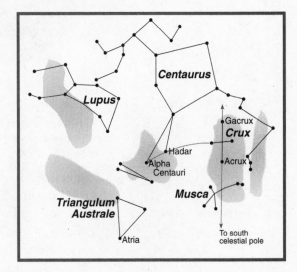

SOME OF THE NEAREST STARS

Name	Distance (light years)
Proxima Centauri	4.3
Centauri A	4.3
Centauri B	4.3
Centauri C	4.3
Barnard's Star	5.9
Wolf 359	7.6
Lalande 21185	8.1
Sirius A	8.6
Sirius B	8.6
Luyten 726-8A	8.9
Luyten 726-8B	8.9
Ross 154	9.4
Ross 248	10.3
Eridani	10.7
Luyten 789-6	10.8
Ross 128	10.8
61 Cygni A	11.22
61 Cygni B	11.2
Indi	11.2
Procyon A	11.4
Procyon B	11.4

The earth is approximately **ninety-three million miles** away from the sun—not your average Sunday drive. A trip from New York to California is approximately 3,000 miles. A trip around the globe at the equator is only about 25,000 miles. This means that if you wanted to travel all the way to the sun, you would have to circumnavigate the earth at the equator more than 3,500 times. The distance between the sun and the earth is called an **astronomical unit**.

The sun is huge by our puny earthly standards. It is about 860,000 miles in diameter, a lot bigger than the earth, which is only about 8,000 miles in diameter.

Our home

6. **What happens when the moon is eclipsed by the earth?**

An **eclipse** is when one object blocks the light of another object. An eclipse of the moon happens when the earth's shadow blocks the light from the sun that normally hits the moon. It is not too exciting to watch. An **eclipse of the sun,** on the other hand, is very exciting. The moon blocks the sun, and if the sun is totally covered, the light that appears around the edge of the moon is quite spectacular. Eclipses were once thought to bring bad luck. If an object as predictable as the sun suddenly behaved in an unpredictable manner, what else might go wrong? Of course, we now know that eclipses themselves are very predictable.

7. Approximately how long does it take for light to travel from the nearest star (excepting the Sun) to the Earth?

   (A) 9 minutes
   (B) 2 days
   (C) 4 years
   (D) 100 years

The star closest to earth is the sun, but the next closest star is Proxima Centauri, which is approximately 4.3 light years away (twenty-five trillion miles). A light year is the distance covered by light traveling for one year. It is almost impossible for us to conceive just how far away from here Proxima Centauri really is.

To try to understand the distance, let's look at how long it would take us to get there. The Space Shuttle, the fastest fixed-wing plane ever flown, travels at a speed of 16,600 miles an hour. The speed of light is approximately 684,931,507 miles per hour, so if we were to ride the Space Shuttle until we got to Proxima Centauri, it would take us approximately 170,000 years. So until we can travel a lot faster than we do today, a vacation there is out of the question.

THE NIGHT SKY

A constellation is a group of stars that forms a shape when connected. If you look up at night, you will see many constellations, including the Big Dipper, the Little Dipper and Orion's Belt. The constellations were viewed many years ago by the Greeks (pp 141-144) who would look up at the night sky and imagine that the stars were the endpoints of lines. When the stars formed a shape, the Greeks would give it a name. For example, when the Greeks saw a group of stars that looked kind of like a lion, they named it Leo. We still use many of these names today.

SCIENCE & TECHNOLOGY

"Jupiter" Symphony by Wolfgang Amadeus Mozart. "The Planets" by Gustav Holst.

8. Name the planets in our solar system.

The planets, beginning with the one closest to the sun, are **Mercury, Venus, Earth, Mars, Jupiter, Saturn, Uranus, Neptune,** and **Pluto** (Neptune and Pluto switch places from time to time). With the exception of the earth, the planets are all named after Greek and Roman gods (p. 386). The Greeks and Romans felt that the gods resided in the solar system, and the names stuck. Between the planets Mars and Jupiter there is an asteroid belt. Asteroids are tiny planetoids that orbit the sun.

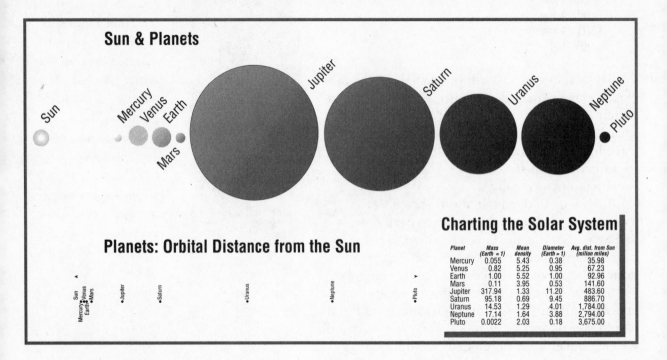

Sun & Planets

Planets: Orbital Distance from the Sun

Charting the Solar System

Planet	Mass (Earth = 1)	Mean density	Diameter (Earth = 1)	Avg. dist. from Sun (million miles)
Mercury	0.055	5.43	0.38	35.98
Venus	0.82	5.25	0.95	67.23
Earth	1.00	5.52	1.00	92.96
Mars	0.11	3.95	0.53	141.60
Jupiter	317.94	1.33	11.20	483.60
Saturn	95.18	0.69	9.45	886.70
Uranus	14.53	1.29	4.01	1,784.00
Neptune	17.14	1.64	3.88	2,794.00
Pluto	0.0022	2.03	0.18	3,675.00

ANSWERS

1. B   2. A   3. B   4. B   5. D   7. C

Earth Science

1. **Water takes up approximately what percentage of the earth's surface?**

   (A) 25%
   (B) 50%
   (C) 70%
   (D) 90%

Silent Spring, by Rachel Carson. A great book on ecology.

When we think of the earth, we think of earth—dirt, mountains, rocks, and such. We don't live in the water, so we can easily forget that more than seventy percent of the earth's surface is ocean. Water, and the fact that most of it's in a liquid state on earth is what makes it possible for humans to survive. If the earth were closer to the sun, like Venus or Mercury (p. 272), all the water would evaporate, and if the earth were farther away, it would all freeze.

We are lucky that water is the liquid filling the oceans, because it is one of the few liquids that become lighter when they freeze. Ice floats, keeping the oceans from freezing solid and allowing for animals to survive underneath the frozen water.

SCIENCE & TECHNOLOGY

2. **The process by which water forms into clouds is called**

   (A) Condensation
   (B) Evaporation
   (C) Boiling
   (D) Dissolving

The ocean is responsible for many of the climatic changes that occur on earth. Clouds are formed through a process that begins with the evaporation of the water from the oceans. Water vapor rises off the surface of the ocean and eventually reaches the colder upper atmosphere where it condenses into clouds. Clouds are masses of tiny water droplets that eventually coalesce into rain or snow or sleet or other things that fall on your head if you forget your umbrella.

3. **The polar ice in Antarctica is approximately how deep at its thickest point?**

   (A) 140 feet
   (B) 1,400 feet
   (C) 14,000 feet
   (D) 140,000 feet

The polar ice cap in **Antarctica** is truly a wonder. The ice at its thickest point is over 14,000 feet thick. On average the ice is about 4,000 to 6,000 feet thick and if it melted would raise the level of the oceans about 200 feet. When people worry about global warming (pp. 277-278), one of their worries is that the polar ice caps might melt.

4. **Which of the following is NOT a renewable resource?**

   (A) Energy from the sun
   (B) Energy from the wind
   (C) Energy from fossil fuels
   (D) Hydroelectric power

A **renewable resource** is one that will always be available or that can be replaced. In practical terms there will always be energy from the sun, and its energy causes a lot of other activities from which man can draw power. The heat from the sun causes the oceans to evaporate and the resultant rain forms the rivers, which allow for the construction of hydroelectric dams. The heat from the sun is also instrumental in making wind.

The energy from burning fossil fuels, however, is limited. **Fossil fuels** are **oil**, **natural gas**, and **coal**, which were all formed out of fossilized plants and animals millions of years ago. **Photosynthesis**, the process by which plants create energy from the sun, is what gives fossil fuels their energy. Unfortunately, it is a slow process, and it will take millions of years for new oil to be formed. So, when you are driving your car or heating your home, you are reaping the benefit of all the millions of creatures that died millions of years ago. One day, perhaps, your fossilized remains will be powering some car driven by a teenager millions of years in the future.

5. **What is the approximate temperature of the earth's core?**

(A) 27° C
(B) 100° C
(C) 212° C
(D) 2450° C

The interior of the earth is incredibly hot, averaging about 2450 ° C. The surface of the earth, although appearing predominantly stable, is actually in constant motion above the earth's molten interior. If we could look at the earth in fast-motion, we would view an image of huge sections of the earth colliding and rubbing into each other, mountains forming out of the buckling earth, erupting out of nowhere. Sometimes moving as much as several inches each year, these plates shape the earth. When they rub up against each other we get earthquakes. The **San Andreas fault** in California is a meeting of two very active plates grinding into each other.

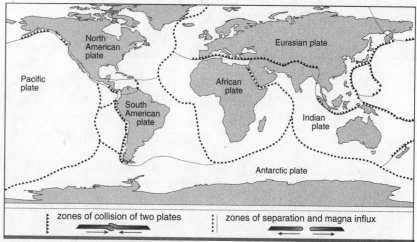

zones of collision of two plates   zones of separation and magna influx

One theory that explains the formation of the Earth's continents is called "continental drift." In 1915, Alfred Wegener (1880-1930) theorized that the earth used to be made up of one big super-continent, and that gradually, as the plates below the surface moved, the super-continent (that Wegener named "Pangaea") broke up into the current continents.

SCIENCE & TECHNOLOGY

Superman (1978), starring Marlon Brando and Christopher Reeve. Lex Luthor, the villain, hatches a dastardly plot involving nuclear warheads and the San Andreas fault. Superman must come to the rescue.

6. The island of Hawaii was formed by

(A) volcanic activity
(B) a buildup of organisms into a coral reef
(C) breaking off from nearby California
(D) changes in the earth's gravitational pull

Most of the Hawaiian islands grew as the result of **volcanic activity.** Tectonic plates in the ocean pulled apart and allowed the molten inner layers of the earth to escape into the ocean. As the rock cooled, it formed land.

Some land is formed through the shifting of huge plates that hold the continents and also through the associated volcanic activity. Often, changes in the surface of the land have been caused by the growth and shrinkage of **glaciers.** Many features of America, like the Grand Canyon, were caused by such movement over millions of years. Other land is formed when the shells of dead animals and sand are gradually buried and compressed into rocks by the weight of the land. Eventually these rocks can be pushed back up to the surface again and turned into mountains.

Plants and animals form into a complex arrangement that creates soil and allows for more plants and animals to exist. For example, the earth's atmosphere originally contained little oxygen, but the process of plant respiration gradually produced the oxygen that we breathe today.

The eruption of Mount Saint Helen's in 1980 sent ash and steam 60,000 feet into the air.

7. How has recent deforestation of the environment affected the atmosphere?

(A) There has been an increase in acid rain caused by a break in the ozone layer.
(B) There has been an increase in the percentage of the atmosphere that is carbon dioxide.
(C) There has been a decrease in arable land suitable for agricultural production.
(D) There has been an increase in volcanic activity throughout the world.

Considering how short a time human beings have lived on the planet, our activities have had an enormous impact on the shape of the earth. The earth has been around for about 4.6 billion years. Modern humans have been around in the form they are today for only 40,000 years. To put that in perspective, if the earth was five minutes old, humans would have existed for only three-one-thousandths of a second. In that small amount of time, we have made huge changes in the environment; we have wiped out numerous species; and we have polluted untold numbers of acres of land and ocean.

One example of the changes caused by man is the destruction of forests throughout the world. This **deforestation** has reduced the amount of oxygen produced by plants and has therefore increased the proportion of CO_2 in the atmosphere.

8. **Which of the following is thought to be a cause of global warming?**

    (A) Burning of fossil fuels
    (B) Acid rain
    (C) Melting of polar ice caps
    (D) Pollution from nuclear power plants

Global warming is caused by an increase in atmospheric carbon dioxide which is sometimes called the **greenhouse effect**. The theory (and it is only a theory) is that carbon dioxide and water vapor in the atmosphere contribute to keeping the temperature of the earth at a livable level. When the sun shines through the atmosphere, it heats the earth, but the CO_2 (carbon dioxide) and the H_2O (water) keep the heat from escaping. It's just like a greenhouse, where the sun warms the air, but the heat cannot escape because of the glass.

Scientists worry that a sharp increase in CO_2 caused by the burning of fossil fuels will increase the insulating properties of the atmosphere. Even a slight increase in temperature could have a devastating effect on the environment: the polar ice caps would melt and many coastal cities would be flooded; arable land would turn into desert; and people would be starving everywhere.

However, scientists aren't sure what will happen if there is an increase in carbon dioxide. There could be factors that keep the temperature from going up. For example, plankton in the oceans might increase their activity because of the increase in CO_2 and temperature, thereby creating more oxygen and canceling out the greenhouse effect.

As we become more concerned with the environment, we come up with different terms to describe it. What used to be jungles are now called rain forests; what used to be swamps are now called wetlands. Although there is a difference in meaning between the term rain forest and jungle (a rain forest has a high canopy and less undergrowth), for all intents and purposes they both refer to the same thing. It is just that a rain forest sounds much more appealing than a jungle. As William Safire, who writes about language for "The New York Times," put it, "If you call it a jungle nobody would want to preserve it. But a forest has nice ring to it—there was Robin Hood with his merry men robbing the rich in Sherwood Forest . . . If a pollster asks, 'Is it O.K. to mow down the jungle?' the answer will be 'Sure, who needs it?'; if the same pollster asks, 'Do you approve of destruction of the rain forest?' the answer will be 'No, it will lead to global warming or a new ice age.'"

The deforestation and destruction of the rain forests causes approximately two species to become extinct every hour. The Butterfly Effect (so called from the notion that the fluttering of a butterfly's wings may set off currents that will eventually grow into a large storm) states that a very small natural force may cause a cumulatively large effect over a period of time and illustrates that the loss of a single species can have a profound effect on our global ecosystem.

The greenhouse effect is a global problem. The entire world must work together to reduce the emission of CO_2 in order to effect change.

9. **Which of the following is a major cause of acid rain?**
   (A) Changes in atmospheric pressure caused by global warming
   (B) Deforestation
   (C) Water pollution caused by runoff from toxic waste dumps
   (D) Automobile exhaust

Those darned fossil fuels. **Acid rain** is believed to be caused by the interaction of sulfur and nitrogen dioxides in rain and snow. Auto exhaust and the burning of coal have added to the problems of acid rain.

When acid rain falls, it changes the pH level (p. 297) of streams and lakes, killing the natural vegetation and the fish. While there is some debate as to the extent of the damage, most scientists agree that some bodies of water have been adversely affected by this rain. There are lakes in which all the fish have died.

Acid rain has some political importance. Because of the way in which it travels, the emissions from one country can cause damage in another country. For example, coal burning in England has caused acid rain in Scandinavia. This makes acid rain a global problem.

A traffic jam in Jakarta, Indonesia. Overuse of fossil fuels occurs throughout the world.

10. **Which of the following is considered a cause of the destruction of the ozone layer?**
    (A) The burning of fossil fuels
    (B) The emission of chlorofluorocarbons
    (C) The melting of the polar ice caps
    (D) The destruction of the rain forests

The ozone layer is a protective layer in the upper atmosphere that shields the world from the ultraviolet light of the sun. Ultraviolet light (p. 306) is responsible for suntans, sunburns, skin cancer, and certain damage to the eye. If the ozone layer were to disappear, scientists would expect an increase in incidences of skin cancer and cataracts and a decrease in the ability of man to grow food. One possible cause of the dissolution of the ozone layer is chlorofluorocarbons, or CFCs, which are used in aerosol sprays and air conditioning. A worldwide effort to reduce the use of CFCs is in process, but so far, there is no alternative that is as versatile or as inexpensive as chlorofluorocarbons.

11. **Where is the biggest rain forest in the world?**
    (A) Mexico
    (B) Brazil
    (C) Russia
    (D) Zaire

Eva Luna, by Isabel Allende. A very exciting novel about love, sex, and guerrilla warfare in the jungles of South America. Allende also wrote *The House of the Spirits*, which was recently made into a movie.

The largest rain forest in the world is the **Amazon rain forest** in South America. Located mostly in Brazil (pp. 235-236), the Amazon rain forest is almost as big as the entire United States, excepting Alaska and Hawaii, and is immensely important in the global ecosystem. The Amazon rain forest contains more species of animals and plants than any other place on earth. It contains one third of the earth's trees and is responsible for producing much of the world's oxygen.

The Amazon rain forest is gradually being destroyed by human acts. People are developing the forest into farms and cities, and as vast numbers of trees are burned, four percent of the rain forest is disappearing every year. This is no small thing. If the rain forests disappear, there could be a huge change in the ecological balance of the planet.

The Mission (1986), starring Jeremy Irons and Robert De Niro. It's kind of a long movie about missionaries in late eighteenth-century Brazil, but there's some good action and beautiful shots of the lush Brazilian rain forests.

As the forest is burned to the ground, many species of plants and animals will become extinct. In addition to being a bad thing in itself, this reduction in biodiversity could make it harder to find cures to diseases (certain tropical plants have proven useful to doctors recently) and might otherwise hamper the efforts of science. Burning the trees contributes to the amount of carbon dioxide in the air and could contribute to the greenhouse effect.

ANSWERS

1. C   2. A   3. C   4. C   5. D   6. A   7. B   8. A   9. D
10. B   11. B

Weather

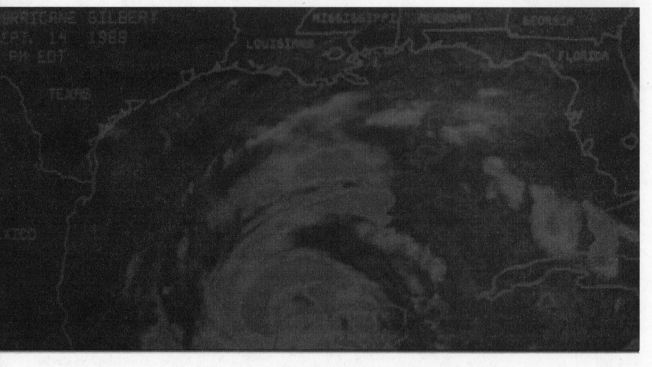

1. **The different temperatures associated with winter and summer are caused by**

    (A) the tilt of the earth
    (B) the change in distance between the earth and the sun
         caused by irregularities in the earth's orbit
    (C) the jet stream
    (D) evaporation of the ocean

The earth orbits around the sun, and the earth rotates around its axis, but the seasonal differences found in the areas north and south of the equator are caused by the tilt of the earth. The earth is so tilted that in the months of September to March, the northern hemisphere of the earth is tilted away from the sun and only gets its sunlight at an angle. As the earth continues its trip around the sun, the rest of the earth's northern side ends up presenting its face to the sun, receiving the sunlight head on.

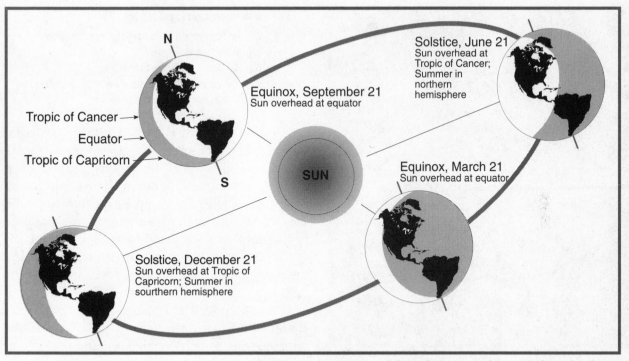

Tropic of Cancer →

Equator →

Tropic of Capricorn →

N

S

Equinox, September 21
Sun overhead at equator

Solstice, June 21
Sun overhead at
Tropic of Cancer;
Summer in
northern
hemisphere

SUN

Equinox, March 21
Sun overhead at equator

Solstice, December 21
Sun overhead at Tropic of
Capricorn; Summer in
sourthern hemisphere

This diagram represents the seasonal changes that occur on earth as a result of its angle to the sun.

2. **The effect of a high pressure system on the weather is**

(A) Warm dry weather
(B) Thunderstorms
(C) Light rain
(D) Fog

As you watch the weather forecast on TV, the forecasters are constantly using words like low pressure systems, high pressure systems, warm fronts and cold fronts, but what does it all mean?

Pressure refers to **barometric pressure,** which is basically a measure of how much air is above you at a given time. A **high-pressure system** consists of a column of air that has heavier gas molecules than the surrounding area. Because of this, the air in such a system flows downward. As the air falls down, it heats up and becomes relatively dry. High-pressure regions are usually a sign of good clear weather.

A **low-pressure system,** on the other hand, is one in which the air moves gradually up. In moving up, the air from a low-pressure system cools and its moisture condenses. Low-pressure systems are the cause of tornadoes and hurricanes and other wet weather.

Bolts of lighting in the night sky

3. **A thunderstorm is caused by**
   - (A) updrafts caused by heating of the earth's surface
   - (B) a high pressure system
   - (C) the destruction of the ozone layer
   - (D) the immense weight of the water vapor present in the atmosphere at any given time

A **thunderstorm** is caused by the condensation of warm air as it moves upward in what are called thermals. The hot air rises rapidly and when it reaches a certain point, it forms into water droplets and falls. The rapid air movement within the clouds of a thunderstorm causes the separation of charges that leads to lightning and thunder.

While most **lightning** occurs within clouds, the lightning that we are most familiar with is the lightning that strikes the ground. The updraft that causes a thunderstorm also separates positively charged particles from negative ones. The positive particles are usually carried up into the cloud with the draft. When the negatively charged bottom of the cloud gets close enough to the positively charged ground, there is a movement of electricity from the cloud to the ground. Thunder is caused by the explosion formed by the release of energy.

4. **How can you tell how far away a thunderstorm is?**

Since sound travels about one mile every five seconds, you can figure out how far away a lightning strike is by counting from the time you see it until the time you hear it. When you hear the boom of the thunder, divide the number of seconds by five. The result is the number of miles away that the storm is. For example, if it took ten seconds for you to hear the sound, the storm would be two miles away, but if the thunder and lightning happen at the same time, and you feel the hair on your neck standing up, you might not survive to read the next chapter of this book.

5. **A hurricane is caused by**
   (A) a shift in the ozone layer
   (B) an increase in atmospheric pressure
   (C) the condensation of huge amounts of moisture
   (D) increased wind caused by the lack of obstruction
       over the ocean

 The Hurricane (1937), starring John Ford and Dorothy Lamour. An escapist love story set on a fictional island. The special effects make it worth watching.

A **hurricane** is caused by the condensation of moisture that evaporates from warm ocean areas. Usually starting in a low pressure area, warm, moist air is drawn up into the atmosphere, where it condenses. The process of condensation releases heat. An average hurricane makes more energy in a day than all the people in the United States use in a year.

Devastation wrought by Hurricane Andrew

ANSWERS
....

1. C   2. A   3. C   5. D

Chemistry

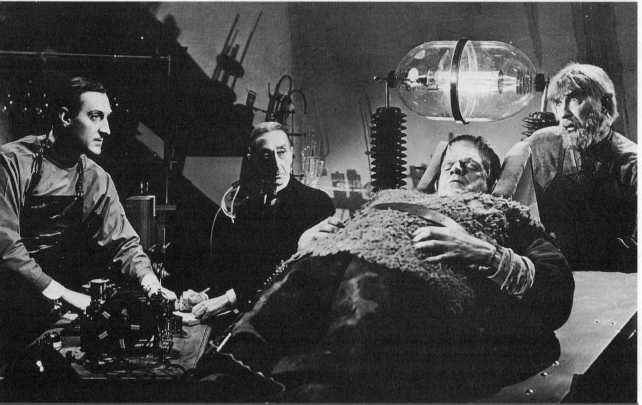

1. **What is the difference between a compound and an element?**

    (A) Compounds are more volatile than elements.
    (B) A compound is not subject to the laws of relativity while an element is.
    (C) A compound is a more dangerous form of an element.
    (D) A compound can be decomposed into another substance by chemical means while an element can't be.

Everything: you, your cat, your car, your house, a dust mite, a baseball, everything is made up of zillions of small particles called atoms or molecules. A compound is a chemical combination of several elements and can be broken down, while an element is a piece of matter in its purest form.

2. **Which of the following characteristics differentiates an organic compound from an inorganic compound?**
   - (A) An organic compound lives, while an inorganic compound is dead.
   - (B) An organic compound contains carbon, an inorganic compound does not.
   - (C) An organic compound is less complicated than an inorganic one.
   - (D) An organic compound cannot be poisonous to living creatures, while an inorganic compound can be.

It took only a few minutes for the Hindenburg to be consumed by hydrogen-fueled flames.

Organic compounds are what make up living beings. They are usually fairly complicated and have the element carbon in their makeup. Organic chemistry is the study of these compounds. Because they are the basic building blocks of life, organic compounds are studied by biologists interested in understanding the basic functions of the cell and of life.

3. **Which of the following substances is an element?**
   - (A) Hydrogen
   - (B) Sodium chloride
   - (C) Carbon dioxide
   - (D) Water

An element is a substance which cannot be broken down into other elements. Sodium chloride (NaCl), carbon dioxide (CO_2), and water (H_2O) can all be broken down into other elements, but hydrogen is a type of atom and is thus impossible to change into another atom by chemical means. (Hydrogen can be changed into other types of atoms by nuclear fusion (pp. 292-293), but we'll get to that later.)

4. **Approximately how many known elements are there?**
   - (A) 4
   - (B) 40
   - (C) 100
   - (D) 300

THEY BOTH START WITH "H"

Noble gases (p. 289) don't react very easily with other gases. In one instance, this advantage would have been life-saving. In 1936, the Hindenburg, a giant zeppelin, went down in a fiery mess after being hit by lightning in New Jersey. The blimp was filled with hydrogen, which burns very easily. Had the blimp been filled with helium (as blimps are today), which is a noble gas, thirty-six people would not have died when it crashed.

5. The table that shows the elements and their
   properties is known as
   (A) the table of the atoms
   (B) the periodic table
   (C) the list of elements
   (D) the endurable

There are approximately 100 known elements and they are listed in the periodic table (p. 287). The periodic table gives a great deal of information about each element, and is useful to scientists for determining how elements behave.

Of the 100 or so known elements, only a few of them show up often in the known universe. The following chart shows the most common elements.

UNIVERSE	SUN'S ATMOSPHERE	EARTH'S CRUST
Hydrogen	Hydrogen	Oxygen
Helium	Helium	Silicon
Oxygen	Oxygen	Aluminum
Neon	Carbon	Hydrogen
Nitrogen	Nitrogen	Sodium
Carbon	Silicon	Calcium
Silicon	Magnesium	Iron
Magnesium	Sulfur	Magnesium
Iron		Potassium
Sulfur		

What's the most common compound in the universe? Water! Its molecule consists of one oxygen atom and two hydrogen atoms. Hydrogen is the most common material in the universe, and oxygen is the third most common, so, using the law of averages, water is the most common compound. The second most common atom is helium, which is an inert substance and forms no compounds.

6. Which of the following characterizes an electron?
   (A) Mass: 1 AMU; charge: positive
   (B) Mass: almost nothing; charge: positive
   (C) Mass: 1 AMU; charge: negative
   (D) Mass: almost nothing; charge: negative

An electron is a negatively charged particle with almost no mass that moves about the nucleus of an atom. The nucleus is composed of protons, which are positively charged particles that weigh one atomic mass unit, and neutrons, which have weight but no charge.

7. The number 18 above Ar stands for

(A) The number of protons in the nucleus of an atom of Ar
(B) The exact weight of an atom of Ar
(C) The radioactivity of an atom of Ar
(D) The number of electrons in an atom of Ar when it forms a compound with another substance

 "The Elements," from *An Evening Wasted*, by Tom Lehrer. Incredibly, Lehrer manages to get all the elements on the periodic table to the tune of "Modern Major General" from the *Pirates of Penzance*. The rest of the album is pretty funny, too.

S subshell area

P subshell area

D subshell area

Period 1	1 H 1.0																	2 He 4.0	Period 1
Period 2	3 Li 6.9	4 Be 9.0											5 B 10.8	6 C 12.0	7 N 14.0	8 O 16.0	9 F 19.0	10 Ne 20.0	Period 2
Period 3	11 Na 22.0	12 Mg 24.3											13 Al 27.0	14 Si 28.1	15 P 31.0	16 S 32.1	17 Cl 35.5	18 Ar 39.0	Period 3
Period 4	19 K 39.1	20 Ca 40.1	21 Sc 45.0	22 Ti 47.9	23 V 50.9	24 Cr 52.0	25 Mn 54.9	26 Fe 55.8	27 Co 58.9	28 Ni 58.7	29 Cu 63.5	30 Zn 65.4	31 Ga 69.7	32 Ge 72.6	33 As 74.9	34 Se 79.0	35 Br 79.9	36 Kr 83.8	Period 4
Period 5	37 Rb 85.5	38 Sr 87.6	39 Y 88.9	40 Zr 91.2	41 Nb 92.9	42 Mo 95.9	43 Tc 97.0	44 Ru 101.0	45 Rh 102.9	46 Pd 106.4	47 Ag 107.9	48 Cd 112.4	49 In 114.8	50 Sn 118.7	51 Sb 121.8	52 Te 127.6	53 I 126.9	54 Xe 131.3	Period 5
Period 6	55 Cs 132.9	56 Ba 137.3	57 La 138.9	72 Hf 178.5	73 Ta 180.9	74 W 183.9	75 Re 186.2	76 Os 190.2	77 Ir 192.2	78 Pt 195.1	79 Au 197.0	80 Hg 200.6	81 Tl 204.4	82 Pb 207.2	83 Bi 209.0	84 Po 209.0	85 At 210.0	86 Rn 222.0	Period 6
Period 7	87 Fr 223.0	88 Ra 226.0	89 Ac 227.0																Period 7

| 58 Ce 140.1 | 59 Pr 140.9 | 60 Nd 144.2 | 61 Pm 145.0 | 62 Sm 150.4 | 63 Eu 152.0 | 64 Gd 157.3 | 65 Tb 158.9 | 66 Dy 162.5 | 67 Ho 164.9 | 68 Er 167.3 | 69 Tm 168.9 | 70 Yb 173.0 | 71 Lu 175.0 |
| 90 Th 232.0 | 91 Pa 231.0 | 92 U 238.0 | 93 Np 237.0 | 94 Pu 244.0 | 95 Am 243.0 | 96 Cm 247.0 | 97 Bk 247.0 | 98 Cf 251.0 | 99 Es 254.0 | 100 Fm 253.0 | 101 Md 256.0 | 102 No 253.0 | 103 Lr 257.0 |

F subshell area

The **periodic table** arranges the elements in a form that is useful to scientists. The elements are arranged in ascending order according to their atomic number. The atomic number refers to the number of protons—positively charged particles—in the nucleus of the atom. An oxygen atom has 8 protons and is thus given the atomic number of 8.

8. **Why do elements in the same column of the periodic table exhibit similar properties?**
    (A) They just do, which is why they were put in the table in the first place.
    (B) An element in a column has the same number of electrons as the other elements in the column.
    (C) Elements in the same column share the same quantum mechanics.
    (D) Elements in the same column have a similar number of electrons in their outer shells.

The order in nature that is represented by the periodic table is astounding. Why should an element like neon with ten electrons have anything to do with an element like argon with eighteen electrons? Why would carbon and silicon share similar properties?

To understand why these elements exhibit similar properties, we must first understand how the electrons that move about the nucleus of an atom behave. Scientists used to think that the electrons orbited around the nucleus in much the same way that the planets orbit around the sun. **Neils Bohr** (1885-1962), a Dutch physicist, theorized that atoms moved only in certain orbits. The closer to the nucleus the orbit is, the fewer electrons that can fit into the orbit. So, the first orbit can only hold two electrons. The second can hold eight. It turns out that the electrons don't move in orbits like the planets, but the general idea of the theory holds true (see quantum mechanics p. 294). There is only a certain amount of room at each level for electrons.

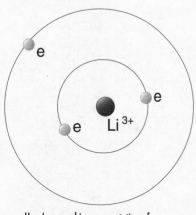

Here's a graphic representation of electron shells in a lithium atom.

Each level of electrons is called a **shell**, and each shell can only hold a certain number of atoms. When a shell is full, the atom is happy and stable and does not need to react with another atom. When the shell is not completely full, the atom is unstable and wants to react with another atom. The reason that atoms within the same column of the periodic table function in similar ways is that their outer shells have the same number of electrons in them. For example, both lithium and sodium have one electron roaming about their outer shells, so they like to form compounds with the same atoms.

9. **The substances Ne, Ar, Kr, Xe, and Rn in column 8 share which one of the following properties in common?**

(A) They are all radioactive
(B) They are all missing at least one electron
(C) They are all inert gases
(D) They are all easily transformed into superconductors

Elements with similar properties are in the same column, thus neon, argon, krypton, xenon, and radon all have similar properties. They are all noble, or inert, gases. A noble gas is one that does not react with other elements (think of it as a snooty member of the aristocracy who would not deign to deal with anyone else). The reason the noble gases are stable is that all of their shells are full.

10. **The name for the discrete unit with which energy is added to or taken away from an electron at the molecular level is**

(A) A joule
(B) A quantum
(C) A calorie
(D) Fusion

At the molecular level, when an atom is excited, its electrons move farther away from the nucleus. The energy that excites the atom must come in discrete steps; that is, a certain amount of energy is necessary to change the state of an atom. (An increase in energy pushes electrons to a shell that is farther away.) If even a tiny bit less energy is supplied, there is no change in the position of the electron. The amount of energy needed to change the state of an electron is called a **quantum**.

Elements give off energy in the same way, and this leads to the distinct spectrum of different elements. Armed with this information, you can determine the elements that make up something that is very far away, like a star or Mars.

Three Mile Island nuclear power plant was the site of a major nuclear accident in 1979.

11. **What does it mean to say that an element has a half-life of 5000 years?**

(A) The element is a substance that will last approximately 2500 years.

(B) Half of a given amount of the element is expected to decay in 5000 years.

(C) For the first half of the element's life, it will exist as a radioactive isotope.

(D) In 5000 years, the element will completely transform into another element.

The warning symbol placed on radioactive material

Certain forms of many elements are **radioactive.** An element's nucleus is made up of protons and neutrons. The protons exist in a fixed number for each element, but if an element has too many or too few neutrons, it gets uncomfortable and begins to decay. ^{235}U is an example of a radioactive isotope of uranium. ^{235}U decays and forms into two smaller elements, and in the process, it releases huge amounts of energy. In fact, using one pound of ^{235}U in this manner can produce as much energy as burning 2.5 million pounds of coal. This process is called fission, and was used in the atomic bomb (p. 292)

Actor Lou Ferrigno portrays the Incredible Hulk, a gamma ray casualty.

A **half-life** is the amount of time it takes for half of a given amount of an element to decay. The reason that scientists talk in terms of half-lives is that radioactive decay is a random event, and it is impossible to determine exactly when a particular particle will decay.

The emissions from radioactive material consist of different particles. There are alpha particles, which are positive electrons, beta particles, which are negative, and gamma radiation, which has a high frequency. On TV and in the comics gamma radiation transformed Dr. Bruce Banner into the Incredible Hulk. (It's just fictional though; gamma rays don't really turn people into green body builders). Radiation exists in nature, so even without a man-made event, there is a certain amount of background radiation that can always be detected.

Silkwood (1983), starring Meryl Streep, Cher, and Kurt Russell. True and scary story of Karen Silkwood, a worker in a nuclear parts plant who was contaminated by radiation due to lax safety procedures. She tried to produce evidence of wrongdoing and died in a mysterious car crash.

12. **What does the c stand for in E=mc^2?**

   (A) The energy from a carbon atom
   (B) Celsius
   (C) The speed of light
   (D) A constant derived from the explosion of 1 kilogram of TNT

One of **Albert Einstein**'s (1879-1955) many achievements was the conception of the formula **E=mc^2**. E stands for energy, m for mass, and c stands for the speed of light (see light years p. 271). This formula implies that a small amount of matter has a huge amount of energy because c, the speed of light, is such a large number (186,000 miles a second).

The theory was brought to reality in the **atomic bomb** (Hiroshima pp. 202-203). The A-bomb creates a huge amount of energy by splitting atoms (a process called **fission**). That this much energy was in a tiny amount of matter was foretold by Einstein's theory. The A-bomb works by creating a chain reaction in which certain atoms split apart, releasing particles that split other atoms which, in turn, split, releasing more particles until . . .

BOOM!!!

Usually a certain **critical mass** is necessary to create such an explosion. A critical mass is the minimum amount of material necessary to sustain a **chain reaction.**

13. **Which of the following substances is used in the H-Bomb?**

    (A) Helium
    (B) Gamma rays
    (C) Hydrogen
    (D) Radon

An **H-bomb** fuses hydrogen atoms together to make another substance in a process called, obviously enough, **fusion.** It requires an incredible amount of activation energy (p. 293, below) to explode an H-bomb. Therefore, a bomb engineer must use an old-fashioned fission explosion to cause the primary explosion, which then releases huge amounts of energy.

14. What is a catalyst?

(A) A disease of the eye that results in poor vision
(B) A substance that helps increase the rate of a molecular reaction
(C) The chemical property of a hydrogen atom
(D) The means by which substances enter a phase change

When two or more substances react chemically and turn into another substance, the resulting substance can have totally different properties than its component parts. Energy can be given off or used up when a chemical change takes place, but in either case a certain amount of **activation energy** is needed. The activation energy is the amount of energy needed to begin a reaction and a catalyst reduces this amount. We run into catalysts every day. For example, the vitamins that everyone tells us to take are simply catalysts that help certain reactions happen in the body.

15. Heisenberg's Principle of Uncertainty states that

(A) some elements will never be discovered.
(B) a scientist can never be sure of the results of an experiment.
(C) it is impossible to determine both the position and the direction of movement of an electron.
(D) a positron is unlike an electron in a scientifically uncertain way.

Heisenberg's (1901-76) **Uncertainty Principle** states that we can never know both the position and the direction in which an electron moves. No matter what scientific instruments are developed, no matter how much more advanced our technology becomes, there are some things that we just won't be able to figure out.

16. When does a substance have more energy?

(A) When it is warm
(B) When it is cold

Science & Technology

Energy is defined as the ability to do work. The more energy available, the more work that can be completed. The temperature of a substance is a measure of its energy, and the hotter the substance, the greater its energy. Energy is divided into a number of different forms: kinetic energy (which is energy of movement), light energy, electrical energy, chemical energy, heat energy, potential energy (p. 299), mechanical energy, and atomic or nuclear energy (p. 292).

No matter what happens in a reaction, there is the same amount of energy at the end as there was at the beginning. Energy is neither created nor destroyed, but transformed or converted into other types of energy. When you slam on the brakes in your car when a cop pulls you over for speeding, the kinetic energy of your car—the energy derived from the movement of the car—does not disappear. It is converted into heat energy, which is dissipated through the brake shoes.

Just as H_2O exists as ice, water, or steam, other substances also exist in three phases depending on the amount of heat energy within the substance. Almost every substance can exist as a solid, a liquid, and a gas.

17. Entropy is

    (A) a measure of the disorder present within a system
    (B) the gradual weakening of a muscle caused by disuse
    (C) a measure of the energy present during radioactive decay
    (D) a measure of the complexity of proteins

Entropy is the measure of disorder within a system. There is a certain amount of randomness within anything, and entropy is what is used to describe it. For example, a solid has less entropy, less randomness, than a gas in which all the molecules are careening around and bumping into each other.

There is a law in physics that states that everything tends to move toward entropy. In other words, over the course of time, things will become more chaotic.

A good way to understand the concept of entropy is to assume that you and your room are a substance. Without effort, your room decays to a state of random disorder. It takes effort to keep it organized. Matter works the same way. Given its druthers, it would rather just spread out and hang out doing nothing but bouncing off the walls, but given time and energy and some luck, it forms itself into compounds and surfaces and life forms.

The theory of quantum mechanics has had a big influence outside of the sciences. Here is a theory that tells us that some things are not knowable. Science is admitting a certain amount of randomness in the world, and this randomness allows for some unusual possibilities. **Albert Einstein (pp. 291-292)**, a smart customer if there ever was one, was not fond of the theory of quantum mechanics. In response to the Principle of Uncertainty, Einstein remarked that "God doesn't play dice," meaning that God would not base his universe on a theory without any certainty.

Mindwalk (1991), starring Liv Ullman, Sam Waterston, and John Heard. A poet, a physicist, and a politician have a sometimes fascinating, sometimes snooty discussion about the earth, atoms, ecology and the nature of time. There's a lot of interesting stuff, though, if you don't mind fast forwarding from time to time.

18. **What happens to the temperature of boiling water as more heat is added?**

    (A) The temperature increases.
    (B) The temperature stays the same.
    (C) The temperature decreases.
    (D) It cannot be determined.

When a substance changes phase from a liquid to a gas, the added heat energy is used to convert it into a gas and has no effect on the temperature. This temperature is called the **boiling point** and the **condensation point**. When water is at the boiling point and heat is added, the temperature of the water doesn't change; the water is converted to steam.

The conversion to steam leaves a bunch of contaminants behind; this is how **distilled** water is made. Water is boiled and the resulting steam is collected in another container where it is cooled and condensed. This process removes many impurities from the water.

19. **Which takes longer to boil, a pot of cold water or a pot of lukewarm water? (Assume that all other experimental variables are the same.)**

    (A) The cold water
    (B) The lukewarm water
    (C) It cannot be determined.
    (D) They both boil at the same time.

You may have heard somewhere that cold tap water will boil faster than hot tap water. Well, you heard wrong. The warm water already possesses more energy than the cold water, and it needs less heat to reach the boiling point.

Two units of energy are used to measure heat: the **BTU** (British Thermal Unit) and the **calorie**. A BTU increases one pound of water by one degree Fahrenheit. A calorie increases a kilogram of water by one degree Celsius.

20. **Does a watched pot ever boil?**

No. Never. Try it.

The coldest spot in Antarctica is still 200°F warmer than absolute zero.

21.   **What is a mole in chemistry?**

(A)   The number of molecules of a gas necessary to take up exactly 22.4 liters of space at standard pressure and temperature

(B)   The number of years it takes for a radioactive particle to decay

(C)   The rate of a chemical reaction

(D)   The gradual warming of the atmosphere as caused by an increase in released carbon dioxide

Things work out in strange ways in the world of science. Certain numbers keep popping up. A **mole** is 6×10^{23}, (That's right, six followed by twenty-three zeros) and it describes the number of atoms within a certain weight of a gas. Any gas has exactly one mole of atoms in 22.4 liters of space (assuming standard atmospheric pressure).

22.   **Absolute zero is**

(A)   the number of degrees in a straight line

(B)   the lowest point above sea level

(C)   the temperature at which water freezes

(D)   the temperature at which all molecular motion ceases

As objects cool, the motion of their molecules decreases and when it gets really cold, the motion actually ceases altogether. **Absolute zero** is –273° C, and it is so cold that at this temperature, everything would freeze. It is impossible to reach absolute zero, so you will never get the pleasure of experiencing it.

23. Which of the following substances is a base?
    (A) Sulfuric acid
    (B) Ammonia
    (C) Vinegar
    (D) RNA

A solution can either be **acidic** or **basic.** An acidic solution produces positive ions while a basic one produces negative ions. An **ion** is an atom that is either missing an extra electron or in possession of an extra electron.

Vinegar is a common acid and soap and lye are common bases. Acids are usually sour (citric acid is what makes a lemon sour) and strong acids can even dissolve metal. Bases like ammonia hydroxide are used for cleaning. Ammonium, as it is commonly called, is a poisonous gas that dissolves in water and forms a basic solution.

The pH scale is used to measure whether something is acidic or basic. Water's pH is 7 and is therefore a neutral solution because its pH falls dead center on the scale. A solution with a lower pH (1-6) is acidic and one with a higher pH (8-12) is basic. Sometimes bases are called alkaline.

ANSWERS

1. D 2. A 3. A 4. C 5. B 6. D 7. A 8. D 9. C 10. B
11. B 12. C 13 C 14. B 15. C 16. A 17. A 18. B 19. A 21. A
22. D 23. B

Physics
Physical Motion

1. If you walked 5 mph north while traveling in a train traveling 60 mph south, how fast would you be going relative to the ground?

(A) 55
(B) 60
(C) 62.342
(D) 65

Motion is relative. When we say that something is moving at a certain speed, we usually mean that it is moving at that speed relative to the earth's surface. But every movement can be measured as relative to something else. A person standing still on the earth's equator is really moving about 1,000 mph relative to the center of the earth. In the question above, your speed relative to the ground is fifty-five mph. If somebody standing on the ground could see you walking, it would appear to her that you were traveling fifty-five mph. Another place where relative speed is important is on an escalator. Say you are walking up the down escalator at such a rate that you are neither moving up nor down relative to the ground. If you look at your feet, it appears that you are moving, but if you look at the top of the escalator, it appears that you are not moving at all.

You might wonder what practical purpose knowing relative speeds might serve, so we are going to set up a situation that is familiar to many of you. Let's say that you are driving a little too fast on the highway and a traffic cop pulls you over. Instead of meekly paying the ticket, suppose you engage the cop in a discussion of relativity. You might say something like, "It may have appeared to you that I was going ninety-five mph, but really, I was looking at the other cars, and compared to them, I was only doing forty." The cop will look a bit puzzled, so you might try again: "Ma'am, I don't see how you can give me a ticket . . . the sign says 'speed limit fifty-five mph.' I was only going forty relative to the other cars." (By the way, this is not Einstein's theory of relativity (pp. 304-305).)

2. **What is potential energy?**
   (A) The energy used to set off a chain reaction in a nuclear power plant
   (B) Energy not yet found, such as fossil fuels that are still in the ground
   (C) An object's energy of motion
   (D) Energy possessed by an object due to its position or condition

An object is said to have potential energy when its position or condition could lead to a release of energy. For example, if you lift a 100-pound weight from the ground to a table, you have increased its potential energy. If the weight were to fall, it would release that energy.

3. **What happens to the speed of a car when it goes around an unbalanced curve (assume that the driver keeps the same pressure on the gas pedal; i.e. the energy given to the car is unchanged)?**
   (A) It stays the same.
   (B) It speeds up.
   (C) It slows down.
   (D) It crashes into the big ol' oak tree in front of the Ryscheks' house.

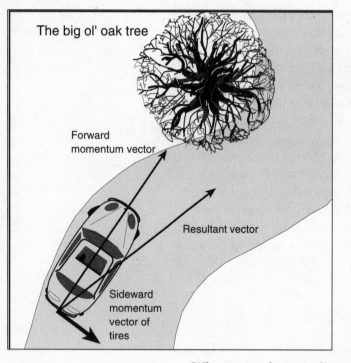

The big ol' oak tree

Forward momentum vector

Resultant vector

Sideward momentum vector of tires

When a car (or any object for that matter) turns, some energy that was being used to go forward must be used to go sideways. This means that assuming no extra energy is added, a car going around a curve will slow down. So if you don't accelerate around a curve, you will slow down. (This might be a good thing. You don't want to run into that big ol' oak tree in front of the Ryscheks' house.) And that sideways energy can be felt as you go around the curve. This force is called **centrifugal force**.

Say you attached a string to a ball and started whirling it around in a circle. The force that seems to be pulling the ball away from the center of the circle (you) is called centrifugal. The tension of the string, which is the force moving inwards, towards the center of the circle, is called **centripetal force**.

When a car changes direction or changes velocity, it is said to be accelerating. Acceleration is defined as the change of speed divided by the time, so if you were to drive a car from 0 to 60 mph in ten seconds, the acceleration would be (60/10) miles per hour per second.

4. **Why is it harder to stop a 2-ton truck moving 5 miles an hour than it is to stop a 180-pound bicyclist moving 5 miles an hour?**

    (A) Inertia
    (B) Momentum
    (C) Gravity
    (D) Volume

Because the truck weighs more than the bicycle, it has more **momentum** and is more difficult to stop. The amount of force needed to stop a moving truck is much greater than that needed to stop a bicycle.

Every action produces a reaction, so if the bicyclist drove headfirst into the truck, the truck would slow down a little. (Don't try this at home.)

5. If a 2-pound ball and a 20-pound ball of the same size
   are both dropped from the same height at the same
   time, which will land first? (Assume no air resistance.)

   (A) The 2-pound ball
   (B) The 20-pound ball
   (C) They will both land at the same time.
   (D) It cannot be determined from the information given.

Assuming that we are dropping the balls on Earth, the balls will land simultaneously. Although the mass of an object is part of the formula for determining the gravitational pull on an object, the weight of the earth is so great, that the difference between the 20-pound ball and the 2-pound ball is insignificant. Because the earth is so much heavier than the two balls, their weight will have only a minuscule effect on the force of gravity. This may seem to defy common sense; in most of our experiences, a heavy object falls faster than a light object. Let's say you dropped a rock and a feather. Obviously, the feather will land second. But this is because the air slows it down. If you dropped the two objects in a **vacuum**, an area without gas, you would find that they dropped at the same rate.

Near the surface of the earth, the rate at which objects accelerate due to gravity is about 9.8 meters per second (or 32 feet per second). That means that in every second of time, an object will speed up approximately 9.8 meters per second. In theory, an object's speed would continue to increase until it hit the ground, but an object's speed is usually limited by air resistance. The top speed achievable by an object is called its **terminal velocity**. A human being's terminal velocity is approximately 185 miles an hour. That is, no matter how high off the ground a person is when he falls, he will hit the ground going no faster than 185 miles an hour. (This is assuming that the person is diving in a head-down free-falling position. The speed would be much slower if the person spread his or her arms and tried to slow down.)

6. Why do objects fall slower on the moon than on the earth?

   (A) The moon lacks oxygen
   (B) The moon is smaller in diameter than the earth
   (C) The moon has less mass than the earth
   (D) The moon spins much slower around its axis than the
        earth

SCIENCE & TECHNOLOGY

IT SHOULD HAVE BEEN CATASTROPHIC

Veterinarians in New York City discovered an interesting phenomenon when they noticed patterns in the injuries sustained by cats who fell from tall buildings. They found that cats who fell from five to nine stories were the most likely to be seriously injured or killed. The cats who fell fewer stories, as you might imagine, were not as likely to be seriously injured because they were not traveling as fast as those that fell from greater heights. But why would the cats who fell from farther up be more likely to survive?

It turns out that a cat reaches a terminal velocity of about sixty miles an hour after falling five stories. It doesn't matter from how high the cat falls; its velocity will never reach more than sixty miles an hour. When the cat falls from a height greater than nine stories, it has enough extra time that it relaxes somewhat and is injured less seriously. There are reports of cats surviving falls from over forty stories. Any wonder they supposedly have nine lives?

Gravity is a force of attraction between two objects. The effect of gravity is determined by the mass and position of the two objects. Because the moon has less mass than the earth, its gravitational pull on smaller objects is much less than that of the earth. Conversely, if we were on Jupiter or some other planet bigger than Earth, the gravitational force would be much greater.

7. **Who discovered the Law of Universal Gravitation?**
   (A) Galileo Galilei
   (B) Sir Isaac Newton
   (C) Charles Darwin
   (D) Albert Einstein

That things fall is a well-known fact and has been for generations. Even primitive man, without the benefit of a written language, was aware that when he or she dropped something, it fell. And so for thousands of years, man has tried to find ways to explain this amazing force. Aristotle (p. 268) came up with a theory which lasted for over 1,000 years that stated that the four elements—earth, water, air, and fire—tend toward each other. So the more earth in an element, the more quickly it moves to earth. He was wrong, but so respected that people did not try to disprove his theories until **Galileo Galilei** started studying dropped objects. He found that gravity was about acceleration and not velocity. But the crowning achievement in the attempts to understand gravity was the **Law of Universal Gravitation**, discovered by Sir Isaac Newton, who figured out that gravity was the force that attracted the moon, the earth, and the apples in the trees. (The falling of an apple supposedly inspired his theory.) A man of immense talents, Newton also invented calculus.

NEWTON'S LAWS OF MOTION

1. *A body at rest tends to stay at rest, unless acted upon by a force. A body in motion tends to stay in motion.*
2. *The force applied to a body causes a momentum in the body that is proportional to the force.*
3. *For every action, there is an equal and opposite reaction.*

ANSWERS

1. A   2. D   3. C   4. B   5. C   6. C   7. B

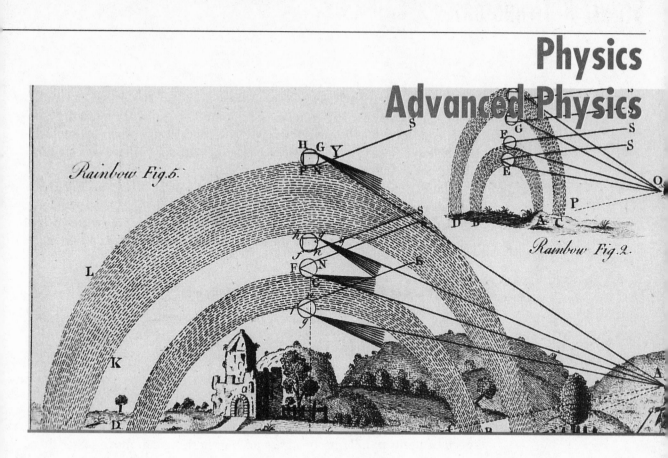

Rainbow Fig. 5.

Rainbow Fig. 2.

1. **What is a black hole?**

    (A) A collapsed star with a gravitational field so strong that not even light can escape it

    (B) The difference between the money spent by the United States government and the money collected from taxes

    (C) The emptiness that exists between different types of matter in space

    (D) The shadow cast by one star when its light is blocked by another

Sometimes the gravity produced by an object becomes so great that not even light can escape. When this happens, the object is usually referred to as a **black hole**. Because the gravity in a black hole is strong enough to suck in light, nothing can escape. Black holes are like a one-way street: Everything can go in, but nothing ever comes out.

Any star can become a black hole if its radius is compressed enough.

If our sun were compressed to a radius of about two miles, it would become a black hole. This will never happen. The sun will eventually collapse and become a white dwarf. But don't worry too much about such things. We have a good 5 billion years before the sun will be making any significant changes.

Stars can also change into other forms. If the mass of a star is not great enough to create a black hole, it can still collapse into what is known as a **white dwarf** (as we mentioned), which is a much smaller star with a huge amount of mass, or a **neutron star**, a super-dense star formed when really massive stars explode.

2. **Based on Einstein's Special Theory of Relativity it is possible to conclude that**

   (A) the maximum velocity attainable is that of light
   (B) some things weigh more than others
   (C) f = ma
   (D) it is impossible to determine the exact location of an electron

Albert Einstein's Special Theory of Relativity postulates that the speed of light (p. 271) is constant and that nothing can move faster than the speed of light. Once you accept this fact, some rather strange conclusions are possible. Suppose you are standing on Earth shining a light at a departing rocket screaming into space. The light moves away from you at 186,000 miles per second, but at what speed does it overtake the rocket? Again, the answer is 186,000 miles per second. Why is this true? The rocket is moving slower in *time*. Its seconds are longer relative to beam of light than are yours.

As things approach the speed of light, weird things start to happen. We see everything through light, so when an object moves at nearly the speed of light, our perception of the object changes. It appears taller and thinner, and its color changes.

Many of Einstein's theories have been tested and proved correct. One method of testing the Theory of Relativity is to place an atomic clock on the equator and another one near the North Pole. An atomic clock is incredibly accurate and is able to measure even the most minute difference in time. The clock at the equator is moving a great deal faster than the clock at the North Pole, so Einstein's theory would lead us to expect that the clock moving faster would show time moving slower. In fact, a clock moving around the equator ticks away a little slower than one on the North Pole.

Albert Einstein in a playful mood on his birthday

3. What is the name of the effect that is produced when the sound of a car horn seems to change pitch as the car passes by?
   (A) The pitch-change effect
   (B) The Doppler effect
   (C) The Octavia effect
   (D) The Optimal effect

FREQUENCY AND MUSIC

You can easily see the effects of frequency on pitch with stringed instruments. On a guitar (or violin, bass or whatever) the strings that are wound tightest have the highest pitch. That's because the tighter something is pulled, the faster it will vibrate when plucked. The faster it vibrates, the closer together the sound waves; the closer together the sound waves, the higher the pitch. You might not be able to see this on a guitar, so try this: Get a big rubber band, stretch it between your fingers and have someone pluck it. Then stretch it tighter and pluck it again. Notice that as you pull tighter, the rubber band vibrates faster and gives off a higher "twang."

Sound is caused by vibrations that spread away from its source. The faster the vibration, the higher the pitch. The way that sound emanates from a source resembles the waves on a puddle, and so the vibrations are usually referred to as **sound waves**. When the source of a sound wave is coming toward you, it sounds as if it has a higher pitch than if it were moving away from you. This is because the waves of sound hit you faster, and appear to you to be closer together. When the object moves away from you, the sound waves seem farther apart, and it appears that their frequency has decreased. This makes the sound seem to have a lower pitch. This whole phenomenon is called the **Doppler effect**.

Light is also a wave, so by measuring the change in wavelength in stars, it is possible to determine whether they are moving away from us or toward us.

4. Place the following in order of frequency from fastest to slowest:

   I. Infrared Radiation
   II. Visible Light
   III. X-rays
   IV. Ultraviolet radiation

   (A) I, II, III, IV
   (B) IV, I, II, III
   (C) I, II, IV, III
   (D) III, II, I, IV

Waves are measured by the frequency in which their vibrations are repeated. Sound waves vibrate fairly slowly while **x-rays** vibrate quickly. The faster the frequency of vibration, the shorter the wavelength of the vibration. X-rays have a short wavelength and can thus go through skin and other objects, while visible light's wavelength is fairly long and bounces off of skin. The chart below shows the various wavelengths and frequencies of different radiation.

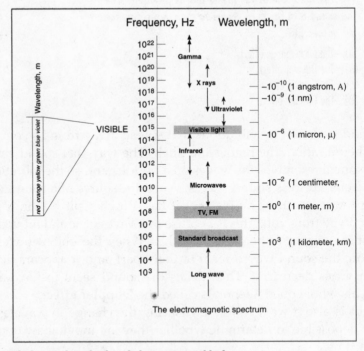

The electromagnetic spectrum

5. Which wavelength of sunlight is responsible for producing sunburn?

(A) Red light
(B) Infrared light
(C) Ultraviolet light
(D) X-rays

Ultraviolet light is the wavelength of light that causes sunburn. It is usually screened out by the protective layer of ozone in the upper atmosphere, but this layer has been disappearing in part because of the use of chlorofluorocarbons (p. 279) (CFC for short), which are chemicals used in aerosols and in refrigerators and air conditioners. **Infrared** is the wavelength of heat energy.

Different materials reflect or absorb different frequencies of radiation at different rates. For example, our atmosphere allows for the penetration of visible light from the sun, but doesn't allow for heat to escape into space. This is one of the reasons that life can survive on the earth.

6. **Which of the following is the best conductor of electricity?**

   (A) Wood
   (B) Aluminum
   (C) Glass
   (D) Plastic

Aluminum is the best of the above substances for conducting electricity. **Electricity** is basically the movement of free electrons through a medium. Certain media allow this type of movement. The most common conductors are metals. That's why they're used in electrical wire. The human body is also a pretty good conductor of electricity. This is why you experience electrical shocks when your body comes in contact with an electric current—a charge is trying to move through your body to the ground.

7. **The electricity in your area costs 14¢ per kilowatt-hour. How much does it cost to keep two 100-watt lights on for ten hours?**

   (A) 7¢
   (B) 14¢
   (C) 21¢
   (D) 28¢

Electricity is measured in **watts**. A kilowatt-hour is the equivalent of using 1,000 watts for one hour, and electric companies use this unit of measure to charge us for electricity. To figure out how much using an appliance or a light bulb costs, figure out how long it is on and how many watts it uses. Then set up an equation to determine how much you have to pay: $2(100) \times 10 = 2{,}000$ watt-hours = 2 kilowatt hours, or 28¢. This may not seem like a lot of money, but over a month, it would be $8.40. And over a year, it would be a little more than a hundred dollars.

LIGHTBULB SCIENCE

When electricity passes through the bulb's tungsten filament, it glows white hot, stimulating an inert mixture of nitrogen and argon gas held within the bulb, which gives off a nice amount of visible light.

ANSWERS

1. A   2. A   3. B   4. D   5. C   6. B   7. D

Biology
Classification

1. **What is the essential difference between plants and animals?**

   (A)   Plants are green; animals are not.
   (B)   Plants are not alive; animals are.
   (C)   Plants make their energy directly from sunlight; animals do not.
   (D)   Plants don't move by themselves; animals do.

2. **The process by which plants make energy is called**

   (A)   Digestion
   (B)   Photosynthesis
   (C)   Reproduction
   (D)   Activation

Almost all living creatures with which we are familiar can be divided into the **animal kingdom** and the **plant kingdom**. The plant kingdom is composed of beings that generate their energy by synthesizing energy from the sun. This process is called **photosynthesis** and is one of the fundamental processes by which life is made possible.

 Many people have repeated the oft-quoted and only half-correct statement that a tomato is not a vegetable, but actually a fruit. It turns out, as with most things, that these people are only half right—a tomato is a fruit and a vegetable. Vegetables are any edible herbaceous plant, or part of such a plant. Fruits are the seed and the stuff surrounding the seed of a plant. Thus, while a tomato is a fruit, so are peas, string beans, and corn.

3. **Which of the following organisms is neither a plant nor an animal?**

   (A) Bacteria
   (B) Venus fly traps
   (C) Slugs
   (D) Cockroaches

Some creatures are neither plant nor animal. These can be unicellular organisms such as bacteria and blue-green algae, or multi-cellular like most fungi. A mushroom is not a plant, even though you can find it in the produce section in your supermarket.

SCIENCE & TECHNOLOGY

4. **Which of the following is NOT a defining characteristic of a mammal?**

   (A) Hair
   (B) Giving birth to live young
   (C) Eating both plants and animals
   (D) Females having milk-producing glands

5. **Which of the following creatures is NOT a mammal?**

   (A) Blue whale
   (B) Bat
   (C) Shark
   (D) Human

WHAT'S YOUR PHYLUM?

*Living creatures are classified in terms of certain characteristics. All organisms have a **kingdom**, a **phylum**, a **class**, an **order**, a **family**, a **genus**, and a **species**. For example, a dog is in the animal kingdom of the Chordata phylum, the Mammalian class, the Carnivore order, the Canidae family, the Canis genus, and the canis familiaris species. Humans are of the species **homo sapien** and like the dog are in the Mammalian class. Scientists use this system of classification to differentiate species and denote the relationships among organisms. A scientist can look at the full name of an unfamiliar plant or animal and know some of its characteristics just from the name.*

Humans are of the Mammalian class. This means we share certain characteristics with other mammals—we have hair, give birth to our offspring live rather than in eggs, and our females produce milk. Other mammals are cows, horses, mice, rats, dogs, cats, whales, dolphins, and even bats.

6. **All organisms that mate with each other and produce viable offspring can be classified as**

   (A) a species
   (B) a class
   (C) a genus
   (D) an animal

The classification system designed by scientists defines a **species** as a group of organisms that can mate with one another to produce offspring that can then go on and mate again. For example, dogs and cats are different species. They can try to mate, but they can't produce offspring.

When horse and donkeys mate, a mule is born, but it is sterile and can't reproduce. That's because horses and donkeys are not part of the same species.

The classification of some animals becomes somewhat problematic and the definition of species is not always hard and fast. For example, while Chihuahuas and Great Danes are both dogs and belong to the same species, they are members of divergent subspecies genetically distinct enough so that one could not produce offspring with the other, even through artificial insemination.

7. In which of the following locations might a scientist find the most diversity of species?

    (A) A northern forest
    (B) A suburban backyard
    (C) A tropical rain forest
    (D) A tidal basin

The diversity among living things is truly astounding. There are animals that eat plants, plants that eat animals, animals that are so specialized that they can only survive in a twenty-by-twenty-foot area, and others, like man and certain insects, that can survive almost anywhere.

The greatest degree of **biodiversity** can be found in the tropical rain forests, where thousands of species of plants and animals live side by side. Scientists fear that by destroying the rain forests (p. 279), we will severely reduce the earth's biodiversity. Study of all these different animals and plants could lead to new knowledge as well as some practical applications. We might find better ways to cure diseases as well as better ways to grow food.

 Four percent of the rain forest disappearing a year may sound small, but it translates into 35.2 million acres a year. That means that sixty-seven acres are being wiped out each minute--a football field a second. It is estimated that this incredible mass destruction also obliterates 17,000 species of plants and animals per year. That means forty-eight species are made extinct every day—two every hour. If you know of the "Butterfly Effect" (p. 278) you realize the potential danger of the absence of even one species from the earth's global ecosystem.

8. An ecosystem is

    (A) the best way to recycle aluminum and other metals
    (B) an interdependent group of organisms and their environment
    (C) a method for collecting insects and other biota
    (D) an environmentally correct way of producing fossil fuels

Much of nature is interdependent. No organism could survive without the aid of other organisms. Some flowers need a bee's help to reproduce. The minerals provided by the waste products of certain animals, most notably the earthworm, help plants grow. Animals rely on the food created by plants to survive. Each incredibly complex web of nature, with organisms interacting with each other and their environment, is called an **ecosystem**.

9. Which is considered higher up on the food chain?

    (A) Chicken
    (B) Human

A food chain is the succession of organisms through which energy passes. Grain, chickens, and

Don't be chicken.

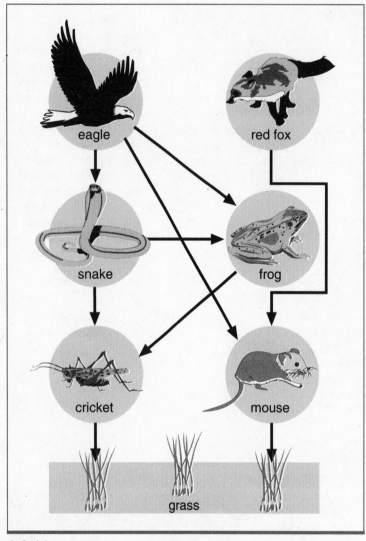

The food chain

humans are ascending links on that chain. Chickens eat grain, then humans eat chickens. Usually there is a loss of energy as you go up a food chain. For example, while one pound of meat contains about twice the energy content of one pound of grain, it takes approximately twenty pounds of grain to feed the cow to create that one pound of meat.

10. **An organism that inhabits another organism and depends on the host organism for nutrition and metabolic need is called**

    (A) A predator
    (B) A scavenger
    (C) A parasite
    (D) An omnivore

The interaction between organisms in an ecosystem can be complex. There is the predator-prey relationship in which one organism depends on eating another organism for survival. There are mutually beneficial relationships, called **symbiosis**, in which two species are dependent on each other. (Bees use a flower's pollen to create food and in so doing fertilize the flowers.) There are relationships in which a **parasite** lives off of a host organism. A particularly gruesome example is the tapeworm. These creatures live in the small intestine (p. 333) and can grow as long as thirty-three feet. They survive by eating the partially digested food that passes through a body. A bunch of creatures called **scavengers** and **decomposers** survive by eating dead plants and animals.

11. Without any influence from humans, an ecosystem would most likely be

   (A) stable, with little change over time
   (B) changeable, with some species dying out and being replaced by others
   (C) a desert, with the area eventually unable to support life
   (D) full of plants that are impossible to classify

Even without the intervention of humans, ecosystems would be constantly changing. As climate changes or migration from different areas influence the balance of an ecosystem, new creatures prosper while others might have trouble. Most ecosystems are in a constant state of flux.

NOT SUCH A GOOD HOUSE PLANT

Some flowers imitate the scent of rotten meat in order to attract flies to help in pollination.

ANSWERS

1. C   2. B   3. A   4. C   5. C   6. A
7. C   8. B   9. B   10. C   11. B

Biology
Evolution

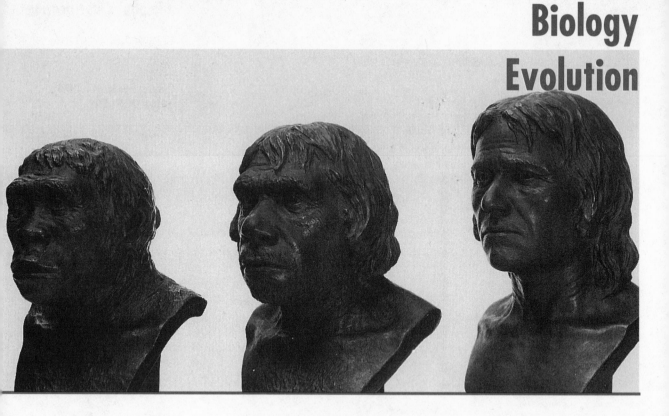

1. **The process by which different characteristics are passed from a parent to its offspring is called**

    (A) Distillation
    (B) Heredity
    (C) Love
    (D) Descending

The process by which a parent passes on characteristics to its offspring is called **heredity**. Although a parent's offspring will have many of the parent's traits, there will be some differences as well. Through successive generations, these differences can increase. This is how we breed animals and plants. After a time, these differences can increase to the point where different descendants of an organism cannot mate and are not of the same species.

2. **The person who discovered genetics is**
   (A) Gregor Mendel
   (B) Isaac Asimov
   (C) Antoine Laurent Lavoisier
   (D) Thomas Robert Malthus

The son of farmers, **Gregor Mendel** (1822-1884) developed the theory of the gene, which has come a long way toward explaining how different traits are passed on from generation to generation. Through experiments with pea plants, Mendel discovered that traits were passed on in a systematic fashion.

Austrian monk and scientist, Gregor Mendel

3. **If a pea plant with the homogeneous dominant trait of a smooth pea pod mates with one with the recessive trait of a wrinkled pea pod, what type of pea pod will the offspring have?**
   (A) Wrinkled
   (B) Partly Wrinkled
   (C) Smooth

Before Mendel's day, most naturalists agreed that if two different pea plants were mated, the resulting pea plant would have traits somewhere between the two original plants. They believed that if a plant with wrinkled pea pods was mated with one with smooth pea pods, the resulting plant would have pea pods that were somewhere between wrinkled and smooth.

Mendel proved them wrong. Through a series of carefully planned experiments, he showed that an offspring's traits are not a mixture of the parents' traits. When two plants, one with wrinkled pods and one with smooth pods, mated, the resulting plants had either smooth pods or wrinkled pods. There were no plants with pods that were slightly wrinkled. He found the same thing to be true for height. If a very tall plant were mixed with a short plant, no medium height plants resulted. For all characteristics that he tested, the same result occurred. (If this all seems to fly in the face of conventional wisdom, think about what happens when males and females reproduce.

Heredity: The tall and short of it

We don't end up with an animal that is both male and female.)

Mendel decided that certain traits were **dominant** and others **recessive**. He found that when two parent plants each had different characteristics, all of the offspring would end up with the dominant trait. But if the offspring mated, the resulting plants would be a mixture with $3/4$ having the dominant trait and $1/4$ having the recessive.

Some genetic traits are not so simple. For example eyecolor in humans is handled by a bunch of genes, and so determining how each parent affects the color of a baby's eyes is difficult.

4. **Which type of reproduction produces the most variation among offspring?**

   (A) Asexual
   (B) Sexual

Mendel studied pea plants that reproduce sexually. This means that the male and female of the species each contributed genes to form an offspring. If an organism reproduces asexually, the offspring keeps the parent's entire DNA and therefore all of its characteristics. Because **sexual reproduction** takes genes from both the mother and the father, it allows for a greater variety of offspring within one species. The explosion of species during recent geological time may be partially because of the development of sexual reproduction in animals.

5. **What is the primary function of DNA?**

   (A) To protect individuals from disease
   (B) To help in passing different traits from a parent to its offspring
   (C) To mutate the original function of an organism
   (D) To exchange oxygen for energy

The different traits a parent contributes to its offspring are encoded in genes now known to be segments of the **DNA** (deoxyribonucleic acid) molecule. DNA is an enormous molecule containing the genetic codes that determine how an organism will develop. Because every cell in an

WHAT ABOUT THE DINOSAURS?

Over sixty-five million years ago, dinosaurs ruled the earth. Most of these reptiles were large, but some were very small -- about the size of birds and lizards. Their closest surviving relatives are birds and crocodiles. Since the human species began to evolve only about six million years ago, humans and dinosaurs have never co-existed on the planet (contrary to the plots of some of the movies you may have seen). Though it is not known exactly what killed the dinosaurs, the most accepted theory is that a huge comet smashed into the earth, kicked a lot of dirt into the atmosphere, and caused dramatic shifts in the climate, which killed most of them off. The remains of prehistoric creatures, dinosaurs included, create what are called fossil fuels (p. 275), like petroleum and coal, on which the world is so dependent today.

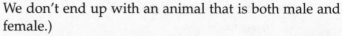

For a long time, scientists knew of the existence of the DNA molecule but not its form. Although they knew the essential ingredients of the molecule, they were unable to view its actual structure. This all changed when the team of James Watson and Francis Crick determined that the DNA molecule is in the form of a **double helix (pp. 320-321)**. Knowing this form gave scientists much insight into how heredity works. And its discovery provided Watson with an excuse to write a very good book that tells something about the way in which scientists work. *The Double Helix* reads like an adventure novel and is a must read for scientists and non-scientists alike.

organism has DNA in it, each cell of every organism contains all the information necessary to develop a copy of the organism. This concept is the foundation of the theory of **cloning**.

But, you might wonder, if all of these cells have the same genetic information, how can they do different things? We all know that muscle cells act differently from skin cells, for example. Scientists are not quite sure, but the prevailing theory is that the environment around the cell determines which parts of the DNA are used to generate the cell's specific function. As an organism develops, more and more complex arrangements of cells become evident.

Double your helix, double your fun: James Watson (left) and Francis Crick (right)

6. **The process by which the information encoded in a gene is changed by some external means is called**

   (A) Changeability
   (B) Variegation
   (C) Mutation
   (D) Depletion

Invasion of the Body Snatchers (1956). A sci-fi movie, twice re-made, revolving around the dastardly cloning of human beings.

Normally, in sexual reproduction, there is some variety. Some of an organism's characteristics may come from one parent, some from the other. Sometimes, however, the DNA may become damaged or be encoded incorrectly. When this happens, a **mutation** occurs (Hiroshima, pp. 202-203). Most mutations are either insignificant or produce life forms that soon die. But every once in a while, a new species is created that is even better able to survive than an older species. This can lead to the process of **evolution**.

7. **The theory of natural selection was developed by**

   (A) Albert Einstein
   (B) Gregor Mendel
   (C) Charles Darwin
   (D) Thomas Mann

All you have to do is look around to be astounded by the variety and complexity of nature's creatures. Even in a suburban backyard, you will see hundreds of different species. How

Mr. Evolution himself, Charles Darwin

SCIENCE & TECHNOLOGY

Inherit the Wind (1960), starring Spencer Tracy. Courtroom drama based on the real Scopes Monkey Trial of 1925 in which a school teacher is prosecuted for teaching Darwin's theory of evolution. Great performances.

did these species develop? What caused them to have the form and function that they have today?

An early theory by **Jean Baptiste Lamarck (1744-1829)** held that evolution works through a process of "**acquired characteristics**." This theory, now known as Lamarckism, suggests that a giraffe developed its long neck when generation after generation stretched their necks to reach the leaves high up in the trees. Gradually, their necks became longer and longer. This theory has not proven viable. Physical traits modified during an organism's lifetime are not passed on to offspring.

Charles Darwin (1809-82) and **Alfred Wallace** (1823-1913) both formulated theories of **evolution** independently. Darwin made his discovery while exploring the **Galapagos Islands** on the **H.M.S. Beagle**. There he discovered among the enormous variety of life on the islands several species of finches all apparently descended from the same birds that arrived on the islands years ago. Because the islands were somewhat isolated, the finches developed different characteristics, and Darwin recognized that the finches most adapted to living in their environment were the ones to survive. From this he decided that evolution provided for the **survival of the fittest**. The most fit offspring were able to reproduce, and they passed on their desirable traits to their young.

Darwin did not publish his discovery until he was forced to by the discoveries of Alfred Wallace, who came up with a similar theory while studying the variety of life in the Amazon River (p. 235) twenty years later. Darwin had some idea as to how the public would react to the theory of evolution and had given instructions that the theory be published after he died, but when he realized that Wallace had a similar theory, they published a joint paper. Ironically, both Darwin and Wallace were influenced by the theories of Thomas Robert Malthus (1766-1834) (p. 181) who believed that the continuing increase in the population of humans would eventually lead to starvation and death.

Thomas Malthus, an early proponent of population control

8. What was the name of the book that explained the theory of evolution?

(A) *The Theory of Evolution*
(B) *The Origin of Species*
(C) *The Strong Will Survive*
(D) *The End of the World as We Know It*

The book that catapulted the theory of evolution into the eyes of the public was *The Origin of Species,* written by Charles Darwin and published in 1859. One of the most influential books ever, *The Origin of Species* established that the natural world was not static, but in constant flux. The theory shocked millions. How could we be related to chimpanzees and fish and bacteria? Many people in the Western world believed in the theory of Creationism (p. 364): God created Man and the world as they are and neither have substantially changed.

Even today, roughly half of all of Americans do not believe in the theory of evolution. (Just about 100 percent of scientists believe in it.) Maybe this is because the theory seems downright counterintuitive. We have an understanding of heredity that implies an offspring will be something like her parent, and yet evolution seems to say that all living things are descendents of the same unicellular creatures. With our limited perspective of time, this doesn't make any sense.

Well it ain't bananas, but I guess it'll do.

Evolution, however, has been going on for four billion years. Four billion years is a lot of time for a descendent to become different from its parent, especially when you consider that we have seen new species created in our own lifetimes.

Some disagreement still exists among biologists as to how evolutionary change actually happens. Some believe in the theory of **gradualism** which states that evolutionary change happens gradually over time. In gradualism, many steps occur in the evolution of a new species. Through natural selection, a change will develop slowly. A giraffe with a neck that is three inches long will be supplanted by one with a neck that is four inches long, and a few tens of thousands of years later, a giraffe with its present enormous neck develops. Other scientists believe in **punctuated equilibria**. This theory holds that a population of an organism will remain in stasis for many thousands of years, and that significant evolutionary changes happen rapidly in response to some external stimuli. A scientist who believes in punctuated equilibria might feel that an occurrence like an ice age (p. 226) created conditions that led to the quick creation of numerous species.

ANSWERS

1. B   2. A   3. C   4. B   5. B   6. C   7. C   8. B

Biology
The Cell

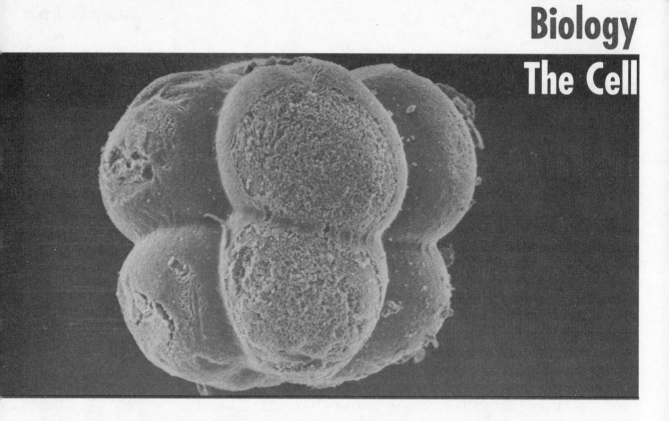

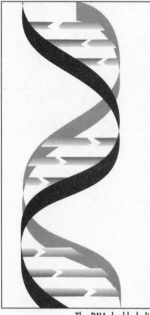

The DNA double helix

1. The unit of structure of all living things is called the

(A) Bacterium
(B) Cell
(C) Building block
(D) Species

Just as all matter is made up of atoms, all living things are made up of **cells**. The cell is the basic structure of all organisms. There is not a huge difference between the cells of a human being and, say, the cells of a mealy bug or a cockroach.

Animal cells and plant cells do have a few fundamental differences, however. Plant cells have a rigid **cell wall**, which allows plant cells to stand up straight, and **chloroplasts**, where photosynthesis takes place.

2. In which of the following organelles
   of a cell is the DNA usually found?

   (A) The mitochondria
   (B) The golgi complex
   (C) The nucleus
   (D) The endoplasmic reticulum

Cells are made up of a variety of **organelles** that take care
of certain functions necessary for the cell to live. A cell has a
nucleus that houses the DNA (pp. 316-317) and **chromosomes**. Chromosomes provide hereditary information, and
direct the cell's biochemical activities.

Outside the nucleus are specialized structures that provide for the rest of the cell's functions, from protein building
to waste disposal to information feedback.

3. Which of the following is a primary
   function of mitochondria?

   (A) Asexual reproduction
   (B) Anaerobic respiration
   (C) Energy production
   (D) RNA replication

Doogie the spastic monkey is surprised to
learn that chromosomes are located in a
cell's nucleus.

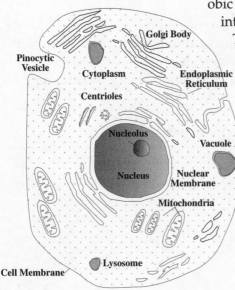

In all **aerobic** animals (an animal is aerobic if it uses oxygen) oxygen is turned
into energy by the **mitochondria**.
These organelles convert oxygen
into **ATP** (adenosine triphosphate), the primary source of
immediate energy in almost all
living things.

Other important organ-
elles are the cytoplasm (the
fluid that holds many of the
organelles of the cell) and the
cell membrane, which separates the outside of the cell
from the inside.

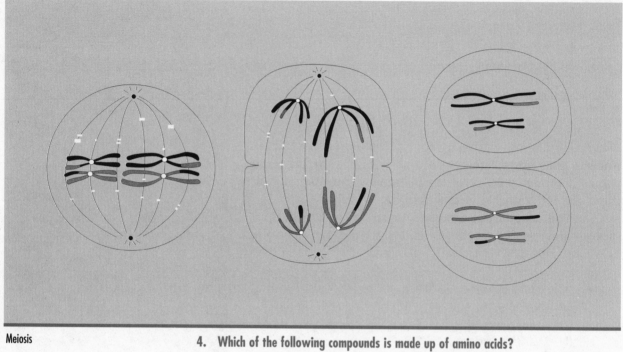

Meiosis

4. **Which of the following compounds is made up of amino acids?**

    (A)   Carbohydrates
    (B)   Lipids
    (C)   Proteins
    (D)   Vinegar

Many of the functions of a cell are carried out by **proteins**. Proteins are compounds made up of big chains of **amino acids**. The order in which the amino acids are connected determines how the molecule acts. Proteins help carry out many different cell functions. They can carry oxygen, respond to stimuli, or become hair and nails.

5. **The process by which a cell splits into two is called**

    (A)   Mitosis
    (B)   Prognosis
    (C)   Ambidextrous
    (D)   Biodiversity

The process of reproduction in complex organisms occurs at a microscopic level when cells divide. Most cells divide in a process called **mitosis** in which all of the chromosomes in the nucleus of a cell are replicated. In mitosis, the cell splits into two identical cells, with each daughter cell containing the same genetic information as the parent. In sexual reproduction, cells divide in a process called **meiosis**. During sexual reproduction a cell splits and creates **gametes**, each of which holds only half of the genetic information of a parent. During **fertilization** two gametes, one from each parent, unite and the full complement of chromosomes is restored.

Humans
Classification

1. **Humans can be classified as**

   (A) Reptiles
   (B) Primates
   (C) Invertebrates
   (D) Canines

Humans are classified just like other animals and plants. We are **Homo sapiens** of the **primate** order. Primates also include chimpanzees and gorillas. Humans began to evolve about five million years ago. Originally, several different types of human-like organisms were around; eventually all but Homo sapiens became extinct.

2. **Are all human beings of the same species?**

   (A) Yes
   (B) No

All of the different races of humans are part of the same species (p. 310). People of different races might have different body proportions or different skin color or more or less body hair, but any two people of opposite sexes from anywhere in the world can produce a child.

Certain characteristics separate humans from any other species. Humans are the smartest of all known creatures and the only species that can communicate complex thoughts and ideas. Other creatures can have relatively complex social organizations, but only in fixed patterns. Human beings are adept at adapting to many circumstances.

3. **Which of the following physical characteristics allows humans to use and make tools?**
   (A) Having an opposable thumb
   (B) Standing on two feet
   (C) The ability to distinguish between dangerous and helpful organisms
   (D) The ability to lift heavy objects

One of the distinguishing characteristics of the human species is our ability to use our hands. Because of the way our thumbs are positioned on our hands we can grasp objects that other animals cannot. Other primates share this characteristic **opposable thumb,** but humans, in combination with their intellect, have used it to make all kinds of tools and weapons (Weapons Technology Timeline pp. 138-140).

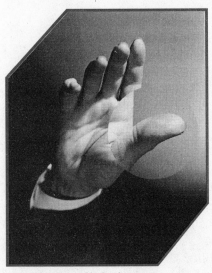

This manufacturing of tools and other technologies is what distinguishes humans from other animals. We are not especially fast or strong. We do not have particularly powerful hearing or sight. It is through the use of technology that we are able to outrun, outlift, outhear, and outsee any other animal.

Humans have opposable thumbs. Yipee!

Humans Sexuality

1. **Which of the following organs produces sperm cells?**

   (A) The penis
   (B) The testes
   (C) The ovaries
   (D) The uterus

All of us develop from a single cell formed by combining the genetic information in a male **sperm** cell with the genetic information in a female **egg** cell. The sperm cells are produced in a man's **testes**, which produce millions of sperm cells and are deposited in a woman during sexual intercourse. The testes become active after a male passes through **puberty** (somewhere between the ages of twelve and seventeen). A woman is born with all of the egg cells that she will ever produce, but the cells do not become mature until puberty, after which the cells are brought to maturity in a woman's **ovaries**. The ovaries release one egg per **menstrual cycle** (approximately one month).

Even with sexual intercourse, the millions of sperm cells deposited in a woman's **vagina** may not result in fertilization. Other factors such as when the intercourse takes place as well as whether contraceptive devices are used may prevent fertilization from taking place.

2. Which of the following forms of contraception is the most effective at preventing pregnancy?

(A) Condoms
(B) Birth control pills
(C) Diaphragms
(D) Spermicidal gels

While the most effective way to prevent pregnancy is to avoid having sex, certain methods of contraception are extremely effective in preventing fertilization. Birth control pills and other hormonal devices such as Norplant® are up to 99.5 percent effective if used as directed. Condoms, cervical caps, sponges, and diaphragms also work well, especially when combined with spermicidal gels. Condoms also have the benefit of preventing the transmission of some sexually transmitted diseases (STDs) such as AIDS, gonorrhea, syphilis, and genital herpes.

One not-so-great contraceptive method often used is the withdrawal method. Before the man reaches orgasm, he pulls his penis out, thereby keeping the sperm from entering the woman's vagina. Aside from the fact that getting the timing right is difficult, men usually emit a certain amount of semen, the liquid material containing sperm, when aroused. These tiny drops can contain thousands of those little suckers and may cause pregnancy.

How the human egg is often deceived.

Another method used to avoid pregnancy with a little more success is the **rhythm method.** In this method, a woman keeps track of when her period is and avoids sex during the few days during her menstrual cycle in which she is actually ovulating. The problem with this method for many couples is that sperm can live for three or four days, and it is difficult to determine just when ovulation is occurring. If the timing is wrong, pregnancy can occur. However, many couples use the rhythm method successfully by combining it with barrier methods. When the woman is fertile, the couple uses condoms or diaphragms.

Package of Birth Control Pills

BIRTH CONTROL, DISEASE PREVENTION

	Percentage of women who did not become pregnant during a year of use	Effectiveness of Method at preventing disease
Abstinence (avoiding sex)	100%	Extremely effective
Norplant®	99.9%	Not effective at all
Male Sterilization	99.9%	Not effective at all
Depo-Provera	99.7%	Not effective at all
Female Sterilization	99.4%	Not effective at all
Condoms in combination with spermicides	**99%**	**The most effective way of protecting yourself if you are going to have sex**
The pill	95%	Not effective at all
I.U.D.	94%	Not effective at all
Condoms	93%	Effective
The diaphragm	90%	Not effective at all
Spermicides alone	87%	Not effective at all
Sponge	85%	Not effective at all
Withdrawal	79%	Not effective at all
No contraception	15%	Not effective at all

The Norplant® birth control capsules. The capsules are placed under the skin in the upper arm and become effective within twenty-four hours when placed during the first seven days of the menstrual cycle. The system has been called an alternative to sterilization and the most innovative contraceptive in thirty years.

If a women does become pregnant, she has choices. She has the legal right to an **abortion,** or she can choose to continue the pregnancy and then either keep the baby or put it up for adoption. Any woman who is pregnant should see a health care provider as soon as possible.

3. **In which of the following ways can a person contract AIDS?**

    I. **Having Sex**
    II. **Hugging**
    III. **Giving Blood**

    (A) I only
    (B) I and II only
    (C) I and III only
    (D) I, II, and III

In recent years, the devastating disease of **AIDS** (Acquired Immuno-deficiency Syndrome) has become more and more prevalent. AIDS is not transmitted through casual contact. A person who hugs someone with AIDS will not catch the disease. Certain kinds of kissing are OK too. (A kiss like you would give your grandmother is safe. Deep kissing may not be.) Giving blood is also safe. Since blood is removed from the body by a clean needle, no germs can be transferred to the donor.

Certain actions, however, put you at risk, namely **unsafe sex** and needle use. Engaging in sex (especially sex in which a condom is not used correctly) or otherwise exchanging body fluids with a person who has the HIV virus can expose you to the disease. Sharing an intravenous needle with someone who is infected is another way to get AIDS. Remember, you can't tell by looking whether someone has the HIV virus, so use safe practices all the time. When AIDS was first diagnosed in the U.S. in the early 1980s, it was associated with and more prevalent in certain groups of people—

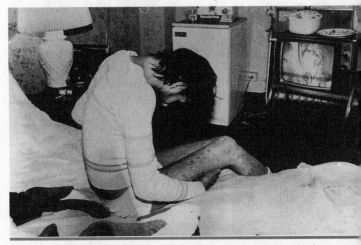

AIDS victim in a Times Square hotel room

intravenous drug users, homosexuals and hemophiliacs. Since that time, we have learned that everyone who engages in unsafe sex or drug practices is at risk for getting the HIV virus. Among the fastest growing groups of people with the disease are teenagers. So be careful and smart.

Everything You Always Wanted to Know About Sex (But Were Afraid to Ask), by Woody Allen. Funny, funny, funny movie.

4. What is the function of the placenta?
(A) To protect the fetus
(B) To nourish the fetus
(C) To generate eggs
(D) To transport the egg to the uterus

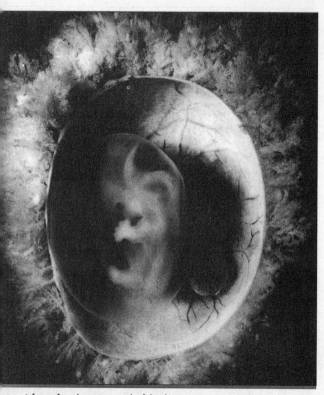

A fetus after about one month of development

The **placenta** is the region where the umbilical cord attaches to the wall of the **uterus** (the place where the fetus grows). A placenta allows for the transfer of food from the mother to the child and is a defining characteristic of a mammal (p. 310). Because the placenta takes care of the nutritional element of feeding the fetus, the eggs of mammals can be small.

5. Approximately how long is the first trimester of a human pregnancy?
(A) One month
(B) Two months
(C) Three months
(D) Four months

Pregnancy is broken down into three three-month **trimesters**. In the first trimester, cells are dividing and organizing into organs. The first trimester is extremely important in the development of the baby. It is also the dividing line in some states for legalized abortion. In the second trimester many of the features of the baby develop. During the last trimester, the fetus becomes a recognizable and viable, if premature, baby.

Prenatal care is care given while a woman is pregnant. It is extremely important that a mother get adequate prenatal care for her child, because during the time of pregnancy, a woman's actions and her environment can have a direct influence on the health of her baby. Smoking, drinking alcohol, taking drugs, malnutrition, and working with dangerous chemicals can lead to a **premature birth**, **miscarriage,** or **stillbirth**. The health of the father at the time of conception may also have an effect on the health of the baby. Studies have shown that a father's exposure to dangerous chemicals can adversely affect his child, leading to birth defects.

6. A "normal" child first learns to read by her

(A) first birthday
(B) sixth birthday
(C) tenth birthday
(D) twentieth birthday

Children learn skills at successive stages. By their second birthday, they may learn to speak. By their sixth birthday, they may be able to read. If a child isn't taken care of or properly stimulated in his youth, he may have some problems later in life. Because so much of our culture depends on our brains, it takes longer for human beings to develop necessary skills than it does for other creatures.

7. The age at which women no longer release eggs and stop having menstrual cycles is called

(A) Puberty
(B) Menstruation
(C) Menopause
(D) Women continue to have menstrual cycles for their entire lives

Women start menstruating at puberty and continue to menstruate until the onset of **menopause** at the age of forty-five to fifty-five. At this point, there is a change in the production of sex hormones and women are no longer able to have children. Menopause may be associated with certain symptoms including headaches, hot flashes, and osteoporosis, a weakening of bone mass. In cases with severe symptoms hormonal therapy is used to supply the menopausal woman with certain hormones that have stopped being produced. Exercising and changing one's diet have also been shown to be effective in relieving some of the symptoms associated with menopause.

Men undergo no comparable change. However, aging can affect men's sexual desire and their ability to engage in the sexual act.

Homosexuality, the attraction towards persons of one's own sex, is the subject of fierce debate among all sorts of groups: religious, military, social, you name it. So why is everyone so up in arms about what people do with their sexual lives? Lesbians (the term for homosexual women) and gays (used for both men and women) feel their sexual preference is something they were born with, like brown hair or blue eyes. The religious right, led by figures like Pat Robertson, Jerry Falwell, and Billy Graham, condemns homosexuality, viewing it as a psychological disorder that can be cured. Many other religious groups that also use the Bible as the basis for their faith do not condemn homosexuality as a sin, but welcome homosexuals, like everyone else, into their places of worship. Until recently, homosexuals were not allowed to serve in the military. Now, the military employs a "don't ask, don't tell" approach to the admittance of gays into their ranks: the military isn't allowed to ask questions regarding sexual preference, but the servicemen and servicewomen can't tell, either. Many states in the U.S. outlaw homosexual acts, but none of the countries in the European Community, except the Isle of Man (the irony!), forbid homosexual acts between consenting adults. Strides by the gay rights movement in the last fifty years have done a lot to reduce discrimination against gays and lesbians, but the rights of gay people are still challenged every day. Famous gay people include Greek philosopher Socrates (pp. 142-143), Renaissance artist Michelangelo (p. 454), author Oscar Wilde (1854-1900), who was imprisoned for two years for "homosexual offenses," playwright Tennessee Williams (1911-1983), author Gertrude Stein (p. 396), performer Sandra Bernhard, singer k.d. lang (1962), tennis star Martina Navratilova (p. 472), and Olympic diver Greg Louganis.

Humans
Bodily Functions

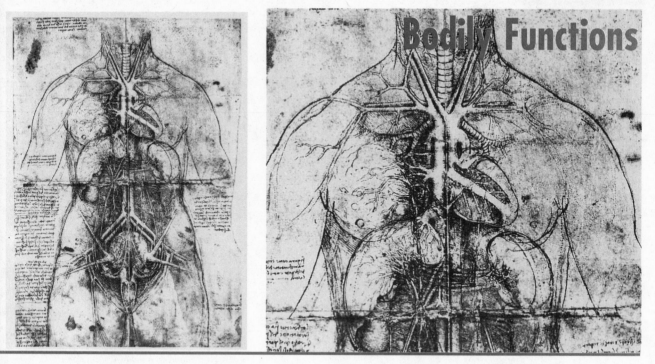

1. **The purpose of digestion is**

   (A) to break down food molecules so that they can be used
        by the body
   (B) to protect the body against invading organisms
   (C) to control the function of different organs
   (D) to help in the movement of the body from place to place

Human beings must eat to survive (no kidding), but the food has to be processed in the body before it is useful. This process of reducing the food to tiny molecules that can be used for energy is called **digestion**. When you eat a granola bar, for instance, your mouth chews the granola until it is small enough to fit down your throat. Chewing stimulates your salivary glands to produce **saliva**, which helps break down starches and also provides a means for those little pieces of nuts and oats to float down your throat. The granola mush then passes through your system by the process of **peristalsis**, wavelike muscular motions that help move food through your body.

2. **Which of the following organs is partly responsible for breaking down proteins so they can be used by the body?**

   (A) The stomach
   (B) The mouth
   (C) The lungs
   (D) The lymph nodes

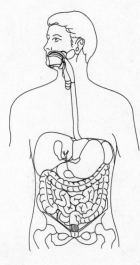

After food moves down your throat, it reaches the **stomach**, a muscular sac filled with **hydrochloric acid** that further breaks down the starches and proteins. There the gunk left from whatever you have eaten is gradually pushed into the **small intestine** where the now-usable bits of food are absorbed by tiny, weird-looking fingerlike things called villi and enter your bloodstream for use. Whatever food is undigested goes through the **large intestine** and is removed when you go well, you know.

3. **Which of the following organs produces bile?**

   (A) The stomach
   (B) The liver
   (C) The heart
   (D) The lungs

Bile is this nasty stuff produced by the **liver** that aids in the digestion of fats. Bile is stored in the **gall bladder** and released into the small intestine when needed for digestion. Because of the vile nature of bile, the term is also used to express bitterness.

 In the Middle Ages (pp. 151-158), the human body was thought to contain four fluids. They were called the **four humors**. The dominance of any of the humors—blood, phlegm, choler, and black bile—determined a person's character and general health. Neat theory, bad medicine.

4. **The system that provides for the transport of dissolved material through the body is called**

   (A) the immune system
   (B) the circulatory system
   (C) the digestive system
   (D) the respiratory system

Dissolved material is transported around the body in the **circulatory system**. Through the muscular action of the heart, blood is pumped through the **arteries** and then back again through the **veins.** The arteries and veins branch off into tiny blood vessels called **capillaries.** These are extremely thin vessels with walls only one cell thick, where material passes between body cells and the blood.

5. Which of the following most helps the human body to defend itself against invading organisms?

(A) Red blood cells
(B) White blood cells
(C) Platelets
(D) Plasma

Blood is composed of four parts: **plasma, red blood cells, white blood cells,** and **platelets.** The plasma is the liquid portion of the blood. Blood is mostly water, many useful nutrients, enzymes, antibodies, and other stuff float around in it.

Red blood cells carry oxygen from the lungs to the rest of the body, while the white blood cells are useful in fighting off infections (immune system, p. 334). Some white blood cells are responsible for producing antibodies, while others leave the blood system to engulf and destroy invading bacteria.

Platelets are used to form blood clots. Whenever you are cut, and blood begins to run out through the hole in your skin, your body forms a blood clot. A blood clot stops the flow of blood and eventually turns into a scab.

6. A response by which of the following causes an allergic reaction?

(A) The respiratory system
(B) The immune system
(C) The digestive system
(D) The excretory system

The immune system is the body's defense against invading forces. The body recognizes certain objects as "foreign" substances or **antigens**. White blood cells create **antibodies** to destroy the antigens. This **immune response** protects us from the damage that might be caused by invading agents. If the immune response is caused by substances that are not particularly dangerous, the resulting disorder is called an **allergy**.

AIDS (Acquired Immunodeficiency Syndrome) (p. 329) gradually weakens the immune system. It is caused by the virus called **HIV** (Human Immunodeficiency Virus). A person can find out if he or she has the HIV virus by taking a blood test. Those infected with the virus are **HIV-positive**. Someone who is HIV-positive might not show symptoms of the diseases associated with AIDS, but can still transmit the virus to others through the exchange of bodily fluids. Some people are HIV-positive for years without getting sick, but their immune systems eventually grow weaker and they can become infected with opportunistic diseases. When this happens the person is said to have full-blown AIDS.

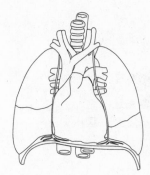

7. **Which of the following is used by human beings for respiration?**

   (A) Alveoli
   (B) Plasma
   (C) Appendix
   (D) Liver

Our **lungs** are the most important organs in the breathing process. To move the air in and out of your body, the diaphragm and rib cage expand and contract to change the pressure inside the lungs. Breathing allows for the exchange of gases with the atmosphere. The air is exchanged between the lungs and the blood by the **alveoli.** These tiny air sacs are surrounded by capillaries that allow oxygen to be brought into the blood.

Sometimes cellular respiration happens without oxygen. If we have a shortage of oxygen, our muscles and liver rely on **anaerobic** respiration. The process of anaerobic respiration produces much less energy and a bunch of **lactic acid.** The pain that you feel after exercising strenuously is caused by this lactic acid.

8. **The gas excreted by the lungs in the process of respiration is called**

   (A) Oxygen
   (B) Carbon monoxide
   (C) Carbon dioxide
   (D) Phlegm

The lungs are part of the excretory system. Our body uses the oxygen taken in by the lungs and then excretes carbon dioxide, which is breathed out. Other organs help in excreting products that are no longer needed. The liver helps get rid of old red blood cells and nitrogenous waste (which later becomes urine). Sweat glands help cool the body and rid it of excess water. The liquid caused by perspiration also helps cool the skin.

SMOKING SUCKS

Smoking is one of the main causes of lung cancer, and if you want to ensure a horrible death for yourself, smoking cigarettes is a good way to start. Not only does smoking cause all kinds of damage, it is also highly addictive. Nicotine is in the same drug family as heroin, cocaine, and morphine. It is considered by health experts to be just as addictive as these substances. So if you haven't started smoking, don't. And if you have started, it's never too late to quit. The body has amazing recuperative powers, and if you stop early enough, your lungs will repair themselves.

9. **Which of the following describes the function of the kidneys?**
   (A) They regulate the concentration of many of the materials present in the blood.
   (B) They produce bile.
   (C) They help pump the blood through the circulatory system.
   (D) They produce the physical material necessary for the nervous system to operate.

Frankenstein, by Mary Shelley. Written way back in 1818, this is still a chilling story about bringing life to a dead body.

The kidneys are responsible for excreting nitrogenous wastes and for making sure that the right concentration of different substances exists in the blood. People can survive without one kidney, but it's nice to have two. A diet that is almost exclusively protein can cause the kidneys to malfunction, so if you're eating steaks for breakfast, lunch, and dinner, you'd better quit.

10. **Which of the following is part of the nervous system?**
    (A) The alveoli
    (B) The lymph nodes
    (C) The brain
    (D) The liver

The nervous system controls your thought processes and reactions to different stimuli. A system of nerve cells called **neurons** help transfer information to, from, and within the **brain.** Many of these neurons run through the **spinal cord,** a thick nerve enclosed in your spine.

Two types of behavior are controlled by the brain: **involuntary behavior** and **voluntary behavior.** Involuntary behavior includes reflexes, heartbeats, breathing, and other things not in your conscious control. Voluntary behavior includes reading, playing poker, and other actions that you choose to undertake.

11. **Which of the following actions is usually associated with the right side of the brain?**

    (A) Calculating
    (B) Drawing
    (C) Speaking
    (D) Control of the right side of the body beneath the head

The right side of the brain controls the left half of the body: The signals are switched in the spinal column. By studying people who have had the pathways between the two halves of their brains severed, scientists have found that in addition to motor control, each side is responsible for different skills. The left side of the brain is responsible for verbal skills and the right side is responsible for non-verbal and spatial skills.

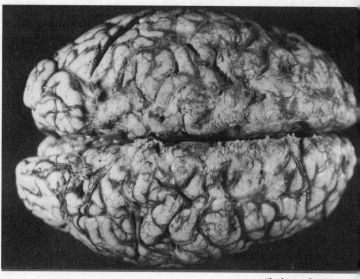

The human brain

The nervous system operates in tandem with the hormonal system. **Hormones** affect brain cells and are in turn affected by commands from the brain. Many drugs work by copying or blocking the effect of hormones or **neurotransmitters** (the chemicals that connect up different nerve cells).

Hormones also play a role in sexual development. The development of both male and female secondary characteristics is controlled by hormones. **Testosterone** causes the development of certain male characteristics such as facial hair and the lowering of the voice's pitch. **Estrogen** causes the development of breasts and other female characteristics. So you gotta love those hormones.

The Man With Two Brains (1983), starring Steve Martin. It has nothing to do with serious brain research, but if you like seeing lots of brains in jars and you like to laugh, this is your movie. *Young Frankenstein* (1974), starring Gene Wilder, directed by Mel Brooks. Another funny scene with a brain. The movie is very funny all the way through.

ANSWERS

1. A   2. A   3. B   4. B   5. B   6. B
7. A   8. C   9. A   10. C   11. B

Technology
Farming

1. Which of the following enabled humans to settle in one place without migrating?

(A) Fire
(B) Agriculture
(C) The spear
(D) Flint

So much of our modern lifestyle is made possible by the development of agriculture. Early man survived by **hunting and gathering**—the only way to get food was by finding it or killing it. Being out in the elements day after day kind of stumbling around and hoping for food may have instilled in early man a capacity for patience unknown today, but it also got pretty lonely, because the number of people who could live together in a small area was severely limited. Researchers have estimated that the maximum density of people who can be sustained without agriculture is two people per square mile. If this is true, the entire earth couldn't sustain the current population of Los Angeles and its surrounding areas.

Agriculture, the process of growing plants and breeding animals, provides food in a much more concentrated area.

2. **Approximately how many years ago was agriculture developed?**
   - (A) 100,000
   - (B) 10,000
   - (C) 5,000
   - (D) 2,000

Two-horse plow

Agriculture was developed about 10,000 years ago. It is not coincidental that the development of agriculture occurred only a short time before the first civilizations of the ancient world, like Mesopotamia (p. 135), came into being. The advent of agriculture led people to settle into permanent towns. This changed the way in which people valued land and objects. Because it was possible to live in the same place for a long time, land became valuable, and because people did not have to carry all their possessions all of the time, bigger objects began to have positive value. This all helped lead to the development of advanced civilizations.

3. **Which of the following is NOT a danger of relying too much on pesticides?**
   - (A) We will soon run out of the chemicals necessary to make pesticides.
   - (B) Through genetic change, pests can generate their own immunity to insecticides.
   - (C) Insecticides can find their way through the food chain into animals that we do not want to kill.
   - (D) Insecticides can kill off the natural predators of creatures they are designed to kill.

Twenty-four-horse harvester

Widespread use of **pesticides** greatly increased the efficiency of farms. Large percentages of crops used to be destroyed by rodents, insects, and fungi (p. 309). Through the use of pesticides, humans have become much more efficient at producing the food necessary for survival. The drawback of pesticides, however, is that they can do more than just kill off their target pests. An insecticide, for example, may poison the natural predators of the insects that the insecticide was meant to kill. These harmful chemicals can also become concentrated as they move up the food chain. **DDT**, a commonly used pesticide in the U.S. during the 1950s,

Wheat is harvested in Colorado. Finally, a machine!

Science & Technology

The development of agriculture proceeded in several steps. First, people discovered how to cultivate wheat or corn, depending on the continent. The first wheat plants were hybrids that happened to have plump seeds. But the plants were not able to survive on their own. Without the help of humans, the much plumper seed would not be borne by the wind, and the species would be unable to reproduce. Through a combination of luck and the ability to recognize the advantage of this species of wheat, early man was able to greatly increase his crop yields.

Next, humans learned how to harness the power of animals. With the help of an ox or a horse, a person was able to cultivate a greater area of land. As time passed, people learned how to breed animals and plants to increase their productivity. Recently, through the use of genetic engineering, a process by which the **genetic code (pp. 316-317)** of an organism is directly affected, scientists have been able to design plants and other organisms that have certain desirable characteristics. Imagine a corn plant with its own defenses built in, rendering pesticides unnecessary. Imagine a blue rose. Genetically engineered tomatoes are already on the market.

was extremely effective at killing insects that fed on crops. The problem, however, was that it was also effective in stopping birds from reproducing. (Its widespread use helped eliminate many bird species.) In 1972, the U.S. banned the use of DDT in this country, but it is still manufactured here and sold to other countries.

Another problem with pesticides is that their targets eventually become immune to the chemicals. Since most insects reproduce at a rapid rate, the process of evolution happens fairly quickly, and the newly resistant creatures not killed by the pesticides stuff themselves with the food that the farmers are trying to get to market.

Recently, farmers have been experimenting with more environmentally friendly forms of pest control. Diversifying crops, taking better care of the soil, and introducing biological means of controlling pests have all been effective in reducing our dependence on pesticides.

4. **Approximately what percentage of workers in the U.S. were engaged in farming in 1900?**

   (A) Sixty percent
   (B) Forty percent
   (C) Ten percent
   (D) Two percent

5. **Approximately what percentage of workers in the U.S. are engaged in farming today?**

   (A) Sixty percent
   (B) Forty percent
   (C) Ten percent
   (D) Two percent

In the past, most people in the U.S. were involved in farming. Until 1870, more than half of the country's workers were involved in producing food. By 1900, it was down to thirty-eight percent, and today only about two-and-a-half percent of people in the country work on farms.

What happened? In the last eighty years there has been an enormous increase in the ability of farmers to produce food. Previously, most farm work was done by hand. Recent innovations have enabled farmers to work much more land with fewer people. The rise of industrialization (pp. 344-345) also created many new jobs in the cities and caused a rapid shift of population from the country to the city.

ANSWERS

....

1. B   2. B   3. A   4. B   5. D

1. **Approximately how many years ago was bronze invented?**

   (A) 10,000
   (B) 5,000
   (C) 2,000
   (D) 1,000

Around the time that agriculture developed, certain peoples discovered the benefits of metal. About 10,000 years ago, people began to construct **copper** tools and artifacts. Suddenly they had a material that could be cast into shapes, melted down, and cast again. But copper is a soft material, and cannot hold an edge. The invention of **bronze** (copper mixed with tin) about 5,000 years later made a huge difference in the ability of humans to make tools, because bronze doesn't bend. The discovery of bronze is one of the most important innovations in the history of mankind. With bronze, people could make weapons (pp. 138-140) like

SCIENCE & TECHNOLOGY

THE RUBBER AGE

Originally, rubber became stiff and brittle in cold weather and malleable and sticky in warm weather. An inventor, Charles Goodyear, who had spent time in prison for debt, decided to try to improve rubber by adding sulfur. Initially, he failed. Then, accidentally, he spilled his failed rubber-sulfur mixture on a stove and discovered the process of vulcanization—which provided dry, flexible rubber at all temperatures. Although Goodyear patented this process in 1844, vulcanization was so simple that many people copied the process without paying Goodyear royalties. When he died in 1860, Goodyear owed hundreds of thousands of dollars again.

 Celluloid is related to the explosive nitrocellulose, so if ignited, it burns like crazy. Several serious fires in movie theaters and hospital X-ray areas occurred before celluloid was replaced by cellulose acetate as a film base.

swords and knives. Bronze also allowed artifacts to be exactly shaped. The invention was so important that anthropologists named the era in which bronze was first used the **Bronze Age.**

2. **Which of the following is a primary advantage of iron over bronze?**

(A) It is easier to manufacture.
(B) It is softer and more easily molded.
(C) It is harder and therefore able to hold an edge for a longer period of time.
(D) It is closer in appearance to gold.

Hard on the heels of bronze, **iron** was first used for materials around 2,500 BC. Iron has a couple of big advantages over bronze: It is more prevalent near the earth's surface, and it is harder. The discovery of iron made it possible for people to develop more durable tools and, when formed into its alloy, **steel,** iron became the material with which many of the machines and tools used by man were made.

3. **In which of the following years was the first synthetic plastic invented?**

(A) 1778
(B) 1856
(C) 1912
(D) 1948

For thousands of years, humans have used materials found in nature or have mixed together different substances found in nature to make new materials. In 1856, Alexander Parkes invented the first **synthetic plastic.** Called **celluloid,** this material could substitute for the ivory used in piano keys, billiard balls, and combs. It was also used as the material for film and motion picture stock. Plastics technology has gone through many changes since 1856. Today, most plastics are constructed from substances contained in oil and natural gas.

4. **A superconductor is**

(A) A material that is superior to steel for use in rail construction

(B) A material that can carry electric current without losing any energy

(C) A material found in nature that is able to withstand enormous temperature fluctuations

(D) A material superior to plastic in its ability to be molded

The Graduate (1967), starring Dustin Hoffman. It's a great flick with a famous line about plastic.

Made by baking clay and other substances, ceramics include pottery, porcelain and other useful objects. One recent innovation in the use of **ceramics** has been in the creation of **superconductors**. Ceramic materials are able to carry electric current without any loss of energy. Because the temperatures at which superconductors operate are very cold (about 77° Kelvin, –196° C, or –321° F) and the materials somewhat brittle, superconductors are just beginning to play a role in industry.

No plastic, no frisbees, no fun.

ANSWERS

1. B   2. C   3. B   4. B

Technology
Energy

1. **Which of the following innovations was most important in enabling the Industrial Revolution to take hold?**

   (A) The ability to make plastics out of petrochemicals
   (B) The ability to make bronze
   (C) The invention of the steam engine
   (D) The invention of the computer

For thousands of years, most manufacturing was done by individual craftspeople who created objects from start to finish by themselves. The innovations that led to the **Industrial Revolution** (p.178) changed all that. England had just experienced a huge population increase and needed more consumer goods. By using machines invented in the 1760s, the textile industry began to mass-produce clothes. A few years later, **James Watt**'s (1736-1819) improvements of the **steam engine** allowed for the use of machine-driven factories to manufacture goods. This new ability

Old steam locomotive

enabled manufacturers to produce previously undreamed-of amounts of power and to increase dramatically the speed with which goods were made.

The Industrial Revolution did not improve the workers' lot, however. Before the revolution, a craftsperson had control over the method with which he produced his goods. Afterwards, a worker was at the mercy of the bosses. Nineteenth-century English industrial towns were not happy places. Soot covered everything. Everyone, including children, worked long hours and life expectancy was not great.

In the long run, however, the Industrial Revolution has led to higher standards of living and it is still championed today as a way to make poorer countries richer.

2. **Put the following in order from greatest to least.**

   I. **The amount of energy released from burning one pound of wood**

   II. **The amount of energy released from causing the fission of one pound of Uranium**

   III. **The amount of energy released from burning one pound of coal**

   (A) I, II, III
   (B) II, I, III
   (C) II, III, I
   (D) III, I, II

In the past, almost all the energy we needed was produced by burning wood. We have since found that by burning fossil fuels such as coal and oil, we can obtain more concentrated energy. In the last thirty years or so, we have also started to make energy from nuclear reactions. In this case, the energy from the fission of uranium atoms is transferred to make steam, which drives a turbine.

A Japanese model of a solar (sun-powered) car

All forms of energy production discovered up to this day have their problems. Burning wood is inefficient. Fossil fuels create pollution and eventually run out. Nuclear power is relatively efficient, but the by-products of nuclear power (p. 292) are extremely dangerous. Lately, scientists have been trying to develop a controlled fusion reaction. Fusion is the combining of different atoms to make energy similar to the energy released by solar energy (pp. 274-275). Even if a controlled fusion reaction were discovered, however, we would still have nuclear by-products to deal with.

Hydroelectric power harnesses the water flowing through rivers. Because the rivers are filled by rain and snow, it is possible to use this type of power indefinitely. Unfortunately, to create a hydroelectric power plant, huge areas of riverfront land must be flooded, and the environmental impact is significant. We can get energy directly from the sun either by using solar cells to convert sunlight into energy, or by using the heat generated by the sun to heat our homes and water. However, large surface areas are required to house the solar panels necessary to create enough concentrated energy for, say, powering a car. **Wind power** is another form of energy, but like solar energy, it is not sufficient for our needs. And there is also **geothermal energy,** energy derived from the warmer temperatures underground. While clean and efficient, geothermal energy is only available in areas where the heat of the interior of the earth is close to the surface and easily accessed. In Iceland (p. 230), for example, geothermal heat is used to heat sixty-five percent of the homes.

The Hoover Dam, built 1931-36, is on the Colorado River between Arizona and Nevada.

3. **Which of the following nations uses the most energy?**

   (A) Japan
   (B) The United States
   (C) Germany
   (D) China

As you might have guessed, the U.S. uses the most energy, consuming twenty-three percent of the world's entire energy production while making up only five percent of the world's population.

French hydroelectric plant

Technology
Communication

1. **Approximately how long ago was the first full writing system invented?**

   (A) 50,000 years ago
   (B) 5,000 years ago
   (C) 2,000 years ago
   (D) 1,000 years ago

One of the features that distinguishes us from the rest of the animal kingdom is our use of language. Through speech, people have been communicating for much of the time that we have existed as a species. In fact, some anthropologists believe that the development of the species and language happened at the same time.

The invention of writing (p. 135), however, is a relatively recent phenomenon. While simple marks made for counting and other limited forms of writing have been around for 30,000 years or so, a writing system that allows for the recording of thoughts and spoken language has only been around for about 5,000 years. The invention of writing affected the very fabric of human society. Suddenly, we were not limited to the confines of memory. We could write things down if we wanted a permanent record. Books could be written, ideas could be codified and then later remarked on.

2. What was one advantage of the telegraph?

(A) It allowed for the transmission of the sounds of a person's voice.

(B) It allowed for communication without wires.

(C) It allowed for the almost instantaneous communication of language over great distances.

(D) It allowed for ships to communicate to shore.

Even with the convenience of language and writing, it could still take a long time for a message to reach its recipient. Before the invention of the **telegraph**, a system that allowed for the communication of information through electricity (p. 307), it was impossible to communicate any faster than a person could travel. This made for some interesting historical events like the Battle of New Orleans (p. 56), in which Andrew Jackson defeated the British even though the war was technically over .

The telegraph was limited, however, to a code of dots and dashes that were then converted into simple messages.

3. Who invented the telephone?

(A) Thomas Edison

(B) Alexander Graham Bell

(C) Albert Einstein

(D) Guglielmo Marconi

Some of the limitations of the telegraph were exploded by the invention of the **telephone**. **Alexander Graham Bell** (1847-1922) created a working device that allowed for the communication of voice over long distances. Telephones were limited only by their means of transmission: the wire.

HOMER WAS ILLITERATE

A blind poet who could neither read nor write, Homer (8th century BC) was able to recount the tales of Greek mythology (pp. 381-392) and history through an amazing feat of memory and through some techniques still used in societies today. Homer's words are recorded in the Iliad and the Odyssey (pp. 389-391). Many pre-literate cultures have enormously complex oral traditions consisting of complicated stories that are passed on from generation to generation. Homer's work was eventually written down and it became one of the cornerstones for much of Western literature. In the process, it became accessible to a much greater number of people.

Alexander Graham Bell

4. Who invented radio?

(A) Thomas Edison
(B) Alexander Graham Bell
(C) Albert Einstein
(D) Guglielmo Marconi

In 1895, Guglielmo Marconi (1874-1937) invented **radio**. Suddenly people could communicate over great distances without wires. Called **wireless** communication, the radio allowed for ships to communicate with the shore and eventually evolved into the huge entertainment and information industry we all know and love.

Receiving set used by Marconi

5. When was television invented?

(A) In the 1880s
(B) In the 1910s
(C) In the 1930s
(D) In the 1950s

Although simple **televisions** had been invented in the 1930s, it wasn't until 1941 that the FCC allowed for the broadcast of commercial black-and-white television images. The industry caught on, and after WWII (pp. 95, 193), the number of televisions in America multiplied rapidly. Now, there are more televisions in the U.S. than there are indoor toilets.

It is hard today to imagine life without the television. Through satellite broadcasts, we can take a peek at things happening all over the world. We can see history taking place. The advent of television has been criticized by many because of tv's mindless programming and its tendency to suck away valuable leisure time. The television revolution, for better or for worse, has changed the way we live our lives.

6. **A digital signal is different from an analog signal because**

    (A) A digital signal can travel long distances
    (B) A digital signal can be transmitted over telephone wires and through wireless communication.
    (C) A digital signal is either on or off while an analog signal allows for modulation
    (D) A digital signal is able to be recorded; an analog signal is not.

Recently, the big push in communications technology is to go **digital,** which means "coded as numbers." A digital signal is one in which only two possibilities exist: on or off. Data is coded as a series of these "on" or "off" signals, usually transmitted as pulses of light or voltage. Because computers (pp. 352-355) use such signals, digital systems allow for much more control over the information sent. Compact discs use a laser beam to read an encoded digital signal which is then transformed into music or computer information (**CD-ROM**). Because of the high quality of digital sound recorded on compact discs, older sound systems have become virtually obsolete. (Ask your parents about eight-track tapes. It will make them feel old.)

7. **What is the purpose of fiber-optic cable?**

    (A) To aid in the exchange of digital information
    (B) To aid in the transfer of power from electrical lines
    (C) To increase the power of intergalactic telescopes
    (D) To physically strengthen already existing underwater copper telephone wires

Lately, there has been a lot of talk about the **information superhighway.** As we develop more and more ways of using information, we have developed a need to transmit this information over long distances. **Fiber-optic cables** are one way of accomplishing this goal. The cables are made up of a bunch of transparent fibers that transmit light (pp. 305-307). A fiber-optic cable can transmit much more digital information than traditional copper cables, and the installation of these cables will eventually allow for all kinds of technological wizardry.

ANSWERS

1. B   2. C   3. B   4. D   5. C   6. C   7. A

Technology

Computers

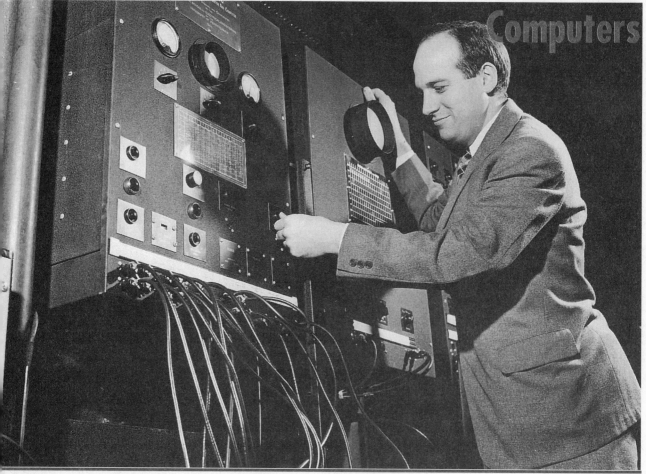

War Games, (1983), starring Matthew Broderick and Ally Sheedy. Story of a young computer hacker who breaks into the military computer system and almost starts World War III. Their only hope is for the central computer to develop its own intelligence.

1. **In a computer, what is the difference between ROM and RAM?**

   (A) ROM is many times faster than RAM.
   (B) ROM cannot be changed by software, while RAM can.
   (C) ROM and RAM are the same thing.
   (D) ROM is removable, but RAM is soldered into the motherboard of a computer.

Just as the middle of the nineteenth century in England is often referred to as the Industrial Revolution (pp. 344-345), we are now going through what some people call the information revolution. Most of this so-called revolution is based on the technological innovation of the computer. Using a **binary system** in which all information is converted into ones and zeroes, **digital computers** can hold and process huge amounts of information.

A computer, at its most basic level, is a series of switches that are either on or off. Technological innovations have made it possible to increase greatly the number of switches that can be placed in a small area, and computers today can perform much faster than they could in the past. All of these on/off switches are programmed so that they can perform different commands.

Many of these commands are **hard-wired** into the machine. That is, these commands are part of the physical makeup of the machine. These commands cannot be changed without supplying new parts to the inside of the machine, and many of them are stored in **ROM,** Read Only Memory, which cannot be erased.

As you work on a computer, however, you make changes in the memory held by the computer. These changes affect the **RAM,** Random Access Memory, and while the computer is on, the changes are remembered. Computers also store information that remains even if the computer is turned off. The information can be stored in a number of ways: on **tape drives, floppy discs, hard drives, removable hard drives,** or **optical discs.**

COMPUTER UPGRADE

....

The original ENIAC computer occupied an entire city block with its large machinery. The same computing power and capabilities are now encompassed in a chip of silicon a quarter-inch square.

Burning Chrome, by William Gibson. A collection of cyberpunk short stories.

2. **Put in order from smallest to largest:**

   I. Bit
   II. Gigabyte
   III. Kilobyte
   IV. Megabyte

   (A) I, II, III, IV
   (B) I, III, II, IV
   (C) I, III, IV, II
   (D) III, IV, II, I

Japanese Computer Store '94

As we said before, a computer is a binary system in which different switches are either on or off. A **bit** is this little guy who registers whether things are on (1) or off (0), a kind of yes-man or no-man, depending on what's happening. A bit can only hold the value of 0 or 1. A **byte** is 8 bits and can contain the numbers from 0 to 255 or the letters of the alphabet and other information. Computers are usually wired to accept a number of bits together. Thus, we hear of a 16-bit microprocessor or a 32-bit microprocessor. A **kilobyte** is about 1,000 bytes, a **megabyte** about a million, and a **gigabyte** is about one billion bytes.

Zoolook, by Jean-Michel Jarre. A synthesized suite of twenty sampled languages.

3. **Windows and MS-DOS for IBM computers and System 7 for Macintosh computers are all**
   (A) word processors
   (B) operating systems
   (C) spreadsheets
   (D) hardware

The physical machinery of a computer is called **hardware.** The instructions used to run the system are called **software.** The hardware in a computer is kind of like the paper in a book, while the software is the words on the paper. The basic controls of the computer are controlled by an operating system. An **operating system,** such as Windows or System 7, handles functions such as reading and writing data to the screen or interpreting user commands. A computer would not be able to function without one.

Neuromancer, by William Gibson. The classic, futuristic story of cyberspace, high-tech robbers, and a very clever artificial intelligence.

4. **All of the following are resources on the Internet EXCEPT**
   (A) E-mail
   (B) Gopher
   (C) MS Word
   (D) WWW

The **Internet** is a loosely organized group of computer networks. Today there are millions of people attached **on-line** by their computers to this amazing resource. As more and more computers get connected, more and more information becomes available. Think of it as a giant, expanding web of information. In a few blinks of an eye, your computer can retrieve a tasty morsel of information from any point on the web. To get connected, all you need is a computer, a modem, some software, and a way in. Lists of companies that now sell Internet access are available in almost any book about the Internet.

The Internet is the first step to the information superhighway. As it stands now, most Internet connections are rather slow (usually traveling over existing phone lines), and only text and simple pictures can be sent efficiently. If the bandwidth could be increased, say, by using fiber-optic cables (p. 351), people could send multimedia programs and even video on-line.

These are some of the more popular on-line services.

E-mail—E-mail allows you to send electronic mail all over the world. It is a fast and efficient method of communication that makes old-fashioned letters seem cumbersome. For example, let's say you wanted to have a discussion with your parents (in Kalamazoo) and your brother (in a study program in Greece) at the same time. You can write a note that would reach them all, and they would get it almost immediately.

Listserve—Because it takes no extra effort to send a note to hundreds of people, many e-mail mailing lists have developed. These lists allow you to find people with similar interests and join discussions with them. There are mailing lists for people interested in almost everything.

Internet for Dummies, by John R. Levine and Carol Baroudi. A great guide to the Internet. What William Gibson foretold in *Neuromancer* is coming true.

Usenet—Usenet groups (also called news groups) are like cyberspace bulletin boards for E-mail. To post something to a newsgroup, you submit an E-mail to that group's address and it gets tacked up for everyone to read. As of this writing, there are close to 9,000 different newsgroups on subjects as varied as of the Grateful Dead, arcane science fiction writers, different sports teams, wind surfing, skiing, and anything you might imagine. If you aren't satisfied with the choices, you can start your own group.

Gopher—Gopher is a system that lets you follow different menus until you find the stuff you're looking for. As you "surf" through the net, you don't have to worry about which computer you are getting information from. It is all seamless. From Gopher, you can download all kinds of free software to try at home.

WWW—World Wide Web is a system that makes use of hypertext. In a computer program, hypertext is text highlighted in such a way that if you select it, you get sent to another part of a document. On the Internet, you can be sent anywhere—all WWW information is connected and easily accessible.

ANSWERS

1. A   2. C   3. B   4. C

Mathematics

1. While taking a trip to visit the college of your choice, you look at a map in which the scale is 1 inch for every 75 miles. On the map, the distance from where you are to where you have to go is 3 ½ inches. If you are averaging 50 miles an hour, how long will it take you to get to your destination?

   (A) 1 hour and 15 minutes
   (B) 3 hours and 15 minutes
   (C) 5 hours and 15 minutes
   (D) 6 hours

There are two ways to handle this problem. Your choice depends on how accurate you need to be. Let's say you left home at ten in the morning to get to an interview scheduled for four in the afternoon. Did you blow it?

THE HARD WAY

There are many times in life when you will need to calculate a simple proportion like this. The procedure is relatively straightforward. Set up an equation using two fractions as follows: $1/75 = 3\frac{1}{2} \div x$. To solve this equation, cross multiply. This will leave you with the equation $1x = 3\frac{1}{2} \times 75$, so $x = 262.5$. The entire distance that you will have to cover is 262.5 miles.

Since you will be traveling 50 miles per hour, divide the total number of miles by 50. This gives you 5.25 hours—5 hours and 15 minutes.

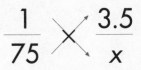

THE EASY WAY

Approximate that you are almost 300 miles from the college (75 miles × 4 inches is 300 miles). At 50 miles an hour this means that you will reach the school in under 6 hours (300 miles ÷ 50 mph. = 6 hours) If you know where the admissions office is, you might make that interview.

2. **At a restaurant, you buy a hamburger and a Coke. The hamburger costs $2.50, and the Coke costs 50¢. If tax is 6% and you leave a 15% tip, approximately how much money did you part with?**

   (A) $3.25
   (B) $3.45
   (C) $3.65
   (D) $3.90

This is an equation you will be grappling with for the rest of your life. In the U.S. we tip for service. (In some other countries, the tip is included.) The standard tip is 15% and there are several short cuts to calculating it.

THE HARD WAY

$3.00 \times {}^{15}/_{100} = .45$
$3.00 \times {}^{6}/_{100} = .20$
$3.00 + .45 + .20 = 3.65$

RENÉ DESCARTES

René Descartes (1596-1650) (p. 169) *believed that the entire material universe could be explained in terms of mathematical physics. He invented coordinate geometry (the x and y axes) as a means of defining and manipulating geometrical shapes in terms of algebraic expressions. The means by which points are represented in this system are therefore called Cartesian coordinates.*

THE EASY WAY

Depending on the local tax rates, sometimes you can double or triple the sales tax to get the correct tip. For example, if tax is 5%, just triple the tax they've calculated for you, and you have your 15% tip. If that doesn't work, try this handy technique. Take the cost:

$$\$3.00$$

Divide by 10.

$$30¢$$

Take half of this number and add.

$$30¢ + 15¢ = 45¢.$$

THIS IS THE TIP

In the problem above, you also have to pay the sales tax. Well, if the 15% tip is 45¢, the 6% tax has to be less than half of that, so the answer must be 3.65.

3. **What are the values for x, such that**
    $$4x^2 + 3x - 7 = 0$$

    (A) $(-\frac{7}{4}, 1)$
    (B) $(-\frac{4}{7}, 1)$
    (C) $(-1, \frac{7}{4})$
    (D) $(-1, \frac{4}{7})$

Factoring is a fundamental skill of algebra, and there is a chance (small though it may be) that someone might stick a gun to your head and tell you to factor or die.

So here's the deal. Set up two sets of parentheses as follows:

$$(4x \ 7) \times (x \ 1)$$

Now you have to decide where the minus signs go. Use trial and error. Let's say that you tried $(-4x + 7) \times (-x - 1) = 0$. By using FOIL (First, Outside, Inside, Last) you would get an answer of $4x^2 - 11x - 7$. The correct factoring is $(4x + 7) \times (x - 1)$. If you FOIL this equation you will end up with the original equation.

The next thing to do is to solve for x. Since any number times zero equals zero, either the first set of parentheses or the second set of parentheses must equal zero. So set each one equal to zero.

$$4x + 7 = 0$$

Subtract 7 from each side

$$4x = -7$$

Divide by 4 on each side.

$$x = -\frac{7}{4}$$

Rosencrantz and Guildenstern Are Dead (1990), starring Gary Oldman and Tim Roth. Rosencrantz and Guildenstern, two friends of Hamlet's, get involved in adventures around the royal castle in Denmark. There is an interesting coin-flipping sequence.

Now do the same for the second set of parentheses:

$$x - 1 = 0$$
$$x = 1.$$

The answer is (A); x can either equal 1 or $-\frac{7}{4}$.

4. Put the following in order from most likely to least likely.

   I. The likelihood of flipping a coin 10 times and getting heads each time
   II. The likelihood of winning a sweepstakes where the odds for winning are 100,000,000 to 1
   III. The probability that when two six-sided dice are rolled, their sum is 7
   IV. The probability that when two six-sided dice are rolled, their sum is 4

   (A) I, II, III, IV
   (B) IV, III, I, II
   (C) III, IV, I, II
   (D) III, IV, II, I

1+1=2	2+1=3	6+1=7
1+2=3	2+2=4	6+2=8
1+3=4	2+3=5	6+3=9
1+4=5	2+4=6	6+4=10
1+5=6	2+5=7	6+5=11
1+6=7	2+6=8	6+6=12

Figure 1

Although only a small amount of time is spent teaching probability in any given math class, an understanding of it can be incredibly useful. Everybody from casino owners to the government gives you odds.

Let's look at the question above. To figure out the probability of getting any roll when using two six-sided dice (assuming of course that the dice are fair), list out all the possibilities (see Figure 1). You should find the following:

This shows that there are thirty-six possible outcomes of a roll of two six-sided dice. Since out of the thirty-six, there are three fours, the probability of getting a four is three in thirty-six or one in twelve. Because there are six sevens, the probability of getting a seven is six in thirty-six or one in six. This means that it is twice as likely to get a seven as it is to get a four.

A similar procedure will work for figuring out the odds of getting heads ten times in a row. The odds of it happening once are one in two (H or T). Twice, one in four (H-H or H-T or T-H or T-T). Three times, one in eight (H-H-H or H-H-T or H-T-H or H-T-T or T-H-H or T-H-T or T-T-H or T-H-H). The odds turn out to be $1/2^n$ with n being the number of flips. So, because there are ten heads in a row, the odds are $1/2^{10}$ which is $1/1024$. I wouldn't be making any bets if I were you.

The odds of winning the sweepstakes in the question above are self-explanatory. If you read the small print, you will find that it is unlikely you will ever win.

Many people have trouble understanding the concept of relative risk. For example, while it is not entirely safe to fly in a plane, the number of people who die in plane accidents is relatively small. Believe it or not, it is far more likely for you to die in a car accident or even to be struck by lightning than it is to die in a plane accident. The chances of dying in a plane accident are still a bit higher than winning the Publisher's Clearinghouse Sweepstakes, but the odds are pretty close. You are more likely to be born a millionaire than to win a sweepstakes like that.

Would you trust this man with your $10 million?

ANSWERS

1. C   2. C   3. A   4. C

When power leads man toward arrogance, poetry reminds him
of his limitations. When power narrows the areas of man's
concern, poetry reminds him of the richness and diversity of
his existence. When power corrupts, poetry cleanses. For art
establishes the basic human truths which must serve as the
touchstones of our judgment.

—**John Fitzgerald Kennedy**

The following chapters deal with the Humanities (mythology, religion, and the arts). These areas of cultural literacy are probably the ones to which you have had the least exposure in school. Very few high schools offer anything about art history, music history, movies, religion, or mythology. Yet, when most people think about culture they think of these things. Almost any movie you see or book you read will make some reference to the Bible or mythology. If you are not familiar with these topics, you will be surprised at how many references elude you.

JUST WATCH "THE SIMPSONS."

An episode of "The Simpsons" featured the curmudgeon Burns looking for his teddy bear Bobo. A huge search was undertaken, and the Simpsons family became involved when Maggie, the baby, fell in love with the teddy bear. The show was very funny, but even more so if you realized that it was a parody of the movie classic *Citizen Kane*.

Now, you have to wonder why a television show would refer to a movie made in 1941. Most Simpsons fans were not even born when the film came out, but *Citizen Kane* is such an icon of American filmmaking that the producers of "The Simpsons" must have figured that almost every American had seen it.

YOU SAY, "BUT I HAVEN'T SEEN *CITIZEN KANE*."

However, you may not have seen *Citizen Kane*. And there are probably a bunch of other important movies, books, music, and art that you haven't experienced. What movies, music, art, and books are culturally important? In this Humanities section, we have provided lists to help you find out. Just work your way through the lists, reading the books and seeing the movies as you can fit them into your schedule. In the visual arts, we have included reproductions of the works, since many of you may not be able to get to the originals.

Religion: The Bible
The Old Testament

1. **From which of the following was Eve created?**

   (A) One of Adam's ribs
   (B) The dust of the earth
   (C) The scales of the serpent
   (D) The womb of God's wife

The Bible is the holy book of Judaism and Christianity, and it is divided into two main sections: the **Old Testament** and the **New Testament.** The Old Testament is accepted by both Jews and Christians, but the New Testament is only accepted by Christians. The biblical story of creation is one of the best known parts of the Old Testament. Everyone has heard the story that God created everything in **six days,** and on the **seventh day,** he rested. The seventh day is known as the **Sabbath,** and Christians and Jews still believe in one day of rest per week. (Christians mostly prefer Sunday. Jews pick Saturday.) God then put the first man, **Adam,** in the **Garden of Eden** with the Tree of Life and the Tree of Knowledge of Good

HUMANITIES

"THE MARK OF CAIN"

God placed a mark on Cain's forehead (referred to as the mark of Cain), so that others would recognize him as a murderer and shun him.

and Evil. God told Adam not to eat of the Tree of Knowledge of Good and Evil, for "in the day that you eat of it, you shall die."

"It is not good that the man should be alone," God decided. So he put Adam to sleep and made the first woman, **Eve**, out of one of Adam's ribs. Now Adam and Eve were living naked in paradise. They were not ashamed of their nakedness, and life, by anyone's standards, was pretty good. But good things never last. One day a serpent came along and told Eve that it would be smart to eat from the tree of knowledge. Then she would know the difference between good and evil and might become a god herself. Eve was swayed by his words. She ate the fruit and gave some to Adam; suddenly things weren't so good. They were ashamed of their nakedness and they made loincloths out of fig leaves. The Greeks have a similar creation story (p. 381).

God, seeing that they had sinned, punished them by making them leave the garden. He also ended the equality that had existed between men and women, making women subservient. Then he punished all women by making them suffer through the pains of childbirth. The serpent suffered punishment as well. He was made to crawl on the ground and eat dust.

2. Who said "Am I my brother's keeper?"

(A) Adam
(B) Cain
(C) Abel
(D) Jacob

Adam and Eve had two children: Cain and Abel. Cain liked to farm, and Abel was a shepherd. The Lord had a certain fondness for sheep that made Cain jealous. So **Cain killed Abel** and when God asked Cain where his brother was, Cain replied "I do not know; **am I my brother's keeper?**"

As you might imagine, God was a bit upset. "What have you done?" he said, "Listen, your brother's blood is crying out to me from the ground!" So he told Cain that he would be forced to wander forever and never be able to grow anything from the ground.

3. According to the Bible, who lived the greatest number of years?

(A) Adam
(B) Abraham
(C) Methuselah
(D) Seth

In the Bible, people lived a long time. Adam lived 930 years. His son Seth lived 912 years. But the oldest of them all was **Methuselah**, who lived 969 years. We still sometimes refer to someone who lives a long time as a Methuselah.

4. **How long did it rain during the great flood?**

   (A) Ten days and ten nights
   (B) Twenty days and twenty nights
   (C) Forty days and forty nights
   (D) Eighty days and eighty nights

After seeing the way people treated each other, God had second thoughts about the creation of the human race. These humans that he had created were not turning out to be good people, so he decided to destroy everyone —with one exception. God decided that Methuselah's grandson **Noah** and his family were not so bad, so he warned Noah of the flood and told him to build an **ark**. After Noah had built the ark, "the fountains of the great deep burst forth, and the windows of the heavens were opened." (In other words, it was a bit more than your average thunderstorm.) Noah, his family, and **two of every creature** boarded the ark. Then it rained for **forty days and forty nights.**

Eventually, after sending out a few birds to see if dry land was available, Noah landed at **Ararat.** After he gave God a burnt offering, Noah was able to get God to promise that he would never kill everything in the world again. (Never underestimate the power of a good barbecue.)

Aftermath of the forty-day flood

5. **What was the name of the city where the people tried to build a tower to heaven?**

   (A) Jerusalem
   (B) Bethlehem
   (C) Babel
   (D) Pisa

In the olden days, everyone spoke the same language. A bunch of people got together and decided that they should build a tower to heaven in the city of **Babel.** God realized that because they could speak the same language, they could achieve anything, so he scattered all the people about and confused their speech so that they could not understand each other. We still think of a "babel" as a state of confusion.

6. **What is Abraham and Sarah's son named?**

   (A) Esau
   (B) Abel
   (C) Isaac
   (D) Joseph

The first patriarch, **Abraham** (c. 2300 BC), was given a covenant by God—a promise that his children would eventually become numerous and ultimately live in Canaan (Israel). Abraham's wife **Sarah** was childless, so Sarah asked Abraham to sire a child through her slave girl, Hagar, an Egyptian. This child was **Ishmael**, who is considered by Arabs to be the forefather of all of Arabs. Sarah was still unhappy; finally, God came to Abraham and told him that he would have a child by Sarah, even though Sarah had passed menopause (p. 331).

God kept his promise, and Sarah had a child named **Isaac.** One day, God decided to test Abraham, and he told him to offer up Isaac as a burnt offering. (Remember, a good barbecue can go a long way.) Isaac was a bit suspicious when he noticed that there was no lamb to offer. "Father, the fire and the wood are here, but where is the lamb for a burnt offering?" Abraham went as far as tying Isaac and placing him on top of some wood. When he reached for the knife to kill Isaac, an angel told Abraham to stop. God, pleased that Abraham proved his fidelity, let him offer up a ram to be sacrificed instead.

7. **What happened to Lot's wife when she turned around to see the destruction at Sodom?**

   (A) She burned up instantly
   (B) She was turned into a pillar of salt
   (C) Nothing
   (D) She ran back to save her children

The people in **Sodom and Gomorrah** were exceedingly evil, and God decided that he would destroy them. But before he did so, he told Abraham of his plan. Abraham convinced God that if one good person should happen to live in the towns, he should not be destroyed. So God sent his angels to Sodom, where they found Lot and his family. Lot treated the Angels well. God decided that he would pardon Lot and his family, so the angels informed them of the imminent destruction of Sodom. Lot and his family fled from the city, but the angels warned that if they looked back, they would be consumed by the destruction. **Lot's wife** could not resist the temptation to look back and was turned into a **pillar of salt.** The word "sodomy," which is used to describe certain sexual acts, comes from the sexual acts allegedly practiced in Sodom.

8. For what did Esau trade his birthright to Jacob?
   (A) Stew
   (B) All the gold in Esau's possession
   (C) A fatted calf
   (D) All the stars in heaven

Isaac, the son of Abraham, married Rebecca. They had two sons, twins named **Esau and Jacob**. Esau, who was born first, was hairy and liked to hunt. Jacob was a quiet man, a mama's boy, and very clever. One day when Esau was returning from a hunt, he was famished and saw that Jacob had made stew. Esau asked Jacob for some stew, but Jacob made Esau trade his birthright (the inheritance due him because he was the first born) for the stew. Esau complied. Later, Jacob tricked Isaac into giving him his blessing. He wore Esau's clothing and put the fur of some animal on his wrists so the then-blind Isaac would think he was his brother. After Jacob received the blessing, Isaac discovered the duplicity—but it was too late. As you might imagine, Esau was upset over Jacob's trickery and he decided that he would kill Jacob as soon as his father died. Rebecca heard of the plot and managed to get Jacob out of the country. After a long life, Jacob eventually reunited with Esau and the brothers made peace.

9. Who was given the coat of many colors?
   (A) Isaac
   (B) Esau
   (C) Joseph
   (D) Moses

Jacob had twelve sons by different wives, but the one he liked the most was **Joseph**, one of two sons by Jacob's beloved wife Rachel. Jacob favored Joseph and gave him a **coat of many colors**. This angered his brothers, who were jealous of their father's preferential treatment toward

"LET MY PEOPLE GO!"

....

The tale of the Hebrews' exodus from Pharaoh's oppression has provided a model for oppressed peoples ever since. Christians and Rastafarians, as well as this century's Jews, have used the language of Exodus to describe their campaigns for justice and freedom. Spirituals, sung by slaves at work and at prayer, served as a vehicle of this rhetoric. They could also function as a means of surreptitious communication in the presence of overseers. "Go Down, Moses" is one of the most famous spirituals.

When Israel was in Egypt's Land,
Let my people go!
Oppressed so hard they could not stand,
Let my people go!

Refrain: *Go down, Moses,*
'Way down in Egypt's Land,
Tell old [or "ole"] Pharaoh,
Let my people go!

"Thus saith [spoke] the Lord,"
bold Moses said,
Let my people go!
"If not I'll smite your first-born dead,"
Let my people go!

No more in bondage shall they toil,
Let my people go!
Let them come out with Egypt's spoil,
Let my people go!

Refrain: *Go down, Moses,*
'Way down in Egypt's Land,
Tell old Pharaoh,
Let my people go!

Joseph. So one day, when Joseph went to meet his brothers in the fields, they decided to kidnap him and sell him into slavery. Joseph was taken to Egypt, where he prospered. He was able to interpret dreams, and God was with him, so, naturally, everything he did was successful.

Meanwhile, a famine struck the entire region. Joseph, who had read the dream of a Pharaoh in Egypt, had predicted the famine, and the Egyptians had been successful in storing food. Because they had the only food in the area, it wasn't long before Joseph's brothers came to buy food. When Joseph met them, he immediately recognized them. They, however, did not know who he was, so Joseph played a little trick. He accused the brothers of lying and framed them for a crime that they didn't commit, causing his brothers a lot of stress.

But then Joseph couldn't contain himself any longer and began to cry, and he told his brothers who he was. The family moved to Egypt, where they stayed until the Exodus some four hundred years later. Joseph was so successful in his work that by the end of the famine, the Pharaoh, with Joseph's help, had enslaved the entire population of Egypt.

Sculpture of Moses by Michelangelo (p. 454-459)

10. Why did Moses's mother put her baby son in a papyrus basket among the reeds on the bank of a river?

(A) Because she wanted to clean the baby
(B) Because it was his first baptism
(C) To hide him from the Egyptians
(D) To take advantage of the nice weather

Eventually, a Pharaoh came to power who did not know Joseph. This Pharaoh thought that the Jews were becoming too numerous and that they would ally themselves against Egypt in the event of a war. So he enslaved them and treated them poorly. The Pharaoh decided that the best way to weaken the Jews was to kill off every male child. At first he tried to get the Egyptian midwives to do it, but they refused, so he passed an edict that every male child should be thrown into the Nile (pp. 246-247)

Now, Moses' mother would have none of that. She thought **Moses** (c. 13th century BC) a perfectly fine baby, and she decided to put him in a papyrus basket in a marsh to protect the boy. The child was discovered by Pharaoh's daughter, who felt pity for the boy, and ended up raising him as her own son. One day Moses saw an Egyptian beating a Hebrew, and because Moses killed the Egyptian, he was forced to go into hiding.

While in hiding, Moses chanced upon a **burning bush** that was not consumed by the flames. From the bush came the voice of God who told Moses that he should help lead the Israelites out of Egypt. Moses went to Egypt and demanded the freedom of the Jews. But Pharaoh, whose heart had been hardened by God, refused, so Moses used a little leverage. God attacked the Egyptians with **ten plagues**. And these weren't your run-of-the-mill plagues. We're talking rivers becoming blood, frogs, locusts, cattle disease, boils, etc. After each one, Pharaoh lied and said he would release the Jews, but then changed his mind. Finally, the tenth plague did the trick. The firstborn of every Egyptian family was killed, and Pharaoh, who had lost a son, finally allowed the Jews to sally forth out of Egypt. The Jews had put blood from a sacrifice on their doorposts, and the angel of death avoided all of the houses with blood on them. (The Jewish celebration of **Passover** is named in honor of this event.)

As the Jews left, Pharaoh had another change of heart. He and the rest of the Egyptians pursued the Jews. The Jews were led by Moses into a position where the entire Egyptian army was on one side, and the Red Sea on the other. Moses lifted his staff and the **Red Sea divided.** The Jews walked across on dry land; when the Egyptians followed, God caused the water to come back upon the Egyptians, drowning all of them.

The Ten Commandments, (1956), starring Charlton Heston, Yul Brenner, and Anne Baxter. Directed by Cecil B. DeMille, this is overblown movie making at its best. The story of Moses' life, with stunning special effects (check out the parting of the Red Sea).

11. What was the name of the food that God provided for the Hebrews who were traveling in the desert after escaping from Egypt?

(A) Cactus
(B) Manna
(C) Torah
(D) Matzoh

After escaping Egypt, Moses and his people spent forty years wandering about the desert. There was little food in the desert, so God provided bread every morning. The Jews called the bread **manna.** Eventually, they reached **Mount Sinai,** where Moses went up to meet God. There God gave him the **Ten Commandments,** but when Moses came down from the mountain, he found that the Jews had constructed a **golden calf** that they were worshipping. Moses was furious, so he smashed the Commandments and upbraided the people. He returned to the mountain, got the laws again, and led the people to Israel. Moses never got to enter the **promised land** of Israel with his people. He died right before they reached it.

The story of the exodus from Egypt is retold each year during the Jewish holiday of Passover. During the holiday, the Jews eat unleavened bread called **Matzoh** to symbolize the flight from Egypt (the speed with which the Jews left Egypt did not allow them time to let their bread rise and it was therefore unleavened). The Last Supper (pp. 376-377) of Jesus Christ was a celebration of Passover.

12. **What was the name of the woman who betrayed Samson?**

    (A) Sarah
    (B) Delilah
    (C) Judah
    (D) Barbaretta

After fleeing Egypt and finding the promised land, the Jews were subjugated by the Philistines, so God gave the Jews **Samson** (11th century BC) to help them escape from oppression. God told Samson's mother that his hair should never be cut because it was the source of Samson's great strength. He killed a lion with his bare hands and was able to beat up people at will. However, Samson had a weakness for Philistine women, and the Philistines used this to try to trap him. When he was with a prostitute, they would try to kill him before he woke, but Samson was too strong.

Finally, Samson met **Delilah** and fell in love with her. The Philistines told Delilah that they would make her rich with silver if she helped capture Samson, so she asked him to tell her the secret of his strength. Samson lied a few times, and made her look pretty stupid, but her persistence finally prevailed He told her that his strength came from his hair. She cut off his hair while he slept with his head on her lap. Samson was captured by the Philistines and his eyes were poked out. They made fun of him and tied him to two pillars during a party. He prayed for one last bout of strength, and God provided. Samson was able to pull down the pillars he was tied to, collapsing the building where all of the Philistines were celebrating, killing them all.

13. **What weapon did David use in slaying the giant Goliath?**

    (A) An enormous boulder
    (B) A bow and arrow
    (C) A sling
    (D) A knife

Goliath loses his head.

The Philistines did not give up and were soon attacking the Jews again. They had a champion named **Goliath** who was over eight feet tall, and he challenged the Jews to kill him. The Jews were fearful, but finally little **David** (c. 1060-970 BC) came with a sling and some small stones and knocked down Goliath. He then took Goliath's sword and killed him. David later became king of Israel, and he and his son **Solomon** (c. 974–937 BC) were both great leaders. David's defeat of Goliath has been a symbol of an underdog's victory ever since.

14. **Which of the following people is known for his devotion to God even under tortures devised by Satan?**

    (A) Abraham
    (B) Job
    (C) John
    (D) Eliphaz

Job (c. 5th century BC) was a good and very rich man who lived in the land of Uz. One day God was bragging to Satan about Job's qualities when Satan countered that it was easy for people to have faith when their lives were easy. So with God's permission, Satan began to tear apart Job's life. He took away his possessions and killed his children, yet Job was able to resist the pressures from Satan and continued to believe in God.

Eventually, God was merciful and he gave Job back double all he had taken from him. We still refer to someone who faces adversity calmly and with dignity as having "the patience of Job."

ANSWERS

1. A 2. B 3. C 4. C 5. C 6. C 7. B 8. A 9. C 10. C
11. B 12. B 13. C 14. B

Religion: The Bible
The New Testament

1. **Name the four writers of the Gospels in the New Testament.**

The four Gospels tell the story of Jesus' (c. 4 BC-AD 29 or 30) life and teachings. The oldest of the Gospels is that of **Mark** (first century AD). Since it was written closer to Jesus's lifetime, it is considered the most reliable. The Gospel according to **Matthew** (first century AD) is placed first in the New Testament, and because of its thoroughness and organization, it is considered the most important of the Gospels in expressing Christian thought. The Gospel according to **Luke** (first century AD) is known for its inclusion of several parables that did not make it into any of the other Gospels. It emphasizes the universal nature of Jesus's teaching. The Gospel according to **John** (first century AD), the most poetic of the four, looks at the occurrences of Jesus' life in a more symbolic manner.

2. **Jesus Christ was born in**

    (A) Mecca
    (B) Bethlehem
    (C) Jerusalem
    (D) Zion

BORN FOUR YEARS BEFORE HIS BIRTH

Our calendar's starting date, determined by monk Dionysius Exiguus in AD 525, was set so that the birth of Jesus would fall on AD 1. Recent historians however, through studying the evidence from the time, believe that Exiguus was wrong in getting the date and that Jesus was actually born BC 4.

Mary of Nazareth, who was engaged to a man named Joseph, had not yet had sexual relations with a man when she was made pregnant by the actions of God. This is the reason that Mary is often called the **Virgin Mary**. **Jesus**, her son, is called the **Son of God**. He was born in Bethlehem in a **manger**, a trough in which hay is kept for horses, because there were no vacancies at the inn.

An angel came to **three wise men** and told them to follow a new star that would be rising in the east over the birthplace of the child born to God. The three wise men followed the **star of Bethlehem** to Jerusalem, where they asked King Herod (74-4 BC) "Where is the child who has been born King of the Jews?" King Herod was not interested in having anyone challenge his power, particularly a little tyke who had God on his side. King Herod instructed the wise men to seek out the child.

When the wise men found Jesus, "they were overwhelmed with joy." They gave the baby gifts of **gold, frankincense, and myrrh**. Joseph was warned by an angel of King Herod's evil intentions toward the child, and he, Mary and the child escaped to Egypt. Herod then killed all of the children in Bethlehem who could possibly have been the child alluded to by the wise men.

When Jesus was twelve and his parents were making their annual pilgrimage to Jerusalem to celebrate Passover (p. 369), he disappeared. His parents looked everywhere and eventually found him sitting among the wise men discussing religion. Everyone was amazed at what the kid knew.

3. **Who baptized Jesus?**

    (A) Mary
    (B) John
    (C) Joseph
    (D) Judas

When Jesus was about thirty years old, he was bap-

The wise men admire newborn Jesus.

tized by **John the Baptist** (c. 12 BC-c. AD 27), who had been born amidst all kinds of fanfare and prophecies six months before Jesus. His parents, like Abraham and Sarah (pp. 366-367), were older than they should have been to conceive a child, but an angel from God told them the name and the importance of their child. It was foretold that John would be the one to "turn many of the people of Israel to the Lord their God."

After being baptized, Jesus spent **forty days** in the wilderness where he ate nothing at all. After all the time without food, Jesus was famished, and the devil took it upon himself to test him by tempting him with the desires of men. Jesus resisted, passed the tests, and was filled with the "power of the Spirit."

4. **The name of the sayings that Jesus made during the "Sermon on the Mount" is**

   (A) The Beatitudes
   (B) The Proverbs
   (C) The Immaculate Revelation
   (D) The Covenant

After his time in the wilderness, Jesus's fame spread as he cured the sick and taught the people the ways of God. A huge crowd gathered to hear Jesus deliver the **Sermon on the Mount,** in which he offered the **Beatitudes**. This collection of sayings included "Blessed are the meek, for they will inherit the earth." At the same sermon, he reinterpreted some ideas from the Old Testament. He said "You have heard that it was said, **'An eye for an eye and a tooth for a tooth.'** But I say to you, do not resist an evildo-

Jesus preaches the Beatitudes.

er. But **if anyone strikes you on the right cheek, turn the other also;** and if anyone wants to sue you and take your coat, give your cloak as well; and if anyone forces you to go one mile, go also the second mile..." He also taught that sin of the heart is as bad as actual sin. It is not enough to avoid committing adultery; "everyone who looks at a woman with lust has already committed adultery with her in his heart."

Jesus then went to teach and perform miracles throughout the area.

At one point in Jesus's travels, a woman who had sinned a great deal came to wash his feet with her tears. When Jesus was questioned for letting such a woman wash his feet, he replied that the more a person has sinned, the more grateful he or she will be to have redemption. Tradition states that this woman was **Mary Magdalene** (first century AD), who was later cured of seven demons, but this interpretation is not clear from the text of the bible.

5. In one of Jesus' parables, he tells the story of a man who had been badly beaten and left for dead. What was the nationality of the "good" man who helped the poor, beaten victim?
   (A) Philistine
   (B) Samaritan
   (C) Israeli
   (D) Pharisean

Jesus taught by using parables. A parable is a story that is meant to teach a lesson. One of these parables concerned the **Good Samaritan.** The Samaritans were a people who practiced a different type of Judaism and were disliked by the Jews. In the parable, Jesus tells the story of a man who is beaten up by robbers and left half-dead on a road. A priest and a Levite walk by and do nothing, but a Samaritan sees him and takes good care of him, cleaning his wounds and paying for his lodging. Jesus then asked his listeners to tell him which of the three men was a good neighbor to the beaten victim.

6. What happens to the prodigal son when he returns home?
   (A) He is killed.
   (B) His father throws a party.
   (C) His brother is happy.
   (D) He kills his father.

"Prodigal Son," by the Rolling Stones, from the album *Beggar's Banquet.* The song is an old spiritual recounting the tale Jesus told, brilliantly reinterpreted by the Stones.

When Jesus was trying to convince his followers of the importance of converting sinners, he told them the story of **the prodigal son.** It seems that the younger of a father's two sons came to him and asked for his inheritance early. His father agreed and the son went on a partying binge. He went "to a distant country, and there he squandered his property in dissolute living." After the son lost all his money, there was a famine, and he got himself a job feeding pigs. While feeding the pigs, he realized that

HUMANITIES

back home his father's hired hands were doing better than he, so he returned home to beg his father to let him work the fields. When he got there, his father was so excited to see him that he killed a fatted calf for him. This was a cool thing. A fatted calf was expensive back then (as it is today).

When the older brother found out about the way in which the father had treated the younger, he became angry. He had always been the good son. While the younger had been away flirting with prostitutes, the older had been doing all the right things. The father said to him "We had to celebrate and rejoice, because this brother of yours was dead and has come to life; he was lost and has been found." The moral of the story: It is important to bring people back to ways of goodness even if they have sinned badly.

7. **What happened after Lazarus died?**
    (A) He was raised from the dead by Jesus.
    (B) He became a symbol of lost hope.
    (C) The Romans blamed Jesus for his death.
    (D) His sister Mary danced on his grave.

Perhaps the most striking of all of the miracles that Jesus performed during his lifetime was the **raising of Lazarus.** Lazarus was the brother of Mary Magdalene (p. 375). When Jesus was told that he was sick, he waited before going to heal him. Lazarus died before Jesus arrived and the people mourned the death. Jesus heard their weeping and went to Lazarus' tomb, where he had been lying for four days, and brought him back to life. This, as you might imagine, caused many non-believers to believe in Jesus.

8. **Which of the apostles betrayed Jesus?**
    (A) John
    (B) Judas
    (C) James
    (D) Simon Peter

Jesus was helped in his teachings by twelve apostles. These people were Jesus's inner circle. The night before his death, Jesus and his apostles celebrated the Passover (p. 369) meal in what is now called the Last Supper (p. 370). It was at this supper that Jesus introduced the sacrament of communion. He informed the apostles that from then on, when they came together in his memory, the bread would be as his flesh and the wine would be as his blood. Jesus then told of his imminent death and said, to everyone's horror, that he would be betrayed by someone present at the supper.

Sure enough, **Judas** (first century AD) betrayed Jesus and led a mob to him. Jesus was accused of blasphemy, arrested, and taken before **Pontius Pilate** (first century AD). He felt that Jesus was innocent, but the mob demanded that he be **crucified.** Crucifixion was one of the preferred methods of execution at the time. A person was hung from a crossbar and died a slow, agonizing death as the muscles in their chests caved in, eventually causing suffocation. The convicted person was usually made to carry the cross from which he would hang to the execution site.

Pontius Pilate agreed to crucify Jesus and washed his hands to symbolize that he would have nothing to do with it. Jesus was forced to wear a crown of thorns as he carried his cross. He was nailed to the cross and while dying said "**Father, forgive them; for they know not what they do.**" Everybody ridiculed him as he was dying. Two thieves were crucified at the same time as Jesus. One scoffed at him, while the other converted and believed in him.

Jesus was taken off the cross by a good man named Joseph (first century AD), and women began the preparations for his burial. But because it was the Sabbath, they rested. When they returned, they found that the stone that had been in front of the tomb had been moved and that Jesus had been **resurrected.**

Answers

....

1. Matthew, Mark , Luke , and John   2. B   3. B   4. A   5. B   6. B   7. A
8. B

Non-Western Religions

1. **What is the name of the holy book of Islam?**

    (A) The Bible
    (B) The Kabbalah
    (C) The Koran
    (D) The Shiite

   Islam is a religion practiced by approximately 950 million people. It is the second-most-practiced religion (after Christianity), and, because the population of **Muslims** (people who believe in Islam) is increasing rapidly, it will soon be the first. The Arabic word *al-islam* means giving all of oneself to God, without reservation. Islam is about total commitment and is more comprehensive than most other religions. A Muslim who follows the dictates of Islam will have guidelines and rules for almost every aspect of his life.

The sacred book of Islam is called the **Koran** (in Arabic it is the Qur'an), and it is supposed to be the word of God as communicated to **Mohammed** (c. 570-632). Mohammed is considered a prophet, but unlike Jesus in the Christian religion, he is not considered to have God-like properties. One of the central tenets of Islam is that there is only one God **(Allah)**, and that people should give their total commitment to him. The Koran refers to Islam as the religion of Abraham. Mohammed is considered the seal of the prophets, the last of a line that includes Abraham, Noah, Moses, and Jesus. Therefore, although Islam began to be practiced in Mohammed's lifetime, most Muslims would argue that the religion was created by God and is a restoration of the original religion of Abraham.

Siddhartha, by Herman Hesse, the story of Buddha's life. *Zen and the Art of Motorcycle Maintenance* by Robert M. Pirsig. An interesting discussion of philosophy and mechanics.

2. **When Muslims pray, they face toward**

   (A) Mohammed
   (B) Mecca
   (C) Japan
   (D) Jerusalem

In the year 610, Mohammed had the first of several revelations from Allah that indicated that he was to be his messenger. He began to preach, but was forced to immigrate to Medina. There he eventually converted the people and adapted the Kaaba (a shrine used for worshipping idols) for the practice of the Muslim religion. The Kaaba

Muslims praying toward Mecca.

was in **Mecca;** to this day, Muslims face toward it when they pray, which they do five times a day. They are also required by Islamic law to make a pilgrimage there at least once in their lifetime.

Another tradition in Islamic law is the fast of **Ramadan**. During Ramadan, a person cannot eat during the daylight hours. It is celebrated during the month in which the Koran is said to have been communicated to Mohammed.

3. **Put the following historical figures into chronological order:**

   I. Jesus
   II. Abraham
   III. Mohammed
   IV. Buddha

   (A) II, I, IV, III
   (B) II, IV, I, III
   (C) IV, III, I, II
   (D) IV, II, I, III

HUMANITIES

KNOWING AND NOT

The Vedic era is one of the earliest in India's history from which documents survive. "The Upanishads" were Vedic treatises written about broad philosophical problems in Hindu thought.

"Who says that Spirit is not known, knows; who claims that he knows, knows nothing. The ignorant think that Spirit lies within knowledge, the wise man knows It beyond knowledge. Spirit is known through revelation. The living man who finds Spirit, finds Truth."

From the Kena-Upanishad

For further exploration into non-Western religion and philosophy, read the *Tao-Te-Ching* by Lao-Tze (c. 600 BC).

Abraham reportedly lived somewhere between 2000 to 3000 BC and the first of the prophets listed above. Buddha lived around 500 BC, and was followed by Jesus, whose birthday should be easy to remember. Finally, there was Mohammed, who lived during the sixth century.

Buddhism is a religion practiced mainly in Asia in which people follow the teaching of the Buddha, a man named Siddhartha Gautama (c. 563-483 BC) who lived in Northern India. The Buddha taught that spiritual discipline should be practiced with the goal of eventually reaching the state of **Nirvana.** Nirvana is a state in which one is not bothered by earthly concerns such as desire and self-consciousness. A person in a state of Nirvana is at peace with himself.

4. **Which of the following are among the sacred writings of Hinduism?**

   I. The Vedas
   II. The Bhagavad Gita
   III. The Koran

   (A) I only
   (B) II only
   (C) I and II only
   (D) I, II, and III

Hinduism is the national religion of India and it counts among its holy books the **Vedas** and the **Bhagavad Gita.** Hindus believe in the transmigration of souls (reincarnation) and the idea of **Karma,** which revolves around the idea of action. Good acts can lead to a rebirth in a better station. Bad acts can lead to rebirth in a poorer station. The Hindu religion divides people up into **castes,** which define a person's position in society.

The Dalai Lama, spiritual leader of the Tibetan Buddhists.

ANSWERS

1. C   2. B   3. B   4. C

Ancient Mythology

1. **According to Greek mythology, which of the following people was responsible for releasing all of the evils and miseries of the world?**

   (A) Athena
   (B) Prometheus
   (C) Pandora
   (D) Oedipus

Mythology, the classic handbook of Greek and Roman mythology, by Edith Hamilton.

In the traditions of Greek mythology, man was created by two **Titans** (the giant offspring of some gods) named **Prometheus** and **Epimetheus**. To give man a head start, Prometheus stole fire from heaven in order to give man special powers. Even though he had the great power associated with fire, man still lacked a mate. **Zeus,** the most powerful of the gods, punished man for stealing the fire in heaven by sending a woman, **Pandora**, to marry Epimetheus and bring about the downfall of man. (Obviously, this tale was not written by a woman.)

Pandora was given many good attributes by all the gods. But she is most remembered for opening a box, given to her by the gods, that contained all of the evils and miseries that could befall mankind. They didn't tell her what was in the box; they just told her not to open it. But she did open it and all the evils flew out into the world. Realizing her mistake, she quickly tried to close the box, but to no avail. It was too late; the bad stuff was out, and to this day, we still use the phrase "opening **Pandora's box**" to mean creating a situation that will cause much pain or grief.

Prometheus paté, anyone?

2   **How was the Greek Titan Prometheus punished for giving man fire?**

(A) He was crucified.
(B) He was made to go to bed without any supper.
(C) He was locked in chains and his liver was fed to an eagle.
(D) His god-like powers were taken away from him.

For his decision to give man fire, Prometheus was punished by Zeus in a diabolical manner. He was chained to a rock where an eagle tore out his liver every night. In the morning, his liver regenerated. Despite the punishment, Prometheus would not give in to Zeus; thus he remains a symbol of an individual's valiant resistance to authority. Later, Prometheus was rescued by Hercules (p. 387).

3.   **Who was given the power to turn everything he or she touched into gold?**

(A) Midas
(B) Goldilocks
(C) Bacchus
(D) Pan

Bacchus, the god of wine, lost track of his foster-father, Silenus, who had been drinking. Silenus stumbled into a kingdom belonging to a man named **Midas**. King Midas was a good host and entertained Silenus for ten days before returning him to Bacchus. As a reward, Bacchus granted Midas one wish, and Midas wished that he be able to turn anything he touched into gold. At first the king was happy. He went around joyously turning anything that got in his way into gold, but when he tried to eat, he realized that there would be some troubles. The bread became hard and cold, the wine went down his throat like melted gold. Midas prayed to Bacchus, who told him to wash in a river to remove the gift. Thereafter, Midas gave up his greed and lived in the countryside in a humble fashion.

GOLD STANDARD

Though Midas's gift did him more harm than good, to this day we refer to a person with extraordinary business sense as having the "Midas touch."

4. Which of the following people tied the knot that Alexander the Great cut with his sword?
    (A) Icarus
    (B) Gordius
    (C) Dionysus
    (D) Athena

Midas' father, **Gordius**, was originally made king when he just happened to enter a town in a wagon. The people of the town had been told by their gods that the next king would arrive in such a manner. He tied his wagon with a complicated knot (called the **Gordian Knot)**, and people said that the first person to untie the wagon would become the ruler of all of Asia. Alexander the Great allegedly tried to untie the knot, but became frustrated, and split the knot with his sword. Today, if you can solve a difficult problem quickly, or find the root of a problem, you are said to have **"cut the Gordian knot."**

The Golden Ass, by Apuleius. A very funny story written back in the second century. The book not only contains the story of Cupid and Psyche, but also tells of the adventures of a young man who gets transformed into an ass and wanders the countryside.

5. What did Psyche do to cause her husband Cupid to fly away?
    (A) She complained
    (B) She used a lamp to try to see him
    (C) She killed their son
    (D) She gave him a magic carpet

Psyche was a beautiful woman who ended up in a mysterious castle with a husband who wouldn't let her see him. He would arrive late at night and leave before she woke in the morning, and he insisted that she not try to look at him. Psyche was satisfied with this agreement for a while, but unfortunately for her, she had sisters who were a tad bit envious of her situation. The sisters convinced Psyche that her "husband" must be a monster fattening her up for the kill. They told her that she should hide away a lamp and a knife so that she could reveal his face with the light. Then, if he turned out to be a monster, she could surprise him and plunge the knife into his body.

So Psyche lit the lamp as her sisters had suggested, but when she looked at her husband, **Cupid** (who happened to be the god of love), she was so shocked at his beauty that she dropped some of the oil from the lamp on his shoulder. Cupid was furious and he flew away to the home of his mother, Venus (p. 389). Venus hated Psyche because her beauty rivaled her own. Venus made Psyche do a bunch of heinous tasks, and she was eventually rescued, allowed to become immortal, and marry Cupid. (If you are wondering, her sisters ended up falling off a cliff.)

I MADE HER MYSELF!

The myth of Pygmalion became the basis for a play called Pygmalion *by George Bernard Shaw Later it was the basis for the musical comedy* My Fair Lady, *in which an aristocratic man teaches a lower-class woman how to speak and act like a lady and then falls in love with her.*

6. **What was the name of the sculptor who created a statue so real that he fell in love with it?**

   (A) Icarus
   (B) Pygmalion
   (C) Michelangelo
   (D) Priam

Pygmalion decided that he did not like women and resolved to live unmarried. He was a sculptor, and with consummate skill had created an ivory statue that looked exactly like a woman. He fell in love with the work and treated it like a woman, buying it gifts and dressing it up and such. He became obsessed with the statue and prayed to Venus to bring the statue to life. She complied, and they got married and had a child.

Pygmalion says, "A hard woman is good to find."

7. Which of the following people fell in love with his or her own reflection?

   (A) Venus
   (B) Madonna
   (C) Narcissus
   (D) Cupid

After rejecting the company of any of the nymphs, the beautiful youth Narcissus found himself in front of a spring that gave a perfect reflection of his image. He was so taken by his reflection that he kept trying to talk to it, but to no avail. The reflection looked upon him with love in its eyes and even reached out its arms when Narcissus tried to embrace it. But when he touched the spring, the reflection disappeared. Narcissus could not bear to leave his reflection, and eventually wasted away and died. We still refer to someone who is stuck on himself as narcissistic.

Narcissus: love at first sight.

8. What is the name of the monster whose face could turn anyone into stone?

   (A) Minerva
   (B) Madonna
   (C) Medusa
   (D) Medea

Because of a conflict with the goddess Athena, Medusa was made so ugly that anyone who saw her would turn to stone. Her hair was turned into snakes, and she caused the kingdom all sorts of problems. The cavern in which she lived was full of stone statues of people who had attempted to kill her. Perseus used a shield so that he could look at her reflection instead of directly at her. In this way he managed to kill her, and he gave the head of the slain monster to Athena.

9. Who was successful in retrieving the Golden Fleece?

   (A) Jason
   (B) Achilles
   (C) Perseus
   (D) Janus

The story of Jason has been used for the foundation of many plays and novels such as Shakespeare's *Macbeth* and Euripides's *Medea*.

Even though he was the rightful heir to the throne, Jason was told by his uncle that he should go out in search of the golden fleece, the magical hair of a once-magical ram. The golden fleece was in another kingdom, and to reach it, Jason embarked on a difficult journey. He got together a group of brave Greeks who traveled together on a great ship called the Argo. Called Argonauts, these soldiers comprised some of the strongest warriors of Greek mythology, including Hercules. The Argonauts traveled through many perils to get to the land of the golden fleece. When they finally got there, the local king made them perform difficult tasks, including sowing a field with dragon's teeth, in order to win the fleece.

Jason was helped by his intended wife, Medea, who gave him charms and potions that made the job easier. He returned to his homeland victorious, but once home he found himself a new wife (bad move). Medea was furious. She killed the new wife and then she killed the children that she had had with Jason. Jason ended up a sad and broken man, forgotten by the gods and eventually killed when his ship, the Argo, fell on him.

SAME GODS, DIFFERENT NAMES

	GREEK	ROMAN
Big Guy	Zeus	Jupiter
God of the Sea	Poseidon	Neptune
God of the Dead	Hades	Pluto
Goddess of Love	Aphrodite	Venus
Goddess of Wisdom	Athena	Minerva
Big Guy's Wife	Hera	Juno
God of the Sun	Apollo	Apollo
Goddess of Hunting	Artemis	Diana
God of Wine	Dionysus	Bacchus
God of Merchants	Hermes	Mercury
God of War	Ares	Mars
Big Guy's Father	Cronus	Saturn
God of the Sky	Uranus	Uranus
Goddess of Harvest	Demeter	Ceres
Wife of Hades	Persephone	Proserpina
Goddess of Victory	Nike	(no equivalent)
Goddess of Hearth	Hestia	Vesta

10. **How many tasks did Hercules undertake?**

   (A) Four
   (B) Six
   (C) Nine
   (D) Twelve

Born with amazing strength, Hercules was one of the many sons of Zeus by different mortal women. Zeus's god-wife, Hera, was a little jealous of her husband's flirtations with mortals and made Hercules a servant to Eurystheus. Eurystheus gave Hercules twelve tasks which became known as the "Labors of Hercules." The labors included everything from heroic deeds to the unenviable task of cleaning a stable that had not been cleaned in years. Hercules was eventually killed when his wife tried to give him a love potion, but was fooled into poisoning him. (Women just don't get many breaks in classical mythology.)

11. **What was the monster that Theseus killed in the Labyrinth?**

   (A) The minotaur
   (B) The dragon
   (C) The three-headed bull
   (D) The many-headed hydra

Theseus slaying the minotaur

Another of the great heroes of classical mythology is Theseus. The king, his father, had commanded that Theseus be raised in another place. When he was old enough, he was to return to Athens. The dreaded Medea (p. 386) almost succeeded in poisoning Theseus, but failed and was expelled to another unsuspecting country.

When Theseus returned, Athens (p. 142) was in turmoil. The city was required to send seven youths and seven maidens to Crete, where they were to be eaten by a Minotaur. The Minotaur was kept in a Labyrinth so complicated that, once inside, it was impossible to escape without assistance. Theseus volunteered to enter the Labyrinth and battle the Minotaur. When the daughter of King Minos of Crete fell in love with him, Theseus was able to get a sword and a clew of thread to use in order to escape the Labyrinth. He used the string to keep track of the way out of the Labyrinth, and he succeeded in killing the Minotaur. On his way home to Athens, Theseus abandoned the daughter of

King Minos on an island because Dionysus, a god, was in love with her. Theseus then ran off with the queen of the Amazons, Hippolyta.

12. **Icarus is known for**

  (A) flying too close to the sun
  (B) invading Troy during the Trojan war
  (C) succeeding Caesar as heir to the throne
  (D) joining with Hamlet in attacking his father

The inventor of the Labyrinth that held the Minotaur, **Daedalus** found himself out of favor with King Minos. Minos imprisoned Daedalus and his son, **Icarus**, in a tower. Daedalus was a master craftsman, and succeeded in building a pair of wings for himself and his son that would allow them both to fly to freedom. Daedalus warned his son not to fly too high because the wax of which the wings were made would melt. Icarus had so much fun flying that he didn't heed the words of his father; he flew too close to the sun and his wings melted. He fell to his death, and Daedalus mourned the loss of his only child.

13. **What is the name of the man who, in classical mythology, killed his father and married his mother?**

  (A) Hercules
  (B) Achilles
  (C) Aeneas
  (D) Oedipus

Later on, the myth of Oedipus took on a bigger meaning when **Sigmund Freud (p. 182)** used it to illustrate one of his theories of human nature. A man with an Oedipus complex has an unnatural attachment to his mother and a dislike of his father.

"Oedipus Rex," by Tom Lehrer from *An Evening with Tom Lehrer.* Funny song about poor Oedipus.

Laius, the King of Thebes, had been informed by the gods that his son would be a danger to him if he grew up. So he gave his baby son to a herdsman who, unable to kill the infant, hung the baby upside down from a tree. The child was picked up by a peasant who named him **Oedipus,** which means swollen foot. When Oedipus grew up he accidentally met his father on a narrow path, and neither of them would get out of the way. The king killed one of Oedipus's horses, and Oedipus, out of anger, killed the king.

In the kingdom where this all happened, there was a **Sphinx**. This winged monster with the body of a lion and the head of a woman was fond of riddles. The Sphinx was causing problems for the people of the kingdom by blocking one of the main roads and refusing to let people pass unless they could solve her riddles, which were not easy. Oedipus decided to challenge the Sphinx, and when he was asked "What animal is it that in the morning goes on four **feet**, at noon on two, and in the evening upon three?" he replied "Man, who in childhood creeps on hands and knees, in manhood walks erect, and in old age with the aid of a staff." The Sphinx was so upset that it jumped off a cliff, and the people of Thebes made Oedipus king.

One of the benefits of being King was that Oedipus could take Jocasta, the former queen, for his wife. But after the kingdom was thrown into famine, it was discovered that Jocasta was Oedipus's mother. When the royal couple found out, Jocasta killed herself, and Oedipus tore out his eyes.

14. What criterion was Paris supposed to use in deciding to whom to give the golden apple?

   (A) Intelligence
   (B) Beauty
   (C) Strength
   (D) Agility

Paris was tending his flocks when three goddesses appeared before him with the instructions that he was supposed to give the most beautiful of the three a golden apple which contained the inscription "For the fairest." Poor Paris. He had to choose between **Juno,** a war goddess, **Minerva,** the goddess of intelligence, and **Venus,** the goddess of love. Each promised him incredible gifts. Venus would give him a beautiful woman for his wife, Minerva glory in war, and Juno power and riches. As we might

Decisions, decisions, decisions

expect, Paris went for the beautiful woman, and gave the apple to Venus. This **Judgment of Paris** led to the **Trojan War,** which was recorded by the great poet **Homer** in the **Iliad.**

Paris ended up with **Helen,** who is said to have "**a face that launched a thousand ships**" because of her part in bringing about the **Trojan War**. Venus helped Paris steal Helen from her Greek husband and take her to Troy. The Greeks were furious and prepared to enter into a huge war to bring her home. Some of the greatest heroes of Greece and Troy battled with assistance from the gods. One person to remember is **Achilles,** who fought for the Greeks. When Achilles was a boy, his mother dipped him in **the river Styx;** he became immortal everywhere except for his heel, where she had held him. Achilles killed the Trojan hero **Hector** after forcing him to run around the town three times. Another character is **Cassandra,** who was given the gift of prophecy—along with the curse that no one would ever believe her.

The Trojan Horse, stuffed with angry Greeks

HORSEPLAY

This is where we get the colloquialism "Beware of Greeks bearing gifts."

15. The Trojan horse

(A) is a two-time winner of the Kentucky Derby
(B) is a horse that, although it pulls slowly, gets the job done
(C) is a wooden horse that concealed Athenian soldiers
(D) is a horse used to pull chariots in the Roman amphitheaters

In the end, the Trojans were able to withstand the Grecian attack, and the Greeks appeared to be leaving. But before they did, they built a huge wooden horse (the Trojans worshipped horses) and left it on the shore after they left. The Trojans were intrigued and even fascinated by this strange gift. However, one of them, **Laocoön,** said "For my part, I fear the Greeks even when they offer gifts." But Laocoön and his sons were suddenly killed by two serpents from the sea, and the Trojans took this as a message that they should bring the **Trojan Horse** into their city.

After darkness fell, a Greek spy opened up the horse, and the Greek soldiers hidden inside went on a rampage. They killed most of the Trojan people who had been celebrating their victory and were fast asleep from eating too much food and drinking too much wine.

16. Which of the following women is known for avenging her father's death by killing her mother?

(A) Helen
(B) Electra
(C) Andromache
(D) Venus

When **Agamemnon,** who had fought for the Greeks at Troy, returned home, his wife **Clytemnestra** was upset that he had sacrificed their daughter, so she killed him. She also planned to kill his son **Orestes,** but she failed. Orestes and his sister, **Electra,** eventually got together and killed both Clytemnestra and her lover. Just like with Oedipus (p. 182), Sigmund Freud used the myth of Electra (p. 182) to illustrate one of his theories.

17. **What is the name of the hero of the Homer's *Odyssey*?**

   (A) Achilles
   (B) Ulysses
   (C) Orestes
   (D) Perseus

The Scylla (right) and Charybdis (left)...

Having conceived of the Trojan Horse trick, **Ulysses** (Odysseus in Greek) still had to travel back to Greece, and what an adventure he had. As chronicled in the *Odyssey*, which was spoken by the blind poet Homer, Ulysses and his men had all kinds of adventures on their wayward cruise back to Greece. They ran into **Circe,** who turned much of the crew into swine. They were captured by a **Cyclops,** a one-eyed creature who delighted in throwing Ulysses' men against his cave's wall to smash out their brains. They had to pass between **Scylla and Charybdis.** Scylla was a many-head-ed monster, and Charybdis is a swirling whirlpool that devours ships. While trying to avoid Charybdis, Ulysses lost many of his men to the monster Scylla. And then there were the **Sirens**, creatures whose music was so beautiful that it lured sailors to jump into the ocean to their deaths.

Ulysses survived the perilous journey, but all of his com-panions were crushed, eaten, speared, or drowned. It's a great story.

18. **Which of the following heroes is known for carrying his father on his back out of the destruction of Troy?**

   (A) Ulysses
   (B) Hercules
   (C) Aeneas
   (D) Perseus

... and those sweet-sounding Sirens

"WHOSE HYMNS?"

Homeric hymns date from the same era as the epic poet and were once believed to be his work. Whoever wrote them was concerned with preserving the basic tales of ancient Greek mythology and offering the reader (or listener) capsule biographies of the gods. Below are three songs to three of the most powerful Greek goddesses.

10. TO APHRODITE
I shall sing of Kythereia, born on Cyprus, who brings sweet gifts to mortals, and whose lovely face ever smiles radiant with lambent beauty on it. Hail, goddess and mistress of well-built Salamis and of sea-laved Cyprus! Grant me enchanting song. And now I will remember you and another song, too.

11. TO ATHENA
I begin to sing of Pallas Athena, defender of cities, awesome goddess; she and Ares care for deeds of war, cities being sacked and cries for battle. And she protects an army going to war and returning. Hail, O goddess, and grant me good fortune and happiness.

12. TO HERA
Of golden-throned Hera I sing, born of Rhea, queen of the gods, unexcelled in beauty, sister and glorious wife of loud-thundering Zeus, All the gods on lofty Olympos reverence her and honor her together with Zeus who delights in thunder.

After the debacle of the Trojan horse, the people of Troy, led by **Aeneas,** fled to a new land. Aeneas carried his father on his back and proceeded through a series of adventures that saw him battling monsters and shipwrecked in Carthage, a part of Egypt (pp. 145-146). While in Carthage, he met **Dido,** the queen of Carthage, and they had an affair for a while. When Aeneas left her, she committed suicide (once again women get no break). Aeneas eventually settled in Rome and was believed by the ancient Romans to be the father of their country.

19. How does the Phoenix reproduce?

(A) It marries another Phoenix and has children.
(B) It burns itself to death.
(C) It finds a helpless mortal, and forces her to be his bride.
(D) It flies to the sun and comes back as two birds.

The **Phoenix,** a mythical bird, reproduces every 500 years by burning itself to death. From the ashes of the bird comes a new bird. A person who "rises Phoenix-like from the ashes" is someone who has surmounted almost impossible difficulties and been "reborn" to a new life.

20. What is the name of the place in Heaven where dead Nordic heroes reside?

(A) Valhalla
(B) Neiffleheim
(C) Sköll
(D) Jutenheim

Although only a small amount of Scandinavian mythology has made it to our culture, there are a couple of things that you should know. If a soldier was lucky enough to be killed in battle, he was sent to **Valhalla,** a wonderful place filled with people who had died bravely in battle. These heroes could drink all the **mead** (wine made with honey) and eat all the wild boar they wanted. And then for fun, they were able to cut each other into pieces over and over again. Everyone else who died and was not a warrior went straight to hell.

Valhalla was located in **Asgard,** the home of the Nordic gods. The god **Odin** ruled Asgard with the assistance of his son **Thor,** the god of thunder, who wielded a mighty hammer. Thursday is named after Thor.

21. **Who pulled the sword Excalibur out of the stone and became King of England?**
    (A) Merlin
    (B) Henry
    (C) Arthur
    (D) Lear

Thor, Norse God of Thunder

One of the greatest and most retold stories of English mythology, the legend of King Arthur is full of **chivalry** and **knights** and fair maidens. King Arthur is known for setting up a court at **Camelot,** which was filled with the noblest warriors of Europe. This group, called the **Knights of the Round Table,** included **Sir Lancelot, Sir Galahad, and Sir Gawain,** among others. Arthur was counseled by **Merlin**, a powerful sorcerer who used his magic to help Arthur achieve prominence.

Arthur's queen was **Guinevere,** whom he met while helping a kingdom defend itself against impossible odds. One of the Knights of the Round Table's most famous adventures was the search for the **Holy Grail,** the cup from which Jesus is said to have drunk during the **Last Supper.** The quest was epic and it cost many of the knights their lives. Eventually, Percival, who had once been Sir Lancelot's squire, found the Grail and its power was used to help restore Arthur's kingdom.

The Once and Future King, by T.H. White. The story of King Arthur's childhood while he was Merlin's pupil.

URBAN MYTHS

While it might seem that myths are the province of superstitious people in the olden days, you might be surprised at how many myths are present in our own lives. These stories are passed through the culture in an **oral tradition** and are usually told as true. The phenomenon of urban myths has been studied by folklorists and authors throughout the U.S. (especially by Jan Harold Brunvand, whose books on the subject are a lot of fun). Just to prove the point, we are going to include a few of the more prevalent ones here. See if you have heard these tales, and ask yourself, honestly, if you believed them when you first heard them.

A friend of a friend of mine, a petite woman only about five feet tall, was house-sitting for a New York City couple who had a big dog. Well, one day she came home from work to discover that the dog had died

Excalibur (1981), starring Helen Mirren, Nicholas Clay, and Gabriel Byrne. Awesome, gorgeous, brutal, sexy version of the Arthurian legend.

unexpectedly. She was a little nervous. What if the owners of the house came home and found their dead dog lying on the floor of the living room of the house? So she decided she had to bring the dog to a vet, or wherever it is you take a big, dead dog.

She placed the dog in a suitcase and lugged it out of the house. The bag was heavy, and she had to use every bit of her strength to carry it. When she got to the subway, she realized that she was not going to be able to carry the dog down the stairs. A young man offered to help her. He lugged the suitcase down the stairs of the subway and helped the woman get the bag into the train. As the doors began to close, the man grabbed the suitcase and sprinted out of the car.

HOW ABOUT THIS ONE?

An old woman who is cleaning her poodle decides that the fastest way to dry it is to put it in the microwave oven. In the past, the woman had used a conventional oven to dry her poodle, but because she was in a hurry...the poodle explodes all over her microwave oven.

OR THIS ONE?

A woman traveling alone in her car notices that a car is following her. She gets a little nervous and tries different maneuvers to lose the car, but to no avail. So she drives to a police station and runs in to tell the cops the problem.

The policeman runs to the other car and says "What the heck are you doing following that woman??!" The man answers, "Relax, I was just trying to tell her that there was a man in her backseat." And sure enough, there was a man sitting there waiting to cause her irreparable harm.

It is likely that you have either heard one of these stories or ones that are similar. An urban myth is usually told as if it were true. Often the story-teller himself believes that the story is true and will begin the tale with a statement such as "This happened to a friend of my aunt..." or "My sister's boyfriend's father is a doctor and he..." or "I read about this somewhere..." When hard-pressed, the storyteller usually can't provide first-hand authenticity. But just as in the Greek period and the Middle Ages, myths still hold power today.

ANSWERS

1. C   2. C   3. A   4. B   5. B   6. B   7. C   8. C   9. A   10. D
11. A   12. A   13. D   14. B   15. C   16. B   17. B   18. C   19. B   20. A
21. C

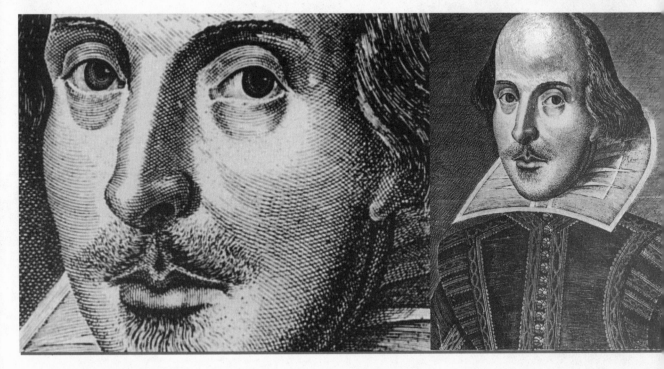

1. **In which centuries did Shakespeare write?**

   (A) The fifteenth and sixteenth centuries
   (B) The sixteenth and seventeenth centuries
   (C) The eighteenth and nineteenth centuries
   (D) The nineteenth and twentieth centuries

Hamlet (1990), with Mel Gibson as 'the melancholy Dane.'

Perhaps the most famous and admired literature in the history of Western Civilization was written by **William Shakespeare (1564-1616)**. So extensive and brilliant was his writing that many have decided that he could not have written everything credited to him, but this is a moot point. The writings that have been attributed to Shakespeare are fabulous. Nobody has said so much so well.

Since Shakespeare wrote his plays for performance, he was not concerned with their publication. Many were reconstructed from the memories of the actors, so it is hard to put an exact date on their creation, but Shakespeare wrote from the end of the sixteenth century until his death in the seventeenth century. His plays range from tragedy to comedy to mixtures of the two. Some of his plays are historic, some are contemporaneous, but all are incredibly well-written and poetic.

Romeo and Juliet (1968), directed by Franco Zeffirelli, starring Olivia Hussey and Leonard Whiting. A touching version of Shakespeare's classic romance. Two previously unknown teenage actors (seventeen and fifteen years old) play the leads.

HUMANITIES

TILTING AT WINDMILLS

Miguel de Cervantes, a contemporary of Shakespeare, created one of the most memorable characters in literature in his novel Don Quixote. *Quixote, an aging, lanky, impoverished noble, becomes so engrossed in tales of medieval knighthood that he comes to believe himself to be a knight in shining armor. His adventures with Sancho Panza in seventeenth-century Spain constitute a rich satire of twisted medieval idealism and the momentous changes of the Renaissance. One of the most famous passages in the book has the deluded Quixote attacking the windmills, which he believes to be giants. The result is a raucous collision of folklore and technology.*

2. **Who killed Julius Caesar in Shakespeare's *Julius Caesar*?**

   (A) Othello
   (B) Lear
   (C) Brutus
   (D) Marc Antony

One of Shakespeare's most famous historical plays is *Julius Caesar* (p. 146), which tells of the life and times of this great leader. In the play, Caesar is betrayed by the Greek senators. When Caesar sees that Brutus, his trusted friend, is helping in the rebellion, he says the famous line **"Et tu Brute,"** which means "And you also, Brutus." The words signify ultimate betrayal.

3. **Which of the following people NEVER hung out with Gertrude Stein?**

   (A) Pablo Picasso
   (B) Ernest Hemingway
   (C) Harriet Beecher Stowe
   (D) F. Scott Fitzgerald

Gertrude Stein (1874-1946), an American writer who lived in Paris, was incredibly influential in twentieth-century American literature. In Paris, she provided a meeting place for the American expatriate "lost generation" (p. 404) who lived there. At her Salons, many now-famous people would gather, including Pablo Picasso (p. 404) (1881-1973), Ernest Hemingway (p. 404) (1898-1961), and F. Scott Fitzgerald (p. 404) (1896-1940). There, they would discuss art and literature, show paintings, discuss poetry, and otherwise pass the time in intellectual pursuits. Besides Stein's contributions to literature, she is also famous for a portrait of her done by Picasso. Picasso, when told that the painting did not look like her, is said to have responded "It will," and he was right.

Expatriate writer Gertrude Stein

4. **What Nobel Prize-winning author wrote Song of Solomon?**

   (A) Toni Morrison
   (B) Thomas Pynchon
   (C) Ernest Hemingway
   (D) Charlotte Brontë

Toni Morrison (1931-), a contemporary American author, won the Nobel Prize in literature in 1993. She has written many novels that chronicle the lives of African-Americans, their history, and their unique struggles. Among these are *Beloved*, *Song of Solomon*, *Sula*, and *The Bluest Eye*. She is a great writer whose books will undoubtedly be among those that continue to affect our culture.

Nobel laureate Toni Morrison

> *I shall be telling this with a sigh*
> *Somewhere ages and ages hence:*
> *Two roads diverged in a wood, and I—*
> *I took the one less traveled by*
> *And that has made all the difference.*

5. **Who wrote the poem from which the lines above were taken?**

   (A) Robert Frost
   (B) Emily Dickinson
   (C) Walt Whitman
   (D) Pat Boone

This is the concluding stanza of the poem "The Road Not Taken" by **Robert Frost** (1874-1963), one of the best-known American poets. Frost, a four-time winner of the Pulitzer Prize, wrote poems that were essentially pastoral, but whose meanings transcended their subject matter. For example, the road not taken can be taken as a metaphor of the poet's life. He took a path in life that had not been followed by many, and that is what made him who he was.

ANSWERS

....

1. B   2. C   3. C   4. A   5. A

TWENTY-THREE BOOKS THAT EVERY HIGH SCHOOL GRADUATE SHOULD HAVE READ

There are some books that everybody should have read by the time he or she graduates from high school. Here is a list of the books we believe are both influential and accessible.

HIGHWAY TO HELL

"The Divine Comedy" by Dante Alighieri (1265-1321) is one of the most famous and most alluded-to works in all of literature. Perhaps only Shakespeare has had more scholars pore over his every word. The magnitude of the influence of "The Divine Comedy" cannot be underestimated. Artists in several other mediums—literature, painting, music, and film—have paid homage to Dante's masterwork and the odds are excellent that you have read, seen, or heard references to "The Divine Comedy" several times already. The best-known and most often read section of "The Divine Comedy" is the "Inferno." Dante's "Inferno" is a series of cantos, or poems, in which he takes pains to describe his vision of hell. He saw hell as having nine circles. You were relegated to one of them, depending on the severity of your sins throughout your lifetime. There are circles and sub-divisions for everyone from alcohol abusers to murderers. Dante's vision of hell has inspired many poets, writers, and painters to expand on his idea and themes, bringing them to life again and again. Fascinating, horrifying, and funny all at once, "Inferno" is a must read. Once you've read it, you will notice how many times references to Dante occur throughout art and literature.

The Bible (Genesis, Exodus, Job, and Matthew)
Author: Many or One depending on how you look at it
Published: Over a period of many years

The most widely distributed book in the world, the Bible is chock-full of stories and parables you will hear quoted and misquoted for the rest of your life. The only way to get the story straight is to go back to the original source. The book is full of adventure stories, and if you skip the long genealogies and the complicated rules, you will find the Good Book great reading.

There are many translations of the Bible floating around. The first important English translation is the **King James Version,** held by many as *the* definitive version. The writing is a bit old-fashioned, with lots of "thees" and "thous" and "begetteths" and "begotteths," so we suggest you get one of the newer translations. The New Revised Standard Version is good, as is the American Standard Version.

Aside from Job, the sections we have selected are the parts of the Bible that have the most stories in them. You will find from reading these that many parts of the Bible seem to contradict each other. Just compare the "Rape of Dinah" in Genesis to the "Turn the Other Cheek" Beatitude (p. 374) in Matthew. But keep in mind that the Bible was written over the course of many years by many different authors, and that the New Testament aims to revise certain aspects of the Old Testament. Those of you who have not read the Bible will be surprised at just how exciting many of the stories are.

Hamlet
Author: William Shakespeare (1564-1616), English
Published: 1603

Hamlet is one of the greatest tragedies ever written. This tale of a Danish prince is about revenge, and Hamlet uses some pretty tricky methods to implicate his mother's new husband in the plot. Reading Shakespeare is a little more difficult than reading the average novel. The plays were written hundreds of years ago in the common language of the day. Many of the words, however, have since left our vocabulary, so we recommend that you use the annotations that are present in most editions of his plays. If you have a little patience, you will find that the play is well worth reading. It has a little of everything: sex, violence, blood, sword-fighting, humor, and ghosts.

Emma
Author: Jane Austen (1775-1817), English
Published: 1816

Jane Austen, a great English novelist known for her penetrating vision of middle-class English society, led a rather eventless life. She did not marry and spent most of her time in the parlor of her family's house writing novels about the lives of all the people around her. Most of Austen's novels consist of the same basic plot: a girl grows into womanhood and enters society, where she eventually marries an older man—a father figure.

Emma does not deviate from this plot line. The title character of the novel is a romantic. She is unable to see reality and envisions herself as a giving and good person, even though she is really self-important and controlling. Unable to see what is really going on with her friends, she meddles in their lives and causes all kinds of trouble. But, eventually, like the rest of Austen's characters, Emma marries the right (older) man. Another famous Austen novel is **Pride and Prejudice**.

Jane Austen

The Tell-Tale Heart and Other Stories
Author: Edgar Allan Poe (1809-49), American
Published: 1843

Edgar Allan Poe is an incredible writer whose fantastic stories are so well told that readers become part of the action. Poe is best known for his short stories, and this collection contains some of the finest ever written. He somehow manages to put a novel's worth of intrigue into a few pages, and because a lot is left to the imagination, we become active participants in the stories. Forget Stephen King; Poe is the master of the horror and suspense tale. In the title story, the narrator is a guilt-obsessed madman who becomes haunted by his employer's evil eye. Suspense and intrigue ensue.

Jane Eyre
Author: Charlotte Brontë (1816-1855), English
Published: 1847

This novel is about a poor servant who is in love with her employer. The heroine, Jane Eyre, is mighty forward for her day, professing her love for the employer before he expresses his feelings for her. This was unusual in Victorian society, and Jane's nerve in approaching a married man made for much controversy when the novel was first published.

The Scarlet Letter
Author: Nathaniel Hawthorne (1804-1864), American
Published: 1850

Nathaniel Hawthorne was born in Salem, Massachusetts, a descendant of Puritans. (That's right, Salem, where all those witch trials (p. 37) were held.) In fact, one member of his family was a judge in the witch trials. So it is not surprising that Hawthorne often wrote about the Puritans.

The Scarlet Letter takes place in Puritan times. Hester Prynne is a young, married, pregnant woman whose hus-

Nathaniel Hawthorne

Wuthering Heights (1939), starring Lawrence Olivier and Merle Oberon. Tear-jerker performance based on the novel by Emily Brontë, Charlotte's sister.

PORNOGRAPHY

Upon its publication in a magazine in 1856, "Madame Bovary" was determined to be pornography. Its author, Gustave Flaubert, was charged with offending the public morality (the book considered issues of adultery). Although he was financially successful, the label haunted Flaubert the rest of his life. He stated that he wanted to "throw them all into the fire and never hear of the book again." "Madame Bovary" stands as one of the most important works of modern literature.

band is away. Because of her condition, she is forced to wear a big red "A" ("A" stands for adultery) on her dress so that everyone knows she is a sinner. Even though the book was written about sex when such things were not discussed, it was not that controversial. Hester, remember, was punished for her deed. You might be wondering why the father was not punished. Finding out is half the fun.

Moby Dick (1956), starring Gregory Peck and Orson Welles. Peck is a perfect Captain Ahab, but the movie doesn't really have that much to do with the novel.

Moby-Dick
Author: Herman Melville (1819-1891), American
Published: 1851

From the opening line, "Call me Ishmael," through pages and pages of brilliantly written prose, *Moby-Dick* is a humdinger of a story. Melville takes many approaches to tell his tale. Parts of the novel are told in verse (poems), parts sound like a textbook for whalers, and parts are in prose (like a regular book). When you read the book (if you aren't reading it for school), feel free to skip some of the technical information on whaling, unless, of course, you find it interesting. Rich in symbolism and in-depth characterization, the book is more than a story of one person's obsession, the search for a whale. It is an epic journey of fixation and desire, pride and fatalism, and what appears to be true and what is truly real.

Call me Herman Melville.

Walden
Author: Henry David Thoreau (1817-1862), American
Published: 1854

The writings of Henry David Thoreau have been influential to people throughout the world. The ideas expressed in Thoreau's essay *On Civil Disobedience* (which was inspired by his refusal to pay taxes) came to influence Mahatma Ghandi (pp. 216-2017) and Martin Luther King, Jr. (p. 111). The concepts presented in Walden helped establish the philosophy of environmentalism and the search for spirituality in nature.

Civilly disobedient Henry Thoreau

Charles Dickens contemplating how something could be the best and worst at the exact same time.

Leo Tolstoy: formidable Russian writer of several massive books

Thoreau built a small cabin in an undeveloped area near Walden Pond, Massachusetts, on land given to him by his close friend and fellow writer, Ralph Waldo Emerson. He kept a garden, read, and wrote. He found that living in such a simple manner gave him clarity of thought and helped him articulate his beliefs.

A Tale of Two Cities
Author: Charles Dickens (1812-1870), English
Published: 1859

One of the most prolific and respected novelists ever, Charles Dickens lived in Victorian Era England. His novels were usually characterized by coincidences in the plots and by a social conscience.

Beginning with the famous line "It was the best of times, it was the worst of times," this novel by Dickens is set in the time of the French Revolution (pp. 173-177). Full of blood and psychological insights, the book gives a sense of what it was like to live in the midst of political upheaval and social chaos.

Anna Karenina
Author: Leo Tolstoy (1828-1910), Russian
Published: 1875

Count Leo Tolstoy, perhaps the greatest of the Russian novelists, wrote novels that were realistic in their depiction of everyday events.

Anna Karenina is the story of a woman in an unfulfilling marriage who gives it up to pursue a passionate affair. The story is like a nineteenth-century soap opera, with heightened passion and all kinds of romantic intrigue. As he developed a complicated storyline, Tolstoy was able to combine the varied elements of the plot into a coherent and fascinating whole.

The Adventures of Huckleberry Finn
Author: Samuel Clemens (1835-1910) a.k.a. Mark Twain, American
Published: 1884

Samuel Clemens, writing under the pseudonym of Mark Twain, had a long and illustrious literary career. His writings, filled with wit and insight, became influential in later American fiction.

Huckleberry Finn is considered by some to be the first modern American novel. The story of Huck Finn and a runaway slave named Jim can be viewed on many levels. It is the adventure story of two young men escaping from their lives, as well as a satire on the conventions of civilization. If you read this when you were younger, try reading it again. Much of the humor and satire is very subtle; you will appreciate it more now that you are older.

Mark Twain

A Portrait of the Artist as a Young Man
Author: James Joyce (1882-1941), Irish
Published: 1916

When you first pick up this book, the writing may seem strange to you. It is written in a **stream-of-consciousness** style; thoughts just seem to roll over one another. But give it a chance. As you read it, you will realize that Joyce's writing approaches the way we actually think much more closely than do other works of literature. The novel tells the story of Stephen Dedalus as he matures from infancy until his early twenties. As Dedalus matures, the writing changes to reflect changes in the narrator's consciousness. Dedalus has an artistic temperament; he feels as if he is a misfit in his own family because of his desire to create art. By confronting his parents and other aspects of his life, he evolves into an artist.

James Joyce

The Fitzgeralds do a jig.

The Great Gatsby
Author: F. Scott Fitzgerald (1896-1940), American
Published: 1925

The writings of F. Scott Fitzgerald exemplify the period of the twenties in America known as the Jazz Age (p. 87). Fitzgerald claims credit for giving the period its name, and *The Great Gatsby* gives a fictional account that demonstrates some of what it was like to live at the time. The rich lived frivolously, spending money and drinking as if they didn't care. (Remember, this was a time when drinking was illegal.)

The novel is about a millionaire who is obsessed with an old girlfriend named Daisy. He goes to all sorts of lengths to win her back, holding lavish parties and involving innocent bystanders (like the narrator) in trying to convince Daisy to leave her husband. The book is fun to read and involving. Fitzgerald is incredible in his ability to create the atmosphere of the millionaire's parties, and, with a subtle cynicism, he evokes the hypocrisies and energy of the Jazz Age.

The Sun Also Rises
Author: Ernest Hemingway (1899-1961), American
Published: 1926

A foreign correspondent and leading voice for the "lost generation" of the 1920s (p. 396), Ernest Hemingway created characters who were cynical and broken. His unemotional, terse, understated writing style became one of the major influences in modern American fiction, and his novel *The Old Man and the Sea* won the Nobel Prize in 1954. Hemingway spent much time abroad, and many of his novels deal with expatriate Americans.

The Sun Also Rises looks at the lives of several Americans living in Europe after WWI (pp. 82-85). They are disillusioned and spend most of their time diverting themselves with love affairs, drinking, and bullfights. The novel is easy to read, dark, and strangely moving.

One of America's most influential writers, Ernest Hemingway

The Grapes of Wrath
Author: John Steinbeck (1902-1968), American
Published: 1939

John Steinbeck, who won the Pulitzer Prize for *The Grapes of Wrath*, wrote about the American experience of the poor, dispossessed, and eccentric. The novel follows a group of sharecroppers who leave the "dust bowl" (p. 93) of Oklahoma in search of better times in California. The families become symbolic of the suffering that the United States was feeling during the Depression (pp. 92-94). Through a strong sense of community, they find a way to transcend the awful things that happen to them.

John Steinbeck

The Heart is a Lonely Hunter
Author: Carson McCullers (1917-1967), American
Published: 1940

Carson McCullers is known for novels that reveal the inner lives of lonely people. *The Heart is a Lonely Hunter* is an incredibly sensitive novel that tells of people who are marginalized in their community. Its protagonist is a deaf-mute who loses his only friend and companion, and ends up becoming a strong presence in the other characters' lives.

Carson McCullers

The Sound and the Fury, by William Faulkner. Very famous novel of a southern family, told from several points of view.

The Fountainhead
Author: Ayn Rand (1905-82), American
Published: 1943

A Russian-born American novelist, Rand originated a philosophy called objectivism. She was a die-hard believer in the individual and in capitalism, and she argued that every individual should seek self-fulfillment. She also believed that altruism bred weakness in a society. This philosophy of self-reliance comes forward in her novels. *The Fountainhead* tells of the life of an architect who many think is based on Frank Lloyd Wright (pp. 405-406). The

Ayn Rand at a press conference

architect is unwilling to compromise his work in the search for perfection. When he feels his designs are being misused, he destroys the work. To Rand, this act makes him authentic.

1984
Author: George Orwell (1903-1950), British
Published: 1949

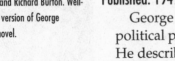

1984 (1984), starring John Hurt and Richard Burton. Well-done version of George Orwell's futuristic novel.

George Orwell's novels are not about relationships; they are about political points of view. *1984* presents the author's view of the future. He describes a world in which bureaucrats control even minor facets of our lives—a world in which Big Brother is always watching us. The novel centers on the lives of two people who attempt to have a private life amidst all the totalitarian controls. Orwell wrote the novel in 1948 and simply reversed the year to come up with his prophetic title. While you're reading the book, think about how many of Orwell's predictions have actually come true. You might find yourself feeling slightly unnerved and paranoid.

Catcher In the Rye
Author: J. D. Salinger (1919-)
Published: 1951

Famous recluse J.D. Salinger in a rare photo

Catcher in the Rye has been a favorite of free-thinking teenagers since it was first written. It expresses young people's desire for things that are not "phony." Set in that phoniest of times, the fifties, *Catcher in the Rye* expresses the adolescent rebellion that was captured in such movies as *Rebel Without a Cause* (p.428). The book tells us the story of Holden Caulfield, a sixteen-year-old who escapes from prep school to the big city. The novel was banned in many school districts for its strong language. One reviewer in *Catholic World* stated, "Not only do some of the events stretch probability but Holden's character is iconoclast, a kind of latter-day Tom Sawyer or Huck Finn (p.403), made monotonous and phony by the excessive use of amateur swearing and coarse language." In other words, the book is a lot of fun.

Invisible Man
Author: Ralph Ellison (1914-1994), American
Published: 1952

Ellison's only novel at the time of his death, *Invisible Man* traces the life of a young black man and his struggle for identity in a society that does not see him as an individual. The book was influential in the civil rights movement (pp.109-113), and it is expertly written. It gives a startling portrait of what it is like to grow up black in America. Ellison was interested in music, and through the use of richly symbolic metaphorical language, he manages to inject a rhythm and emotion into the writing that make the book a magnificent work of art.

Wise Blood (1979). John Huston's adaptation of Flannery O'Connor's novel.

A Good Man is Hard to Find
Author: Flannery O'Connor (1925-1964), American
Published: 1955

A southern writer, Flannery O'Connor is known for her strangely touching stories about characters who are often "freaks" of some kind. Her stories are intensely spiritual, with many of the characters desiring redemption and receiving some type of grace at the moment of their deaths. Even though the characters are not superficially attractive, we find that we are curious about their actions, and that we identify with them.

O'Connor stands with her portrait.

The Autobiography of Malcolm X
Author: Malcolm X, as told to Alex Haley (1921-92), American
Published: 1965

Roots scholar Alex Haley

The Autobiography of Malcolm X is a description of Malcolm X's (p. 112) life as told to Alex Haley, who is probably best known for the history of his family, *Roots*. One of the most compelling works from the civil rights movement of the sixties, the book recounts Malcolm's life—from growing up in poverty to being in

Malcom X (1992), by Spike Lee. A sweeping film based on *The Autobiography of Malcolm X*.

prison to becoming one of the leaders of the Black Muslim (p. 112) organization. The book is a fascinating portrayal of one man's political and personal transformation as he becomes one of the most influential leaders of the late twentieth century.

The Bluest Eye
Author: Toni Morrison (1931-), American
Published: 1969

The Bluest Eye is Toni Morrison's first novel. It tells the story of racism in an Ohio community, and its effect on one African-American family. The central character is a young African-American girl who becomes obsessed with mainstream notions of beauty (including blue eyes). Like all of Morrison's novels, *The Bluest Eye* is both lyrical and profound.

GREAT TEEN NOVELS

Forever • Judy Blume
Go Ask Alice • Anonymous
Lisa, Bright and Dark • John Neufeld
I Never Promised You a Rose Garden • Joanne Greenberg
The Pigman • Paul Zindel

POEMS

"Leda and the Swan" • William Butler Yeats (1865-1939)
"I'm Nobody! Who are You?" • Emily Dickinson (1830-1886)
"Weary Blues" • Langston Hughes (1902-1967)
"Song of Myself" • Walt Whitman (1819-1892)
"The Road Not Taken" • Robert Frost (1874-1963)
"The Love Song of J. Alfred Prufrock" • T. S. Eliot (1888-1965)
"next to of course god america i" • e. e. cummings (1894-1962)
"After the Funeral" • Dylan Thomas (1914-1953)
"The Poems of Our Climate" • Wallace Stevens (1879-1955)

1. The movie *Modern Times* was made by

    (A) Charlie Chaplin
    (B) Steven Spielberg
    (C) Howard Hawks
    (D) Orson Welles

Considered by many to be Charlie Chaplin's best film, *Modern Times* (1936) is an excellent example of what can be accomplished in film without dialogue. Even though we don't hear the Tramp (Chaplin's immortal character with the funny walk, big shoes, and a cane), we still feel for him and can enjoy the actions that follow.

The first films were silent, and the arrival of talkies in 1927 with the movie *The Jazz Singer* dramatically changed the industry. *Modern Times*, made in 1936, came after the technology for talkies had already been introduced. Chaplin, however, preferred to work in silent films. If you want to get a sense of how the new technology affected film stars and directors, see *Chaplin* (1992), *Sunset Boulevard* (1950), or *Singin' in the Rain* (1952).

REJECTING CHAPLIN

Of the many victims of Cold War (pp. 104-108) hysteria, none is more famous than Charlie Chaplin, the film pioneer whose liberal politics aroused the suspicion and hostility of many powerful politicians. In this 1953 editorial on the occasion of Chaplin's voluntary exile to his native England, the writer I.F. Stone bids farewell to Chaplin:

CHARLIE CHAPLIN'S FAREWELL CUSTARD

There are two voices of America. One is the Voice with a capital V, which broadcasts in so many languages so many hours a day what we would like people abroad to think about us. The other, the voice with a small v, is the inadvertent message of our own actions. This, the real voice of America, broadcast a strange message last week about Charlie Chaplin.

It told the world that the little funny man on whom we were brought up could no longer bear the spirit of contemporary America and had turned in his re-entry permit. It said there must be something seriously wrong with our America if Chaplin could no longer live in it.

The "voluntary" exile of Chaplin is a measure of how America has changed since we were children. He never became an American citizen but Charlie Chaplin was and will remain more truly American than the blackguards and fanatics who hounded him, the cheap politicians who warned him not to come back.

We do not blame Charlie Chaplin for leaving us. Who could blame a comic genius—one of the greatest of all time—for being unwilling to live in a country which seems to have lost its sense of humor? But we ask him not to desert us altogether.

The man who made "The Great Dictator" owes it to us and himself to put into a new film the tragicomedy overtaking America where greasy informers are public heroes, protectors of gambling dens set themselves up as guardians of public morality, and a Senator who is afraid to answer questions about his own financial accounts becomes the great investigator of others. Come to think of it, "The Great Investigator" would be a worthy successor to "The Great Dictator."

Turn the laugh on them, Charlie, for our country's sake. This capital needs nothing so badly as one final well-flung custard pie.

April 25, 1953
I.F. Stone, "The Haunted Fifties"

2. **What was the name of the actor who said "Frankly my dear, I don't give a damn" in *Gone with the Wind*?**
   (A) Frank Sinatra
   (B) Clark Gable
   (C) Jimmy Stewart
   (D) John Wayne

If you negate inflation, *Gone with the Wind* (1939) has made more money than any other film. When you see it, you will understand why. The story is romantic, the plot uncomplicated, and the characters simple. Clark Gable's line "Frankly my dear, I don't give a damn" gave the censors trouble but was eventually allowed in the film.

3. **What is "Rosebud" in *Citizen Kane*?**
   (A) Kane's girlfriend
   (B) Kane's wife
   (C) Kane's suburban mansion
   (D) Kane's sled

If we told you, we would ruin the movie for you. Suffice it to say that Orson Welles's *Citizen Kane* (1941) is well worth seeing, and you will probably enjoy it more not knowing what Rosebud is. Considered one of the finest achievements in film history, *Citizen Kane* is a beautiful film that changed the way movies were made.

4. *The Empire Strikes Back* is the sequel to which of the
    following movies?
    (A) *Star Wars*
    (B) *Enter the Dragon*
    (C) *Empire of the Sun*
    (D) *Millennium*

Star Wars (1977) was a huge sensation when it first came out and is still one of ten most successful films ever made. The special effects and the story are exciting, and the movie is incredibly fun to watch. If you haven't seen it (and we have found that most of you have), definitely find time to watch it. Its sequel was entitled *The Empire Strikes Back* (1980).

TWENTY-ONE FILMS THAT EVERY HIGH SCHOOL GRADUATE SHOULD HAVE SEEN

The following is a list of twenty-one films that we think every high school student should see before graduating. This is just a start; we realize that over ninety years of movie-making cannot be encapsulated into a list of twenty movies. But if you do take the time to rent these films, you will definitely have a better understanding of our country's film history. The list covers many of the important genres of American film, and besides, all the films are fun to watch. The term "genre" is used to describe the particular style in which a movie is made. For instance, a Western is a genre of film.

Because the films on the list are famous, you should have no trouble finding them at your local video store. If your parents give you any trouble about watching too much TV, just tell them that you are doing your homework. Enjoy.

By the way, we are not giving away the endings to any of these films. So read this guide without fear that we will spoil the fun.

The General
Director: Buster Keaton and Clyde Bruckman
Starring: Buster Keaton, Marion Mack
1927/BW

Buster Keaton plays a shy locomotive engineer in this comedy set during the Civil War. Considered by some critics to be a better physical comedian than Charlie Chaplin, Keaton's athleticism is astounding to watch—especially when you bear in mind that he performed all of his own stunts without the benefit of modern safety equipment. The humor in this type of film is not subtle, so don't think too much. As this movie is only a little over an hour long, you might try a double bill with *Modern Times*.

Surprisingly, Keaton plays a hero for the South during the Civil War (pp.66-68), helping to make the world safe for slavery. The slavery issue is not addressed in the film, but it adds a bit of tension. Here we are rooting for this guy who is supporting a cause that we most likely do not believe in.

See also: *The Great Train Robbery* (1903); *The Great Locomotive Chase* (1956); *Silver Streak* (1976), starring Gene Wilder and Richard Pryor; *The Great Train Robbery* (1979), starring Sean Connery; and *Steamboat Bill, Jr.* (1928), Buster's hilarious follow-up to *The General*.

Comic duo Margaret Dumont (center) and Groucho Marx (right).

A Night at the Opera
Director: Sam Wood
Starring: Groucho, Chico, and Harpo Marx, Kitty Carlisle, Allan Jones, Walter Wolf King, Margaret Dumont, Sigfried Rumann
1935/BW

Argued by many to be the best Marx Brothers film, *A Night at the Opera* is composed of one funny bit followed by another. The Marx Brothers were so influential that you may have seen some of their comedic routines without realizing where they originated. Since the one-liners fly so fast, you might want to watch a few scenes more than once. You will find it well worth it to get the finer points of the dialogue. See also: *Duck Soup* (1933) and *Horse Feathers* (1932). Both are Marx Brothers films.

Modern Times
Director: Charlie Chaplin
Starring: Charlie Chaplin, Paulette Goddard
1936/BW

Charlie Chaplin, famous for his inimitable Tramp, a ne'er-do-well with a funny walk, directed this film about the dehumanizing effect of industry. The movie is not a silent in the strictest sense: it has a soundtrack that consists of sound effects, music (credited to Chaplin), and gibberish. The movie is hilarious and a little bit scary, and is an excellent introduction to Chaplin's work.

See also: *The Kid* (1921), *The Gold Rush* (1925), and *Monsieur Verdoux* (1947, not silent). These three are all Chaplin films that show the great variety of his work. For a contemporary take on the same theme, check out *The Terminator* (1984) and *Terminator II: Judgment Day* (1991), starring Arnold Schwarzenegger, and *Robocop* (1987), with Peter Weller.

Bringing Up Baby
Director: Howard Hawks
Starring: Katharine Hepburn, Cary Grant
1938/BW

A wacky "screwball" comedy about paleontologists and a leopard, this film stars Cary Grant and Katharine Hepburn, two of the most famous film stars of all time. When you watch the film, remind yourself that the leopard and the actors never actually appeared in the same scene together during the filming. The camera effects still hold up, even today.

Katharine Hepburn and Cary Grant contemplate their "baby."

Howard Hawks's movies range from the funny to the scary, and if you like this film (or even if you don't), you should try some of his other films such as *Scarface* (1932), *His Girl Friday* (1940), *The Big Sleep* (1946), *The Thing* (1951), and *Rio Bravo* (1959). All of these films have been remade by other filmmakers in some form.

The most famous kiss in screen history, this scene from *Gone With the Wind* swept them away.

See also: *The Thin Man* (1934), which features the same annoying dog from *Bringing up Baby*; *Mr. Blandings Builds His Dream House* (1948), with Cary Grant; and these more modern takes on the screwball comedies of the thirties and forties: *What's Up, Doc?* (1972), with Barbra Streisand; *Something Wild* (1986) with Melanie Griffith; and *The Hudsucker Proxy* (1993), by the Coen brothers.

Gone With the Wind
Director: Victor Fleming
Starring: Vivien Leigh, Clark Gable, Leslie Howard, Hattie McDaniel, Butterfly McQueen, Olivia de Havilland
1939/Technicolor

Gone with the Wind is a whirlwind of an emotional drama that depicts the life of Scarlett O'Hara as she lives through the South's defeat during the Civil War. If you are lucky enough to get the chance, view this film in a theater; it's great to see with a crowd. The filmmaking is superb, and the simple romantic story can leave even jaded modern audiences in tears.

Gone With The Wind won tons of Oscars—including Best Picture, Best Screenplay, Best Director, Best Actress, and Best Supporting Actress for Hattie McDaniel (the first black woman to win such an award). In a way, *Gone with the Wind* created a new genre of motion picture: the movie conceived and budgeted to win Academy Awards. The movie is long, but has an intermission, so don't be afraid to take a break to pop some popcorn.

The most famous line from the film, "Frankly my dear, I don't give a damn" was almost dropped because it was deemed offensive. The new line would have read "Frankly, I don't care." Luckily for us, the line was left as it was. Also watch for the line "As God is my witness,

If *Gone With the Wind* is your cup of tea, you will probably want to read the book by Margaret Mitchell which, obviously, inspired the most successful film in Hollywood history.

I'll never be hungry again." It is quoted again and again, and it might be of use to you someday.

See also: *A Streetcar Named Desire* (1951) with Vivien Leigh and Marlon Brando; *The Deer Hunter* (1978), another epic Oscar-sweeper, this time set during the Vietnam War, with Robert De Niro, Meryl Streep and Christopher Walken; *The Beguiled* (1971) with Clint Eastwood; and *Glory* (1989) with Denzel Washington, both about the Civil War.

Citizen Kane
Director: Orson Welles
Starring: Orson Welles, Joseph Cotten, Dorothy Comingore, Agnes Moorehead
1941/BW

Over the years, this film has been the consistent choice of film critics, directors, and movie fanatics as the best movie ever made. And it is a doozie of a movie. Everything about this film is big, from the performances to the scope of the story to Kane himself. Innovations abound. Just watch the way that the camera follows Kane as he walks through hallways: beautiful, scary, and big. Also look carefully at the sets. Most of them were small, but through ingenious matte photography and other special effects, they were made to appear enormous in the film.

If you haven't seen the film, see if you can guess what Rosebud is. Try to imagine what would be so significant that it would cause the great Kane to utter these words on his deathbed. While watching *Citizen Kane*, remember that the director of this film, Orson Welles, was twenty-five years old. Unbelievable.

See also: *The Magnificent Ambersons* (1942), directed by Orson Welles; *The Third Man* (1949), starring Welles and Joseph Cotten; and *Touch of Evil* (1958), Welles's brilliant, brutal film noir.

Orson Welles (center) as Charles Foster Kane

Sam (Dooley Wilson) plays it
for Bogie and Bergman.

Casablanca
Director: Michael Curtiz
Starring: Humphrey Bogart (a.k.a.
"Bogie"), Ingrid Bergman, and a whole
mess of people who were either famous
then or went on to become famous.
1942/ BW

One of the most quoted and copied movies of all time, *Casablanca* set a standard for quality that has yet to be surpassed. What a film! Bogie, Bergman, and everyone else give excellent performances. The music is great. The photography is superb. The story is exciting. It is considered by many the best Hollywood movie of all time. If you haven't seen it, you are in for a treat. The film is famous for a number of immortal lines, although nobody in the picture ever says, "Play it again, Sam." Ever.

Before you see it, you might spend a few minutes reading through the section in this book on WWII (pp. 95-103). The context for this film can give you some further insight into what's going on in the movie. The film is set in Casablanca, a city in Morocco which was on the path for refugees trying to get out of occupied France to America. Even though the area has yet to be taken over by the Germans, the Nazis had a large influence on politics there. If you miss this film, you will regret it, maybe not tomorrow or the next day, but soon ... and for the rest of your life.

See also: *To Have and Have Not* (1944), directed by Howard Hawks, screenplay by Joan Forthman and William Faulkner (p.408), based on Ernest Hemingway's (p. 404) novel, and starring Bogie and Lauren Bacall, who fell in love making the film and were married a year later; and *Play It Again, Sam* (1972), starring Woody Allen as a shy guy who gets advice from Bogie.

Double Indemnity
Director: Billy Wilder
Starring: Fred MacMurray (of *My Three Sons* fame), Barbara Stanwyck (who isn't really a blonde), Edward G. Robinson
1944/ BW

An excellent example of classic "film noir" (French for "dark film") with jagged angles, harsh lighting, crime, and low-life characters, *Double Indemnity* is thrilling and somewhat depressing at the same time. Film noir films are dark thrillers which were made during the forties and fifties (although people still make them today). Usually, they depict a world without redemption where morality is in constant question. Usually set in mundane places (like the suburbs) these films capture a darker side of life (hence the name of the genre). They have many plot twists and the heroes, if you can call them that, find danger around every corner. Your heart will beat a little faster after watching this film.

Watch how the characters smoke. People used to think it was cool and sexy. (Today we know better.) When this film was made, it was not legal to show any kind of sex on screen, so filmmakers developed a type of shorthand using cigarettes. In this film, any kind of intimacy between the leads is suggested through the lighting and sharing of smokes. Notice that MacMurray lights matches with his thumbnail. Before the advent of safety matches, a match could be lit off of anything: teeth, a zipper, a heel.

See also these great examples of film noir: *The Maltese Falcon* (1941, Huston) with Bogie; *The Big Sleep* (1946, Hawks) with Bogie and Bacall; *Touch of Evil* (1958, Welles); *Chinatown* (1974) with Jack Nicholson; *Body Heat* (1981), a remake of *Double Indemnity* with Kathleen Turner; and *Blade Runner* (1982), a futuristic film noir with Harrison Ford.

Sneaky lady Stanwyck plots MacMurray's fall from grace.

All About Eve
Director: Joseph L. Mankiewicz
Starring: Anne Baxter and Bette Davis, with Marilyn Monroe in a bit part
1950/BW

Bette Davis (center) eyes the road in *All About Eve*.

A classic film filled with classic lines, this Mankiewicz movie stars Bette Davis, who is fantastic as an aging star being supplanted by a young starlet. The dialogue (and the delivery of said dialogue) is amazing. If you can learn how to say "Fasten your seatbelts. It's gonna to be a bumpy night" with the flair and presence that Davis does, you will go far.

This is a movie with strong female characters. Although the men are ostensibly in positions of power—directors, and writers and so forth—it is the stars, the women, who are important in this film. Listen carefully; the lines contain some insults that are fairly subtle, but the film is a riot, with a thoroughly satisfying ending.

See also: *The Women* (1939), with Joan Crawford; and *The Philadelphia Story* (1940), with Katharine Hepburn, Cary Grant, and Jimmy Stewart.

High Noon
Director: Fred Zinnemann
Starring: Gary Cooper, Grace Kelly, Lee van Cleef
1952/BW

Set in real time, *High Noon* begins at 10:40 AM and the tension rises with the sun. It is an excellent Western. With the grand themes of good versus evil and with a solitary hero faced with a choice between doing his duty and living his own life, the movie ticks along to an exciting climax. Watch the onscreen clocks; see if they match your own. This movie is nerve-racking, and you may find yourself so far

Gary Cooper in his Oscar-winning performance as Sheriff Will Kane in *High Noon*

off the edge of your seat that you are sitting on the floor.

So what's the deal with Gary Cooper and Grace Kelly anyway? He does seem a little old for her, but that is a pattern well established in Hollywood—older male leads ending up with younger women.

See also: *The Searchers* (1956), a classic Western with John Wayne directed by the great John Ford; *Red River* (1948, Hawks), also with John Wayne; and *Blazing Saddles* (1973), a hilarious send-up of all things Western.

Don't bother with the sequel of *High Noon*; it sucks.

Singin' in the Rain
Director: Gene Kelly and Stanley Donen
Starring: Gene Kelly, Donald O'Connor, Debbie Reynolds, Cyd Charisse, Rita Moreno
1952/C

Considered by many critics to be the best movie musical ever made, *Singin' in the Rain* has some of the most exciting and energetic dancing ever to grace the silver screen. Gene Kelly is terrific, an athletic dancer who can sing and act (a rare find in the art of musicals). The plot is relatively interesting (also rare in musicals). And the cinematography is fantastic, with brilliant color, cool sets, and film angles. The most famous part of the film is when Kelly uses his umbrella as a dance partner and (you guessed it) sings and dances in the rain. (No doubles here. Kelly gets soaking wet.)

See also: *Top Hat* (1935), with Fred Astaire and Ginger Rogers, or any other Astaire film; *All that Jazz* (1979), another musical with a great plot; *Hairspray* (1988), a

Gene Kelly *dancing* in the rain

wacky look at high school; and *Sunset Boulevard* (1950), set in the same time of transition between silent and talkie films.

Some Like It Hot
Director: Billy Wilder
Starring: Tony Curtis, Jack Lemmon, Marilyn Monroe, Joe E. Brown
1959/BW

A funny film about men dressing in drag, *Some Like It Hot* is about as wacky a movie as was ever made. Marilyn Monroe, whose film persona has become an integral part of our culture and has influenced everyone from Andy Warhol (p.466-467—plate 26) to Madonna, is wonderful. Tony Curtis and Jack Lemmon keep the audience laughing with great comic performances. Don't miss this one.

See also: *Bus Stop* (1956), starring Marilyn in her best performance; *Glen or Glenda* (1953), a film about a transvestite that's so bad it's good; *Jules et Jim* (1961) by Francois Truffaut; and *Victor/Victoria* (1982), a cross-dressing farce by Blake Edwards.

Psycho
Director: Alfred Hitchcock
Starring: Anthony Perkins, Janet Leigh, Vera Miles, John Gavin, John McIntire, Martin Balsam
1960/BW

Hitchcock's most notorious film, *Psycho* is a psychological thriller based on a novel by Robert Bloch. Even if you haven't seen it, you have seen many reinterpretations of it in more recent thrillers. Although many do not consider it Hitchcock's greatest film (most critics pick *Vertigo* or *North by Northwest*), *Psycho* is still a good introduction to the master's work. If you can find a copy with the original trailer for the film attached, rent it (or buy it) if at all possible. The publicity for the movie was a scream (no pun intended) with the tag line "The picture you must see from the beginning—or not at all." (Theaters were instructed to refuse admission to people who showed up late.)

Hitchcock made a cameo appearance in all his films. Look for him in this one. He's a rather heavy man with a distinctive profile. Few filmmakers have had a greater effect on our culture than

Hitchcock, who had more than fifty films to his credit.

See also: *Dressed to Kill* (1980), a modern version by Brian DePalma, and these other Hitchcock films: *The 39 Steps* (1935); *Spellbound* (1945); *Notorious* (1946); *Rear Window* (1954); *To Catch a Thief* (1955); *Vertigo* (1958); and *North by Northwest* (1959). These films are all excellent and have great casts, including Ingrid Bergman, Gregory Peck, Cary Grant, Jimmy Stewart, and Grace Kelly.

Don't bother with: *Psycho II, Psycho III, Psycho IV: The Beginning.* All are awful.

Psycho's Anthony Perkins takes Oedipus (p.182) a step further.

2001: A Space Odyssey
Director: Stanley Kubrick
Starring: Keir Dullea, Douglas Rain as HAL
1968/C

2001 is a cerebral science fiction film that, although slow-moving, is a milestone in filmmaking. Beautifully filmed with groundbreaking spectacular special effects (for the time), *2001* spans all of human evolution, from primitive man making his first weapon to men flying through space.

One of the main characters in the film, HAL, is a computer that develops its own personality. (The name "HAL" is a play on IBM. Think about it.) The film is about technology, and in some of the slower moments, you might ask yourself how they could film some of the effects. Remember, there were no computer-aided digital effects when this film was made.

When you watch this film, turn the volume up. The music is all-important (and of a type that probably won't offend your parents); without the full effect of sound, the movie loses some of its grandeur. Also watch for changes in technology. Some things that seemed modern in 1968 are commonplace today.

See also: *Forbidden Planet* (1956) with Leslie Nielsen; *Silent Running* (1971), with Bruce Dern; *Star Wars* (1977) by George Lucas; *Close Encounters of the Third Kind* (1977) by Steven Spielberg; *Alien* (1979) by Ridley Scott with Sigourney Weaver; and *Blade Runner* (1982), also by Scott.

Don't bother with the sequel, *2010*. It's lame.

M*A*S*H
Director: Robert Altman
Starring: Donald Sutherland, Elliot Gould, Tom Skerritt, Sally Kellerman, Rene Auberjonois, Jo Ann Pflug, Gary Burghoff
1970/C

Not a typical war movie, *M*A*S*H* is an entertaining black comedy (a black comedy is one that finds humor in awful situations like war, death, or poverty) about a mobile hospital set near the front lines during the Korean War (pp. 106-107). Stuck in a horrible situation, the characters manage to entertain themselves (and us, as well) by engaging in a series of pranks and activities that are hilarious. Director Robert Altman manages to create a comedy that is entertaining at the same time as it tackles a number of big issues. If you have seen the TV show and not the film, you don't know what you're missing. The film is different: funnier, faster, better.

See also: *The Bridge On the River Kwai* (1957), with Alec Guiness; *Catch-22* (1970), by Mike Nichols (based on the Joseph Heller novel); and *Apocalypse Now* (1979), by Francis Ford Coppola (based on Joseph Conrad's book *Heart of Darkness*).

Some other great Altman films: *McCabe and Mrs. Miller* (1971), a western with Warren Beatty; *Nashville* (1975), with a large cast of stars; and *The Player* (1992), another black comedy with an even larger cast of stars.

The principal cast of *M*A*S*H*

Dirty Harry
Director: Don Siegel
Starring: Clint Eastwood, Andy Robinson
1971/C

Harry Callahan is a tough cop who makes his own rules. He sets off on the trail of a psycho-hippie on the streets of San Francisco, and fights the liberal establishment all the way. With a remarkable presence on the screen, Eastwood plays Callahan straight up, tough, and quiet. Every word he says counts, and we have no doubt that he will round up the bad guy. A violent film, *Dirty Harry* is not for the squeamish, but its characters and action are so well put together that the movie never becomes disgusting.

Surprisingly, most of the sequels are pretty good: *Magnum Force* (1973); *The Enforcer* (1976); and *Sudden Impact* (1983) are all worth a look. Go ahead. Make his day.

See also: *Bullitt* (1968), with Steve McQueen; and *Thunderbolt and Lightfoot* (1974) with Eastwood and Jeff Bridges.

The Godfather
Director: Francis Ford Coppola
Starring: Marlon Brando, Al Pacino, Talia Shire, Diane Keaton, Robert Duvall, James Caan, and countless others, all great.
1972/C

The Godfather, Part II
Director: Francis Ford Coppola
Starring: Robert De Niro, Al Pacino, Talia Shire, Diane Keaton, Robert Duvall, James Caan, Bruno Kirby, Harry Dean Stanton, and countless others, all great.
1974/C

The seventies answer to *Gone with the Wind*, (p. 414-415) these two epic films tell the story of the Corleones, a Mafia family in which everybody is involved in the "family business," like it or not. Based on the Mario Puzo novel *The Godfather*, these films set a standard for gangster films that will be hard to beat. With breathtaking vision, Coppola has managed to turn the story of a gangster family into an analogy of the American Dream. Don Vito Corleone, tied to ritual and in love with his country, is searching for the same respectability sought by every other American. Tied up in this tale is the contemporaneous story of a nation emerging triumphantly from WWII.

Notice the way in which Coppola juxtaposes beautiful music or religious themes with bloody violence and murder. It is a Coppola trademark and serves to make these horrible acts majestic. Both films are spectacular (with many critics liking the second over the first), and both films won Academy Awards as best picture.

See also: *The Public Enemy* (1931) with James Cagney; *Scarface* (1932), the Howard Hawks original; *Once Upon a Time in America* (1984), with Robert De Niro; and *GoodFellas* (1990) by Martin Scorsese (again with De Niro).

Jaws
Director: Steven Spielberg
Starring: Roy Scheider, Robert Shaw, Richard Dreyfuss
1975/C

This film, which is about a shark that harasses a small New England beach town, is among the scariest ever made. It helped establish Spielberg as one of the most popular filmmakers of all time. The acting is terrific, and the scenes of the shark attacks scared a generation of beach-goers. The music that the audience hears when the shark is approaching has been used in countless comedy sketches and advertisements and has become an icon in its own right.

See also: *Raiders of the Lost Ark* (1981), which George Lucas and Speilberg produced together; and *1941* (1979), with John Belushi, notable as Speilberg's only unsuccessful film, in which he spoofs *Jaws*, among other films.

Annie Hall
Director: Woody Allen
Starring: Woody Allen, Diane Keaton, Tony Roberts, Carol Kane, Paul Simon, Shelley Duvall
1977/C

A romantic comedy about New York City and Los Angeles, intellectuals and anti-intellectuals, *Annie Hall* is the story of two mismatched lovers whose only common trait is neurosis. This is a playground of a movie, jokey and light, with moments of tender humor mixed in. Listen carefully; some of Allen's jibes are so quick and so nasty that it takes a minute to understand them. The scene in which the characters wait in a movie line is particularly funny, and the line "What I wouldn't give for a large sock of horse manure" may come in handy some day.

See also: *The Goodbye Girl* (1977), a Neil Simon comedy; *The Sure Thing* (1985) with John Cusack; and *When Harry Met Sally* (1989), a Woody Allen rip-off with Billy Crystal and Meg Ryan.

Art imitates life or vice versa?

Some other great Allen films: *Everything You Always Wanted to Know About Sex *(*but were afraid to ask)* (1972); and *Manhattan* (1979), Allen's great follow-up to *Annie Hall*.

Raging Bull
Director: Martin Scorsese
Starring: Robert De Niro, Cathy Moriarty, Joe Pesci
1980/BW

Not for the faint of heart, this disturbing film is about the world champion boxer Jake LaMotta. The film is emotionally brutal, and the boxing scenes are incredible—blunt, noisy, sweaty, bloody. Scorsese's camera captures every nuance of every blow. There is nothing romantic here. The acting is epic, the visuals beautiful, but don't expect to be happy at the end.

Robert De Niro's performance is a great example of method acting. He lives the part, gaining thirty pounds through weight training to look like a boxer, and then gaining even more weight to look like the fat ex-boxer that he becomes in the end. There are no make-up effects aiding his characterization.

See also: *Fat City* (1972), John Huston's tale of a small-town boxer; *Rocky* (1976), for contrast with *Raging Bull*; and *Taxi Driver* (1976) by Scorsese, with De Niro and Jodie Foster. *Taxi Driver* inspired John Hinckley to attempt to assassinate President Reagan (p.127) in 1981.

De Niro in his Oscar-winning performance as Jake LaMotta

FIFTEEN FOREIGN FILMS THAT DON'T SUCK

We realize that most high-school students would rather do their homework than watch a movie with subtitles, but some of the best films ever made were not made in America. Many foreign films are hugely entertaining, and some provided ideas that Hollywood borrowed in making American films. The following is a list of twelve films in which the language spoken is not English, but that you will enjoy watching anyway. Try a few.

The Bicycle Thief (1947, Italian). A classic, a tear-jerker, and a must-see.

Wages of Fear (1952, French-Italian). Four men are hired to drive trucks filled with nitroglycerine through some very rough country. Very nerve-racking.

The Four Hundred Blows (1959, French). The haunting film about a youth who turns to crime to escape his derelict parents that established director Francois Truffaut as a master of his art.

Jules et Jim (1961, French). Another Truffaut masterpiece.

Knife in the Water (1962, Polish). Director Roman Polanski's first film is a harrowing tale of a boat trip gone horribly wrong.

High and Low (1966, Japanese). A complicated, exciting tale of kidnapping and extortion told by world-renowned filmmaker Akira Kurosawa.

King of Hearts (1966, French-British). It is WWI and a Scotsman wanders into a French town abandoned by all but the inhabitants of the local insane asylum. Sound interesting? It is.

Aguirre: The Wrath of God (1972, German). A Spanish conquistador leads his men through the Amazon on an insane quest for cities of gold. Involving and spectacular.

Return of the Dragon (1973, Hong Kong). He directed it, stars in it, and choreographed the fights. He's Bruce Lee. Enough said.

The Soldier of Orange (1979, Dutch). Epic, exciting, educational, and emotional, this film is based on the real life experiences of Erik Hazelhoff, a Dutch spy during WWII. One of the best war films ever made.

The Gods Must Be Crazy (1981, Botswana). This comedy uses two languages—English and a bushman dialect. It concerns the cross-cultural problems that occur after a litterbug pilot drops a Coke bottle out of his plane into the middle of a community of bushmen. You'll never look at a Coke bottle the same way again.

Gregory's Girl (1981, Scottish). A thoroughly enjoyable film about a high school crush.

Diva (1982, French). A bootlegged tape of an opera diva causes a young, French music lover a lot of problems. Fast and funny.

Fanny and Alexander (1983, Swedish). Ingmar Bergman's somewhat autobiographical tale of a family as seen through the eyes of a young boy.

La Femme Nikita (1990, French). While more or less inspired by American action films, this highly stylized, very entertaining thriller is still distinctly French. It inspired American and Japanese remakes.

THE FOURTEEN BEST FILMS ABOUT HIGH SCHOOL

Many movies have been made about high school, but most are poorly made and have plots as deep as a puddle in the Sahara. We have sifted through most of these films, and here provide you with a list of high-school films that we feel are of superior quality.

Blackboard Jungle (1955). The New York City public school system was always tough. The first high school movie to have a rock 'n' roll soundtrack—a big deal back when it was made.

Rebel Without A Cause (1955). The classic, although dated, is still fun to watch because James Dean is so cool.

To Sir, With Love (1967). Sidney Poitier struggles to win over his mod, sixties, disillusioned high school class. Much better than it sounds.

American Graffiti (1973). Considered a classic. George Lucas wrote and directed this perceptive and entertaining film about graduating from high school in the early sixties. This film inspired the TV series "Happy Days." Lucas followed it up with *Star Wars*.

Grease (1978). High school sweethearts John Travolta and Olivia Newton-John, a gang leader named Crater Face, and the highest-grossing film musical of all time. Why not?

Rock 'n' Roll High School (1979). The punk rock group The Ramones cause untold havoc in a high school full of less than inspired students. Very silly. A lot of fun.

My Bodyguard (1980). A funny movie about a friendship that develops between the new kid in school and the huge loner who everyone thinks is psychotic.

Fast Times at Ridgemont High (1982). Probably the perfect high school movie, thanks to Mr. Hand, Jeff Spicolli (played by Sean Penn), and a great cast.

Risky Business (1983). A young Tom Cruise is an honors student and a member of the young entrepreneurs club, but he's also somewhat . . . frustrated. Needless to say, he gets into a lot of trouble and comes up with a rather original business solution to his problems.

Sixteen Candles (1984). Stupid, crude, obnoxious, and thoroughly silly. It is about high school after all.

Hairspray (1988). Cult director John Waters creates a wild, goofy, and very entertaining look at high school in the fifties.

Heathers (1989). A black comedy about high school that is occasionally right on the mark.

House Party (1990). A raucous house party sets the stage for plenty of hijinks, pranks, and great dancing in this energetic and very funny film, starring rappers Kid N Play.

FIVE GREAT MONSTER FILMS

Hollywood has a long tradition of making films about monsters, and here are five that we really like:

Frankenstein (1931). The original is a classic, and it's easy to see why.

King Kong (1933). The grandaddy of all monster films, *King Kong* is undeniably a classic. Its effects, though long since surpassed, are still great fun.

Godzilla (1956, Japanese). Godzilla inspired countless sequels and also supplied not-so-subtle commentary about the effects of atomic weapons (pp. 202-03).

The Thing (From Another World) (1951) and *The Thing* (1982). The 1951 version is a Howard Hawks production and a classic of the genre. The 1982 remake starring Kurt Russell is one of the scariest, creepiest, bleakest, grossest films ever made. In other words, it's great.

Alien (1979). Ridley Scott's sci-fi/horror film is rich with atmosphere, full of chills, and has one of the scariest monsters in film history. It also launched Sigourney Weaver's career. The sequel, *Aliens*, while different, is also great. Avoid the third one.

Six Cult Films

When you get to college, you will find that some people are obsessed with certain films. It may seem hard to believe after you see these films, but they represent some of the most popular "cult" films—films that have inspired thousands of obsessed fans who view them time after time and know every line, word for word.

The Rocky Horror Picture Show (1975). Dr. Frankenfurter is a mad, love-crazy transvestite scientist who lives in Transylvania. Did we mention that this is a musical?

Eraserhead (1978). David Lynch is a strange man. After you've seen *Eraserhead*, you'll be both confused and disgusted—although parts of this film are very funny. Lynch also directed the cult favorite *Blue Velvet* (1986).

The Life of Brian (1979). The Monty Python troupe tell the story of the kid who grew up across the street from Jesus. Blasphemous and hilarious.

The Wall (1982). Pink Floyd's album comes to the big screen. Need we say more?

Repo Man (1984). What's a young, acerbic, not-so-smart L.A. punk to do with himself after his parents give away his savings to a tele-vangelist? Why, get a job repossessing cars, of course. Little does he know there are aliens in the trunk of one of his repos.

Spinal Tap (1984). A fictional documentary on the heavy metal band *Spinal Tap*, this film spoofs the rock 'n' roll world so well you're not sure if what you're seeing is truth or fiction.

Answers

1. A   2. B   3. D   4. A

1. **Put the following people in chronological order:**

   I. Ludwig van Beethoven
   II. Johann Sebastian Bach
   III. Wolfgang Amadeus Mozart

   (A) I, II, III
   (B) II, I, III
   (C) III, I, II
   (D) II, III, I

Perhaps the three most influential composers in Western classical music are **Johann Sebastian Bach** (1685-1750), **Wolfgang Amadeus Mozart** (1756-1791), and **Ludwig van Beethoven** (1770-1827). Their music has been heard by millions and to some it defines the classical music of Europe. Bach was one of the most important Baroque composers. Mozart's music became associated with the Classical period. Beethoven wrote music that bridged the Classical and the Romantic period of classi-

THE ANTHEM MAN

*As a novel use of court aides, **King Alfonso** of **Spain** (1886-1931) created a new position in his court. He appointed one of his subjects the Anthem Man. Apparently King Alfonso was so tone-deaf he was unable to recognize his own national anthem. This man's sole job was to indicate when the national anthem of Spain was played, so the King could rise.*

HUMANITIES

BUILDING ON A GOOD BASS

Charles Mingus (1922-1978) stood out prominently among musicians of his generation. A bass player and composer, he worked for Duke Ellington among others before going on to lead his own groups. By many accounts he was cranky and eccentric, but beneath these labels we can detect a man of enormous intellect, creativity, and individualism.

cal music. Each of these composers was influenced by the preceding masters, and they all built on the artistic creativity of their elders.

2. **Of the following, who is NOT considered to be a jazz musician?**
   - (A) Louis Armstrong
   - (B) Ella Fitzgerald
   - (C) Redd Foxx
   - (D) Thelonious Monk

A truly American music, jazz has had an enormous influence on music throughout the rest of the world. It all began in **New Orleans, Louisiana,** where a new style of music developed out of blues music and the ragtime style piano-playing that were both popular in the area. This early jazz was different from traditional European music in that the musicians improvised as they went along, playing solos that were moving and surprising because they were made up on the spot. The early New Orleans music is known as **Dixieland jazz.** It is vibrant and rich, with complicated arrangements of several instruments, each improvised by a musician but seamlessly come together to form a beautiful whole. One of the most famous jazz musicians ever, **Louis Armstrong** (1901-1971) started out playing Dixieland jazz and is known for his improvisations. A trumpet player and a singer, he helped invent and then popularize jazz.

Dizzy Gillespie (middle right) and Charlie "Bird" Parker (middle left) circa 1950

The next phase of jazz music was the big band era of the 1930s and 1940s—sometimes referred to as swing—which was widely popular because of its danceability. Among the great swing bands are those led by **Duke Ellington** (1899-1974), **Count Basie** (1904-1984), and **Benny Goodman** (1909-1986). **Swing** has had a huge impact on American music, and it is still being danced to today. Often these bands would feature a singer, and among the best are **Billie Holiday** (1915-1959), **Ella Fitzgerald** (1918-), **Frank Sinatra** (1915-), and **Sarah Vaughan** (1924-1990).

After Swing, a new style of jazz was created by the saxophonist **Charlie Parker** (1920-1955). Noted for its complex melodies and an even greater emphasis on improvisation, **bebop jazz** is exciting and challenging. Almost impossible to dance to, bebop is about sophisticated harmonies and complicated rhythms. Many jazz aficionados consider it to be the beginning of "serious" jazz music. Among its best musicians are **Thelonious Monk** (1917-1982), **Charles Mingus** (1922-1979), **Miles Davis** (1926-1991), and **Dizzy Gillespie** (1917-1993). Much of the jazz you hear today is a form of bebop.

After bebop came several other styles of jazz. **Fusion**, (again with Miles Davis) is a combination of rock-and-roll rhythms and jazz; **free jazz** (**Ornette Coleman** (1930-) and **John Coltrane** (1926-1967)) is almost unstructured and allows for free interpretation; and **cool jazz**, (Miles again...) is mellow and easy to listen to.

The Blues Brothers (1980). Extravagant comedy starring John Belushi and Dan Akroyd is not only funny, it also features performances by Aretha Franklin, Ray Charles, James Brown, and Cab Calloway. Great soundtrack.

3. **Which of the following people is known for her recording of the song "Crazy"?**

   (A) Ella Fitzgerald
   (B) Patsy Cline
   (C) Madonna
   (D) Naomi Judd

Although not the most famous of country musicians, **Patsy Cline** (1932-1963) has been one of the most influential. She was a heroine to **Loretta Lynn**, and the songs that she sang have been covered by many other musicians. "Crazy," written by **Willie Nelson** (1933-), is one of her most famous songs and was recorded in 1961. You probably have already heard it somewhere, but if not, you should find a way. It is one of the classic performances of American music.

Coal Miner's Daughter (1980), Bio-pic of the life of Loretta Lynn, starring Tommy Lee Jones and Oscar-winner Sissy Spacek.

4. **Which of the following performers made the song "Respect" famous?**

   (A) Aretha Franklin
   (B) Elvis Presley
   (C) The Rolling Stones
   (D) Billie Holiday

MEETING THE BEATLES?

Beatlemania stands as one of the most popular teenage trends of the century. Pamela des Barres, who made her reputation as a groupie in the sixties, offers this extract from her childhood diary in her memoirs I'm With the Band.

Friday, May 8, 1964...I Love Paul. I'm in love with his body and everything that's on it. I love you, I love you, I love you, my precious precious Paully Waully Paul Paul!! Oh, my bee bee, my own lover.

May 10...I love Paul. Sad News! He's with PigFace in The Virgin Islands and I thought they had broken up. That's not all! Ringo is with Maureen Cox and George is with Patti Boyd. No parental consent. No chaperones.

June 3...My seats at the Bowl, Oh My God!! I'm about 20 feet from the stage...fifth row!!! There's an actual day this year that is called August 23rd! It comes in 83 days!!

June 24...Paul McCartney is the man I love. If he got the chance I know he would love me. I just know it. I love every muscle and fiber and ligament in his thigh. I know that sounds odd, but that's the way I feel.

August 2...It's been a Hard Day's Night and The Beatles are the greatest actors alive. First off, Paul is MY lover, he was such a doll. George was SEX, John was very mental and Ringo is truly a beautiful man. In 21 ravishing days, Oh My God!!

August 23...Day of All!! Tonight I saw Paul, I actually looked at his lean slender body and unique too-long legs. I saw his dimples and pearly white teeth. I saw his wavy, yet straight lengthy hair, I saw his doe-like eyes...and they saw me. Maybe it's fate that brought him to our sunny shores...for I am here too.

Considered by many as the greatest **soul** singer ever, **Aretha Franklin** (1942-) is probably most famous for her recording of "Respect." Although the song originally written by **Otis Redding** (1941-1967) (who was also a great soul singer), Franklin made it her own by infusing it with her Gospel-influenced style. If you like Franklin's music, you might try listening to some **Gospel** music. It is spiritual, and yet some of it can really rock.

5. **Which of the following bands is from the United States?**
   (A) The Beatles
   (B) The Rolling Stones
   (C) The Doors
   (D) Led Zeppelin

Although **rock and roll** comes from blues and country music, both of which developed in the United States, many of its early pioneers are from England. **The Beatles**, **The Rolling Stones**, and **Led Zeppelin** are all originally from Great Britain. During the British Invasion of the sixties (pp. 434-435), these bands transformed rock and roll and American popular music.

The Doors, led by Jim Morrison (1943-1971), is an American band.

6. **Name as many of the Beatles as you can.**
   1. Paul McCartney
   2. John Lennon
   3. George Harrison
   4. Ringo Starr

The tale of the Beatles goes beyond music. They were a pop-culture phenomenon. Their music was listened to by people who had no interest in rock music, and their popularity was unique in the way in which it transcended traditional categories. The Beatles listeners ranged from concert-mad, screaming teenagers to fans of classical music, who were intrigued by their vocal harmonies. Through their experimentation with different instruments and musical styles from around the world, they extended the realm of popular music and legitimized it.

They also had a good deal to do with the social revolution of the sixties (p. 121). The Beatles wore their hair long (well, it wasn't exactly long, just over their ears, but to people back then it seemed long), and they wore bizarre fashions and experimented with drugs. Not exactly great role models, but emblems of the culture, nonetheless. Led by singers **Paul McCartney** (1942-), bass, and John Lennon (1940-1980), guitar, and backed by Ringo Starr (1940-), drums, and George Harrison (1943-), guitar, the Beatles were one of the first modern bands to transcend the music world and become actual cultural icons.

7. **Disco music is associated with what decade?**
    (A) The fifties
    (B) The sixties
    (C) The seventies
    (D) The eighties

Disco, one of the musical forms popular in the seventies, is made with one thing in mind: dancing. A hard beat, a simple melody, and emphasis on percussion and bass (combined with some really "loud" clothes) define disco. Popularized by the movie *Saturday Night Fever*, which featured music by the Bee Gees, disco became the rage throughout the United States. If you are curious about the music, listen to the soundtrack of *Saturday Night Fever*. Other famous disco singers include Diana Ross (1944-), Donna Summer, Gloria Gaynor, and the Swedish sensation ABBA.

8. **MTV first started in which of the following years?**
    (A) 1972
    (B) 1976
    (C) 1981
    (D) 1986

Although the music videos that play on **MTV** are associated with the eighties and nineties, the music video has a long history. In the late forties, opera was being broadcast on TV; in the fifties and sixties, Ed Sullivan would sometimes feature musicians on his show (the most famous of his guests were **Elvis Presley** (1935-1977) and the Beatles). But music videos first came to be the monumental sales instruments that they are today when MTV was established in 1981. It broadcasts music videos twenty-four hours a day and is structured much like a radio station, with VJ's (instead of DJ's) who play the most popular music of the day. Some of the videos have helped launch the careers of rock musicians. Most notably, in the early eighties, a then little-known singer named **Madonna** (1958-) was one of the first musicians who became famous through her well-produced videos. They helped make her one of the most famous singers today.

TWENTY-SEVEN MUSICAL ARTISTS THAT EVERY HIGH-SCHOOL GRADUATE SHOULD HAVE HEARD.

The following is a list of twenty-six musicians whose music has been influential to American culture. Much of their work is available in stores and libraries. We have made suggestions of particular pieces that you might want to listen to. We've tried to make the list eclectic, featuring a wide range of styles, and accessible, in that the music will be fun and easy to find.

Antonio Vivaldi (1678-1741)
The Four Seasons (1725)

Nicknamed "The Red Priest" because he was a member of the clergy and had red hair, Antonio Vivaldi had a great deal to do with the development of Baroque music. Bach, who was a friend and admirer of Vivaldi, even arranged some of his pieces for piano. *The Four Seasons* is a collection of four concerti, which succeeds through music in conjuring up the images associated with the different seasons. Birds chirp, plants blossom, storms rage, hunters hunt, and snow falls.

Johann Sebastian Bach
Brandenburg Concertos (1721)

Johann Sebastian Bach is one of the best and most well-known composers of the Baroque period. His enormous body of work ranges from concertos to religious pieces for the organ. The Brandenburg Concertos are an incredible example of the range of music produced in the Baroque period of the eighteenth century. If you are not familiar with classical music, this is a good introduction. The music is sad, happy, energetic, religious, and just plain beautiful. Give yourself some time to devote exclusively to it and enjoy.

J.S. Bach really went for Baroque.

Wolfgang Amadeus Mozart
The Marriage of Figaro (1786)

Wolfgang Amadeus Mozart, a child prodigy, is still considered without peer among composers. His work is characterized by an easy-going brilliance that is emotional while at the same time melodic. The 1984 film *Amadeus* is a great introduction to his life and music.

The Marriage of Figaro is an opera, and if you have heard opera (and made fun of it), you might try taking some time to listen to this one (or see it; it's available on videotape). Operas are not about plot, but about singing. Don't feel that you have to listen to the whole thing at once. Listen to it until you are tired and can't concentrate any more, and then give it another chance. It will be well worth it.

Also try Mozart's *Requiem*, a mass written near the end of his life.

Wolfgang Amadeus Mozart

Ludwig van Beethoven
Symphony No. 9, in D minor, Op. 125 (1824)

Also try any of Beethoven's other symphonies, particularly his Third Symphony. Dedicated to Napoleon Bonaparte (pp. 176-77), it is known as *Eroica*.

Beethoven's symphonies are considered among the best ever written, and his Ninth Symphony is considered by many to be his best. This music is about drama, tension, suspense, and energy. The music rises and falls and brings you to different emotional heights—only to surpass them later on. The final movement, set to the poem "Ode to Joy" by German poet Johann Schiller, makes you want to sing along with it (of course, the poem is not in English, which makes it a bit harder).

Beethoven was completely deaf when he wrote his Ninth Symphony.

You have probably heard parts of the Ninth Symphony in different commercials and movies (it was in *Die Hard* and *A Clockwork Orange),* but to hear the whole piece together is a new experience. When you listen, try to give all your attention to the music—but don't feel that you have to hear the whole thing at once. Take it one movement at a time, and listen to parts of it over and over. And most of all, turn it up. This symphony is meant to be heard at ear-shattering volume. (Best of all, your parents won't really be able to complain. You are trying to learn about culture, aren't you?)

Igor Stravinsky (1882-1971)
The Rite of Spring (1913)

Also try Stravinsky's *Firebird Suite*, written in 1910.

Disney's animated classic *Fantasia* (1940) features an incredible sequence animated to *The Rite of Spring* and other great classical pieces.

The Russian composer Igor Stravinsky (1882-1971) is one of the greatest twentieth-century composers. Atmospheric and full of irregular rhythms, his music was different enough from what preceded it to shock and enrage the conservatives among his audience. *The Rite of Spring* inspired a riot when it was first performed in Paris on May 29, 1913. So when you listen to it, try to imagine what was so shocking about this piece of music.

Louis Armstrong
Louis Armstrong and Earl Hines, The Genius of Louis Armstrong, Volume I, 1923-1933

Louis Armstrong, known as Satchmo—for "Satchel mouth" because his was as big as a suitcase—was one of the first to develop the jazz solo into an improvised art form. To experience his remarkable abilities, listen to any of his Hot Five or Hot Seven recordings and you will get a sense of how Armstrong turned a popular art form into high art. If you haven't heard much jazz, or have only heard more recent stuff, you are in for a treat. Armstrong's music has heart and is moving and entertaining at the same time.

Ol' Satchmo

Duke Ellington
Any greatest hits package (1940s - 1950s)

Duke Ellington is considered by many to be the best American composer ever. His original music ranges from danceable swing like "Take the 'A' Train" or "Satin Doll" to more serious pieces like "Harlem Air Shaft." But mostly, his music is about swing, and boy does it ever. Ellington's music is the kind that you can imagine your grandparents doing the fox-trot to; indeed, it is hard to listen to without tapping your feet.

Try also *Ellington Indigos,* on the Contemporary Jazz Masters label and *New Orleans Suite.* The music on these two albums was written more than thirty years apart and shows Duke's brilliance and growth beautifully.

Also try "Louis and Duke: The Complete Sessions," the only recording that features both Louis Armstrong and Duke Ellington playing together. It's great.

The Duke

Benny Goodman
Best hits or, if you can find it, *Carnegie Hall Jazz Concert—1938*
(Late 1930s)

Benny Goodman swings.

In the late thirties, Benny Goodman was the most popular musician in the United States. His band achieved the type of popularity that foreshadowed the hysteria created by Elvis Presley and the Beatles years later. Everyone knew who he was, and most people could name some of the people in his band. Goodman's music was known for its swingability; listening to it, it is not hard to imagine how it could get a room full of people to dance.

The 1938 Carnegie Hall concert was important because it featured the first multiracial group of musicians in that prestigious hall. Goodman was white and Jewish, and he played with African-American musicians from the bands of Count Basie and Duke Ellington.

LADY SINGS THE BLUES?

A lot of people mistakenly refer to Billie Holiday as a blues singer. She sang with a blues feeling, but Holiday sang jazz and popular music. Blues refers to a specific form of music. A typical blues song might go as follows:

> *I hate to see / the evening sun go down.*
> *I hate to see / the evening sun go down.*
> *Cause my man done left me / done left this town.*

If you want to hear blues, you should go back to Bessie Smith (1894-1937), an incredibly popular blues singer of the twenties.

Billie Holiday
Anything before 1942

Billie Holiday's abilities as a singer are truly amazing. Before 1942, she sang with bands that rocked, and the music is lively, exciting and moving. Especially with the saxophone player Lester Young, Lady Day (as she was called) sang the heck out of some terrific songs. After 1942, Holiday switched to singing in front of string instruments. She became a bit more sappy, although she still did some fine recordings. After many bouts with drugs, she recorded some of the most moving recordings ever. Some people like the "late" era of Holiday because they consider the music more bluesy, filled with heart-wrenching emotion. Others hear only the depressing remnants of a woman ravaged by drugs and a hard life. You decide.

Ella Fitzgerald
Compact Jazz or other Verve label compilations (Late 1950s, Early 1960s)

Ella Fitzgerald is all about joy and exhilaration. Her recordings during the sixties were done when her voice was at its strongest. If you can find her singing "Mack The Knife" live in Berlin, you will get a sense of just how good she is. She can hit notes in a huge range and imbue each of them with enough warmth and emotion to send shivers down your spine.

Soundtrack to *Oklahoma!* or *Carousel* by Oscar Hammerstein and Richard Rodgers

The American answer to opera, these musicals embody the tradition of musical comedy in America. The lyrics are the important thing. Don't worry about the plot as much as the clever writing of the songs. After listening to these musicals a few times, you'll be singing right along. That's what this music is

Ella and some famous friends, clockwise from top right, Max Roach (a famous drummer), Roy Eldridge, and Oscar Peterson

all about. The melodies are not complex, and anyone off the street can sing along.

The song writing team of Rodgers and Hammerstein collaborating wrote some of the most popular American musicals and, in 1943, their musical *Oklahoma!* won the Pulitzer Prize for musical achievement. If you like these, you might try other Broadway musicals and anything by Cole Porter (1891-1964).

A still from the film musical *Oklahoma!*

George Gershwin (1898-1937)
Rhapsody in Blue (1924) or *Porgy and Bess* (1935)

One of America's most beloved and popular composers, George Gershwin wrote music for many popular Broadway shows. One of his most famous pieces is *Rhapsody in Blue*, an extended jazz composition that combines many of the elements of European classical music with American jazz music of the twenties. The piece was so popular that it inspired a film of the same name in 1945, and has been used in films and commercials ever since it was written.

Porgy and Bess is an American opera exploring the lives of people in an African-American community. The opera combines elements from the blues and classical music and is incredibly popular.

Hank Williams, Sr. (1923-1953)
Greatest Hits from the 1950s

Considered by many to be the greatest figure in country music, Hank Williams was one of the first people to bridge the gap between country and pop music. His songs have been re-recorded by numerous musicians of all disciplines, and his style of singing became the basis for many of the country acts to follow. Other important country musicians are Johnny Cash (1932-) and George Jones (1931-).

Hank is smiling even though his songs are sad.

Folsom Prison Blues, I Walk the Line, and *Ring of Fire*, by Johnny Cash. Great country standards featuring Cash's famous baritone.

Elvis Presley
Elvis, The Sun Sessions (1950s)

Able to mix the bluesy quality of black music with the country-western, hillbilly tradition, Elvis Presley was the first person to popularize rock and roll. It is hard for us to imagine just what kind of reaction his music brought about. A southern white man doing black music was enough to send racist southerners into a tizzy. Various anti-rock and roll organizations started declaring that Elvis's records were "nigger music, bestial and vulgar." Today, in Memphis,

Tennessee, one of the former hotbeds of such racist vitriol, Elvis's home, **Graceland**, sits as a mecca for the lovers of the man, and rock and roll.

Until the arrival of **Michael Jackson** (1958-), Elvis was the most successful musician the world had ever known. Known as "the King," Elvis was also a popular phenomenon outside of his music. He captured America's imagination, developing his own fashions and persona. Even now, years after his death, some people have trouble believing that he is not still alive.

For those of you who have heard of the Elvis phenomenon but have not heard his music, listening to him may be somewhat of a revelation. He was really good. The music is gritty and emotive, and he was able to generate a lot of excitement. Maybe you can understand why this was a man who will not die (so to speak).

If you like this music, you might try **Sun's Greatest Hits** which includes performances by Elvis, Carl Perkins, Johnny Cash, Jerry Lee Lewis, Roy Orbison, Bill Justis, Carl Mann, and Charlie Rich—all of whom had a huge influence on future rock and roll.

The King was reportedly seen nearly one hundred times last year by rather excited fans.

Chuck Berry (1926-)
Chuck Berry Golden Decade, Vols. 1, 2, and 3 (Chess 1967, 1973, 1974)

At the same time that Elvis Presley was adding black rhythm and blues (R&B) to white country-western music, Chuck Berry was going from the other side, adding white country music to his R & B roots. If not for racism and segregation in the music industry, he would probably have been as popular as Elvis. His music serves as the foundation for rock and roll. It is filled with energy and practically screams out from his guitar.

ELVIS CENSORED ON ED SULLIVAN

Elvis's peculiar (and some would say sexy) way of shaking his hips when he gave a concert was a little too racy for network television. When he gave a performance on the Ed Sullivan show, the camera operators were instructed not to shoot footage of his hips, and the TV audience only saw him from the waist up.

BERRY BE GOOD

At the height of his career, Berry was arrested and put in jail for two years. Berry was charged with rape because he had crossed into a southern state in the company of some white female fans. There was no "rape" involved, but white southerners could not stand to think of white women socializing with black men.

Chuck Berry

Unlike Elvis and many of the other performers of the time, Berry wrote many of his own songs. When you hear this CD, you will get a sense of why he was so popular and influential. Many musicians have done their own versions of his songs, and his lyrics have become part of rock's legacy. Some of his famous songs include "Johnny B. Goode" and "Brown-Eyed Handsome Man."

Loretta Lynn (1935-)
Greatest Hits (1960s)

Immortalized in the movie *Coal Miner's Daughter*, Loretta Lynn is a true American legend. She overcame poverty, traveling the country along the way, promoting herself by giving away albums to radio disk jockeys. Her singing and song-writing were so good that she began to attract followers, and eventually her music became incredibly popular. Her singing style became the signature style of country music.

If you like her music, you might try Patsy Cline, one of the singers who most influenced Loretta Lynn. Both singers knew how to put life into a song.

James Brown (1928-)
Live at the Apollo (1962) or *In the Jungle Groove* (1970)

These two albums will give you an idea of the range and ability of James Brown, the greatest and most influential soul singer of the twentieth century. Brown's music is about rhythm and percussion. Everything—his voice, his guitar, the horns—has taken on a rhythmic quality. The **"Live at the Apollo"** album gives you an idea of the way in which Brown could inject his voice with emotion and lead an amazingly versatile band. "In the Jungle Groove" is the ultimate in danceable funk music. If you have listened

"I got soul and I'm super bad."
—James Brown

to any rap or current dance music, you will notice that many of the sampled sections of rhythm come from this album. "Funky Drummer" is the most sampled piece of music ever.

The Beatles
Sergeant Pepper's Lonely Hearts Club Band (June 1967)

Perhaps the most famous of all pop musicians, the Beatles had a huge impact on American culture. Their music, a combination of English choral music and American rhythm and blues, had an enormous effect on the development of rock and roll, country, and jazz. Millions of young people obsessed over John, Paul, George, and Ringo, copying their hair styles and clothing, screaming at their concerts, and studying their every move in fan magazines.

A Hard Day's Night (1964), and *Yellow Submarine* (1968), starring the Beatles.

John, Paul, George & Ringo

Paul McCartney and John Lennon were superb songwriters who enlarged the potential subject matter available to rock music. *Sergeant Pepper's Lonely Hearts Club Band*, recorded in 1967, upped the stakes of what could be done with popular music. They combined elements of classical music, world music, jazz, and poetry, and brought new respectability to modern popular music. The importance of this album cannot be overstated.

Other CDs to get include *The Beatles*—nicknamed *The White Album* (1968), *Abbey Road* (1969), *Revolver* (1966), *The Beatles 1962-1966,* and *The Beatles 1967-1970.*

The Stones in 1972

The Rolling Stones admit to the influence of American blues artists on their music. Many of their songs (and the songs of Led Zeppelin) are covers of blues standards. If you're interested in the roots of rock, listen to any recordings of John Lee Hooker, Willie Dixon, Muddy Waters, Howlin' Wolf, B.B. King, or Robert Johnson.

Gimme Shelter (1970). Great documentary on the Stones' free concert at Altamont, where chaos erupted thanks to rowdy fans, the security patrol of Hell's Angels, and "Sympathy for the Devil."

The Rolling Stones
Exile on Main Street (1972) or a greatest hits record

The most famous and enduring rock and roll band, The Rolling Stones, popularized American rhythm and blues and had a huge influence on American counter-culture. Part of the "British Invasion" of the sixties, the Stones transformed and invigorated American rock and roll.

Exile on Main Street has a country, bluesy feel and is different from any other Rolling Stones music you have heard. *Exile* is thoughtful and moving, and shows the artistry and versatility of the group at their creative peak.

Woodstock
1969 (NOT 1994!)

The recording of the Woodstock festival features many of the important rock musicians of the sixties. The 1969 festival was over-run by rock-and-rolling, free-loving hippies (p.121), and it turned into the defining moment of a generation. With more than 400,000 fans on hand, musicians such as **Jimi Hendrix** (1942-1970), who practically invented modern rock-and-roll guitar, The Who, and Sly and the Family Stone played a few memorable songs during the three memorable days of peace, love, and music. The disc will give you a

It's 1969. Do you know where your mother is?

THE ROCKETS' RED GLARE

During the music festival at Woodstock (pp. 446-447) in 1969, Jimi Hendrix did a version of "The Star-Spangled Banner" that had Francis Scott Key (the original writer) turning over in his grave. Playing his electric guitar at incredibly high volumes, Hendrix turned this sacred piece of American music into his own. Hendrix's rendition was not parody, however; he took a well-known piece of music and gave it new life. His version of the national anthem, distorted and angry, could be seen as a comment on the Vietnam war (pp.117-118), the Civil Rights movement (pp. 109-113), or any of the social disillusionment of the time.

sense of the music that was happening at the time and of the character of the sixties' generation. Also, you might want to see the movie, which shows your parents' generation rolling around naked in the rain and mud of upstate New York.

The Temptations
All the Million Sellers or Any Album From the Late 1960s and 1970s

The Temptations were one of the first bands to combine danceable, funky music with sophisticated melodies in what became known as the Motown sound. Recording for Detroit-based Motown recording studio, the Temptations sold millions of records and helped popularize this type of music. Other important bands from this period included The Supremes (with Diana Ross, who later launched her own solo career) and The Jackson Five (starring a very young Michael Jackson, who ended up with the most successful solo career ever). If you want an easy route to the Motown sound, try listening to the soundtrack from the movie The Big Chill, which has lots of the music from this period, or one of Motown's own greatest hits compilations.

Motown sound pioneers, The Temptations

Hard rock icons and truly talented musicians, the members of Led Zeppelin

Led Zeppelin
Led Zeppelin II, IV, or *Houses of the Holy* (1969, 1971, and 1973 respectively)

A British band that had a huge influence on rock and roll, Led Zeppelin created a loud, distorted, yet bluesy music with a screaming vocal track. The music is intense, emotional, and rhythmic. The screaming guitar solos of Jimmy Page and the high-pitched voice of Robert Plant combine to create a music that has become the foundation of "hard rock" and "heavy metal" music. But even for people who don't like heavy metal, Led Zeppelin's music is vital, exciting, and emotional.

The Song Remains the Same (1973), Zeppelin's concert film showing just how raucous those guys were live.

Bob Dylan (1941-)
Highway 61 Revisited (1965) or *Blonde on Blonde* (1966)

Combining elements of **folk music** and poetry with rock and roll, Bob Dylan changed the face of popular music. Besides dealing with a number of important political issues, Dylan used poetic imagery in his lyrics. Instantly recognizable because of his idiosyncratic vocal twang, Dylan became a type of rock guru for a generation, defining causes and ideas and providing inspiration for the sixties "cultural" revolution. When you listen to this music, pay special attention to the words. Dylan's work became the rallying cry of a generation of rock listeners.

The typically pensive Bob Dylan

Willie Colon (1950)
The Musical History of Willie Colon (1970s -1980s)

Willie Colon is a trombonist who plays **salsa** music, a Latino American music that is a cross between Puerto Rican and Afro-Cuban music with some rock and jazz mixed in. Salsa developed in the seventies in New York City's Latino community, and has had a huge influence on other music genres. This album traces some of Willie Colon's collaboration with different artists, and it will give you a good sense of the best of this music. Although the songs are in Spanish, the music is purely American, and you will recognize elements of it in other music that you hear today. If you like Colon, try Tito Puente, too.

Sex Pistols
Never Mind the Bullocks,
Here's The Sex Pistols! (1977)

Most of the "alternative" music and "college" music in the last fifteen years owes a unique debt to this band. The Sex Pistols reinvigorated rock and roll and popular music, injecting an enormous amount of energy into a medium that was becoming moribund. Disliked by the authorities, The Sex Pistols and band members Johnny Rotten and Sid Vicious became yet another symbol of the coming decline of Western civilization.

Sid Vicious looking better than usual

The first punk album, *Never Mind the Bullocks* is an intense CD with an incredible amount of energy. Listen to it a few times. The first time you hear it, it might sound like noise. The second time, you may find yourself slam dancing. If you like this type of music, try listening to the Clash or the Ramones or the New York Dolls.

Sid and Nancy (1986), a film about Sid Vicious, his girlfriend Nancy, and the Sex Pistols. It captures the seventies punk scene quite well. Also see *The Great Rock and Roll Swindle* (1980), the story of the Sex Pistols, starring the Sex Pistols, as told to us by Malcom MacClaren.

Bob Marley (1945-1981)
Legend (1972-1980)

Not the first reggae musician, Bob Marley was by far the most popular and influential. His music is danceable, but also political. It covers a wide range of issues and does so with a beat. Reggae, according to reggae singer Toots of Toots and the Maytalls, comes from the word "regular." Reggae came out of the ghettos of Jamaica and it is meant to be music for the regular people. Many of its performers believe in the Rastafarian religion that called for a great exodus to Africa.

Marley's music was copied by many popular musicians and became a major part of the music that we hear today. Even if you haven't heard Bob Marley before, his music will sound familiar, as it has influenced everything from jazz to country to funk and rap. If you like Marley, you might try listening to Jimmy Cliff, who was one of the first reggae performers. If Marley does it for you, also check out Toots and the Maytalls, Ziggy Marley, Steel Pulse, Burning Spear, and Alpha Blondy.

RASTAMAN BOB MARLEY

Marley's political lyrics continue a long history of rock as a revolutionary force, and they have been heard in protests all over the world. Check out these words from "Get Up, Stand Up," recorded in 1973:

> *Get up, stand up,*
> *Stand up for your rights,*
> *Get up, stand up,*
> *Don't give up the fight.*

Public Enemy
It Takes a Nation of Millions to Hold Us Back (1988)

In the past fifteen years, rap music has come to dominate the popular music scene in America. While early hip-hop artists, such as Afrikaa Bambaata and Grandmaster Flash, are regarded as pioneers—and such recording artists from the sixties and seventies as Gil Scott-Heron and the Last Poets are obvious forerunners—no rap act has generated more interest from the wider musical world than Public Enemy, consisting of Chuck D, Flava Flav, and Terminator X.

"It Takes a Nation of Millions..." has had a huge impact on rap music and on non-rap music. Recorded by Public Enemy, this CD upped the ante in rap music. Rap musicians like Grandmaster Flash had dealt with political issues, but Public Enemy made rage into poetry. The song "Black Steel in the Hour of Chaos" became a rallying song for bombers during the Gulf War (pp. 130-131). When you listen to it, you will understand. It is about power and pride.

If you like Public Enemy, you might also try: Run DMC, Queen Latifah, A Tribe Called Quest, and Jamal Ski.

ANSWERS

1. D   2. C   3. B   4. A   5. C   7. C   8. C

Visual Arts

1. Put the following constructions in chronological order according to when they were built:

   I. The Berlin Wall
   II. Chartres Cathedral
   III. The Great Wall of China
   IV. Stonehenge

   (A) III, IV, II, I
   (B) IV, III, II, I
   (C) IV, II, III, I
   (D) IV, I, II, III

Certain structures have become so associated with a time or a place that they have become visual symbols. **Stonehenge** is a mysterious structure, built between 2800 BC and 1100 BC, that stands on Salisbury Plain in Wiltshire, England. The huge stones were carried from great distances (almost twenty miles) and erected without the help of modern machines.

Stonehenge is pointed toward the sunrise during the summer solstice, (pp. 280-281) but its purpose is unknown.

The Great Wall of China (p. 252) was built in the third century BC to help thwart invasion. It is an enormous edifice stretching some 1,500 miles through China. The wall was not entirely successful in protecting China from invasion. It is also the only man-made structure that can be seen from space with the naked eye.

The Cathedral of **Chartres** is considered by some to be the supreme example of High Gothic Art. It is enormous and beautiful, and is an excellent example of the transition between the Romanesque style and the Gothic style. It was rebuilt in 1194-1220 and one of the towers is still of the old-fashioned Romanesque style. The inside is beautiful, with resplendent stained glass casting a spiritual light upon the inside of the church.

The Berlin Wall, built in 1961 and destroyed in 1989, is one of the most potent symbols of the Cold War. Erected by communist East Germany to keep its people from escaping to the West, the wall was destroyed when Germany was reunited (p. 116).

2. **In which of the following countries is the Parthenon located?**

   (A) Greece
   (B) Armenia
   (C) Rumania
   (D) Italy

The Parthenon (p. 142), an incredible temple built by the Greeks in the fifth century BC, is a fascinating piece of architecture. The design is so meticulous that certain supporting beams are curved slightly so that they appear straight to the eye. The Parthenon is in the Acropolis, a walled city within Athens, which was supposed to be used when the city was attacked.

3. **Who painted the Mona Lisa?**

   (A) Leonardo da Vinci
   (B) Michelangelo
   (C) Rembrandt van Rijn
   (D) Sandro Botticelli

ART SUPPORT

George Washington challenged Congress in 1789 to attempt its "best endeavors to improve the education and manners of a people to accelerate the progress of art and science; to patronize works of Genius, to confer rewards for inventions of utility and to cherish institutions favorable to humanity." Sadly, no official policy was forthcoming from Washington's government, or any president's government for that matter, until 1962, when John F. Kennedy appointed August Hecksher as a special consultant in the arts. Today the NEA (National Endowment of the Arts), a federal organization, provides grants to artists in all creative disciplines.

Scala/Art Resource NY

The **Mona Lisa** was painted by **Leonardo da Vinci** during the Italian Renaissance (pp. 159-162). Da Vinci is known as a **Renaissance Man** (it probably should be Renaissance Person, but it isn't yet) because he could do so many things so well. Aside from his obvious artistic talents, he made startling discoveries in science as well.

4. Who painted the Sistine Chapel Ceiling?

(A) Leonardo da Vinci
(B) Michelangelo
(C) Raphael
(D) Lorenzo di Medici

The Ceiling of the Sistine Chapel (p. 459), which is located in the Vatican in Rome, is one of the most studied paintings ever. Done in fresco by **Michelangelo** so that the painting is actually part of the walls, the ceiling depicts a number of scenes from the Bible.

Scala/Art Resource NY

5. The artwork pictured above was created during which of the following time periods?

(A) 1800-1850
(B) 1850-1900
(C) 1900-1950
(D) 1950-present

The Painted Word, by Tom Wolfe. A scathing, hilarious critique of modern art by one of our country's great creative journalists.

Guernica (pp. 465-466), painted in 1937, is a poignant memorial to the Spanish Civil War. It depicts the horrors of war and makes use of some of the innovations in modern art developed by painter Pablo Picasso (pp. 463, 465)

TWENTY-EIGHT PIECES OF ART THAT EVERY HIGH SCHOOL GRADUATE SHOULD KNOW

As you read the following descriptions, flip to the color insert in the middle of this book for full color reproductions of the pieces.

Plate 1
Cave Painting
Artist: Unknown
15,000 – 10,000 BC

Found on the walls of a cave in Les Trois Frères, France, this cave painting is one of the earliest images found anywhere in the world, and it is similar to other cave images of the time. It predates writing, agriculture, bronze, and many other signs of early civilization, and it shows that there is some innate desire among humans to create art. Anthropologists have theorized that these drawings might have had some spiritual qualities. Perhaps the images of animals and spears were made to ensure the success of a hunt and not merely to record the event of a hunt.

Plate 2
Discus Thrower
Roman copy of bronze
450 BC (original)

The original bronze sculpture of the "Discus Thrower" was converted into weapons or some other bronze object years after it was created, but the copy gives us an idea of what the original looked like. Among the most famous works of the ancient Greeks, this sculpture captures the power of a man in motion. The original, which was most likely a more skillful version of this one, must have been quite dynamic. Notice how it seems like the athlete is about to let go of the disc, like he is on the verge of an explosive act of motion.

Plate 3
Nike of Samothrace
Artist: Unknown
200-190 BC

This sculpture is of Nike, the Greek goddess of victory. (Yes, the sneaker is named after her.) She has just stepped onto the prow of a ship. Notice the way the wind seems to throw her clothing behind her. The stone has taken on the quality of fabric. If you ever get the chance to go to Paris, make it a point to see this sculpture in the Louvre. It is truly spectacular.

Plate 4
The Laocoön Group
Artist: Unknown
First century AD after Greek original

This sculpture represents the death of Laocoön and his two sons. They all died when Laocoön argued that the Trojan horse (pp. 390-391) was an evil gift that should not be accepted. A serpent came up from the sea and strangled them to death. Notice the pathos, the way in which the figures scream and toil to free themselves from their bonds.

Plate 5
Wedding Portrait
Oil on Panel, 33" x 22 ¹/₂" (83.7 x 57 cm)
Artist: Jan van Eyck (1390-1441)
1434

At first glance, it appears that the couple is alone, but look closely at the mirror. There, you will see two people witnessing the wedding. One of these people is the artist in miniature self-portrait. Inscribed immediately above the mirror are the words "Jan van Eyck was here." (Of course it's in Latin, so if you tried to read it you might see "Johannes de Eyck fuit hic.") Notice that the woman looks pregnant. Many woman of the time would wear clothes that accentuated their stomachs in order to show a kinship with the Virgin Mary. What is remarkable about this painting and others of its time is that every object in the painting has a certain symbolism. The shoes indicate that the couple is on holy ground; the dog, that they will be faithful.

Plate 6
The Birth of Venus
Tempera on Canvas, 5'8 ⁷/₈" x 9'1 ⁷/₈" (1.8 x 2.8 m)
Artist: Sandro Botticelli (1444-1510)
1480

This painting, one of the most well-known of the Renaissance, was done by Sandro Botticelli. It depicts the birth of Venus (p. 389) who, according to Greek mythology, rose from the foam of the sea. Painters have been fascinated with the female form for centuries and this is one of many images of Venus.

Plate 7
The Last Supper
Tempera Wall Mural, 15'2" x 28'10" (4.6 x 8.8 m)
Artist: Leonardo da Vinci (1452-1519)
1495-1498

A **fresco** is a style of painting in which the colors actually become part of the plaster on the wall. Da Vinci, a scientist as well as a painter, had been experimenting with different methods to achieve fresco, and unfortunately arrived at one that did not adhere to the wall too well. Thus, we can only see a shadow of this original piece of art. Considered by many to be the first great painting of the high Renaissance (pp. 159-162), "The Last Supper" is incredible. It shows the moment when Jesus said "One of you will betray me," (pp. 376-377) and if you look carefully you will see the bearded Judas reacting to the accusation. He is the one with his elbow on the table. Not only did he precipitate the death of Jesus, but he had poor manners as well. When you first look at this painting, it seems to be in perfect stability, balanced with an equal amount of weight and energy on each side, but if you look carefully, you will see that there is an incredible amount of dramatic tension. Notice how each person has his own personality and how the architecture forms a halo around Jesus. Renaissance painters were concerned with perspective (the way in which objects appear smaller as they become farther away) and you will notice that the exact center of the painting is where the vanishing point of the perspective lies. If you drew diagonal lines from the tops of the black architectural forms on the sides of the painting, they would meet at Jesus's head. This also helps to make him the focal point of the painting.

Plate 8
David
Marble, height 13'5" (4.08 m)
Artist: Michelangelo (1475-1564)
1501-1504

This statue of David, the young man who defeated Goliath (p. 371), was sculpted by Michelangelo. Considering that David was supposed to be much smaller than Goliath, we have to wonder just how big Goliath would stand next to this fourteen-foot-high sculpture. The sculpture is supposed to be symbolic of Michelangelo's home town of Florence. Florence was a small city surrounded by powerful neighbors, and by making David into an enormous and powerful man, Michelangelo could have been demonstrating civic pride.

If you ever get a chance to see this sculpture in person, you will know why it is a famous piece of art. Like most of Michelangelo's work, the marble is so finely crafted that it looks like skin. He had a miraculous ability to give life to inanimate stone.

Plate 9
Mona Lisa
Oil on Panel, 30 $\frac{1}{4}$" x 21" (77 x 53.5 cm)
Artist: Leonardo da Vinci
15031505

This is probably the most famous piece of art in Western culture. It has been fascinating people for centuries. Looking at this photograph of the painting, you might wonder "Why this painting?" What is it about the Mona Lisa that makes it so mysterious and valuable? First there is the technique. Da Vinci used a technique called "sfumato," in which thin glazes of paint are added a little at a time until the figure forms out of the layers. If you ever get a chance to see the painting in person, you will notice an almost unearthly light emanating from the subject's face. (Unfortunately, the painting is in the Louvre in Paris behind a thick pane of bulletproof glass, so you will never be able to see its full expressive power.) Her eyes seem to follow you as you move about the room. It is an eerie experience.

The other factor that has fascinated art lovers for centuries is the sitter's expression. She is idealized, but she is also an individual. Is the smile alluring or aloof? Take a minute to figure out what you think this woman is up to.

Plate 10
Sistine Chapel Ceiling (The Creation of Adam)
9'2" x 18'8" (2.8 x 5.69 m) detail of Adam;
Entire Chapel ceiling 45' x 128' (13.72 x 39 m)
Artist: Michelangelo
1508-1512

This image, from the ceiling of the Sistine Chapel in the Vatican (p. 232) in Rome, is of God giving the spark of life to Adam (pp. 363-365). It is one of the most recognizable images of art in the world. Its depiction of man as a powerful being continued the stylistic developments achieved by Michelangelo in his sculpture of David. Michelangelo was not entirely psyched about doing the ceiling, but the Pope convinced him, and he created an amazing piece of art. This painting is about drama. Notice that as Adam reaches his hand out to receive the spark of life from God, who is hurtling through space, Adam sees his future mate, Eve, under God's arm. Also, take a second to look at the hands in the fresco. Notice how the limp outstretched hand of Adam is contrasted by the powerful gesture made by God as he creates life.

Plate 11
Sistine Chapel Altar Wall (The Last Judgment)
48' x 44' (14.68 x 13.41 m)
Artist: Michelangelo
1534-1541

This image of a wrathful Jesus raising his hand shows an entirely different view of him. In the past, Jesus was always depicted as suffering, but here he is shown angry. He is about to swat a sinner so hard that he will be forced out of kingdom-come. If you notice the man to the right of Jesus, you will notice that he is holding a human skin. This is the Apostle Bartholomew, who was flayed and became a martyr. Look closely at the face on the limp skin. It is a self-portrait of the artist Michelangelo, who was most likely not feeling too good about himself when he painted it.

Plate 12
Self-Portrait
Oil on Canvas, 31 $^5/_8$" x 26 $^1/_2$" (80.3 x 67.3 cm)
Artist: Rembrandt van Rijn (1606-1669)
1660

This self-portrait by Rembrandt is an excellent example of his painting style. Done late in his career, it is remarkably expressive and striking. Notice how the paint seems to have taken on the quality of flesh. If you get up close to this painting, you can see that the paint is thick and that the imprint of the brush is still visible. Rembrandt's work is remarkable for its ability to capture complex emotions and the way he makes a painting resonate with more than the original energy put into it. Rembrandt was fond of the self-portrait, and his work provides an unusual and intense view of his aging process. A viewing of some of his sixty or so self-portraits makes one feel as if he actually knew Rembrandt.

Plate 13
Water Lilies, Giverny
Oil on Canvas, 6'6 $^1/_2$" x 19'7 $^1/_2$" (2 x 6 m)
Artist: Claude Monet (1840-1926)
1907

Vincent and Theo (1990), a film on the life of Van Gogh by Robert Altman (p.422-423).

To really appreciate this painting, you have to see it in person. It is huge, a series of paintings that, when connected, takes up an entire wall. When you stand in front of it you feel as if you are in the midst of a great pond with water lilies and their flowers mixed with the reflection of the trees above. Claude Monet, the artist, was obsessed with the play of light and color on an object. He was an **Impressionist** and was attempting to capture a momentary view of an object. He spent years trying to perfect the view of the water lilies. If you get a chance to go to New York City, make a pilgrimage to see this work at the Museum of Modern Art.

Plate 14
Dancers Practicing at the Barre
Oil on Canvas, Colors Freely Mixed with Turpentine
29 ³/₄" x 32" (75.6 x 81.3 cm)
Artist: Edgar Degas (1834-1917)
1876

This painting of ballerinas rehearsing is an excellent example of Degas's work. Notice the strange balance and angles with which he worked. Degas was influenced by Japanese prints, which used similar angles in forming the composition of a picture. Notice the grace and balance with which the ballerinas support themselves. Degas contrasted the balance with the awkwardness of their stance. How comfortable could it be for them to stand that way?

Plate 15
Sunflowers
Oil on Canvas, 17" x 24" (43.2 x 61 cm)
Artist: Vincent van Gogh (1853-1890)
1887

Vincent van Gogh was the artist who most profoundly expressed the spirit of the approaching twentieth century. Not only was his work incredibly expressive, but he lived a life that became a bizarre symbol of the embattled artist, attempting to create against all odds. Mostly self-taught, van Gogh was able to create a body of work in his short lifetime that still feels modern and essential to this day.

This painting is of sunflowers. Notice how the stems and the flowers seem to release energy. It is as if this "still-life" is moving, exploding with emotion. If you could run your hand over the surface of the painting, you would feel the actual marks made by van Gogh. The texture adds to the work, increasing the connection between us and the artist.

Van Gogh lived to be thirty-seven, but only painted in his last ten years. He was never successful in his lifetime, and only a few people ever saw his work. Suffering from madness, he is known to have cut off his ear to send it to a woman. He eventually committed suicide. Rather than taking away from his reputation, his madness has intrigued twentieth-century art-lovers. Twentieth-century history is so full of death and destruction that many people view it as a time of madness. Why shouldn't it value art produced by mad people?

Plate 16
The Scream
Tempera and Casein on Cardboard, 36" x 29" (91.3 x 73.7 cm)
Artist: Edvard Munch (1863-1944)
1893

Arrgghhhhhhhh!!!!!!!!!!! This painting of a scream is a nightmare of intensity that borders on the humorous. Munch intended it to be an expression of fear. He was an **Expressionist** who was trying to show the uncontrollable terror of a nightmare. Notice how the bridge on which the man (or woman) is standing seems to be falling off the canvas. Everything in the painting seems to be falling on this poor person, causing the figure to open his or her mouth in terror.

This type of intense experience is the essence of expressionism and much of twentieth-century art. The artist is not trying to depict reality (for that, there is the camera). He is trying to express something that cannot be seen through normal means, something that exists in the imagination.

Plate 17
Arrangement in Black and Gray: The Artist's Mother
Oil on Canvas, 57" x 64 1/2" (144.6 x 163.8 cm)
Artist: James McNeill Whistler (1834-1904)
1871

This painting is by an American artist who was concerned with the composition of a painting as well as the actual subject. Notice how the forms in the painting strike a perfect balance; the black dress of the woman is used to balance the curtain to the side.

Although Whistler would most likely have wanted the painting to be considered predominantly for its abstract qualities, the expression of his mother and the way she is sitting brings about a strong feeling of melancholy in the viewer.

Plate 18
The Thinker
Bronze, height 27 ¹/₂" (69.8cm)
Artist: August Rodin (1840-1917)
1879-1889

Rodin, considered by many critics to be the best sculptor since Michelangelo, made this piece to be part of a larger sculpture, a gate that depicted hell. This thinker was supposed to sit on top of the sculpture, which was never finished. "The Thinker," however, has become one of the most recognizable pieces of sculpture in the world.

Rodin was not concerned with capturing the exact appearance of a subject. He attempted to make the working process itself part of the art piece. "The Thinker" still has the marks of Rodin's hands on its surfaces.

Plate 19
Les Demoiselles d'Avignon
Oil on Canvas, 8' x 7'8" (2.43 x 2.33 m)
Artist: Pablo Picasso (1881-1974)
1906-1907

This painting created quite a stir when it was first exhibited. It destroyed the classical ideal of beauty and created its own aesthetic environment. When people first saw the painting they were shocked. Originally intended to be a temptation scene in a brothel, the piece took on a life of its own. The women in the painting are gradually made more and more abstract. The first three women on the left are relatively normal, but as Picasso continued with the work, the women became more and more distorted.

It's hard to understand today just how radical a departure from traditional painting this was. Just imagine if all you had ever seen were the paintings on the previous pages. Picasso's women, especially the woman whose faces resemble masks, are just not pretty. Picasso changed the rules of the art game. Painting was relieved from representing the outside world and was able to stand on its own. The forms and shapes of the women's faces become more important than the women depicted. Picasso had succeeded in creating his own pictorial language for expression.

Plate 20
The Dance
Oil on Canvas, 8′5 $^3/_4$″ x12′9 $^1/_2$″ (2.59 x 3.9m)
Artist: Henri Matisse (1869-1954)
1910

Henri Matisse, one of the best painters of the twentieth century, is often compared with Picasso. They both had long careers at about the same time, but while Picasso would use mainly lines and forms to make unforgettable images, Matisse used color. When you see his work in person, it is so bright, it practically glows. This painting, one of his earlier works, shows the incredible amount of energy that Matisse could generate from rather simple forms. The painting is huge, and when you stand in front of it, you feel drawn into the dance.

Plate 21
Black Iris III
Oil on Canvas, 36″ x 29 $^7/_8$″ (91.4 x 75.9 cm)
Artist: Georgia O'Keeffe (1887-1986)
1926

This painting of a flower by Georgia O'Keeffe exemplifies some of the best qualities of the art of the 1920s. By magnifying the essential features of the flower, O'Keeffe turned a very real thing into an abstract form. The painting is vibrant and full of energy, and dare we say, a little sexy.

Plate 22
American Gothic
Oil on Beaverboard, 29 $^7/_8$″ x 24 $^7/_8$″ (75.9 x 63.14 cm)
Artist: Grant Wood (1892-1941)
1930

This painting of two American farmers was painted by Grant Wood, an American artist who rejected many of the tenets of modernism. The people are depicted realistically with severe expressions that might make you think twice before talking to them. It might be interesting to compare this work with "Wedding Portrait" by Jan van Eyck (Plate 5 in the color insert). However, the couple in "American Gothic" are father and daughter, not husband and wife. Wood was strongly influenced by van Eyck, and you will notice that American Gothic has much more in common with van Eyck's work than with that of Wood's contemporaries, like Picasso.

Plate 23
Persistence of Memory
Oil on Canvas, 9 ¹/₂" x 13" (24 x 33 cm)
Artist: Salvador Dali (1904-1989)
1931

This painting was done by the **Surrealist** Salvador Dali, an eccentric who wore capes and a funny mustache. Surrealism is a style of art with images that are based on fantasy and dreams, and many times the works feature objects that are just plain absurd. One famous piece done by Meret Oppenheim is of a cup and saucer covered by fur.

Persistence of Memory shows watches bending around the forms of a forbidden landscape. The image shows what looks like real objects fashioned in an impossible way, and there is something haunting about it.

This all reminds us of the classic joke about surrealists: How many surrealists does it take to screw in a light bulb?

The answer: Fish.

Plate 24
Guernica
Oil on Canvas, 11'6" x 25'8" (3.5 x 7.8 cm)
Artist: Pablo Picasso (1881-1974)
1937

This mural, and it is huge at eleven by twenty-five feet, memorializes the bombing of Guernica during the Spanish Civil War in the thirties. The bombing was one of the first instances in which civilians were attacked with the same force as the military. The painting depicts the horrors of this type of warfare. It doesn't show a particular event but instead demonstrates the all-out terror that the bombing of a city can generate.

Look at the woman on the far left of the painting whose head is immediately under the bull. Picasso has successfully represented a scream in its most basic form. Her mouth is open, her neck extended, her tongue vibrates with the expression of pain and anguish. This scream and this painting have become an all too accurate representation of the battles of the twentieth century.

Plate 25
One (#31)
Oil and Enamel on Unprimed Canvas, 8'10" x 17' ⁵/₈" (2.69 x 5.32 m)
Artist: Jackson Pollock (1912-1956)
1950

At first glance, it seems that the artist has simply dripped paint over a canvas. You will have to trust us when we say your two-year-old brother could not do a painting like this.

When you stand in front of the actual painting, the first thing you notice is the size. The painting is nine by seventeen feet. When you stand in front of it, it takes over your entire world. All you can see is the dripping paint flung at the canvas. Nothing seems to stand still. A splat of paint will come forward and move around in space. You feel as if you are surrounded by raw energy and the floor may feel a bit unsteady.

This style of painting is called **Abstract Expressionism.** It is about the use of paint and color to express emotion, not objects or events. Not all abstract expressionist paintings are formed by dripping paint, but they all share the same search for emotive expression and some can be incredibly moving.

Plate 26
Campbell's Soup
Oil Silk Screen on Canvas, 36 ¹/₈" x 24" (91.7 x 60.9 cm)
Artist: Andy Warhol (1928-1987)
1965

Andy Warhol was one of the founders of **Pop Art.** Pop artists take familiar images from popular culture and transform them into art. By so doing, they comment on the banality of life. Warhol depicts an everyday object that we have seen a million times in a new light. Our culture has made soup cans as recognizable as religious and mythological figures used to be, and by pointing this out, Warhol demonstrates just how empty our lives have become.

Warhol himself was famous, and several of his comments and

ideas have weaved themselves into the annals of pop culture. He once said that everyone would have fifteen minutes of fame in our new media-influenced times. He helped sponsor the rock band The Velvet Underground headed by Lou Reed, a widely influential band among rock-and-rollers. He also made a number of experimental films which are not much fun to watch. In one called *Empire*, he points a camera up at the Empire State Building and lets it film the scene for hours and hours. The viewer sits in front of the screen wondering if anything is going to change. Every once in a while, a bird will fly by or a cloud will appear in the sky. That's it.

Plate 27
Three Flags
Encaustic on Canvas, 30 $^7/_8$" x 45 $^1/_4$"" (78.4 x 115.6 cm)
Artist: Jasper Johns (1930-)
1958

Jasper Johns was into symbols. When is a flag not a flag? If you look closely at his work, you will find that the stars and stripes are formed through the thick application of encaustic, which is pigment mixed with wax, and have a palpable thickness that adds to the image. There is something about the texture of the paint that is truly beautiful and meaningful.

Plate 28
Lobster Trap and Fish Tail (mobile)
Painted Steel Wire and Sheet Aluminum 8'6" x 9'6" (2.6 x 2.9 m)
Artist: Alexander Calder (1898-1976)
1939

This enormous contraption is a **mobile**, a sculpture that moves with the breeze. As the sculpture moves it forms different compositions and different balances, all of which work to create art. With the slightest breeze, the sculpture comes alive. These pieces, when seen in real life, are exciting and vibrant and move with infinite grace despite the weight of the material.

Answers

1. B   2. A   3. A   4. B   5. C

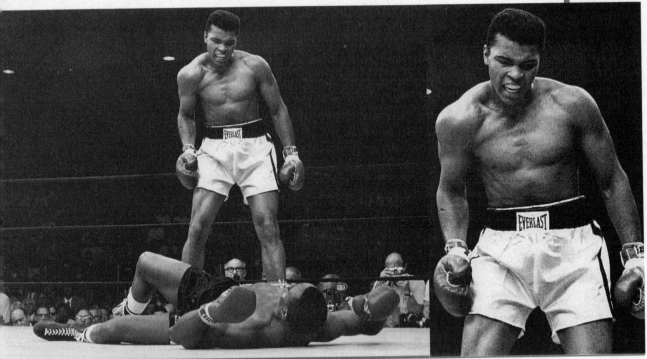

1. **For how many seconds must a professional fighter be on the ground before he is officially "knocked out?"**

   (A) Three seconds
   (B) Five seconds
   (C) Eight seconds
   (D) Ten seconds

The rules in boxing are fairly simple. Two people are put in a square "ring" with fingerless gloves on their fists and they punch each other in sets of three-minute rounds. The fight is over when a certain predetermined number of rounds has passed, when one of the contestants is knocked out for ten seconds, or when one fighter is deemed too messed up to continue.

Raging Bull (1980).
Devastating film about the life of boxer Jake La Motta, featuring an Oscar-winning performance by Robert De Niro (p. 426).

2. Who said "float like a butterfly, sting like a bee?"

    (A) Babe Ruth
    (B) Mohammed Ali
    (C) Tom Clancy
    (D) Robert Frost

Perhaps the most well-known boxer is **Mohammed Ali**. Born Cassius Clay, he changed his name when he became a Muslim (p. 112). Ali became heavyweight champion of the world a record three times, and for this reason he was nicknamed "the Greatest." Ali, a born showman, was a hero for many Americans. He refused to go to Vietnam when drafted and was stripped of his title as a result. He then went on to regain the title after an appeal to the Supreme Court. Ali was also known for his wit and skill with words. His most enduring quote remains his description of his boxing style: "I float like a butterfly, sting like a bee."

Other famous boxers include Joe Louis, known as "the Brown Bomber," and Jack Dempsey.

3. A grand slam in baseball is

    (A) when the ball bounces over the outfield wall
    (B) when two players collide at third base
    (C) when a batter hits a home run while the bases are
         loaded
    (D) when a team wins the World Series in four straight
         games

The rules in baseball are fairly complex. There are nine players on a team and the teams take turns playing offense and defense. When a team is playing offense it tries to score as many runs as possible, and the defensive team (you guessed it) tries to stop them. A **run** is scored when a player advances around the three **bases** and reaches **home plate** without being tagged with the ball.

The offensive team always has one player who is up **at bat**. He tries to hit the ball thrown by the pitcher in such a way that none of the players on defense can catch it. The batter must also decide if he wants to swing at the ball. If the ball is not in the strike zone and he doesn't swing, it is called a **ball** by the umpire, a referee who stands behind the plate. If the batter is pitched four balls he gets to **walk** to first base without even hitting the ball. If the ball is thrown over the plate it is called a **strike**. Any time the batter swings and misses it is considered a strike regardless of whether the ball is in the strike zone. Three strikes and (that's right) he's

**KNOCK-DOWN,
DRAG-OUT**
....

Before the turn of the century, it was not unusual for boxing matches to last more than a hundred rounds. Rounds were determined by knockdowns. Additionally, fighters fought with bare knuckles—they used no gloves.

The Bad News Bears (1976), starring Walter Matthau. A hilarious comedy about a little league team led by an unorthodox, i.e. inebriated, coach who decides to put a girl on the team, much to the dismay of his foul-mouthed pre-adolescent players.

HUMANITIES

Eight Men Out (1988). The story of the 1919 Chicago White Sox, who threw the World Series and caused America to lose some of its innocence.

Pride of the Yankees (1942). The story of Lou Gehrig, with Gary Cooper and Babe Ruth playing himself. One of the best baseball films ever made.

Baseball (1994). Ken Burns, the man who made the vivid documentary *The Civil War* (p. 67), scores again with this extensive and lovingly detailed documentary on the national pastime.

The Sultan of Swat sits on a fastball.

out. A good hitter will be successful about thirty percent of the time.

If a player hits the ball out of the ball park and it is not foul, he has hit a **home run.** If the **bases are loaded** with players and he hits the home run, it is called a **grand slam.**

Baseball, known as the **national pastime,** has been hugely popular throughout the twentieth century. It has supplied America with heroes and controversy, and is still America's most widely attended sport.

4. **Which of the following baseball players was nicknamed the "Sultan of Swat?"**
   (A) Lou Gehrig
   (B) Babe Ruth
   (C) Ty Cobb
   (D) Joe Di Maggio

The greatest star ever to play the game, **George Herman "Babe" Ruth** (1895-1948) transcended the sports world and became a national legend. Not only was he an incredible baseball player, possibly the best hitter ever, but he was well-loved by the fans, and helped save baseball from the aftermath of a few scandals. The Babe, also nicknamed the Sultan of Swat (people were quite imaginative with nicknames back then), still holds several records for his achievements in baseball even though he stopped playing in 1935. Legends concerning his prodigious skills abound.

The Babe's team, the **New York Yankees,** has dominated baseball like no other team has dominated any professional sport. Professional baseball is divided into two leagues, the National League and the American League. The teams that win in each division are said to have "won the pennant." The Yankees have won the American League pennant and made it to the World Series, as of this writing, thirty-three times. They won the Series twenty-three out of those thirty-three times. The Yankees have been world champions in baseball for almost a quarter of the time that such a championship has existed.

5. **The first African-American baseball player in the major leagues was**
   (A) Babe Ruth
   (B) Hank Aaron
   (C) Jackie Robinson
   (D) Willie Mays

For years after major league baseball got started at the turn of the century, African-Americans were not allowed to play. African-Americans played in the Negro Leagues, but the big money was made by the white players. All of this changed in 1947, when **Jackie Robinson** stood for the National Anthem at Ebbets Field in Brooklyn, destroying the race barrier in professional sports.

Robinson's entry into major league baseball was facilitated by the owner of the Brooklyn Dodgers, Branch Rickey, and it was not without controversy. Opposing players called him names and taunted him; some even tried to get a strike going to stop the entry of blacks into professional baseball. Robinson, with his characteristic dignity and forthrightness, was successful at diverting the controversy and became one of the best baseball players of all time. His Brooklyn Dodgers were one of the biggest box-office draws when they played in opposing cities. The team was a sensation, and had it not been for their arch-rivals, the New York Yankees, they would have won more than one World Series during Robinson's tenure.

There have been other heroes of baseball. Among them are **Lou Gehrig**, who played alongside Babe Ruth, and was known for playing 2,130 games in a row (and for whom a debilitating disease is named); **Ty Cobb**, one of the greatest hitters in the early years of baseball; **Joe DiMaggio**, who hit in fifty-six consecutive games and married Marilyn Monroe (p. 420) in 1954; and **Cy Young**, who won an astounding number of games as a pitcher.

DiMaggio and Monroe kiss at their wedding.

6. **If a player in a tennis game is ahead by a score of 40-love, how many points has she scored in that game?**

   (A) 1
   (B) 2
   (C) 3
   (D) 4

Tennis's unique system for scoring works as follows: **love** means zero points; **fifteen** means one point; **thirty** means two points; **forty** means three points; and **game** means four points. A player can't win a game in tennis unless she is ahead by more than one point. So, if both players reach forty, the situation is called **deuce**. When one player gets the next point, it is said that he or she has the **advantage**, or "ad" for short. The person who is serving is more likely to win, so if the other player is about to win, the point is called a **break point**. If a player who is not serving is ahead love-forty, the point is called triple break point because he or she has three chances to break the opponent's serve.

The four most prestigious tennis tournaments are known as the **Grand Slam**. The Grand Slam consists of the U.S. Open, Wimbledon, the Australian Open, and the French Open. If a player wins all four, he or she has captured the Grand Slam of tennis.

Martina wins Wimbledon (again).

7. Who has won the most Grand Slam titles (including singles and doubles)?

(A) Billie Jean King
(B) John McEnroe
(C) Björn Borg
(D) Martina Navratilova

Perhaps the most dominating of all tennis players was **Martina Navratilova**. Born in Czechoslovakia (when it was under the dominance of the USSR (pp. 205-206)), she eventually defected to the United States and won a world-record fifty-five Grand Slam titles (eighteen singles, thirty-one women's doubles, and six mixed doubles). Other famous tennis players include Maureen Conolly, Arthur Ashe, Jimmy Connors, Björn Borg, and Billie Jean King. Billie Jean King is known for a match called the "battle of the sexes" that she played against Bobby Riggs, a former Wimbledon champion who had insisted that he could beat any woman. He lost.

8. How many points does a team score in football if it makes a field goal?

(A) One
(B) Three
(C) Six
(D) Seven

The rules in American football are complex, but here are the basics. Two teams compete with eleven players on each side. One team is on offense, which means that is has the ball and tries to keep it within its possession and get it to one end of a one-hundred-yard field. The team on offense can use one of two of techniques to move the ball: passing, which means that one player throws the ball forward to a teammate, or running while carrying the ball. The team without the ball, the team on defense, tries to tackle the person with the ball. The game is violent, often brutal, with players ramming into each other all over the field. The team on offense has four **downs** in which to try to move the ball at least ten yards. If it fails, the other team gets the ball. So usually, on fourth down, the offensive team chooses to kick the ball way down field so that the other team will have farther to go to score. A team scores in one of four ways. It can score a **field goal** (three points) by kicking the ball between the uprights, two poles positioned beyond the other team's **goal line**. If the ball is caught or run into the **end zone**, a ten-yard area beyond the other team's goal line, a six-point **touchdown** is scored. The team on defense can score by tackling someone on the offensive team behind their own goal line for a **safety** (two points). After scoring, a team gets the ball only a yard or two from the other team's goal line, and it can either kick the ball between the uprights (one point) for an **extra point** or run the ball into the end zone for a two-point conversion.

Football is a uniquely American sport. It is not played anywhere else, but it is extremely popular here. Its championships all include the word "bowl." There is the **Rose Bowl**, the **Cotton Bowl**, and the **Sugar Bowl** in college football, and the **Super Bowl** in the professional league. The winner of the Super Bowl is considered the world champion, and all the players on the team get gaudy rings.

The Longest Yard (1974). Burt Reynolds is a former football pro who gets thrown in jail and is forced to put together a team of convicts to play a semi-pro team consisting of prison guards. A great football flick and full of big laughs.

North Dallas Forty (1977), starring Nick Nolte. One of the best sports movies ever made, this film takes a look at labor abuse inside the NFL and is dramatic and funny at the same time.

Black Sunday (1977). If you've ever watched the half-time show during the Super Bowl, you can probably sympathize with the terrorists in this film who plot to blow up the whole shebang on Super Sunday.

9. A field goal in basketball is worth

    (A)   two points if taken in front of the three-point line
    (B)   one point
    (C)   three points if dunked
    (D)   the same as one free throw

One of the fastest-growing sports in the United States, **basketball** is played on a hard court with two baskets made out of metal from which white netting is suspended. The object is to get the ball in your own basket. In the NBA (National Basketball Association), each team has five players, and the team with the ball works together to score. The player with the ball must dribble the ball when he moves; if he moves without dribbling the ball, the other team gets it. When a player shoots the ball in the basket, it is called a **field goal**. A normal field goal is worth two points, but if the player makes the shot from beyond the three-point line

Michael Jordan skies over Charles Barkley (again).

(thirty feet away from the basket) it is worth three points.

10. **Which of the following basketball players has averaged the most points per game over his entire career in the NBA?**

(A) Michael Jordan
(B) Wilt Chamberlain
(C) Kareem Abdul-Jabbar
(D) Bill Russell

The most famous basketball player ever is **Michael Jordan**, who set all kinds of records as he dominated the league from the late eighties until his retirement at the top of his game in 1993. Jordan changed the game with his incredible athletic ability, adding an almost balletic grace to the sport. Seemingly at will, he could take over a game and score a massive number of points, often more than fifty in a game. A 6'6" guard, Jordan was able to leap high in the air, and inexplicably float as he flummoxed his opponents.

After winning an incredible, but not unprecedented, third straight championship (for the Chicago Bulls in 1993), Jordan retired to pursue his lifelong dream of becoming a major-league baseball player. Twenty-one months later, disillusioned with baseball, Jordan returned to basketball for "the love of the game."

Jordan's career is also remarkable for all of the endorsement money he received from advertisers. Through ads for Nike® shoes, Wheaties®, and Gatorade®, to name a few, he became one of the most famous men on the planet, opening the lucrative doors of advertising to many African American athletes. Even while in his temporary retirement, Jordan pulled in a sweet 30 million dollars a year in endorsement revenue.

Before Jordan, Wilt Chamberlain, a 7'1" center dominated the league. He was virtually unstoppable, and in one season during his career averaged over fifty points a game.

11. **How many players are on each team during a soccer match?**

    (A) Nine
    (B) Ten
    (C) Eleven
    (D) Twelve

In **soccer**, which is called **football** in the rest of the world, each team has eleven players who do their darnedest to get a ball into the other team's goal. The players are not allowed to use their hands, so they must rely on their feet, heads, or any other useful body part. In front of the goal is a goalie who is allowed to use his hands to stop the ball from going into the net. Soccer is the most popular game in the world; countries from Europe and South America are wildly supportive of their national teams. The world championship of soccer is called the **World Cup**, and it is played once every four years. In 1994, Brazil won its record fourth World Cup when the tournament was played in the U.S. for the first time ever.

Perhaps the best soccer player ever is **Pelé**, a Brazilian who was almost impossible to stop. He led Brazil to its first three World Cups, and then came out of retirement to play for a newly founded American league. Pelé is one of the primary reasons that soccer has achieved popularity in the United States.

Victory (1981). Legendary director John Huston brought Sylvester Stallone, Michael Caine, and soccer great Pelé together to make this absolutely ridiculous film about WWII POWs who play soccer. Recommended solely for the reason that it does capture Pelé's astonishing grace on the soccer field.

12. **The champion of the National Hockey League receives the**

    (A) Gold Medal of Hockey
    (B) Stanley Cup
    (C) National Hockey Trophy
    (D) Golden Puck

Hockey is a game in which players try to use sticks to hit a hard rubber disk, called a puck, into the net of the opposing team. The game is played on ice,

Pelé leaves another defender in the dust.

"The Great One," Wayne Gretzky

Slap Shot (1977). Paul Newman stars in this very funny comedy about a bush-league hockey team's rise in popularity.

so it is naturally fast-paced and somewhat violent. The major professional league in the United States and Canada is the National Hockey League (**NHL**). The winner of the championship gets the **Stanley Cup**.

The most famous hockey player is **Wayne Gretsky**, who holds numerous NHL records and is called "the Great One." Other famous hockey players include Gordie Howe, who played more games than anyone else, Bobby Orr, and Bobby Hull.

13. **Which of the following is NOT part of horse racing's Triple Crown?**

(A) The Kentucky Derby
(B) The Preakness
(C) The Indianapolis 500
(D) The Belmont Stakes

America's second-most-attended sport (after baseball) is horse racing. Basically, in thoroughbred racing, a bunch of horses, each carrying a jockey, race around a track. The first one to cross the finish line wins. In harness racing, the horse pulls a chariot that holds a driver. Besides its beauty and excitement, horse racing has the additional attraction of offering legal gambling. People bet on horses to **win** (come in first), **place** (come in first or second), or **show** (come in first, second, or third). Different amounts of money are given depending on the odds of a particular horse to finish. The odds are figured out according to the bettors: The more people who bet on a horse, the lower the odds and the less money paid out if that horse wins.

One of the most famous thoroughbred horses is **Secretariat**, who won the **Triple Crown** in amazing fashion. To win the Triple Crown, a horse must win the **Kentucky Derby**, the **Preakness**, and the **Belmont Stakes** in the same year. This has only been done eleven times since 1875. Not only did Secretariat win the three races but he won them in spectacular style, capturing the Belmont with an enormous lead, more than thirty-one lengths ahead of his nearest rival. Other famous thoroughbred horses include **Man o' War** and **Citation.**

ANSWERS

1. D   2. B   3. C   4. B   5. C   6. C   7. D
8. B   9. A   10. A   11. C   12. B   13. C

Index

appeasement, 197
Arab nations, 218
Ararat, 365
Archimedes, 289
architecture
    cathedral, 154–155, 453
    Greek, 142, 144, 453
    pyramid, 136, 238, 247
Argonauts, 386
Aristotle, 142, 143, 144, *268*, 302
Ark, Noah's, 365
Arkansas, Little Rock, 111
armed forces
    in civil rights movement, 110–111
    Civil War, 66–68
    Commander in Chief of, 51
    Korean War, 106–107
    and Native Americans, 72–73, 74
    Persian Gulf War, 130–131
    Revolutionary War, *42–48*
    SpanishAmerican War, 79–80
    student protests, 118
    Vietnam War, *117–118*, 120, 121
    and warfare technology, *138–140*, 156, 187, 199–200, 325
    World War I, 82–85
    World War II, 95–103, 200–204
Armstrong, Louis, 432, 439
Armstrong, Neil, 122
Arouet, FrançoisMarie, 172
Arrangement in Black and Gray: The Artist's Mother (Whistler), 462
arteries, 333
Articles of Confederation, *42–43*, *49–50*
Aryan race, 195
Asgard, 393
Asia, 213–217
    European exploration of, 161
    geography, 249–252
    map quiz, 249–250
    see also names of specific countries
asp, 148
assassination
    of Julius Caesar, 146
    of Archduke Ferdinand, 82, 187
    of Mahatma Gandhi, 217
    of John F. Kennedy, 119–120
    of Lincoln, 69–70
    of Malcolm X, 112
    of McKinley, 81
    score card, 119
assembly lines, 89–90

asteroids, 272
astronomical unit, 270
astronomy, 267–272, 303–304
at bat, in baseball, 469
Athena, 385
Athens, *142*, 387–388, 453
athletes. *see* sports
Atlantic City, New Jersey, 222
atomic bomb, 102, 140, 202–203, 207, 251, 290, *292–293*, 294
ATP (adenosine triphosphate), 321
Augustus, Emperor of Rome, 146, 148
Auschwitz, 96, 197
Austen, Jane, 399
Australia
    geography, 258–259
    map quiz, 257–258
Austria, 172, 197
    and World War I, 187, 188, 190
Autobiography of Malcolm X, The (Haley), 407–408
automobiles, 89–90
    and OPEC, 126
Axis powers, 199, 200–201
Aztecs, 136, 137, 238

Baatan Death March, 98
Babel, tower of, 365–366
Bacchus, 383
Bach, Johann Sebastian, 160, 431–432, 437
bacteria, 309
Balboa, Vasco, 162
Balkanization, 208
Balkans, 208, 263
ball, in baseball, 469
balloons, 139
Baltic states, 207–208, 263
banking, 230–231
barometric pressure, 281
baseball, 469–471
    players, 470–471
    terms, 469–470
bases, in baseball, 469
bases are loaded, in baseball, 470
basic solution, 296–297
basketball, 473–474
    players, 474
    terms, 473
Bastille, 175
Bastille Day, 175
Battle of Bunker Hill, 44
Battle of New Orleans, *56*, 349
Bay of Pigs invasion (1961), 115–116

Calvinism, *164*, 168
Cambodia, 96, *215–216*
Camelot, 393
Campbell's Soup (Warhol), 466–467
Canada
    geography, *241–244*
    map quiz, 241–242
    and Revolutionary War, 42
cannon, 138
Cantonese, 252
capillaries, 333
capital, 180
capitalism, 179
Capone, Al, 87
carbon dioxide, 335
Carousel (musical), 441
Carter, Jimmy, 125–126
Carthage, 145–146, 392
cartography, 161
Casablanca (movie), 416
Cassandra, 390
castes, Hindu, 380
Castro, Fidel, 115–116, 208
catalysts, 293
Catcher in the Rye (Salinger), 406
cathedrals, 154–155, 453
Catherine the Great, 171
cats, falls by, 302
Catt, Carrie Chapman, 87
cavalry, 138
Cave Painting (Les Trois Frères, France), 455
Cavour, Camillo, 184
CBGBs (nightclub), 224
CDROM, 351
cells, living, 320–323
celluloid, 342
cell wall, 320
Central America
    geography, 237–240
    map quiz, 237–238
    see also names of specific countries
Central Intelligence Agency (CIA), 115
Central Pacific Railroad, 76
Central Powers, World War I, 188
centrifugal force, 300
centripetal force, 300
ceramics, 343
Cervantes, Miguel de, 396
chain reaction, 292
Chamberlain, Neville, 197–198
Chamberlain, Wilt, 474
Chaplin, Charlie, 75, 409–410

chariots, 138
Charlemagne, Holy Roman Emperor, *152–153*, 176, 183, 195, 196
Chartres, Cathedral of, 453
Charybdis, 391
chemistry, 284–297
Chiang Kaishek, 214
Chicago, Illinois, 224
China
    ancient, 137
    Beijing, 252
    Boxer Rebellion, 185, *213*, 252
    communism, 214
    Great Wall, *252*, 453
    invention of gunpowder, 138
    languages of, 251–252
    Opium War, 213
    Russo–Japanese War, *185*, 190
    and Tibet, 215
    Tienanmen Square uprising, 252
    and World War II, 200
chivalry, 393
chlorofluorocarbons (CFCs), *279*, 306
chloroplasts, 320
chocolate, 230–231
Christianity, 161
    Anglican Church, 165, 166
    early years, 149–150
    in the Middle Ages, 153–155
    missionaries, 210
    Reformation, 163–166
    Roman Catholic, 163–164, 232
    see also Jesus Christ
chromosomes, 321
Churchill, Winston, 100, 104, *198*, 199, 202, 206
Cicero, Marcus Tullius, 149
Circe, 391
circulatory system, 333–334
Citation (race horse), 476
cities
    migration of farm laborers to, 178–179
    urban mythology, 393–394
    see also names of specific cities
Citizen Kane (movie), 410, 415
citizenship, 52
citystates, Greek, 142–143
civilization, 135
civil rights movement, *109–113*, 121, 217, 407, 447
Civil War, *66–68*, 139, 412
    antebellum period, 60–65
    Reconstruction, 67, *69*
Clark, William, 55

Darrow, Clarence, 89
Darwin, Charles, 88–89, 318–319
David, 371
David (Michelangelo), 458
da Vinci, Leonardo, *454*
Davis, Jefferson, 70
Dawes Severalty Act (1887), 73–74
DDay, 200–201
DDT, 339–340
Declaration of Independence, 39, 42, *45*
    and Constitution, 52, 53
decomposers, 312
deficit, national, 129–130
deforestation, 276–277, 279
Degas, Edgar, 461
De Klerk, F. W., 212
Delilah, 370
Democratic Party, 57, 58
Les Demoiselles d'Avignon (Picasso), 463
Denmark, 200, 230
deoxyribonucleic acid (DNA), 316–317, 321
Depression. *see* Great Depression
Descartes, René, 169, 172, 357
despot, enlightened, 172
détente, 207
dialects, Chinese, 252
diaphragms, 88, 328
Dickens, Charles, 402
Dido, 392
digestion, 332–333
digital signals, 351, 352
DiMaggio, Joe, 471
dinosaurs, 316
Directory, 176
Dirty Harry (movie), 423–424
disco, 435
discs
    floppy, 353
    optical, 353
Discus Thrower (Roman sculpture), 455
diseases
    AIDS (Acquired Immunodeficiency Syndrome), *329*,
        334–335
    Black Death, 157–158
    in New World, 33, 35
    polio, 94
    sexually transmitted (STDs), *327–329*
    in ten plagues, 369
distance and time calculations, 356–357
distilled water, 295
Diva (movie), 428
Divine Comedy, The (Dante), 398

Divine right, 168
Dixieland jazz, 432
DNA (deoxyribonucleic acid), 316–317, 321
dominant trait, genetic, 316
Doors, The, 434
Doppler effect, 305
double helix (DNA molecule), 316
Double Indemnity (movie), 417
Douglas, Stephen, 65
Douglass, Frederick, 64
downs, in football, 473
drama, Greek, 144
dreams, 182
drives (computer)
    hard, 353
    removable hard, 353
    tape, 353
drugs
    nicotine, 335
    Opium War, 213
Dublin, Ireland, 229
Du Bois, W. E. B., 71
Duce, Il (Benito Mussolini), 160, *195*
Due process, 52
dust bowl, *93*, 405
Dylan, Bob, 448

Earhart, Amelia, 91
Earth, 268–271, 272
    seasons, 280
earth science, 273–279
eclipse, 270–271
economic imperialism, 40
economics
    Keynesian, 94
    laissezfaire, *179*, 183
    national deficit in, 129–130
    supplyside, 128–129
ecosystem, *311*, 313
egg cell, *326*
ego, 182
Egypt
    ancient, *136*, 141, 147–148, 247
    Hebrews in, 368–370
    language of, 211
Eighteenth Amendment, 86–87
Einstein, Albert, *291–292*, 294, 304–305
Eisenhower, Dwight, 111
Elba, 177
Electra, 391
Electra complex, *182*, 391
electricity, *307*, 349

Ford, Gerald, 125, 126
Ford, Henry, 89–90
forty, in tennis scoring, 471
40 acres and a mule, 69
forty days (Jesus in the wilderness), 374
forty days and forty nights (great flood), 365
fossil fuels, *275, 277, 278*, 345
Fountainhead, The (Rand), 405–406
Four Humors, 333
Four Hundred Blows, The (movie), 427
Four Seasons, The (Vivaldi), 436
1492 (discovery of America), 34
Fourteen Points plan, 85, 190
Fourteenth Amendment, 52, 70
France
     Bourbon dynasty, 169–170
     cave painting, 455
     in French and Indian War (1756–1763), 38–39
     in Hundred Years War, 156
     Louisiana Purchase from, 54–55
     during Revolutionary War, 47, 48
     and World War I, 84–85, 187, 188
FrancoPrussian War, 186
Frankenstein (movie), 429
Franklin, Aretha, 433–434
Franklin, Benjamin, 46, 47
Frederick the Great, King of Prussia, 172
free jazz, 433
French and Indian War (1756–1763), 38–39
French Revolution, 53, *173–177*
French sector (in Germany), 100
frequency
     light wave, 305–306
     sound wave, 305
fresco, 457
Freud, Sigmund, *182–183*, 388, 391
Frost, Robert, *397*
fungi, *309*, 339
fusion, nuclear, 103, 285, *292–293*
fusion jazz, 433

Gable, Clark, 410
Gagarin, Yuri, 122
Galahad, Sir, 393
Galapagos Islands, 318
Galilei, Galileo, 88, 155, *269, 302*
gall bladder, 333
Gama, Vasco da, 162
gametes, 323
Gandhi, Mahatma, 111, *216–217*, 401
Garden of Eden, 363–364

Garrison, William Lloyd, 63
gas chambers, 197
Gates, Horatio, 48
Gautama, Buddha, 380
Gawain, Sir, 393
Gay Rights movement, 111, 331
Gaza strip, 218
Gehrig, Lou, 471
General, The (movie), 412
genetic code, 316–317, 340
genetic engineering, 340
Genghis Khan, 157, 161
genus of an organism, 310
geography, 219–264
     Africa, 245–248
     Asia, 249–252
     Australia, New Zealand, Indonesia, 257–260
     Canada, 241–244
     Central America and West Indies, 237–240
     Europe, 200, 227–232
     Middle East, 253–256
     Russia and the Republics, 261–264
     South America, 233–236
     United States, 221–226
geology, 273–279
geometry, 357
George III, King of England, 45
geothermal energy, 346
Germany, *180*
     Berlin Wall, 116, 206, 453
     colonies of, 185
     division of, 100, 116
     Hapsburg family, 170
     Nazi, 30, 96, 104, 182, *195–202*, 204
     Nazi-Soviet Non-Aggression Pact, 199
     during Revolutionary War, 47–48
     after Thirty Years War, 172
     unification, 19th century, 183
     and World War I, 83–85, 95–96, 187, 188, 190
Geronimo, 74
Gershwin, George, 442
Gestapo, 196
Gettysburg Address, 68
geysers, 225
gigabyte, 353
glaciers, 226, 276
global warming, 274, 277–278
Glorious Revolution, 168
goal line, in football, 473
Godfather, The (movie), 424
Godfather, The, Part II (movie), 424
Gods Must Be Crazy, The (movie), 209, *428*

Super Bowl football championship, 473
superconductors, 343
superego, 182
"superpowers," 105
supplyside economics, 128–129
Supreme Court, 51
    and abortion, 123–124
    and civil rights, 109–110
Surrealists, 465
survival of the fittest, 318
Sweden, 230
Swift, Jonathan, 229
swing, 432–433
Switzerland, 200, 230–231
symbiosis, 312
synthetic plastic, 342

Taft, William H., 81
Tale of Two Cities, A (Dickens), 402
tanks, 140
taxes
    in calculation of tips, 357–358
    colonial, 41
    in supply-side economics, 128–129
Tea Act, 41
Teamsters, 77
telegraph, 139, 184, *349*
telephone, 349
telescope, 139, 269
television, 350, 435–436
Tell-Tale Heart and Other Stories, The (Poe), 400
temperature
    absolute zero, 296
    boiling point, 295
    condensation point, 295
    and energy, 293–294
    and seasons, 280
Temptations, The, 447
1066, Norman Conquest, 153
Ten Commandments, 370
tennis
    players, 472
    terms, 471–472
ten plagues, 369
terminal velocity, *301*, 302
terrorism
    Iranian hostage crisis, *125–126*, 255
    Irish Republican Army, 230
testes, 326
testosterone, 337
Texas, battle of the Alamo, 58
"That was one small step for man, one giant leap for

mankind" (Neil Armstrong), 122
theocracy, 37
Theseus, *387–388*
Thing, The (From Another World) (movie), 430
Thinker, The (Rodin), 463
Third Estate, 174–175
Third Reich, 196
Thirteenth Amendment, 52, 68, 70
thirty, in tennis scoring, 471
Thirty Years War, 170, 172
Thor, 393
Thoreau, Henry David, 111, *401–402*
threefifths compromise, *52–53*, 61, 70
Three Flags (Johns), 467
three wise men, 373
thumb, opposable, 325
thunderstorms, 282–283
Tiananmen Square uprising, 252
Tibet, 96, *215*, 251
time and distance calculations, 356–357
tips, calculation for, 357–359
Titans, 381
tobacco, 61
Tokyo, Japan, 251
Tolstoy, Leo, 402
Toltecs, 137, 238
Tonkin, Gulf of, Resolution, 117
To Sir, With Love (movie), 428
touchdown, in football, 473
trade unions, 77–78
transportation
    airplane, 90–91
    automobile, 89–90, 126
    Panama Canal, 81, 239
    railroad, 76, 77
Treaty of Versailles, 85, 189–190, 195, 197
trench warfare, 187
trimesters of pregnancy, 330
Triple Alliance, 187
Triple Crown, 476
Triple Entente, 187
Trojan Horse, *390–391*, 392, 456
Trojan War, 389–392
tropical rain forests, 277, 278, *279*, 311
Trotsky, Leon, 192
Truman, Harry S, 101–102
    Cold War, 105, 107
Truman Doctrine, 105, 206
Tubman, Harriet, 64
Tudor family, 167
Turkey, and World War I, 188
Turner, Nat, 64

PHOTO CREDITS
(In order of appearance)

The Bettmann Archive
The Bettmann Archive
The Bettmann Archive
The Bettmann Archive
The Bettmann Archive
The Bettmann Archive
The Bettmann Archive
The Bettmann Archive
The Bettmann Archive
The Bettmann Archive
The Bettmann Archive
The Bettmann Archive
The Bettmann Archive
The Bettmann Archive
The Bettmann Archive
The Bettmann Archive
The Bettmann Archive
The Bettmann Archive
UPI/Bettmann
The Bettmann Archive
The Bettmann Archive
The Bettmann Archvie
The Bettmann Archive
UPI/Bettmann
UPI/Bettmann
The Bettmann Archive
The Bettmann Archive
The Bettmann Archive
The Bettmann Archive
The Bettmann Archive
The Bettmann Archive
The Bettmann Arhcive
The Bettmann Archive
The Bettmann Archive
The Bettmann Archive
McCord Museum of Canadian History,
  Notman Photographic Archive
The Bettmann Archive
The Bettmann Archive
Collection of the New-York Historical
  Society
The Bettmann Archive
The Bettmann Arhcive
UPI/Bettmann
The Bettmann Archive
AP/Wide World Photos
Collection of the New-York Historical
  Society
The Bettmann Archive
The Bettmann Archive
UPI/Bettmann
UPI/Bettmann
The Bettmann Archive
The Bettmann Archive
The Bettmann Archive

The Bettmann Archive
AP/Wide World Photos
Photo: Time/Life, Inc.

UPI/Bettmann
UPI/Bettmann
UPI/Bettmann
UPI/Bettmann
AP/Wide World Photos
The Bettmann Archive
UPI/Bettmann
The Bettmann Arhcive
UPI/Bettmann
The Bettmann Archive
UPI/Bettmann
UPI/Bettmann
AP/Wide World Photos
UPI/Bettmann
UPI/Bettmann
UPI/Bettmann
UPI/Bettmann
UPI/Bettmann
AP/Wide World Photos
UPI/Bettmann
AP/Wide World Photos
UPI/Bettmann
UPI/Bettmann
UPI/Bettmann
UPI/Bettmann
UPI/Bettmann
The Bettmann Archive
UPI/Bettmann
UPI/Bettmann
Reuters/Bettmann
UPI/Bettmann
Reuters/Bettmann
Reuters/Bettmann
The Bettmann Archive

Neg. No. 335885
Courtesy Department Library Services
American Museum of Natural History

The Bettmann Archive
The Bettmann Archive
The Bettmann Archive
The Bettmann Archive
The Bettmann Archive

Neg. No. 335887
Courtesy Department Library Services
American Museum of Natural History

The Bettmann Archive
The Bettmann Archive
The Bettmann Archive
The Bettmann Archive
The Bettmann Archive
The Bettmann Archive

The Bettmann Archive
The Bettmann Archive
The Bettmann Archive
UPI/Bettmann
The Bettmann Archive
Alinari/Art Resource NY
The Bettmann Archive
The Bettmann Archive
The Bettmann Archive
The Bettmann Archive
The Bettmann Archive
The Bettmann Archive
Bridgeman/Art Resource NY
Alinari/Art Resource NY
Scala/Art Resource NY
Alinari/Art Resource NY
Alinari/Art Resource NY
Alinari/Art Resource NY
Alinari/Art Resource NY
Alinari/Art Resource NY
Alinari/Art Resource NY
Giraudon/Art Resource NY
The Bettmann Archive
The Bettmann Archive
The Bettmann Archive
The Bettmann Archive
The Bettmann Archive
The Bettmann Archive
UPI/Bettmann
UPI/Bettmann
UPI/Bettmann
UPI/Bettmann
UPI Bettmann
The Bettmann Archive
The Bettmann Archive
UPI/Bettmann
UPI/Bettmann
UPI/Bettmann
UPI/Bettmann
UPI/Bettmann
UPI/Bettmann
Reuters/Bettmann
UPI/Bettmann
The Bettmann Archive
Reuters/Bettmann
Reuters/Bettmann
The Bettmann Archive
UPI/Bettmann
UPI/Bettmann
UPI/Bettmann
UPI/Bettmann
UPI/Bettmann
UPI/Bettmann
The Bettmann Archive
The Bettmann Archive
The Bettmann Archive

UPI/Bettmann
UPI/Bettmann
UPI/Bettmann
The Bettmann Archive
The Bettmann Archive
The Bettmann Archive
UPI/Bettmann
Photo by Celeste Ganderson
UPI/Bettmann
The Bettmann Archive
UPI/Bettmann
UPI/Bettmann
UPI/Bettmann
Reuters/Bettmann
UPI/Bettmann
Reuters/Bettmann
Springer/Bettman Film Archive
The Bettmann Archive
UPI/Bettmann
The Bettmann Archive
UPI/Bettmann
The Bettmann Archive
The Bettmann Archive
The Bettmann Archive
The Bettmann Archive

Neg. No. 323721
Courtesy Department Library Services
American Museum of Natural History

The Bettmann Archive
UPI/Bettmann

Neg. No. 108781
Courtesy Department Library Services
American Museum of Natural History

The Bettmann Archive
UPI/Bettmann
The Bettmann Archive
Photo by Grace Roegner
UPI/Bettmann
The Bettmann Archive
UPI Bettmann

FAR SIDE
© 1988 FARWORKS, INC./Dist. by UNI-
    VERSAL PRESS SYNDICATE.
Reprinted with permission. All rights
    reserved.
UPI/Bettmann
Reuters/Bettmann
Reuters/Bettmann
UPI/Bettmann
The Bettmann Archive
The Bettmann Archive
UPI/Bettmann
UPI/Bettmann
Reuters/Bettmann

UPI/Bettmann
The Bettmann Archive
UPI/Bettmann
UPI/Bettmann
Reuters/Bettmann
The Bettmann Archive
UPI/Bettmann
The Bettmann Archive
The Bettmann Archive
The Bettmann Archive
The Bettmann Archive
Scala/Art Resource NY
The Bettmann Archive
The Bettmann Archive
The Bettmann Archive
Reuters/Bettmann
UPI/Bettmann
The Bettmann Archive
UPI/Bettmann
The Bettmann Archive
UPI/Bettmann
The Bettmann Archive
The Bettmann Archive
The Bettmann Archive
The Bettmann Archive
The Bettmann Archive
The Bettmann Archive
The Bettmann Archive
The Bettmann Archive
The Bettmann Archive
The Bettmann Archive
The Bettmann Archive
UPI/Bettmann
UPI/Bettmann
The Bettmann Archive

The Bettmann Archive
The Bettmann Archive
The Bettmann Archive
The Bettmann Archive
The Bettmann Archive
The Bettmann Archive
The Bettmann Archive
UPI/Bettmann
UPI/Bettmann
UPI/Bettmann
UPI/Bettmann
The Bettmann Archive
UPI/Bettmann
The Bettmann Archive
Springer/Bettmann Film Archive
Springer/Bettmann Film Archive
Springer/Bettmann Film Archive
The Bettmann Archive
The Bettmann Archive
The Bettmann Archive
Springer/Bettmann Film Archive
The Bettmann Archive
Springer/Bettmann Film Archive

UPI/Bettmann
UPI/Bettmann
Springer/Bettmann Film Archive
UPI/Bettmann
The Bettmann Archive
The Bettmann Archive
The Bettmann Archive
The Bettmann Archive
UPI/Bettmann
The Bettmann Archive
UPI/Bettmann
UPI/Bettmann
Springer/Bettmann Film Archive
The Bettmann Archive
UPI/Bettmann
UPI/Bettmann
Amalie R. Rothschild/The Bettman
    Archive
UPI/Bettmann
UPI/Bettmann
UPI/Bettmann
The Bettmann Archive
UPI/Bettmann
UPI/Bettmann
UPI/Bettmann
The Bettmann Archive
Scala/Art Resource NY
Scala/Art Resource NY
UPI/Bettmann
UPI/Bettmann
UPI/Bettmann
Reuters/Bettmann
Reuters/Bettmann
UPI/Bettmann
Reuters/Bettmann

ABOUT THE AUTHOR

Michael Freedman has been a writer and a teacher with The Princeton Reviewfor many years, and in the process he has worked on a number of their books. He is also pursuing a career as an artist, and his paintings appear in many private collections. Freedman graduated from New College of the University of South Florida where he studied fine arts, mathematics, and the liberal arts. He is now living in Brooklyn, New York with his wife Grace Roegner Freedman, their son Jacob D Freedman, and their two cats. Freedman is also the author of *Word Smart: Genius Edition*, a vocabulary book for those with good vocabularies.